Ascetic Images

Ascetic Images

Anna Maria Ortese and Roberto Rossellini in the Underworld

ACHILLE CASTALDO

Published by State University of New York Press, Albany

EU GPSR Authorised Representative:
Logos Europe, 9 rue Nicolas Poussin, 17000, La Rochelle, France
contact@logoseurope.eu

For information, contact State University of New York Press, Albany, NY
www.sunypress.edu

Library of Congress Cataloging-in-Publication Data

Name: Castaldo, Achille, 1981– author.
Title: Ascetic images : Anna Maria Ortese and Roberto Rossellini in the underworld / Achille Castaldo.
Description: Albany : State University of New York Press, [2026]. | Series: SUNY series, literature . . . in theory | Includes bibliographical references and index.
Identifiers: LCCN 2025023988 | ISBN 9798855805000 (hardcover : alk. paper) | ISBN 9798855805024 (PDF) | ISBN 9798855806939 (epub) | ISBN 9798855805017 (pbk. : alk. paper)
Subjects: LCSH: Ortese, Anna Maria Silenzio della ragione. | Rossellini, Roberto, 1906–1977—Criticism and interpretation. | Viaggio in Italia (Motion picture). | Poor in literature. | Poor in motion pictures. | Naples (Italy)—In literature. | Naples (Italy)—In motion pictures. | LCGFT: Literary criticism. | Film criticism.
Classification: LCC PQ4875.R8 Z59 2025
LC record available at https://lccn.loc.gov/2025023988

To the memory of Fredric Jameson

Contents

List of Illustrations

Acknowledgments

Many friends and colleagues contributed to making this book possible. My gratitude goes to those who read parts of the manuscript and helped me shape it with their feedback: Rosa Barotsi, Daria Biagi, Fiammetta Di Lorenzo, Guido Mattia Gallerani, Mónica García Blizzard, Ezio Puglia, and Saskia Ziolkowski. No less important have been those who offered support and advice at different stages of the project: Geoffrey Bennington, Vincent Bruyere, Ciro Incoronato, Elissa Marder, Alex Mendes, Thomas Rogers, and Giulia Spina. Besides reading my work for years, well before the beginning of this project, Mimmo Cangiano, Danila Cannamela, Francesco Frisari, and Vittorio Martone have been vital interlocutors who helped me develop ideas and navigate this strange form of life.

A special thanks goes to those who read parts of the manuscript and offered key insights at the most critical moment of its itinerary: Chad Córdova, Valérie Loichot, Liran Razinsky, and Eugenio Santangelo.

I am grateful to all my friends and colleagues in the French and Italian Department at Emory; I wish to thank, in particular, my colleagues of the Italian program, who created the best possible environment for work and collaboration: Antonietta Di Pietrio, Stefano Maranzana, Simona Muratore, Angela Porcarelli, Christine Ristaino, and Garrett Waters.

I am grateful to David Bell, Roberto Dainotto, and Anne-Gaëlle Saliot, for helping me find the initial thread of what would later become this book, and whose mentorship defined my intellectual itinerary. At Duke, Fredric Jameson's classes have been the place of a discovery that has yet to end and continues through his inexhaustible work. This book is dedicated to his memory.

My gratitude also goes to Hilary Ilkay, for her precious work on the text of the manuscript, and to David E. Johnson and Scott Michaelsen, who accepted it in their series. SUNY Press's editors Rebecca Colesworthy and Caitlin Bean offered constant support at the different stages of this journey; and I also wish to express gratitude to the anonymous readers who took the time to review the manuscript and helped me improve it.

A precious support came from friends and family who helped me find information about the shooting of *Journey to Italy* in Maiori: in particular, my aunt Enzina Spina, my brother Guglielmo, my sister Viola, and my friend Raffaele Proto (and thanks also to all those who keep the memory of that event alive).

On a personal note, I want to thank my parents for their invaluable support. And my partner Ilaria, who went through this whole thing with me. *Quem o escreveu não importa.*

Parts of chapter 2 have previously appeared, in a different form, in my essay "Trauma and Literary Experience in Anna Maria Ortese's 'Oro a Forcella,'" published as a chapter in the collection *Trauma Narratives in Italian and Transnational Women's Writing*, edited by Tiziana de Rogatis and Katrin Wehling-Giorgi (2022). I thank Sapienza University Press for the permission to republish, and both the editors of the volume for their suggestions in developing the essay in its original form, which proved important for the continuation of the project as well. Many thanks to Antonio Maraldi and the Centro Cinema Città di Cesena, Fondo Pietrangeli, for allowing me to examine the original screenplay of what would later become *Journey to Italy*.

Finally, I want to thank the Center for Faculty Development and Excellence at Emory University for supporting the editing stage through the Scholarly Writing and Publishing Fund, and the Fox Center for Humanistic Inquiry at Emory University, which made this book available in open access with the support of the Andrew W. Mellon Foundation.

Introduction

Condemned to See

The Creature

In the revised 1831 edition of her most famous novel, Mary Shelley added a seemingly incidental detail to the protagonist's biography: Victor Frankenstein was born in Naples. Why, years after the first publication in 1818, did she feel the need to specify the birthplace of the man who would upset the order of things with his Creature? What does this tell us about the city in which the author spent some chaotic months between 1818 and 1819,[1] while fleeing from the same social stigma, the same cruel isolation that had tormented the Creature in her novel to the point of its becoming monstrous? What had she seen there, in the mild winter months spent in a villa in the neighborhood of Chiaia, which ended with the abandonment of a baby girl adopted by her husband perhaps to soothe the mourning for the recent loss of their own child (Seymour 2000, 227)? Maybe the memory of this other "creature," also briefly exposed to the light of glory—Percy Shelley had her baptized and officially recorded her as Elena Adelaide Shelley—and then immediately thrust back into obscurity, can serve as an entry point into this study. It is worth mentioning that "criatura" (creature) is the term commonly used to refer to children in the Neapolitan dialect.

Like Frankenstein's Creature, the lumpenproletariat that lives in the dark alleys of Naples had been produced by the obscure operations of a foreign and incomprehensible power—in this case, the administration of the Spanish Viceroyalty. Since the seventeenth century, this crowd became an entity perceived with dismay by foreign visitors and constitutes to this day a source of constant fear for the local privileged classes. According to the Neapolitan writer Raffaele La Capria, "the fear of the underclass [plebe]" is the secret core of the city's own ideology (2003, 696–738). Yet the presence of this vast social stratum is evanescent throughout the history of the city. If it becomes visible in periods of crisis—revolts, famines, epidemics, wars—it immediately disappears again behind the picturesque images of an urban reality crowded with a people drunk on sun and music, capable of surviving with the bare minimum, which shuns work and any care for the future.

This book addresses the flip side of this idyllic image in two authors—Anna Maria Ortese and Roberto Rossellini—who put the Neapolitan reality at the center of their works in a historical moment particularly favorable to the observation of this ordinary, permanent exception that is the city's lowest class, that is, in the early 1950s, when the traumatic excesses of the war began to fade and just before economic development clouded memories once more. Through the two objects that will constitute the main focus of this book—Ortese's fictional reportage "The Silence of Reason" ("Il silenzio della ragione," 1953) and Rossellini's film *Journey to Italy* (*Viaggio in Italia*, 1954)—I will investigate the functioning of the ideological machine that, since the dawn of the modern age, makes this underclass invisible, hiding the foundation of oppression and exploitation on which the city rests. What is the textual operation that enables this ideological device to conceal an object in plain sight? To answer this question, I draw on the works of Fredric Jameson, Louis Althusser, and György Lukács to put forth a conception of ideology as a device of both vision and blindness. According to this line of Marxist thinkers, ideology goes beyond false consciousness and becomes the mental structure through which human beings locate themselves in their social context, a "mapping mechanism" to quote Jameson (2009b, 341), which functions as an a priori schema of connection with the external world, permeating all aspects of behavior, to the point that it becomes indistinguishable from that *lex insita* (immanent law) that for Bourdieu (2000a, 272) is the class habitus.

The model of reading I theorize below begins by identifying a repressed element, explores that element as the origin of a work's contradictions, and then traces the development of their narrative articulation. But a text's contradictions are not simply expressed on the surface: The ideological drives that determine them are present at all levels of a text's structure, from their obscurity at the deep level of value oppositions to their emergence in the light of the figurative plane, in space, time, characters, and actions. For this reason, the tools of narrative semiotics will be indispensable and will allow for a comparative analysis of literary and filmic texts, from the outer surface of expression, which naturally requires distinct means for cinema and for literature, to the deepest layer, where it will be possible to find common patterns through which the two works address the disorienting reality of extreme poverty and systemic trauma.

According to the most probable reconstruction of the Neapolitan events of the Shelley family, put forth by Miranda Seymour (2000, 227), the little girl adopted and then immediately abandoned belonged to the large number of newborns easily given up for adoption among the ranks of the Neapolitan poor.[2] Thus, Elena Adelaide appears to be forced to confront in real life the traumatic core that fueled her adoptive mother's fantasy—the arbitrary, miraculous selection followed by an incomprehensible abandonment. Similarly, the lower-class children we will meet throughout this book will often be momentarily extracted from their obscurity to be admired as a spectacle, before being returned to the nameless crowd. However, as we will observe, at least some of them will reject this role and attempt to sabotage the ideological mechanism of the "picturesque." This mechanism, which Raffaele Milani defined as "the encounter of the physical eye with the mental image" (2009, 63), tends to make the misery exposed in plain sight invisible: In Ortese's story, we will see how the Neapolitan intellectuals were able to enjoy the "colorful" spectacle of children begging for alms, while in Rossellini's film one of the protagonists will cheerfully comment on the beauty of street children intent on performing manual labor. My reading will show how, in both cases, the textual mechanism itself deconstructs the obliterating perspective it presents. As will become clear, it does so through the dissemination of a series of traces that allow us to reconstruct the virtual presence of the experience of the lowest stratum of the urban population. Following a clue from *Journey to Italy*, I will call this textual inscription "ascetic images."[3]

Shortly before the final sequence of *Afire* (*Roter Himmel*), a 2023 film by Christian Petzold, at the end of a brief summer vacation a man and a woman observe two charred corpses in the morgue: their friends, a young couple surprised by a fire in the middle of the forest. The bodies are intertwined; the young men had tried to protect each other from the flames. We are only shown their hands, which are still holding each other. While the two are intent on observing the corpses, the man's offscreen voice reveals that, rather than crying, in that circumstance his overwhelming emotions manifested themselves as a mental image, which is then presented to us as a photographic illustration in a school book: "The Pompeii Lovers," that is, one of the many casts recreated from voids left underground by the dissolved bodies of couples who had died together during the eruption of

79 CE, and whose negative imprint the soil has preserved over the centuries (figure I.1). A similar image is presented to us in the emotional climax shortly before the final sequence in Rossellini's *Journey to Italy*, also in this case at the end of a brief holiday.

Critics such as Raymond Bellour (1990) and Laura Mulvey (2000) have read the surfacing of these bodies in Rossellini's film as an allusion to the "indexical" power of cinema itself, following André Bazin's well-known ontological interpretation of the photographic image.[4] I will focus on a different allegorical aspect implicit in this figure: the void to be filled that precedes the image itself. This suggests an understanding of the textual experience as the matrix of a series of possibilities—the "ascetic images"—that the viewing (and reading) process can actualize. In line with Lukács's conception of ideology, the possibility of seeing a reality obscured by the dominant ideological perspective passes here through the sharing of a different standpoint—what in narratology is defined as *point of view*—rather than through the mere communication of discursive information. That is, it consists in offering the recipient the possibility of coinciding with a perspective that the text constructs through its overall experience. In this sense, as will become clear only after carrying out an in-depth analysis, in the filmic and the literary text, of the organization of space and the way in which bodies interact in it, the casts emerging from the depths of the subsoil will become

Figure I.1. "The Pompeii Lovers" from a textbook. *Source:* Christian Petzold, *Afire*, 2023.

the figuration of the position occupied by the city's lowest social stratum: trapped in the darkness of an "underworld" and devoid of any possibility of movement other than a desperate gesture of survival or a senseless one of anguish. If this image has therefore continued to haunt the history of cinema—to such an extent that it reemerges in Petzold's film exactly seventy years after it was first shot—it is not so much because it has become an emblem of cinema itself, but rather because it represents the return of a repressed element specularly opposed to the privilege of bodies endowed with light and freedom. Just like Elena Adelaide, for a moment admitted to the free movement without boundaries that comes with wealth and celebrity, and then immediately returned to the mass of bodies condemned to inhabit the dark spaces where every gesture is compulsory; just like the two corpses in the morgue, trapped forever in gestures of despair and anguish. Without open possibilities for the future, they are nothing more than a negative space that questions us.[5]

This book does not take place solely in Naples, however. In the next section of this introduction, we move to a classroom at the University of Lviv (Ukraine), where the Polish phenomenologist Roman Ingarden held his aesthetics seminar in the academic year 1935–36,[6] not many years before the war wiped out most of the participants.[7] In his seminar, Ingarden outlines the idea of an "original emotion" of aesthetic experience, which will then play a central role in his book on the cognition of the literary work of art (1937). My reading overturns and appropriates this idea, using it as an analytical tool to identify the place in a text where the latter signals the onset of its own ideological contradictions. While Ingarden, from within his classicist obsession, saw in the "original emotion" the first manifestation of the "truth" of art, I will read it materialistically as an *original anxiety*, a trace we can follow to locate the work's contact with its historical context. This methodological premise is followed by a brief historical excursus on the Neapolitan lumpenproletariat and on the ideology that has always attempted to "domesticate" and hide it. We then move on to the introduction of Ortese and Rossellini and the context in which the works that will be the focus of this book were created. The textual analysis begins with the fourth section: a "scherzo," as it were, in which, for each of the two works, I identify a scene where the "original emotion" is located at a precise point in space and time. In the case of Ortese's story, the scene follows the spit of a beggar girl—a "creature," again—who, with her irreverent gesture, makes visible the screen (a window) through which the Neapolitan intellectuals were enjoying her "colorful" sight, protected by the lens of the picturesque.

In the case of Rossellini's film, the "original emotion" spills from a blood-stain left by a mosquito splattered on the windshield of the protagonists' car headed for Naples. Here too the protective barrier through which rich tourists can enjoy the spectacle of poverty is brought to light. Finally, I close with a reflection on the possibility of communicating historical reality through the text, which draws on the lectures about literary expression that Merleau-Ponty held in the early 1950s, the same period during which the two works studied here were made, the brief window of opportunity this book has chosen as its privileged time frame.

Original Emotion

The moment we start to experience a work of art is marked by a sudden surge of emotional intensity, according to Ingarden, who defines it as "original emotion" (Ursprungsemotion). In his rather classicist view, this should function as a "spark" capable of igniting a process of serene and harmonious contemplation, separating it from the contradictory and painful underlying materiality of everyday life. However, an attentive examination of Ingarden's text shows how this concept points to a repressed element below the dry surface of his philosophical discourse, to an anxiety breaking the apparently objective and detached shell of theory, creating a passage for the chaos of history. Following this clue, and against the grain of Ingarden's own argument, the original emotion can become a critical tool to map the connections between narrative forms and their historical context.

In a footnote added to the German reedition of the *Cognition of the Literary Work of Art* (*Vom Erkennen des literarischen Kunstwerks*,[8] 1968), Ingarden draws a somber historical picture of the emergence of the original emotion. Conceived in an advanced seminar at the University of Lviv in the academic year 1935–36, this difficult theoretical knot had been worked out during discussions with the seminar participants, to whom, after more than thirty years, the philosopher reiterates here his gratitude. Then he adds, "The war, which broke out a few years later, and the following years had the result that, of the study group, which then consisted of thirty people (in which several professors, art critics, and also several young postdoctoral students took part), only a few remain alive" (Ingarden 1973, 189n14). As the shadow of mass destruction thus looms over the quiet and lofty atmosphere we are inclined to imagine for a seminar devoted to aesthetics, we cannot help but read this contrast in the philosophical text itself, which—this will be my interpretation—only in this sinister light releases all its theoretical potential.

According to Ingarden, the first task of a reflection on the aesthetic event should be "to clarify wherein the transition from the perception of a real object (thing) to the aesthetic experience [ästhetische Erlebnis] consists" (1973, 188). In other words, he asks how our ordinary perception can suddenly shift toward the "aesthetic attitude" (ästhetische Einstellung). The idea of an original emotion is meant to provide a solution for the theoretical difficulty of this transition, whose initial phase he described as follows: "In the perception of, say, a real thing, we are struck by a peculiar quality, or a multiplicity of qualities, or, finally, a particular Gestalt quality (e.g., a color or a harmony of colors, or a quality of a melody or of a rhythm, etc.) which not only draws our attention to itself and concentrates our attention on itself but, in addition, does not leave us cold" (Ingarden 1973, 188). We can note two things right away. First, the low intensity of the reaction being described, qualified as nothing more than a form of attention, further diminished by the litotes (it "does not leave us cold"): As we will see, this understatement will soon be contradicted. Second, this reflection seems to pertain to visual arts and music, but one would have to sensibly stretch it to think of a connection with the "literary work of art"—that is, the very subject of the book—as the translators aptly note in the introduction: "His treatment of the aesthetic experience was based on an earlier paper which was not concerned mainly with the literary work of art, and little attempt has been made to integrate it into the present book" (Ingarden 1973, xxvi). Indeed, another footnote added to the German edition informs us that the chapter under consideration, titled "The Aesthetic Experience and the Aesthetic Object" ("Das ästhetische Erlebnis und der ästhetische Gegenstand"), and whose first conception emerged in the 1935–36 seminar, had been initially presented as a paper[9] read at the Second International Congress of Aesthetics and Science of Art (Deuxième congrès international d'esthétique et de science de l'art) in Paris, in summer 1937. Moreover, in the first pages of the chapter, Ingarden makes clear that the primary example of his reflection is a sculpture, and specifically the *Venus of Milo*, which frequently returns throughout.

I will argue here that this series of "disturbances" to the otherwise smooth and pedantic flow of the phenomenological description can help us uncover an unforeseen critical potential in the concept of an original emotion of the aesthetic experience, which will go beyond the literary domain and will become relevant for narrative forms in general, helping us to connect them to their historical context. Let us start with the reaction to the initial stimulation. First, we should note that the "original" (ursprünglich) character of the emotion is immediately complicated by a redoubling of the process itself. This consists of the initial phase we have seen, with its passive stimulation in which a "quality" in the object affects the subject—thus already eliciting emotional reactions not yet defined as "original"—and a subsequent response finally deemed as "original emotion." Moreover, if we look closely at the expressions used in the first phase, in evident contradiction to the litotes, we note the emergence of a figurative isotopy[10] of violent imposition of physical contact: "The quality strikes us, forces itself upon us, grips us"[11] (Ingarden 1973, 189; the first two verbs are repeated two times in two adjacent paragraphs), and is "distinguished by a peculiar aggressiveness in relation to us" (189). Switching to the side of the perceiving subject, the author notices that "the reception of the quality is passive," and that "[it] brings us out of our equilibrium; we experience it too strongly to be able actually to apprehend it" (189). This is already substantially more than not being left cold. Subsequently, the inter-action is rearticulated as follows: "We feel that it attracts us, that it wants to move us to advert to it in order to possess it in a direct contact (as by touch). . . . To express this at first in a metaphorical way, it touches, rouses, or excites us in a peculiar way rather than being given to us"[12] (189). As it is evident, at a more abstract level these expressions are connected to ideas of aggression and seduction on the one hand, and to being overpowered and submitting to a subliminal influence on the other.

Only now, as a reaction to the initial stimulation, what Ingarden has named "original emotion" properly starts, first as a form of "being in love" (189; "Verliebtsein," 196 [All terms in German in this section refer to Ingarden 1968]), then as "a certain hunger" (190; "ein gewisser Hunger," 196) and a "growing striving for satisfaction from this quality, for lasting possession of it."[13] Soon the palette of sensations grows darker, with "displeasure or discomfort" (191; "Unlust oder Unbehagen" 198), "being unsatisfied" (191; "Unbefriedigtsein," 198), "inner unrest" (191; "innere Unruhe," 198), and three more mentions of "hunger" (191, 197), which anchor it steadily to the bodily dimension. How should we understand this way of depicting the very emotion that is here supposed to make us shift from an "everyday attitude" to the "aesthetic" one? In a footnote, Ingarden clarifies: "Of course, all the expressions used here are metaphorical and have something of a poetic character. This is only the result of the peculiar nature of the phenomenon appearing here, which cannot be named directly because language has not yet found such specialized designations" (1973,

190n15). In other words, the start of the aesthetic experience appears as an emotional excess that philosophical discourse fails to properly define in rational terms, and therefore attempts to allude to, through poetic, that is rhetorical, means. However, this gap in the coherent progression of the philosophical argument does not prevent the author from continuing a detailed description of the aesthetic experience's subsequent phases,[14] culminating in the constitution and contemplation of a "quality of harmony" (204; "Qualität des Zusammenklanges," 212), which places Ingarden's aesthetics in the territory of a rather outmoded classicism, as critics have often noted.[15] What is important for my present purposes is that, in view of such an ideal *telos* for the aesthetic experience, what he has described—and ultimately failed to define ("not purely conceptual determination can help us here," 190)—as the original emotion appears to be more the signal of an obstacle, the result of a *friction* produced by the unsmooth beginning of the process, than a positive start to it. If we now move away from following Ingarden's argument and consider his text as a literary work—which he himself suggests, after all, by admitting the "poetic" character of his descriptions—we can see how it bears within a pathetic intensity that is not only thematized, but inscribed in the text itself, where it is perceivable in the here and now of the reading experience. As we have seen from the quoted passages above, even beyond the choice of lyrical expressions and poetic metaphors, the description has a distinct narrative structure in which abstract or generic entities (the "quality," the "object," "us") are visually represented as engaging in violent interactions. At a deeper level of abstraction, these correspond to forms of manipulation, conjunction, and disjunction with an object of value, all basic narrative semiotic functions connected with the development of a pathetic intensity (Greimas and Fontanille 1991; Bertrand 2000, 225–38). Such emotional intensity is in this case further enhanced by a rhythmic syntactic structure building toward the culminating admission of a lack of defining terms, as if following an emotional stream that finally has proved to be in excess of the enunciator's strength. To sum up, while the original emotion, as thematized in the text, seems to be produced by an obstacle on the way to achieving a final contemplative harmony, in turn, the pathetic intensity produced by the process of defining it signals the presence of a disturbance in the development of the phenomenological description. The meaning of this resistance remains obscure for now; however, as it evokes an abstract structure that we do not fully understand, it conveys the pressure of another reality, the tension of an unsaid element striving to reach the surface of the text.

To see through the opacity of the text, we need to look at the other narrative elements that exceed its theoretical configuration, that is, those proposed by the contextual scenario pictured by the footnotes Ingarden added to the German edition. As I will show, these notes mirror and clarify the idiosyncratic narrative progression of the philosophical argument. In them we learn, as already mentioned, that the chapter we are discussing was presented as a paper at the Second International Congress of Aesthetics in Paris in the summer of 1937—an incidental detail, it would seem. Nevertheless, when connected with the allusion to the tragic destiny of the participants in the Lviv seminar in which the paper itself was first elaborated, this detail cannot avoid directing our attention to the historical context of that congress, that is, the International Exposition of Art and Technology in Modern Life (Exposition Internationale des Arts et Techniques dans la Vie Moderne), of which it was an affiliated event, in fact marketed to international scholars as an opportunity to visit the exposition (Basch 1936). Within this scenario, it is entirely plausible to imagine Ingarden pausing, like any other visitor, at the base of the Trocadero in the most dramatic spot of the exposition, where the German and Soviet pavilions, violently facing off, instantly disproved the rhetoric of peaceful international progress officially proposed by the exposition itself.[16] In his case, however, that specific standpoint was particularly significant, since only a few years later the seat of his seminar, Lviv, would be swallowed up by the violent confrontation between precisely these two powers, first occupied by the Soviets, then by the Nazis, then by the Soviets again (Amar 2015, 44–184), with the university being a major hotspot for political violence and atrocities (Schenk 2007, 113–41). Moreover, besides being in strong symbolic relation with his personal situation and his academic career (which would be interrupted for years and would have to be relocated to Krakow), the particular, heavily politicized aesthetic expressed by the Parisian exposition in the summer of '37—that is, the equally violent aggression and seduction, which all pavilions seemed to communicate to different degrees, as noted by the press of the time[17]—resonates with the two tendencies we have seen emerging in the narrative structure of the philosophical argument, which thus starts acquiring a historical grounding.

However, going back to the philosophical text, we notice that the violent and seductive confrontation returns, as a basic narrative element, at an even deeper level of condensation in the encounter with the *Venus of Milo* at the Louvre, which, as mentioned, is Ingarden's preferred example throughout the chapter. At one single moment, again in a note added to the

German edition, a specific historical encounter with this work is narrated in personal terms and with a reference to prewar Paris: "We remember how the room looked in which the *Venus de Milo* was once exhibited. At that time the walls were covered with red cloth, which contrasted in a very unpleasant way with the color of the statue. Now the *Venus* stands in a room of neutral color, which forms an unobtrusive background for the work of art" (Ingarden 1973, 179–80n5). To sum up, in this encounter where the theoretical elaboration of the original emotion is grounded, we find a trace of the same coexistence of seduction (the pleasant, classical forms) and violence, as exemplified by the red cloth ("which contrasted in a very unpleasant way"). Moreover, if we read the encounter with the *Venus* as the intended epitome of a harmonious contemplative experience, the episode rather testifies to its impossibility in that specific context, where we can read the "red cloth" as symbolically summarizing the larger historical background of prewar Paris ("at that time" as opposed to "now"), a time certainly more inclined to heavily politicized, aggressive conceptions of art linked to the Avant-Garde (and Modernism more broadly) than to Winckelmannian nostalgia. Again, what should entail the rise of an emotional intensity leading to a peaceful contemplation (the classicist ideal) proves instead to be the expression of a disturbance resulting from the ambiguous, unpleasant encounter with a contrasting element.

At this point, we can thus formulate the following hypothesis: While attempting to define a universal reaction that marks a qualitative transition from the "everyday attitude" to the "aesthetic" one, where the first would be discontinued to give way to the second, Ingarden's text in fact describes the dialectical persistence of historical experience within the relationship with the aesthetic object. This manifests itself precisely in the emotional disturbance we have seen, which disrupts the path supposedly leading to the "realization of an emotional contemplative experience of the harmony of aesthetically valuable qualities" (Ingarden 1973, 213). More importantly, we witness here a concrete staging of the philosophical argument in the narrative construction of the text. Indeed, this was already implicit in the almost delirious rhetorical personification of the "qualities" of the aesthetic object that act on the perceiving subject to elicit an emotional reaction, which Ingarden sketched in the phenomenological description of the process. In other words—and this will be decisive for my own use of the concept of an original emotion—Ingarden's text shows, *a parte obiecti*, the inscription of this same emotional experience (the nature of which remains to be determined) in the text itself, where it signals the insistence, beneath the surface, of an anxiety linked to a historical content that is striving for expression. This content—the politicization of art that makes the classicist ideal obsolete, the enormous scale of an epochal disaster that makes philosophical reflection irrelevant—explodes at the core of his work as an internal negation, menacing its own existence.

Following Althusser, Jameson has shown how the aesthetic act participates in the ideological cognitive mapping through which humans situate themselves in the social context, thus resolving, at the imaginary level, the contradictions and shortcomings of their own historicity.[18] It is precisely this model, to which I will return throughout this book, that allows us to understand how Ingarden's work outgrows its own contradiction: The aporetic element—the contrast between theoretical thought and historical context—is absorbed and articulated inside a narrative supplement. This goes beyond the mere insertion of footnotes. It enters, as we have seen, the structure of the philosophical argument itself, from the abstract-thematic to the concrete-figurative level, where it figures ideas of seduction and aggression in the interaction between a perceiving subject and the qualities of an object. As Jameson clarifies, "The *aporia* or the *antinomy*" of a historical situation, what "comes before the purely contemplative mind as logical scandal or double bind, the unthinkable and the conceptually paradoxical . . . must therefore generate a whole more properly narrative apparatus—the text itself—to square its circles and to dispel, through narrative movement, its intolerable closure" (2002, 68). In other words, articulated in the narrative dimension, this contradictory presence can at the same time be acknowledged and hidden in plain sight, allowing the work itself to resist its own aporetic knots.

However, the disruptive emotional intensity we perceive in the text cannot be solely considered as the trace of a form of self-censorship on Ingarden's part. On the contrary, it must also be linked to an opposite ideological thrust, one aimed at revealing the object at the core of the very process of erasure. This is because the necessity to displace and repress here logically coexists with a tendency toward expression, without which the content would have simply not entered his text. This contrast, which traverses the whole work, appears in the clearest way in the narrative condensation we have just examined, where the visit to the museum is recounted. Here not only is one of the most emblematic artifacts of the classicist ideal presented together with the displeasing background that makes its harmonious contemplation uncomfortable, but the contradictory composition is directly indicated and offered as an object for meditation by the gaze of an observer—one coinciding, in this case, with the self-diegetic narrator himself—as if in a cinematic point of view.

As we will see, the formal construction of this scene has a high paradigmatic value that will prove to be key for this book, as it thematizes and pictures both the mechanism of concealment and its undoing. Yet in order to examine how this peculiar scene operates in the text, it is necessary to foreground a second interpretation of ideology as conceptualized by Jameson. It is, in this case, the more literary—or cinematic, as we will see later on—take on ideology originating from Lukács's *History and Class Consciousness* (1923), where it is associated with the notion of "standpoint" (Standpunkt). First developed in his earlier manuscripts on aesthetics, standpoint initially meant the situated opening on the world afforded by the experience of a work of art;[19] later, in *History and Class Consciousness*, the concept is translated into political and epistemological terms to indicate the human mind's structural constraints and capabilities connected with its social position. Following the Marx of *The Eighteenth Brumaire of Louis Bonaparte* (1852), the expression "class consciousness" must be understood here as a subjective genitive, where "consciousness" does not mean the individual's "awareness," but the structure according to which their mind operates under the influence of their social standpoint (the main section of the book is titled "The Standpoint of the Proletariat"). In other words, ideology names here the mental structure deriving from the impact of the social machinery on the connection between the individual and the world. As such, it regulates vision and blindness, the politically distorted perception according to which, for example—and this will be a key example in the chapters that follow—privileged individuals can enjoy a picturesque urban view without being disturbed by the spectacle of misery, while others are able to recognize hunger and distress where the former only see pleasurable exoticism. In sum, for Lukács "ideology was . . . no longer considered false consciousness, but rather a constitutive limitation of the mind . . . the standpoint from which the social totality was masked or distorted" (Jameson 2015, 13). However, this also meant that those who experienced the mechanism of exploitation directly on themselves had the potential to see beyond the limits that complicity and privilege imposed on others. This is why in Lukács's view only the proletariat, the class completely reduced to the status of a commodity, could really *understand* the commodity form (Lukács 1971, 172), and thus the core of capitalist exploitation, from within. In this perspective, ideology must be seen as "an oppressive restriction which turns into a capacity for new kinds of experience and for seeing features and dimensions of the world and of history masked to other social actors" (Jameson 2009b, 221).

Let us head back to the hall of the Louvre, where the philosopher's enjoyment of the *Venus* is disturbed by the red cloth. We can now formulate the hypothesis that his vision was able to disclose the stark contradiction weighing on that piece of cloth precisely because it also incorporates a social standpoint that was deeply influenced by the immense historical dynamic that, first revealed in the aesthetic of the universal exposition, would end up crushing Ingarden's peaceful seminar in Lviv, swallowing up its participants, among which "only a few remain alive." The museum scene thus offers a sort of snapshot of the confrontation between the two opposing tendencies traversing the text: While the first aims to preserve the classicist ideal and the lofty detachment of theoretical discourse from the urgency of the historical context, the second seeks to bring it to the surface. We already know that the latter will succeed, although it will have to "compromise" and be in turn distorted. If we imagine the resistance to a contradictory ideological tendency in terms of mechanics, as a *stiction* (a static friction) resisting the push to initiate the movement of an object, we can see the scene at the Louvre as capturing the instant in which the stiction is overcome and the dialectical movement starts. Indeed, this is directly thematized in the gaze of the narrator focusing on the contradictory image—the *Venus* against the displeasing red background—which foregrounds the entrance of the second tendency into the system of the text, that is, the drive to bring the painful historical context to the surface. In other words, we can see this as an "original" still image, not in chronological terms, as its actual position in the sequence of the text (or in its diegesis) is not relevant, but as the condensation and imaginary reconstruction of that moment, thematized in a gesture. In this sense, as in mechanics, the force necessary to surmount the stiction is higher than the one needed to keep an object in motion. We can thus think of the original emotion as a higher pathetic intensity, signaling the overcoming of ideological standstill in this (non-chronologically) original moment of textualization, where it would correspond to the higher energy released by this initial phase of the process. However, as is evident from the same museum scene, this higher intensity is not textualized as such; rather, the emotion has here a higher degree of precision, of definition, as it is coherently located in the displeasing contrast the narrator feels between the statue and its background.

This marks a qualitative difference between the diffused emotional intensity linked to the presence of an ideological contradiction and the place in the text where this is condensed and thematized, localized in a gesture that indicates its source. We have observed this difference in Ingarden's text, which is chaotically traversed by a pathetic energy that surfaces in places where its appearance puzzles us, as in the examples of the phenomenological description, with its anthropomorphic imagery, while this same energy is suddenly condensed in front of the *Venus* at the Louvre. And what he attempts to define as a universal reaction to the aesthetic object emerges in his narrative as the anxiety of a subject confronted by the inextricability between aesthetic experience and its historical context. This is in turn communicated to readers through the experience of the text, which exposes them to making contact with its repressed historical content. Therefore, appropriating and overturning Ingarden's concept from the domain of reception to that of narratology, what I will call here "original emotion"[20] will be, in the diegesis of a text, the emotional intensity localized in the gesture that points to its origin, situated in the process of overcoming the stiction. This is methodologically important, as the search for the "original emotion" will not mean looking for a spot in the text where emotional intensity is higher—an enterprise always arbitrary and hardly helpful. Again following the script of the encounter with the *Venus*, we will look for the "original emotion" in places where its "origin" is placed in a contradictory element indicated and thematized as such. Indeed, the search for scenes structurally equivalent to this model—in both the literary and the filmic text—will play a key role in this book.

However, I want to clarify immediately that the individuation of such a figurative condensation will not coincide with the goal of my analytical process, but merely with its beginning (again, the overcoming of a stiction from which the dialectical process "painfully" begins). No "truth" is to be found here—to recall Michel Foucault's admonition, whereby to search for truth in the origin is always an " 'adolescent' quest" (Foucault 1977, 143)—but rather a textual hypothesis to be confirmed by the subsequent interpretation. The paradigmatic nature of this element will offer a model to map the ideological contradiction as it is played out in the process of narrativization, and its inner logic. Nevertheless, it will be helpful to preserve the notion of "origin" associated with the emotion that initiates textualization—but "origin" as read through the etymological lens that Martin Heidegger applied to the original German term in the *Introduction to Metaphysics*, seeing in it an "originary leap" (Ur-sprung; Heidegger 2014, 6–7). In this case, it will be the leap between the historical content and the text, through which the force that overcomes the ideological resistance is metaphorically alluded.

Paradise and Underworld

The historical content that will emerge in the works I will investigate is an emblematic example of the function of ideology as a device of visual distortion. "Land of the sun" and underworld, "paradise inhabited by devils," as it has been called for centuries, Naples is a multifaceted shell harboring an enigmatic object: its lower social stratum. This latter, a universally known stereotype and elusive specter at the same time, has been named in many different ways: "lazzari" or "lazzaroni," "plebe" (plebs), "popolino" (little people), "mau mau." I will briefly discuss this terminology in this introduction, where I will also show how the object it names had a paradigmatic function for the modern conceptualization of a lumpenproletariat since Marx and Engels. The story of this anomalous social formation can be traced back to the Spanish Viceroyalty's administration, in the sixteenth and seventeenth centuries, where a series of long-standing policies created a demographic disaster of internal migration, with masses of peasants moving from the whole kingdom to the capital,[21] thus producing "an abnormal and even monstrous urban entity, a unicum in Europe at the time, a land of conquest and colony, where one does not even bother to dress or catechize the most miserable natives" (Mozzillo 1983, 10). Historian Atanasio Mozzillo's reference to the catechization of natives is not a hyperbolic metaphor here, since the Jesuits carried out significant missionary activity in the kingdom, from the mid-sixteenth century until their expulsion more than two centuries later, trying to "civilize" its ungovernable social body, just as they did in the New World.[22] The lack of any structural countermeasure to reorganize the economy of the kingdom resulted in a situation of permanent exception, where the capital was "the monstrous head of a gracile and sick body" (Mozzillo 1983, 18), and reciprocally, "the entire kingdom was, in a sense, the capital's economic hinterland, though one marked by strong territorial discontinuities" (Sabatini 2013, 93). Things did not improve when the kingdom gained autonomy under Bourbon rule in the eighteenth century, and "by the middle of the 19th century the city did not present itself as a modern urban center, sustained by industrial and mercantile development, but, on the contrary, as densely populated agglomerate, artificially held together" (Macry 1997, 60). Since then, countless documents, from historical works to journalistic, fictional, or ethnographic accounts, in various media, have recounted the persistent conditions of misery of the Neapolitan poor, from writer Matilde Serao's post-unitary reportages collected in *The Belly of Naples* (*Il ventre di Napoli*, 1906; "They are monstrous beings, the pity equals the repugnance they inspire" Serao 2021, 44), to journalist and politician Maria Antonietta Macciocchi's letters to Althusser in 1968 ("Since arriving here I have been living in a state of shock, of trauma, pursued everywhere by the fetid odour of Naples' poverty" Macciocchi and Althusser 1973, 14), to anthropologist Thomas Belmonte's 1970s ethnography *The Broken Fountain* ("I managed to settle into one of the most infamous corners of Naples, notorious as a foul-smelling den of thieves and whores" Belmonte 2012, 12). Indeed, writers, intellectuals, and filmmakers have documented this phenomenon up to the present day, with its most recognizable presence in the international media landscape undeniably tied to the portrayal of organized crime in its Neapolitan and Campanian form, the Camorra, which has become, in recent decades, the most common lens through which the ideological machine allows the underclass to become visible. While this study will primarily focus on the early 1950s, it is important to briefly outline the evolution of the portrayal of the Neapolitan underclass in the following decades to connect my analysis with the present, thus clarifying the contemporary perspective through which that past can be viewed today.

The Camorra has roots deeply embedded in the city's lowest social stratum; however, far from functioning as a sort of political organization for the marginalized population, it ultimately reproduces within itself the same class divisions from which it originates, with an elite capable of operating at the high levels of politics and financial capitalism, and a mass kept in poverty and subjugation, at best destined to live and die providing criminal manpower (Barbagallo 2010). The portrayal of contemporary lower classes, shaped and popularized by the media through this lens, is currently split between the historic districts and the new postindustrial suburbs, where its most iconic symbols can be found: no more the dark alleys of the poor neighborhoods in the city center, but the most marginalized housing projects.

The piece of media that undoubtedly gave the greatest impulse to the newfound fame of the current incarnation of the nightmare associated with the Neapolitan underclass—those "devils" who once inhabited the "paradise" have now mutated into members of organized crime—was *Gomorrah* by Roberto Saviano (2006), a collection of narrative reportages and nonfiction stories that unveiled to its international readership the current functioning of the "System" (the name by which the Camorra refers to itself). The book was adapted into a film of the same name by Matteo Garrone (presented at Cannes in 2008, where it won the Grand Prix), and into a television series that spanned five seasons from 2014 to 2021, achieving success both in Italy and internationally. The sociological and documentary impulse, originally present in Saviano's book and Garrone's film, gradually faded in the series in favor of entertainment values—and a similar trajectory was followed by Saviano himself for his subsequent novel *Piranhas* (*La paranza dei bambini*, 2016). However, in the series too, said impulse does not disappear completely, and it remains inscribed above all in the urban settings, in the bodies of the crowds of the extras, and in the thematic elements that refer to the problems of the informal economy in which the underclass survives: violence as endemic to everyday life, drug addiction, unemployment, and precariousness, all elements that filter through the rules of entertainment, exposing its ideological contradictions. It is also important to mention, even only in passing, that the portrayal of these themes as connected to the *habitus* of the Neapolitan underclass—which my research aims to reconstruct in its fundamental structures, albeit with reference to a previous historical moment—was prepared by several authors who have approached this same representational problem with varying intentions and outcomes.

Particularly groundbreaking, in this context, was Salvatore Piscicelli, who, with his first films *Immacolata and Concetta: The Other Jealousy* (*Immacolata e Concetta: L'altra gelosia*, 1980) and *The Opportunities of Rosa* (*Le occasioni di Rosa*, 1981), laid the foundations for a stark portrayal of the living conditions of suburbia's lower classes in their authentic settings, moving away from the clichés of Neapolitan entertainment cinema (Marlow-Mann 2011, 72–74), and bringing to light, above all, a narrative of debt, wherein the story's progression is directed toward the remediation of a structural damage that can never be fully resolved or repaired, and whose momentary relief results in new damage that rekindles the need for repair. The temporal aspect of this narrative structure is, in short, both terminative and inchoative, as seen in stories about drug addiction or the search for money to pay off interest on a (usury) loan, where the completion of the "quest" quickly gives way to the need to start over with the same process, usually carried out through activities involving crime, prostitution, or other endeavors that teeter on the edge of legality.[23]

On a completely different line are two other recent media products with mainstream diffusion, in which the representation of Neapolitan reality plays a major role, namely the last two films by Paolo Sorrentino, *The Hand of God* (*È stata la mano di dio*, 2021) and *Parthenope* (2024). In both cases, the narrative of debt is extinguished, and the protagonists' experiences express the self-realizing temporality of the bourgeois bildungsroman. Significantly, however, in *Parthenope* there is a brief sequence in which the interiors of the Neapolitan "bassi"[24] are explored from the outside, as if the camera was peering into a foreign dimension, where a different temporality evidently corresponds to a different use of space (as these dark, crowded rooms sharply contrast with the vast, sunlit terraces of the protagonist's neighborhood); and yet, devoid of any historical context, the existence of the urban lumpenproletariat here seems to momentarily escape invisibility only to be offered as an enigma. This resonates with recent popular TV shows set in Naples, like those based on Maurizio De Giovanni's novels, where, even when portrayed, the city's lowest social class seems incomprehensible.

The development of the literary representation of the Neapolitan underclass in recent decades follows a framework similar to that just outlined for cinema and television, where the essential link to organized crime can be traced back to the archetypal novel *Il camorrista* (1984) by Giuseppe Marrazzo. In this work, the story of the Camorra boss Raffaele Cutolo is narrated in the first person, reconstructing his persona as the locus of a conscious connection between organized crime and the marginalization of the Neapolitan underclass, which the former drives toward a form of violent and self-destructive redemption. Here, a few years after Piscicelli's first films, the narrative of debt reemerges as a literary representation of an anthropological structure in which social precariousness and organized crime intersect. In opposition to the state's attempt to impose the empty time of prison, the boss organizes an entire society around the illusory reparative structure of debt (while we are, in fact, faced with a form of bad infinity): blood debt (murders to punish those who have betrayed or challenged the boss's authority), economic debt (extortion, corruption), debt of honor (the paradoxical fulfillment of family and friendship obligations). It is no coincidence then that we find all these elements in the non-stereotypical attempts to represent Neapolitan reality from the late 1980s onward, particularly in the two works by Saviano I mentioned previously. But perhaps an even more emblematic case, though less successful, is represented by the stories and novels of Peppe Lanzetta, who sought, with varying degrees of efficacy, to frame Neapolitan reality through the lens of an international imaginary of urban marginalization, spanning from the American ghetto to the French banlieue. Significant, in this sense, are the stories of *Children of a Minor Bronx* (*Figli di un Bronx minore*, 1998), where the three articulations of the narrative of debt noted in Marrazzo's novel are expressed through an "adolescent" tone (Cannamela and Castaldo 2021), with echoes of the first stories of Pier Vittorio Tondelli, from which Lanzetta inherits the lyricism. In Lanzetta's case, however, the focus is not on organized crime but rather on the environment of precariousness, illegality, and marginalization in which it thrives. It is worth mentioning, in this regard, the novel *Tropic of Naples* (*Tropico di Napoli*, 2000), where Tondelli's lyricism vanishes, offering no escape from the endless progression of debt as experienced by a crowd of characters populating marginal spaces, from the city center's historic alleys to the housing projects on the outskirts.

In conclusion to this brief survey, it is important to mention an anomalous product such as Giuseppe Gaudino's film *Moon Orbits Between Land and Sea* (*Giro di lune tra terra e mare*, 1997), which has remained unique in the Neapolitan panorama (although echoes of it can be found today in the work of an author like Pietro Marcello). The film focuses on the erasure of the lower classes of the Phlegraean area (at the western periphery of Naples), where we will soon have to return for two important sequences of *Journey to Italy*. The main storyline revolves around the displacement of a family of fishermen from the ancient center of the town of Pozzuoli (the Rione Terra) to a modern housing project, where their communal life is destined to fade into marginalization. This tale, unsurprisingly marked by the ever-present theme of debt, is intricately woven into a complex layering of historical periods, marked by the inclusion of historical, mythological, and folkloric events that intermittently interrupt the diegetic present with strong formal discontinuities. It is precisely the insertion of private events within the historical discourse that offers here an alternative to the paradigm of the spectacularization of poverty, as the ever-inconclusive narrative of debt can finally be halted through historical knowledge.

It would be certainly possible to extend this analysis further. However, for the scope of this project, it is important to shift focus to a different phenomenon that proceeds in parallel and often overlaps with the documentation of the city's social disaster: the transfiguration or the outright erasure of human suffering from the enchanted scenario of the gulf.

Since the late eighteenth century, when the living memory of the Neapolitan revolt of 1647 to 1648 and of other recent catastrophic events like plagues and famines was beginning to fade, northern European travelers, whose grand tour culminated in Naples,[25] started to shift the tone of their accounts from a more or less horrified description of the Neapolitan poor ("They are the most abominable scoundrel, the most disgusting vermin that has ever crawled on the face of the earth"[26]) to an idealized evocation of a land untouched by progress, where a simple and lazy people lives foreign to history ("One lives on little; in fact, no work and a lot of sleep"[27] Dupaty 1788, 2:216). What had happened in the meantime? To be sure, time partly healed the class panic fueled by the violent revolt of the previous century. However, as suggested by Roberto Dainotto, this change was part of a broader process of creating a European identity in the eighteenth century. Balanced against the external Other identified with the East produced by the ideological machine of Orientalism as described by Edward Said, this identity was at the same time able to liquidate the Other entirely, by a process of incorporation,[28] at the end of which southern Europe emerged as an internal other, a still visible *past*, geographically localized in the places from which Western civilization had emerged (Dainotto 2007, 54–55). Therefore, suddenly, "a myth that often depicted an ungovernable, backward urban jungle, peopled by a bloodthirsty, incorrigible and superstitious population" (Selwyn 2004, 3), without ceasing to be at work, could nevertheless comfortably fade into a different fantasy, one longed for by northern and civilized people absorbed in the discontents of progress and material wealth: contact with nature, primitivism, simplicity, authenticity, strong passions. In other words, we find here all the dreamy traits that enter the field of the "picturesque" as a visual style spanning different media, and which, traversing the romantic era, would find their way into the travel agencies' brochures that still advertise Mediterranean vacations to this day. The "picturesque," a concept that, when it enters the English debate on aesthetics in the eighteenth century, becomes so vastly used that "it can seem so ill-defined as to be virtually meaningless" (Copley and Garside 1994, 1), is nevertheless the obsessively recurring trope through which the south is referred to and depicted by travelers—a catchword indicating something that literally everyone would immediately get.[29] What is most striking in the specific case of the discourse around Neapolitan reality is that, as argued by Melissa Calaresu, in this same time period the category of the "picturesque" is extended from landscape and architecture to "the creation of a modern urban picturesque" (2007, 190), thus becoming able to absorb and domesticate even the fearful crowd of the poor, where ragged, homeless, exhausted bodies can become, in lively descriptions, paintings, illustrations, and postcards, a music-loving, carefree people living off the generosity of the climate. This is a stereotype that, not by chance, is central to Montesquieu's climatological idea of a modern civilization built by northern populations forced to work hard and unite to win a hostile nature (Dainotto 2007, 56–64), and whose positive version in Rousseau's "state of nature" does not change its role in this mechanism.[30]

Thus, when we arrive, at the end of the nineteenth century, at the cultural elaboration of a united Italy, the ideological apparatus destined to include Naples and the south as the nation's internal other is already comfortably in place, and, as shown by John Dickie in his case study of the post-unitary popular magazine *Illustrazione Italiana*, the picturesque works, in this timeframe as well, precisely as an ideological device through which southern reality is absorbed and domesticated, but never really processed in its material, historical features (Dickie 1999, 83–119). However, what matters most for the scope of this book is the appropriation of this ideological device by the Neapolitan elites themselves, with an ambivalent process of defensive self-positioning vis-à-vis the most derogatory depictions produced by foreigners and, at the same time, of eager endorsement of the "positive side" of the stereotype. As an example of this process, Calaresu quotes a guidebook of Naples from the 1780s by the Neapolitan writer Giuseppe Maria Galanti, specifically written "to redress the misinformation and misrepresentation of the city by foreign travel writers," where, in fact, despite describing in more neutral terms the dire conditions of the indigent part of the urban population, the author cannot help concluding "and they go through life sweetly" (Calaresu 2007, 200).

Indeed, this is the point of departure of an ideological process that quickly becomes, for the Neapolitan privileged classes, both an absolutory discourse for living off the exploitation and oppression of the vast majority of the population and a sort of touristic branding *ante litteram*, proposing a luxurious and carefree lifestyle. As we will see in detail in chapter 2 of this book, this will be the basis for what will be called, in the second part of the twentieth century, the "napoletanità": the Neapolitan ideology. Raffaele La Capria has defined it as a "collective performance . . . that social mush in which every difference in class and wealth, even if enormous, becomes secondary in the face of the strongest anthropological-Neapolitan homogeneity" (2003, 654). In his view, in this consolatory self-depiction the Neapolitan elite could see itself reunited, as one single "people," with the fearful crowd of the poor, whose image is tamed through the centuries-old stereotype of the thoughtless "lazzaro," who quietly rests on the seaside, singing traditional songs, not bothered by the weight of tomorrow: "The lazzaroni would embody with only greater force and clarity a general aspiration of all Neapolitans: that of resting and finding all the good opportunities and means to do nothing" (Benigno 2005, 30).

As noted by Ruth Glynn, even recent attempts at rethinking cultural representations of the city and their place in the construction of European modernity have not escaped the allure of such a discourse. In a recent study Glynn has focused, in particular, on how Walter Benjamin and Asja Lacis's essay "Naples" ("Neapel," 1924) has been uncritically received in contemporary reflections. While focusing on the productivity of the concept of "porosity" developed by the two thinkers to interpret Neapolitan reality (in architectural, social, and cultural terms), the contemporary theorists considered by Glynn (Massimo Cacciari and Ian Chambers) failed to see how that seminal essay is fully rooted in the ideological tradition of the Neapolitan picturesque (Glynn 2020, 68). Indeed, Benjamin and Lacis's essay is an excellent example of the ideological device of invisibility through which this discourse is able to hide the city's structural inequality for tourists and privileged inhabitants alike. In it we find, unaltered, the topic of the "collective performance" to which La Capria will refer a few decades later:

> Buildings are used as a popular stage. They are all divided into innumerable, simultaneously animated theaters. Balcony, court-yard, window, gateway, staircase, roof are at the same time stage and boxes. Even the most wretched pauper is sovereign in the dim, dual awareness of participating, in all his destitution, in one of the pictures of Neapolitan street life that will never return, and of enjoying in all his poverty the leisure to follow the great panorama. . . . Similarly dispersed, porous, and commingled is private life. What distinguishes Naples from other large cities is something it has in common with the African *kraal*; each private attitude or act is permeated by streams of communal life. To exist, for the Northern European the most private of affairs, is here, as in the *kraal*, a collective matter. (Benjamin and Lacis 1996, 417–19)

What the two tourists on a one-day excursion from Capri in the summer of 1924 do not seem to realize—and why should they, since on this non-realization the local privileged classes have built their self-understanding for generations?—is that the "collective" character of that form of life is simply produced by inhumane living conditions, and that the "natural theatricality" is rather the effect of some form of endemic anxiety, the exhaustion deriving from surviving in the underworld of informal economy, the Neapolitan "slum economy" described by Allum (1973, 40–41). Some fifty years later, Belmonte will seem to gloss this passage as follows: "The theatrical quality of life in the poor quarters, the loud, gesticulating style and the aggressive hubris of the individual, is the Neapolitans' collective commentary on the instability of the socioeconomic and honorific settings upon which they must stage their lives" (Belmonte 2012, 135). In fact, the two tourists do make the connection between housing and lifestyle toward the end of the essay: "How could anyone sleep in such rooms? To be sure, there are beds, as many as the room will hold. But even if there are six or seven, there are often more than twice as many occupants. For this reason one sees children late at night—at twelve, even at two—still in the streets. At midday they then lie sleeping behind a shop counter or on a stairway" (Benjamin and Lacis 1996, 420). Yet the porosity between private and public dimensions, inner and outer space, waking life and sleep, is no further interrogated in its material foundations.

In 1953, the Neapolitan writer and journalist Anna Maria Ortese, at that time de facto homeless and surviving on precarious publishing activity, on friends' help, and on sporadic patronage, published a collection of short stories titled *Il mare non bagna Napoli—Neapolitan Chronicles* in the most recent English-language edition.[31] In it, one story in particular, "The Silence of Reason," whose title had been inspired by Goya's *El sueño de la razón produce monstruos*, provoked a wave of indignation among Neapolitan intellectuals and in the city's press. She lost almost all her local friends because of it, and since she relied on them for survival, did not set foot in Naples anymore, except on the occasion of her father's death. In the early months of the same year, while Ortese was working on the final draft of "The Silence," Roberto Rossellini was in Naples with his crew, shooting *Journey to Italy*, which would only be released in the fall of the next year because of censorship problems, which had already forced him and his collaborators to drop a fully developed script and to start over almost entirely.[32] Rossellini and Ortese did not meet in those months, although as the writer mentions in an interview from 1996, more than forty years later (Rossellini had been dead for almost two decades; Ortese would survive two more years), they had once met in Naples before the war. Back then, he was a promising young director in the Fascist film industry, and she an even younger—equally promising—writer, who twice had won the national literary competition of the GUF, the League of the Fascist University Students, once for poetry and once for prose narrative, although she was not enrolled in the university and had not even finished middle school. Rossellini wanted to meet her, Ortese recalls, having read one of her articles where she wrote that life is amazing because mandarins and roses exist, both of which are not human-made (Clerici 2002, 117). However, this early longing for something natural *and not artificial* strongly contrasts with the main allegory on which "The Silence" was built, where Nature appears as a monstrous deity keeping the city trapped in its misery, against any attempt of Reason to rescue its population. Yet the point of that allegory, as we will see, was precisely to show how this natural deity is just a fiction: The oppression that weighs on the poorest strata of the population is artificial, and not the result of some unchangeable natural order. Not surprisingly then, her book was accused of being a slanderous attack on Naples (" 'The Silence of Reason' is the story that unleashed hell, so I never went back to Naples. I have had attacks from certain newspapers. And then personal insults. I have not dared to touch Naples anymore" qtd. in Clerici 2002, 240). The main issue was of course the crude representation of the crowd of the poor, which entered "The Silence" together with the Neapolitan intellectuals, many of them mentioned with their real names, caught while exhibiting their peculiar ability not to see that very crowd.

Journey to Italy's problems with censorship were also substantially linked to its depiction of the urban poor, as the script was accused of portraying "a crowd, or rather an anonymous underclass [plebe] . . . according to the abused clichés so dear to the Anglo-Saxons when they intend to vilify Italy and the Italians." That is to say, thus continued the censor's note, "this film, due to its content and its unilateral and sordid representation of a certain southern Italy, as well as harming the prestige and decorum of Italy, could harm the interests of our tourism" (qtd. in Dagrada 2008, 509). This is all very paradoxical, as Rossellini's initial intentions were not too far from seeking to create a positive stereotypical portrayal of the reality of Naples, if we read the interviews he gave about the film throughout his career. And this is also visible in the film finally released in the theaters, which clearly shows the signs of those superficial intentions.

However, in *Journey to Italy*, and more explicitly in Ortese's book, something had happened, something deeply disturbing for their audience and readers. What had remained invisible at the very center of Benjamin and Lacis's philosophical fresco of the Neapolitan reality, even if offered in plain sight ("How could one sleep in similar rooms?"), here suddenly comes into visibility, together with the mechanism that ordinarily makes it invisible. Why such a thing could happen in these two works must be explained historically, not only with reference to the two authors' personal standpoints but also in relation to the unique situation represented by the early 1950s in Italy and in Naples, specifically.

The city suffered greatly during the war due to extensive destruction and chaotic administration before, during, and after the Allied occupation (Ginsborg 1990, 37). Not surprisingly, the weakest sectors of the urban population bore the heaviest burden. Of about the 200,000 people left homeless by the bombings,[33] the majority were the inhabitants of the poorest neighborhoods of the city center. For them, temporary homelessness often became a permanent emergency, well beyond the end of the war (Varriale 2023). In its January 24, 1944 issue *Life* published a photographic reportage by Margaret Bourke-White, which was introduced as follows: "[She] has photographed World War II in Russia, England and North Africa. But nowhere has she seen such desolation and poverty among civilians as she found last month when she visited Naples" (Bourke-White 1944, 17). The dark cave Bourke-White photographs in the opening picture of her reportage would still be populated in the early months of 1946, when Rossellini shot, precisely there, the final sequence of the Neapolitan episode of *Paisan* (*Paisà*, 1946), with the entrance of the American soldier into the abyss of Neapolitan desperation. And the horrible living conditions of another emergency shelter, the infamous Granili, would be described as a fearful underworld by Ortese in 1952, in "The Involuntary City," a story also collected in *Neapolitan Chronicles*. In sum, as had happened in previous centuries with historical crises like revolts, plagues, and famines ("the city acquired a face of degradation and disease that it had not known since the great plagues of the seventeenth century" Ginsborg 1990, 37), the existence of the urban poor suddenly became more visible, thus occasionally escaping the fog of the Neapolitan ideology. Yet, during the war and in the immediate postwar years, the fate of this class was inevitably only a part of a wider catastrophic situation, extending beyond the city's and the country's borders, where the specificity of the lumpenproletariat's own permanent, ancestral catastrophe inevitably risked being lost from view. Therefore, even when narrative representations of the city from those years shift their focus onto this part of the population—thus escaping the picturesque—they tend to frame it inside a much bigger historical picture. This is the case of war memoirs and novels like Norman Lewis's *Naples '44* (1978) and John Horne Burns's *The Gallery* (1947), Carlo Bernari's *Prologue to Darkness* (*Prologo alle tenebre*, 1947) and *Speranzella* (1949), or Curzio Malaparte's *The Skin*[34] (*La pelle*, 1949). However, when this long postwar moment finally came to an end[35] and reconstruction suddenly moved into unprecedented economic development, the need to forget,[36] as quickly as possible, the war and the dark years that had preceded it ("post-war Europe was built upon deliberate mis-memory—upon forgetting as a way of life" Judt 2005, 829) pushed the Neapolitan lumpenproletariat back into its usual invisibility, again confined beyond the screen of the picturesque, where it returned to its role of "the underclass [plebe], the Hidden Thing, always lurking in the unconscious of this city" (La Capria 2003, 652). Therefore, the months between 1952 and 1953, when "The Silence of Reason" and *Journey to Italy* were created, can be considered a brief, privileged window of opportunity in which the conditions of the lowest class could become an object of analysis, after the overwhelming darkness of the war and before the wave of oblivion makes it, once again, increasingly irrelevant. To have a sense of the magnitude of this erasure and its translation into cultural politics, one only needs to consider the astonishing number of romantic musical films that started to be made in Naples in the early 1950s, and whose emblematic figure was the actor and singer Giacomo Rondinella. In 1954 alone, the year when *Journey to Italy* was released, seven such films with Rondinella were also released, all more or less repeating the same plot and situations, with titles like *Longing for the Sun* (*Desiderio di sole*), *Naples Land of Love* (*Napoli terra d'amore*), *One Hundred Serenades* (*Cento serenate*), and so on, where the cinematic version of the picturesque, heavily focused on landscape and music, could triumph, erasing any dissonant trace of misery.

However, despite responding to the same historical situation, "The Silence of Reason" and *Journey to Italy* work in very different ways. If they are both traversed by various degrees of the same ideological contradiction, that is, by opposing drives to reveal and conceal the material conditions of the city's lower classes, the two works embed this first, more elemental contradiction inside a second, wider, less visible but more complex one, which assumes a structural function, and is different in each of the two works. Indeed, if the typical Neapolitan ideology is time and again exposed at different places of the two texts, in order to interpret this second, more personal, structural contradiction where the interpretive key is located, we will need to search for a scene that captures the overcoming of the stiction process—where the "original emotion" is located—following the model traced in the previous section. Yet this will be only a point of departure, and we will need to follow the narrative articulation of this secret contradiction in the wider dimension of the text.

Scherzo: Spit and Blood

"The Silence of Reason" opens with a self-diegetic female narrator who has just returned to Naples after a long period of absence. The signs of the war are still visible, the streets are crowded by an immense lumpenproletariat. She visits her old friends—all young intellectuals with whom, a few years earlier, she had worked on *Sud* (published between 1945 and 1947), a leftist journal deeply committed to a radical renovation of the city's political life. That enterprise had failed, and the young intellectuals disbanded, each embracing a personal career, most of them forgetting political struggle in exchange for personal success. Her presence brings back ghosts of the betrayed ideal. I will closely analyze this work in the next chapters; for now, let us briefly examine the scene where the "original emotion" is located and the overcoming of the stiction is captured.

Luigi Compagnone, the first friend the narrator visits, lives in an upper-class neighborhood, where the presence of the urban poor feels less oppressive. However, as in a nightmare, no place in the city is really free from it. From his ground floor apartment the street is directly visible through a glass "door-window," and while the two friends are discussing, they spot a group of barefoot kids, dressed in rags, carrying, as if in a procession, a pole with a sacred image at the top, as religious brotherhoods sometimes do to raise funds. The kids proceed cheerfully, jokingly begging for alms, their leader "a girl of about seven, her head closely cropped, and wearing a gray rag that, leaving her chest bare, came down to her feet in the manner of a lady"[37] (Ortese 2018, 139). The miserable conditions of the lowest strata of the population had once been the main focus of this group of intellectuals. The unexpected appearance of a specimen of that class should thus evoke some sort of embarrassment, we would think, for the young man in his comfortable, dignified apartment. Yet the apparition does not seem to bother Luigi. In fact, he himself draws the narrator's attention to the children outside ("Look . . . look"), and seems to be amused as he moves to the window, where the narrator joins him: "Truly entertaining," he says; then he adds, "So colorful, so perfect"[38] (139). The color, the perfection mentioned here are an obvious reference to the old obsession with the picturesque. However, something does not go according to script here, and the little beggar, the girl who leads the group, decides to escape the role assigned to her centuries before she was born, when Spanish viceroys ruled over the city: "Like a capricious sideshow freak, [she] swiftly left the group and, with a dirty hand outstretched, feigned begging, her toothless mouth open in a soundless laugh. Having glimpsed Luigi, she came skipping up the steps to the window and, holding up her skirt, curtsied. Then she spat"[39] (139).

Inside the room the two intellectuals remain silent. "Luigi watched as her saliva rolled down the window"[40] (139). They listen to the sound of the children's footsteps fade away, along with their laughs. Here the girl's spit, slowly rolling down the glass, short-circuits the ideological mechanism on which the city's social balance is built. Ideology's invisible lens suddenly becomes visible, the transparent glass becomes opaque. Having stopped the contact between the two classes, it demonstrates its own function as a protective barrier as well as a visualizing screen, operator of a "safe" vision, through which the scary spectacle of poverty becomes "colorful." Thus, metonymically, it invokes the presence of a whole oppressive infrastructure on which the city stands. In other words, what weighs on the silence of the two intellectuals for a long moment is the demonstration of the role of ideology as a modal operator of a social group's capability of vision, because of which some individuals are able to access some contents of reality and others are not. To map its effects on the organization of narrative matter, I will build, in the next chapters, on the semiotic square of the cognitive modalization of space analyzed by Jacques Fontanille in his 1988 work *The Subjective Spaces* (*Les espaces subjectifs*).

Here the space of the picturesque corresponds precisely to the "complex term"[41] of this square (figure I.2), where exposure and inaccessibility coincide. Indeed, through the protective screen, the little beggars are at once visible and invisible, exposed in plain sight yet inaccessible, transfigured by the lens of the picturesque. From his privileged position, the bourgeois intellectual could not avoid their sight and, simultaneously, was not able to see them until the moment in which the girl sabotaged the machine.

Figure I.2. Semiotic square of the cognitive modalization of space. *Source:* Original version in Fontanille 1988, 120. Recreated by the author.

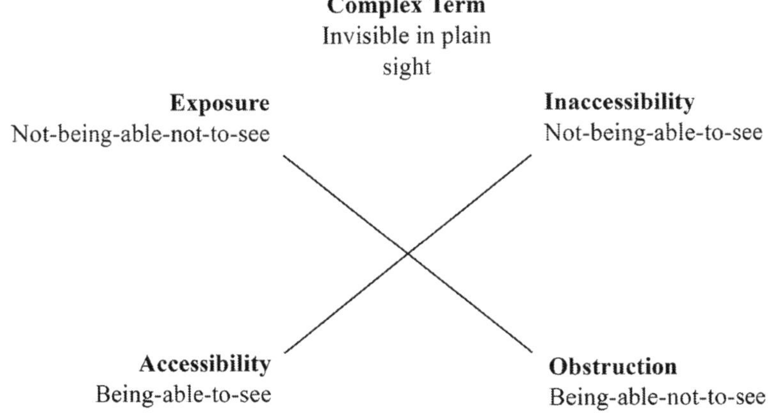

Yet this whole scene is only a premise to the unveiling of the place where the text's inner contradiction is directly indicated, where its "original emotion" is located. As we have learned from the analysis of Ingarden's text, the "original emotion" signals the place in the text where we can locate its central contradiction. Produced by the overcoming of the static friction (the stiction) between two opposing ideological tendencies, one to reveal, the other to conceal, this moment marks the start of the movement that allows the contradictory revelation—contradictory because its trajectory is permanently influenced by the opposing force—to be manifested in the text. This is, in sum, the place where the painful historical content of a text reaches the surface and offers a model to analyze its subsequent articulations. In the case of Ortese's story, while the oppressive function of the Neapolitan ideology is abundantly thematized in the course of the story, its innermost aporia—however linked to the former—lies elsewhere. Therefore, rather than in the scene we have just described, the "original emotion" will be placed in the one that immediately follows, which will reveal the unspeakable relationship between the self-diegetic narrator and the invisible underclass that her presence forces her friends to see. Immediately after that long silence and a brief interruption of the scene due to the entrance of Luigi's wife, the latter is seized by a sudden outburst of panic, fearing that somehow the girl's spit has traversed the window and reached his head: "Luigi asked, 'Would you look at my head?' His voice was a combination of infinite patience and infinite terror, as he struggled to achieve a calm that was completely unnatural 'Is there something . . . something wet?' "[42] (140). The narrator tries to reassure him, but his anxiety is not sedated, and he abruptly and rudely asks her to leave. Once outside, this outburst of anxiety contaminates her as well, and she starts to run. This wet spot Luigi feels on his head, where he asks the narrator to look, seems to be the enigmatic place where the stiction of two opposing ideological drives is located, and where the contradiction starts to move, thus entering the text, releasing the *heat* of the "original emotion" that precisely on this hand tremblingly touching the hair finds its source.

Just as we had to read and reconstruct the entire framework of narrative references in Ingarden's chapter to interpret the scene at the Louvre, here too only a careful examination of internal references between formally similar scenes will allow us to interpret this one properly. However, it is important to clarify immediately that the mysterious physical contact between classes, which has happened despite the barrier, with this ghostly passage of organic matter, points to the identity, at the structural level, of the narrator herself with the bodies of the poor that will populate the story. What should have remained outside has found its way to the inside. She is responsible and must be expelled: The illogical anger with which Luigi asks her to leave speaks of this realization, and her own emotional spasm, which makes her run away, works as a refusal of this painful awareness. I will later explain the narrator's actantial role, in narrative semiotic terms, as coinciding with the ideological "sender" of the failed "quest" for social justice in which Luigi and the other intellectuals were once involved. However, syncretically, her surface character also coincides, at a deeper level, with the very object that the old quest for justice aimed to rescue, now abandoned to its fate: the city's lumpenproletariat, the immense crowd of the poor. Not surprisingly, this has to do with the author's personal social standpoint inscribed in the text, which I will investigate in the first two chapters of this book, where her story of poverty and homelessness will be examined. This will shed light on the inextricable connection of her writing with that same fearful experience of hunger—the necessity to write and get something published for day-to-day survival—which, in different terms, lies at the core of the form of life of the city's poor, whose existential scope is limited to the endlessly repeated project of daily survival.

The shame and the fear that derive from this condition fuel the contradictory drive that runs through this story, and which we have located in the trembling hand of the intellectual pointing to his own head. This entire narrative sequence evokes a situation that had occurred many times during the years Ortese lived in Naples, where she had come to her friends' doors to beg for food, money, and a place to stay. The painful realization is foreshadowed and negated, at the same time, in the narrator's presence inside Luigi's apartment, where it literally completes the performance of the girl, as she is finally treated as an accomplice and sent away. In other words, while the structure of the story will force the protagonists to *see* their own condition as traitors and to look at the object that they had wished to unsee, it will also impose, through a myriad of traces I will pursue across my analysis, the autoptic vision of the narrator as herself a specimen of the lumpenproletariat—a vision that finds its culmination with the apparition of the "hunger artist" in the final pages of the story. This is the content that the trembling hand indicates in the spot where the stiction is overcome and the emotional stream of the story locates its origin.

Another hand, another finger points at a trace of organic matter on a glass barrier at the beginning of *Journey to Italy*. "Is that a streak of blood?" Katherine Joyce (Ingrid Bergman) asks her husband Alex (George Sanders), who is driving their luxury car. The glass barrier is actually the car's windshield, and that trace of blood "is just a bug," as he immediately replies. When the film starts, they are in the countryside of Lazio, around Latina, a malarial swamp until a few decades earlier. They are going to Naples (from England) to sell a villa they just inherited from an eccentric uncle recently deceased. The camera does not show us the stain on the glass; we only measure the disquieting effect it has on Katherine by the frowning of her face, which we see from the side in a lateral medium shot of the interior of the car, where her uneasiness clearly contrasts with her husband's self-assurance (figure I.3).

It is precisely here, I argue, that the "original emotion" of the story is located, ignited by the opposing reactions, almost negligible but clearly articulated with a gesture that indicates the overcoming of the stiction, where the contradiction enters the text. To understand how this process is played out, we need to recall that Rossellini's primary intention for this film was to exploit the positive side of the old stereotype about the South to appeal to a northern—that is, western European and American—audience: As the English couple is facing a marital crisis, at the superficial level the film would show how the southern dimension—Naples and its ancient mysteries—are

Figure I.3. Katherine points to something on the windshield. *Source:* Roberto Rossellini, *Journey to Italy*, 1954.

able to "cure" them, to teach them how to connect again with their inner feelings paralyzed by an excess of rationality. We will see that much more than this is at play in the film. However, in a much-quoted interview with a French radio station from 1960, Rossellini talked about *Journey to Italy* as "an encounter between two civilizations, between two types of education," and explained the difference between them with the allegory of the "draped" people (wearing a toga), corresponding to southerners, and the "sewn" people, the northerners:

> If I could use a paradox to explain myself better, I would take the liberty of dividing civilizations into two categories: that of "draped" men [*sic*], who are always folded in a toga and who continue to wear it (morally, of course), and that of "sewn" men, that is, those who are forced to sew animal skins on themselves in order to survive. They are two very different types of man. It is perfectly logical that the "sewn" man is a truly efficient individual and that the "draped" man has a different concept of life, sweeter, more relaxed. Well . . . I wanted to introduce two examples of "sewn" men into a completely "draped" world, in that world which, among other things, has contributed to the extent we know to the creation of modern civilization. I stopped to observe them, and this is how *Journey to Italy* was born. (Rossellini 1987, 193)

Through the synecdochic element of clothing, Rossellini clearly draws on the old climatological system of metaphors on which Europe's self-understanding was built in opposition to its internal Other, as we have seen in the previous section. However, beyond this surface intention, the film will cut across the system of stereotypes to present a very different reality, in which such mythical racial differences will be brutally reduced to the materiality of class oppression.

Starting from this first sequence in the car, the verbal allusion and the emotional element evoked by Katherine's facial expression elicit a doubt, an alternative hypothesis to the discourse defining the South as a revitalizing, exotic, but ultimately safe tourist destination: "Do you think there is any danger of catching malaria?" she asks. "They say not," he replies. This doubt is immediately translated into the articulation of the filmic space itself: At the moment in which the hand points to the windshield, the latter emerges to visibility as a protective barrier, dividing the safe interior from the unknown, menacing outside. At the same time, the emotional stream traversing the story is clarified as the pressure of an outside on an inside, which the film will communicate through its aesthetic mechanism. Indeed, the story will constantly be rearticulated into the opposition of two different kinds of spaces: one, where the masters can enjoy their leisure, clearly illuminated and open to possibilities, and another, its qualitative inversion into a "lower" dimension, where darkness and material barriers constantly block free movement, forcing bodies into fixed patterns of labor and the satisfaction of needs, leaving room for an expression of vitality only in the frantic outburst of anxiety.

As we will see, this diametrical class opposition will also be strictly characterized in historical terms, as the signs of the recent war will be embedded everywhere. Not by chance, the day after their arrival, when the two will be comfortably seated in the sun on the vast terrace of their villa—a high, brightly lit, vast space opposed to the darkness and constriction of the lower kitchen—Katherine will again break the peace and self-assurance of the touristic discourse by quoting a poem composed by Charles Lewington, a young poet she used to know, who is now dead (precisely here James Joyce's "The Dead"—an unacknowledged debt—starts to contaminate the film, as we will see in detail). Lewington wrote those verses when he was stationed in Naples during the war, and his words acutely contrast with the supposed vitality of the south, evoking ascetic images in opposition to the expected, carefree hedonism of the place. This enigmatic formula will haunt Katherine throughout the story, and I will use it to name the *object* of the quest of both works—the existence of the city's lowest class—whose textual presence my analysis will reconstruct. The squashed bug anticipates this ghostly presence, which will soon be followed by the appearance of bodies seen as belonging to a different species: Do bugs have blood? From the invisible stain in this initial sequence, a dark matter spreads throughout the film, infesting the limits of vision, the screens that here too work as devices both of viewing and of protection.

Lumpen

Bitterly commenting on the failure of revolutionary activities in Vienna and Paris, in an 1848 article published in the *Neue Rheinische Zeitung*, Karl Marx writes, "In Paris the *Guarde mobile*, in Vienna 'Croats'—in both cases *lazzaroni*, lumpenproletariat hired and armed—were used against the working and thinking proletarians" (1975a, 505). As the epitome of "non-working," "non-thinking" proletarians, Neapolitan *lazzaroni*—the city's urban poor—regularly recur in Marx's and Engels's newspaper articles and essays from 1848 onward, as has been noted in a recent historical reexamination of the concept of Lumpenproletariat by Clyde Barrow (2020, 27). It should be noted that the term "lazzaroni" in these writings refers to both a specific historical entity and a general political category: "In Naples the *lazzaroni* are leagued with the monarchy against the bourgeoisie. In Paris the greatest struggle ever known in history is taking place. The bourgeoisie is leagued with the *lazzaroni* against the working class" (Marx 1975b, 17). Finally, in a retrospective reflection on those years of unrest, in the series of articles later collected as *The Class Struggles in France 1848–1850*, the category "lazzaroni" ends up naming a specific "character" of the lumpen-proletariat, which defines it politically beyond the various national contexts: "The lumpen proletariat . . . varying according to the degree of civilization of the nation to which they belong, but never renouncing their *lazzaroni* character" (Marx 1975c, 62). If the use of the category of lumpenproletariat for the poorest stratum of the Neapolitan population seems obvious today, as already suggested since 1895 by Benedetto Croce in a historical essay dedicated to the *lazzari*,[43] Francesco Benigno has proposed, on the basis of a previous study (Meriggi 2002), that the concept of lumpenproletariat was in fact developed starting from the reception, in the German context, of chronicles of the Neapolitan revolution of 1799, "which focused on the role played in those dramatic events by the ragged rabble [plebe], that is, the so-called *lazzari*" (Benigno 2005, 44).

While more than a century separates the two works at the center of this book from the lumpenproletariat to which Marx and Engels referred, several scholars have demonstrated the persistence of this Neapolitan social formation until the postwar years, and up to today—starting, of course, with Allum's classic study on the economy of the alley and the structure of Neapolitan urban classes (Allum 1973, 46–53). Indeed, scholarship has shown how the Neapolitan case is a local variant of the kind of urban population linked to the informal economy,[44] one that could be defined as *precariat*, at least according to the category as recently described by Loic Wacquant,[45] whose definition is certainly appropriate for the Neapolitan urban lowest class, commonly called, in the city, "sottoproletariato" (sub-proletariat), "popolino" (little people), "plebe" (plebs) (Pardo 1993; Goddard 1996; Morlicchio and Pugliese 2006), or "mau mau."[46] In this book I will refer to this social formation with the term *lumpenproletariat*, as it historically names such socioeconomic positions. However, I will use the more generic *under-class* when referring to the urban lower classes at large, which might imply a blurring of differences with other contiguous social sectors.[47] As for the possibility of using "plebs" or "plebeian," I will rather avoid an ambiguous overlapping with the positive concept of a "plebeian experience" as proposed by Martin Breaugh (2007) in a study on the progressive political function of the lower strata of the population seeking political participation: The Neapolitan concept of "plebs," as a broader variant of *lazzari* (in turn seen as an avant-garde and synecdoche of the *plebe* [Croce 2006]), has always had reactionary connotations—as we have just seen with Marx—signaling a non-historical evil, resistant to any hope of change. When, however, we leave the Neapolitan urban context, as in the case of the domestic workers in the villa in *Journey to Italy*, or, in that same film, the final procession in Maiori, I will use the more generic "lower classes" or "popular classes," as Nick Dines has done to refer to a broader social sector than that belonging to the urban precariat.[48]

Besides its terminological accuracy, Dines's essay highlights how the Neapolitan underclass has consistently represented a troubling presence for the Italian Communist Party (PCI), in relation to which it had to define itself and its actions, just as Marx and Engels had "invented" the proletariat against the backdrop of this "negative element." This is a process of capital importance, which lasted from the postwar period until the dissolution of the PCI itself after the fall of the Berlin Wall, but in fact continued to be relevant for the left-wing parties that were its heirs, and which governed the city from the 1990s onward. In this regard, it is important to briefly reflect on two volumes curated by Antonio Bove and Francesco Festa (2022a; 2022b), which recently showed how the anomic presence of the lumpen element at the heart of the city continued to represent, despite its marginality to the centers of power, the fulcrum of the city's political life throughout the last decades of the last century. Dedicated to the history of the Neapolitan Autonomy,[49] the two volumes—a third focuses on Autonomy in the rest of southern Italy—feature numerous testimonies from individuals who were directly involved in the political struggles in the city during the 1970s and afterward. From these voices, an effort emerges to interpret the role of the urban lumpenproletariat in the struggles for work and housing: "That 'crowd' . . . from the early 1970s became a significant part of the class conflict for over a decade, thanks to its encounter with political avant-gardes who recognized its potential, acknowledging its role as an actor in that urban production system" (Bove and Festa 2022a, 171).

It is important to specify that, in those years, the urban poor were also the subject of an attempt, only partially successful, of a mass "deportation" to the peripheral neighborhoods. This was aimed at implementing a process of gentrification that would eliminate this Neapolitan anomaly, that is, the presence of the weakest strata of the population within the historic center of the city.[50] This process, which intensified with the outbreak of cholera in 1973, underwent a strong acceleration due to the earthquake in 1980, which caused a huge displacement of people in Naples and other affected areas (De Stefano 2022, 86). This explosive situation drove members of the urban lumpenproletariat to actively engage in the housing struggles led by Neapolitan Autonomy. At the same time, the gradual decline of the traditional informal economy in the poorest neighborhoods boosted the unemployed's involvement in the fight for jobs.

These circumstances mark, on one hand, the entry of this social stratum into active politics, as affirmed by Raffaele Paura, one of the organizers of the neighborhood associations fighting for housing and jobs in the 1970s: "The novelty of the Neapolitan experience lies in the fact that the encounter between revolutionaries and social subjects extraneous to the production cycle is not a minor element; on the contrary, it is central. Given the unique composition of the urban class in Naples, this relationship becomes essential and requires a new approach to addressing the issue of the lumpenproletariat [sottoproletari] as a *fragment* of the class during those years" (Paura 2022, 21). Other testimonies from those who were present in that cycle of struggles, however, point out that this momentary politicization of the lumpenproletariat did not really mark a change in its class relationship with the other social strata of the city, nor did it inaugurate a continuity in its participation in active politics: "Those layers of the metropolitan proletariat without any political affiliation fought as long as there was a real need, without a political perspective."[51] "We can argue that the political construction surrounding the marginal proletariat has frequently been an ideological imposition on a segment of the population that existed outside the official production cycle. However, this approach did not work for 'internal relations.' Everything relied on the mechanism of need."[52]

Finally, it should be noted that even the mass displacement (the "deportation") of the underclass to the peripheral districts, although only partially successful, did not result in a substantial improvement in their housing conditions, even when it meant the abandonment of the infamous "bassi." In fact, in a 1972 article, journalist Giuliano Zincone noted that the "real tragedies of segregation and abandonment explode in peripheral neighborhoods like Secondigliano, like the Rione Traiano. The latter, in particular, has the humiliating characteristics of a ghetto for the dispossessed." In the Rione Traiano, sixty thousand people reside in a number of rooms intended for twenty-six thousand (Zincone 1972). It is no coincidence that, in later years, Secondigliano (and the neighboring Scampia) became the focal point of the collective imagination surrounding Neapolitan urban marginalization, gaining widespread notoriety particularly through the media products mentioned in this introduction. To be sure, even a cursory analysis of the current conditions of the Neapolitan lower classes exceeds the scope of this study. Nevertheless, it is important to note, in conclusion to this excursus, how the ideological machine has never ceased manipulating the visibility of this social group, both through actual removals of individuals (displacement toward outer districts) and through an obsessive effort at media representation—even though in some cases the latter has, willingly or not, highlighted the violence of socioeconomic relationships that continue to uphold the conditions of marginalization.

Throughout this book, I attempt to build a model with which to observe, through both literary and filmic textual analysis, the communication of the inner features of the experience of the Neapolitan underclass, its habitus, in the sense defined by Pierre Bourdieu,[53] that is, precisely what appears mysterious and incomprehensible in a historical object made invisible by the ideological infrastructure. With the expression "ascetic images," used by the poet Lewington in *Journey to Italy* as an enigma, I will refer to the virtual presence of this experience inscribed in the text, whose scattered elements I will investigate. The tools of semiotics will be fundamental for this task, as they will allow us to recognize, in the organization of space and of the bodies that occupy it—on both the figurative and the abstract level of the text—those basic traits that make a form of life understandable in its interaction with the environment. Unsurprisingly—but contrary to the stereotype of the sweet life of the Neapolitan "fainéant"—the nature of such interaction will prove to be violent and oppressive in the case of the lower classes, whose vital acts will appear as a figure of the absence of meaning, reduced to the elementary gestures of mere survival on the one hand, and to those of the pointless expression of anxiety on the other. Both will prove to be inversions of the meaningful gestures of the privileged, which they will reflect as in a nightmarish upside-down underworld. Thus, from the elementary level of "body hexis," "motor function," and "pattern of postures" (Bourdieu 1977, 87) up to the force fields that support the entire social architecture, the ideological infrastructure of society reveals itself as "the very process by which daily life is systematically reorganized on all its levels (the body and the senses, the mind, time, space, work process, and leisure) by that total quasi-programming process that is rationalization, commodification, instrumentalization, and the like"[54] (Jameson 2009b, 331).

Yet if the existence of this underclass is what the ideological gaze normally makes invisible, how is it possible that it can become experienceable in the work of art? The hypothesis on which my analysis is based is that the artistic gesture has, in some cases, the capacity to communicate a specific social standpoint, a habitus, and therefore to make experienceable a historical content, which the ideological screen makes incommunicable as a simple coding and decoding of information in discursive terms. To explain how this can happen in the texts of Ortese and Rossellini, I will draw from the reflections on aesthetic expression and, more specifically, on the literary communication that Merleau-Ponty developed in his courses at the Collège de France in the early 1950s, in particular *The Sensible World and World of Expression* (*Le monde sensible et le monde de l'expression*) in 1953 and *The Problem of Speech* (*Le problème de la parole*) in 1953 and 1954. It is certainly no coincidence that these reflections were developed precisely during the same months as the works at the center of this book. It is evident that they participate in that particular moment of vision mentioned in this introduction, that "window of opportunity" between the fading of the traumatic memory of the war and the advent of the forced amnesia imposed by the subsequent great economic development. It is also important to note, as we will see more in detail (chapter 3), that Merleau-Ponty's courses were prepared at the same time as his reflections on Lukács's *History and Class Consciousness*, which Merleau-Ponty would include in the essay " 'Western' Marxism" ("Le marxisme 'occidental' "), later printed in *Adventures of Dialectics* (*Les aventures de la dialectique*, 1955).

Merleau-Ponty examined the possibility of communicating individual experience since the time of *Phenomenology of Perception* (*Phénoménologie de la perception*), originally published in 1945, in which he used the limit cases of trauma and mental illness to explain how the perception of the environment is always articulated upon a double dimension. This consists of an "affective background,"[55] where the pre-personal substance of the experience is affected by historical-social contents ("the thickness of the pre-objective present, where we find our corporeality, our sociality, and the preexistence of the world" [Merleau-Ponty 2012, 457]), and a subsequent elaboration of such contents in an objective, sharable form. In certain cases, the traumatic experience proves capable of trapping the subject in the first stage, thus creating a fixation on a present that does not pass, and the possibility of communication disappears: "When I preserve through time one of the momentary worlds that I have passed through and that I make into the form of my entire life" (Merleau-Ponty 2012, 86). Once this invasive "form" is able to take hold of private existence, "the passage of time does not . . . seal off the traumatic experience . . . this past that remains our true present does not move away from us; rather, in lieu of being displayed before our gaze, it always hides behind it" (85). This type of mental prison naturally becomes extreme in mental illness, where it imposes itself as a second dimension of reality ("this second space permeating visible space"[56] [300]), which ends up devouring the one where forms of communication are still possible.

In the terms of the ideological analysis that we examined in this introduction, we could speak of this type of experience as one of repressed historical contents that pertain to a specific standpoint, and which therefore could only be communicated through the sharing of the latter, as happens for class experiences that can be classified as "systemic traumatisms," which we will address in detail in chapter 2. It is no coincidence that Merleau-Ponty went back to the problem of communication at the beginning of the 1950s, when the reflection on aesthetic and literary expression was fueled by the analysis developed, in the same months, on the praxis of the proletariat in *History and Class Consciousness*. A few years earlier—and it is no coincidence either, that these reflections from *Phenomenology of Perception* were developed in the midst of World War II—trauma was that type of experience that could not be communicated in discursive terms, as it only appears as a "style of being."[57] However, in the course notes of *The Problem of Speech*, the concept of "style" becomes the key to understanding how the literary gesture, and the aesthetic one in general—since these reflections follow the broader ones from the previous course, which explicitly included cinema—is able to restore the contours of an experience, as well as precisely those contents that cannot be simply communicated through the coding and decoding of information.[58] The key to understanding this evolution is Merleau-Ponty's interpretation of the proletarian praxis as defined by Lukács, which he reads not as a content simply communicable in discursive terms but as "a vector, an attraction, a possible state, a principle of historical selection, and a diagram of existence"[59] (Merleau-Ponty 1973a, 49), that is, as a point of view within which one can *stand*, and which only a very particular gesture—the sharing of situated, historical perspective—will be able to communicate.[60] Quoting Proust, Merleau-Ponty will say that style is "a question, not of technique, but of vision" (2020a, 181),[61] and he will further characterize it as a way of producing a form of presence of the things for others, rather than simply defining them (181). In sum, if ideological discourse can falsify and distort those contents that are normally not allowed to reach the surface of experience (think of the way in which the mechanism of the picturesque is able to make invisible what is offered in plain sight), we should nevertheless avoid understanding ideology in a paranoid sense, as a form of hypnosis.[62] In fact, the specific possibility of artistic expression is to communicate the incommunicable, and, as clarified in the course summary for *The Problem of Speech*, the writer's "task" is "to produce a system of signs whose internal articulation reproduces the contours of experience; the reliefs and sweeping lines of these contours in turn generate a deep syntax, a mode of composition and recital which breaks the mold of the world and everyday language and refashions it"[63] (Merleau-Ponty 1970, 25). Only an analysis that follows the narrative articulation of ideological distortions, from their "origin" to the unfolding of this "deep syntax," will be able to see through the screens that separate us from invisible experiences.

Overview of the Book

Before we delve into the intensive theoretical discussion and textual analysis anticipated in the previous two sections, I will investigate the relationship of Ortese and Rossellini to the reality of the Neapolitan underclass in chapter 1. I will do this not out of biographical curiosity, of course, but to understand how the capacity for vision inscribed in their work originated, that possibility of coming into contact with a reality that remained so tenaciously invisible to many of their contemporaries. In Ortese's case, what played a role was above all the experience of hunger and homelessness, in short of extreme poverty, which, during the war and in the following years effectively erased any protective barrier between her and the lowest stratum of society, while professional writing became her only means of material support. In the case of Rossellini, we will have to reflect on his direct contact with the disasters of war, which the director and his collaborators experienced during the making of his previous films—a contact that leaves here, as we will see, a direct imprint. This chapter also returns to textual analysis, anticipating the conclusion of the ideological contradiction's itinerary, whose beginning was observed in this introduction. In "The Silence of Reason" this coincides with the appearance of the Kafkian hunger artist, in which the self-diegetic narrator's most secret fear is revealed in her mirror image. In *Journey to Italy*, this function will be carried out by a poem present in an early version of the screenplay, which will be excluded in the final version of the film. Here, the touristic gaze on the Neapolitan reality, typical of the protagonists, gives way to the disorienting echoes of the war.

Chapter 2 clarifies in more detail these two works' exemplary character for the historical object at the center of this book, and the history of their composition. After a discussion of the ideology of Neapolitan intellectuals, starting from the writings of Raffaele La Capria, Ortese's work is examined in the context of trauma studies and related to those interpretations of trauma as a systemic experience, through which conditions of collective oppression are enforced on entire sectors of society in terms of class or gender. The examples of Maria Root and Greg Forter will be important here, but also Gyanendra Pandey's reflections on the "routine violence" on which the entire construction of a nation can be based. The relationship of *Journey to Italy* with the conditions of the Neapolitan lower classes is investigated through its issues with censorship, which tormented Rossellini's project from the beginning and forced him to discard a first screenplay—too explicit in its crude characterization of the conditions of this social stratum—and then to delay its release for at least a year. Additionally, due to my archival research, I will be able to develop a hypothesis regarding the division of labor among those who worked on the project. My analysis also clarifies the structural relationships between this film and Colette's novel *Duo*, of which it was originally intended to be an adaptation, an idea that was then abandoned (but, as we will see, only on the surface). In the same way, I examine the relationship between *Journey to Italy* and Joyce's short story "The Dead," which the film explicitly appropriates, even without officially declaring it. Here too I will highlight the profound structural connections that remain between the two works, largely underestimated by critics.

In chapter 3 I analyze the initial sequences of the two works to concretely develop the reading model that I will employ in chapters 4 and 5. I start from a semiotic analysis of deep textual structures, where both works can be traced back to a common model, that of the search for an object of value that is then disturbed and suspended due to the emergence of a narrative anti-program, which in both cases will have the aim of understanding the reality of the Neapolitan underclass. Later, when it comes to examining surface textual structures, interpretation must naturally diversify its tools for the literary text and for the filmic one. In the case of the literary text, I will proceed to the analysis of the self-diegetic narrative voice and the figurative manifestations of the narrated reality: Already in this first sequence it will be possible to carry out a preliminary study of the form of life of the crowd of poor, the "ascetic images" that will appear as a manifestation of the abolition of meaning, to which these existences are condemned by the oppression on which the well-being of the privileged is based. In the case of the film, I will instead show how the presence, not yet visible, of this social group is foreshadowed through cinematic mechanisms that generate anxiety for a still unknown element: elliptical close-ups (whose emotional reaction goes beyond the object shown), the disruption of linear time in favor of the frequentative mode, and the first signs of a soundscape haunted by offscreen sounds that announce a crowd not yet displayed. The chapter concludes with a study of the phenomenological theme of the communicative possibilities of aesthetic expression, thus returning to Merleau-Ponty's lectures at the Collège de France in the early 1950s. I will read them together with the essay " 'Western' Marxism," which he developed in the same months and where the communication of a historical content is explicitly put into dialogue with Lukács's reflections on the praxis of the proletariat in *History and Class Consciousness*. This will bring us back to the conception of ideology at the core of this book.

Chapters 4 and 5 complete the analysis of the two works. The study of the ideological machine sketched in the introduction is continued here by following the transformations of the scene in which the "original emotion" manifests itself for the first time. The virtual experience of the form of life at the center of these works is clarified through a series of semiotic squares that systematize the analysis' results. For "The Silence of Reason," my reading will aim above all at the study of the visual dimension of the text, showing how it problematizes the mechanism of exclusion-inclusion in the visual field of the objects that the dominant ideology wants to hide. I will also focus on the rhetorical structure through which the text produces its peaks of pathetic intensity, which are connected with the emergence of repressed historical elements. Finally, the surface figurative elements will be grouped alongside the deep value contrasts that can be reconstructed on the semiotic square: By this point, it will not be surprising how many of the semantic oppositions identified here will return in *Journey to Italy*. For this latter, the privileged objects of investigation will be space and time interpreted according to semi-symbolic binary oppositions,[64] without forgetting the devices that serve to evoke a non-visible reality into visibility (actors' expressiveness and the soundscape). Moreover, we will investigate the presence of background figures—the bodies of the street crowd—organized as extras and occasionally filmed in documentary mode (meaning, without orchestration and without consent).

The epilogue reflects again on the paradigmatic value of these two works for a study of the relationship between artistic expression and existences made invisible in a specific social context. The idea of the "ascetic images"—as the experience inscribed in the text and reconstructed through the itinerary of the "original emotion"—will be tested one last time. However, we will not return to the objects just investigated; we will focus, instead, on two short sequences of later works by the two authors. Here, near the end, the abolition of meaning at the heart of the form of life of the oppressed becomes a utopian possibility of salvation: an art of dying well, the return to the lost creature that reverses abandonment into a desire for community.

Chapter 1

Of Hunger Artists and Ascetic Images

Writing and Hunger

A man knocks at the door, bearing a message. This marks the beginning of one of the earliest memories in Anna Maria Ortese's life: "One of the first evenings of my life, in a house, almost in the countryside, very poor" (Ortese 1987, 166). Her mother or grandmother—it is unclear which, for as in all early childhood memories, people are shadows, vanishing into each other—opens the door, looks at the man, and immediately rushes inside to fetch the money ready on the table. But the window is open, a storm is approaching, a sudden burst of wind enters the room, and the bill disappears. The grandmother runs outside desperate to retrieve the money, while the mother stays with the child and begs the man for mercy: The rent money was there, just until seconds ago . . . then it was stolen by the wind. "The man did not believe it, he started to threaten" (167). Nothing is said about the child, the one to whom this memory belongs, but she was certainly terrified: "I do not think grandma found the money, it rained harder and harder, and the woods were dark" (167). No wonder the man did not believe the mother, who had claimed that the wind had stolen the money and dragged it into the dark woods: "From an episode like this, minimal and fantastic, I deduced something terrible: *outside* the house, outside the wonderful walls of the rooms, there were 'powers' that demanded a tax (if we wanted to live!) otherwise woe to us! and there were the Woods, the Wind, like marauders, who stole money from houses, and hid it, to put people in despair" (167). Yet something else becomes apparent from this episode, for those who have read through the many similar—if less fantastic—episodes that punctuate the miserable existence Ortese led for much of her life. Some ruthless messenger demands the money for the payment of a debt, or for rent. Suddenly, instead of the paper bill, there is a different kind of paper that is meant to be a substitute for that money, for that "tax": one that carries words ("My mother was begging him"), words like "dark woods," "winds," "stormy night," and so on: the stuff of stories, the stuff of fairytales. But will the man believe this? Will these stories be an acceptable surrogate for the money, the only value that society recognizes?

The passages quoted below, taken from letters Ortese wrote at the end of the 1950s, a period of dire financial hardship particularly well documented in her biography, provide a good example of the misery she endured for long periods of her life:

> I left Milan and went to Rome. Here, for a year, in 1959, I lived in disarray, literally, passing from house to house, and I was always pushed out because I could not pay for the room. The last one was the vestibule of a distinguished home, in via Anneo Lucano, where I had lived for a month, and from which I had to get out within half an hour. It was again November, a useless year had passed.[1]

Ortese wrote such letters like this throughout her life, to friends, to publishers, to journalists, to whomever could send her money in exchange for a story, such as the story she was telling in the present letter or a story she was promising to write. Two years earlier, in 1957, she had asked Alberto Mondadori, the director of one of the largest Italian publishing houses, who had just offered her a steady job, to send her the monthly income he had promised for the job as an advance payment instead, for a book she was about to write, and for which she needed absolute tranquility:

> I need, for four months, the next four months, to be able to sit at a desk, without any extraneous commitment, and without any financial worries. I need to have that salary or monthly salary of 50,000 lire you told me about, but in advance, and all at once, and without the obligation of immediate collaboration. I have in mind a book that summarizes all my experiences of life and style, from the abstractions of '37 to the realism of ten years later, a tender and terrible Milan, the symbol of a civilization that is no longer just Italian. (Clerici 2002, 326)

Was she quoting Virginia Woolf's "A woman must have money and a room of her own if she is to write fiction" (Woolf 2015, 3)? In Ortese's case, not even food and shared accommodation could be taken for granted. However, her argument was convincing, as were previous proofs of her talent: Mondadori trusted her and sent her the money, but two months later, she sent him a notebook with her old poems instead of the promised book. A few months later, she asked for more money, which she received. But there would never be a trace of the book she promised. The next year Mondadori would only be able to publish *The Days of Heaven* (*I giorni del cielo*), a collection of already published stories she had already recycled multiple times, with different titles, in journals and previous book collections. Clerici's reconstruction of Ortese's extremely complex bibliography reveals a labyrinthic activity of continuous republishing of articles and short stories in different formats and with different titles along the years—an operation no doubt dictated by financial need. In those same months between '57 and '58, while she was supposed to work on the book for Mondadori, she was quietly negotiating with another prominent publisher, Laterza, to arrange the publication of a collection of journalistic pieces devoted to Milan, with which the press evidently hoped to repeat the success she had gained with *Neapolitan Chronicles*, published by Einaudi in 1953. After receiving a check as an advance from Laterza as well, she disappears for several months, after which, in physical and emotional distress, she asks for more money: "I'm sick, and I can't stay at home because I have no one and every day there is the problem of eating . . . I go out to look for someone to lend me a thousand lire, every day with a fever, every day weaker than the day before. But do I have to die on the street? Sorry, I'm beyond desperate."[2] And less than a month later: "Today I was able to eat at Quasimodo's house, after two days of nothing, tomorrow I don't know where. . . . It seems impossible to me that one can die of starvation, in a civilized world, but that's right: one can die easily."[3]

When had this miserable existence started for her? What had gone wrong? Was she not, after all, during the 1950s, a well-known author and journalist who had won important accolades, who wrote for prominent journals and newspapers, who was admired by some of the most important Italian intellectuals and writers? (among which were Elio Vittorini, Italo Calvino, and Salvatore Quasimodo, not to speak of Massimo Bontempelli, who had been her first mentor but had by now declined in popularity because of his earlier connection with the fascist regime—a common sin for which he seemed to be one of the few to pay). Her story demonstrates how impossible it was for a woman, alone, without the support of a family or a partner, to make a decent living out of creative writing during those same years in which, despite the difficult postwar situation, many men were able to do just that. Ortese's hardest period had started during World War II, when she had been displaced as a refugee with her family in different places around the country, from north to south, before returning to a destroyed Naples during the Allied occupation. Things did not go any better there: Her family's already modest apartment had been bombed, and they did not have any material support. In an interview with Dacia Maraini from the '70s, she remembers:

> After the war I experienced real hunger. A hunger so full of anguish that I could have eaten a boiled shoe. How I managed to survive I don't know. Even in '47–'48 the sight of a potato enlivened me. There was food everywhere, good food, but we couldn't afford it. I didn't even have a house: with my parents, we wandered like gypsies from one place to the next. In '48 I began to travel on my own to Rome and Milan by train. I would ride in the corridors, next to the toilet,[4] dead on my feet from exhaustion. (Maraini 2015, 466)

As Clerici explains, the reason for these wanderings was her attempt to make a living as a journalist, which was difficult for a person not steadily affiliated with a single newspaper or a political party—although, according to her, she was affiliated with the Communist Party at some point in the late '40s (Clerici 2002, 141). As she explains, "There was a time, between the end of the war and the late 1950s, when I did nothing but travel. My fundamental problem has always been the 'financial' one: a euphemism to avoid mentioning openly the issue of physical survival" (146). Yet there is something more. If one reads carefully her letters from the time, especially those she wrote to her colleague and friend Pasquale Prunas (about whom there will be more to say in this book), which have been recently collected in a volume, it becomes evident that her way to navigate her financial troubles had a recklessness that bordered on a desire to sabotage the social system that held together the intellectual professions in Italy at the time. This was undoubtedly also a form of self-sabotage, as her physical and mental suffering was real and evident. Yet the stubbornness with which she refused any form of rational solution to her problems is striking. Of course, such a "solution" would have meant giving up her freedom and her own creative process.

In Naples, in 1946, at the beginning of their friendship and collaboration, she writes to Prunas: "You can never imagine where and how I write" (Ortese 2006, 41). In subsequent letters we learn that she was living in a room without electricity, running water, or glass in the windows, though this was not uncommon in a city that had been extensively bombed until less than two years before. The first letter is from March 1946, and as soon as December she is asking for cigarettes and money: "I am desperate, because I can no longer continue working, I do not have a cigarette, no one gives me any, not even one or two—and so I cannot write. I am waiting to receive some money, and then I'll give you a package back too, and then half the money you were good enough to lend me" (Ortese 2006, 51). Then the next year, in February, from Rome, where she had moved and was staying as a guest at some acquaintance's place: "I was as hungry and cold as a human creature can bear. . . . Don't think I'm distracted, I'm *hungry*" (56–57). In this same letter she fills all free lateral spaces on the page due to lack of paper, and she will soon thank Prunas for sending her writing supplies. We do not have his replies, but he always tries to help. In 1945, he has founded a new cultural journal, *Sud*, where young, radical Neapolitan intellectuals have united to help finally change the centuries-old misery of the city (Mozzillo 1995). Prunas believes in Ortese's genius and wants her to collaborate. A retrospective reflection on this enterprise will close Ortese's already mentioned major book on Naples, *Neapolitan Chronicles*, in the story "The Silence of Reason." Yet, despite Prunas's attempts to help, Ortese's situation does not improve. In a letter quoted by Clerici, in August 1947 Prunas writes to Enrico Emanuelli, another collaborator of *Sud*, "Anna Maria Ortese is starving, just the real starving" (Clerici 2002, 164).

Despite her absent-mindedness due to physical and mental exhaustion, so vivid in her letters and easy to guess from Clerici's (tactful) reconstruction of her chaotic travels all around the peninsula in these years, homeless, often starting the day without knowing where she would eat or sleep, it is evident that she was also gaining a political awareness of the structural conditions of her poverty. Many years later, in the preface to a collection of her journalistic pieces, titled *The Dark Lens* (*La lente scura*), she would write: "Particularly in the *Roman* pages, I found myself completely free from newspaper commitments, and therefore from partisan commitments, and I wrote only what I saw through the Dark Lens of a youth spent in the class confinement" (Ortese 1991, 1). "Class confinement" ("confino di classe") is a lens through which she will scan Italian society.

In *History and Class Consciousness* Lukács uses journalism to exemplify intellectual professions, where the reification of personal skills, those that are sold by intellectual workers, leads to the incapacity to perceive the structural reality of their own social situation—one that guarantees their own privilege, as well as the privilege not to see this privilege: "The more deeply reification penetrates into the soul of the man [*sic*] who sells his achievement as a commodity the more deceptive appearances are (as in the case of journalism)" (Lukács 1971, 172). In other words, as intellectuals do not sell their impersonal bodily labor but their personal intellectual ability, what becomes commodified is exactly that faculty through which they could see and understand their own material condition. This blindness becomes their ideological standpoint, protecting them from understanding their exploitative relationship with those from whom wealth is extracted. As we have seen in the introduction, Lukács's view of ideology went beyond false consciousness and became, in Jameson's words, "a constitutive limitation of the mind . . . the standpoint from which the social totality was masked or distorted" (Jameson 2015, 18). In this context, Ortese's unique situation, her disadvantage in comparison to her fellow journalists and writers, the fact that she was homeless and poor, becomes the condition of a paradoxical advantage. Despite being an intellectual, the material degradation that forced her to constantly travel and suffer physically and emotionally as she tried to make a living as a writer brought her closer to the social position of those who sold their impersonal physical labor to survive:

> While the process by which the worker is reified and becomes a commodity dehumanizes him [*sic*] and cripples and atrophies his "soul" . . . it remains true that precisely his humanity and his soul are not changed into commodities. He is able therefore to objectify himself completely against his existence while the man reified in the bureaucracy, for instance, is turned into a commodity, mechanized and reified in the only faculties that might enable him to rebel against reification. (Lukács 1971, 172)

In sum, Ortese's proximity with the lower classes relates to her material standpoint and thus her vision. It was this vision, in turn, that sparked the kind of material epiphany that revealed the deep root through which artistic creativity was connected to economic structure, in a way that remained off limits to the "purest Marxists" (170) she discusses in *Neapolitan Chronicles*. However, as we have seen in the introduction, in the scene where the "original emotion" is located, this vision also remains her "secret," her deeper contradiction that only enters the text by way of distortions, reflections, strategies of displacement.

I will conclude this section with a brief foray into the last part of "The Silence of Reason," which will be analyzed extensively in chapter 4 and where a new mirror image of the self-diegetic narrator is presented, replicating and confirming the ideological contradiction that traverses the whole text. Just as it happened at Compagnone's house when he was startled by the girl's spit, here too, the text subtly reveals the complicity between the narrator and the mass of the poor, adumbrating her role as an outsider among friends who have become (almost all of them) incapable of seeing that social caste.

As the narrator wanders the streets of Naples, in the evening that concludes her stay in the city, with Prunas and two other Neapolitan friends, they end up in front of the entrance of a venue where a few years earlier they had organized a leftist cinema club, where such films as Eisenstein's *Battleship Potemkin* (1925) were showed. Like the ephemeral journal *Sud*, that cinema club had represented a moment of hope for those politically engaged youth, a moment that had soon ended together with their hopes of changing the city's atavistic misery. Yet now, they discover, the venue is being used to host a different kind of spectacle, one that is attended not by middle-class intellectuals but by half-starved lower-class people: "A few thin, mesmerized people were standing before the counter staring at the a sign on which was written: 'Entrance 150 lire' " (Ortese 2018, 181). Her sharp eye immediately recognizes these people's main problems and concerns (no doubt because she is familiar with them too): They are *thin*, and they hesitate to pay the small price of the entrance. Immediately after, as her gaze follows those who go in, she will remark again that they are "all poor." Yet what lies behind the dark curtain where everyone's attention is directed and that seems to provoke so much excitement in this miserable audience? Something very different from the high-culture Prunas and his associates had offered to their intellectual audience: "Something clear sparkled, and in that thing—a simple glass coffin—one could see a long form. It was a man in black, smiling, who looked around patiently, smoking a cigarette" (181). The man is a *digiunatore*, a "fakir" in the English translation, someone who fasts for days, offering the spectacle of his own starvation. In other words, a *Hungerkünstler*, the "hunger artist" who gives the title to the short story on which Franz Kafka was working the day he died—of starvation (Stach 2013, 566–67). This story, known in Italian as "Il digiunatore," had been included in the first translation of Kafka's short stories, realized by Anita

Rho and published by Frassinelli in 1935. Ortese was certainly familiar with this translation,[5] and the fact that a hunger artist is presented as the final apparition in a story (and a book) almost exclusively built on disquieting epiphanies cannot be coincidental. The hieratical presence of the man who fasts in the very place where her intellectual friends had tried to build a venue to change society through high culture is a sign of her deeper understanding of the structural misery on which that very society was built. That body in pain is inevitably linked to her own presence among her friends as an extraneous body, a body experiencing hunger and exhaustion among "spectators." In sum, as an autoptic vision, the hunger artist, with his black dress (one of Ortese's typical aesthetic features throughout her life), in his glass coffin, presents her own intrusion in a social sphere where she does not belong. By the same token, this scene once again points to the screen through which onlookers can safely observe the picturesque spectacle of misery, as the glass coffin echoes the window brought to visibility by the girl's spit. Yet, this apparition also offers the chance to reflect further on the central ambiguity on which "The Silence" (but arguably the whole book) is built, that is, a double positionality in class terms: On the one hand the "thin bodies," the presence of the lumpenproletariat, seem to emanate from the narrator's own presence, sharing with her a dark nature that separates both of them from the bourgeois world of her friends and colleagues; on the other hand, an opposite tendency, a sort of recoil she experiences from this very presence of the lower classes' epiphanies. "I wasn't sure if I was on Via Chiaia or in a distant, exotic city, or in Paris, perhaps. I wondered if I had had a drink of something strong while wandering anxiously around Naples" (Ortese 2018, 181), she says while commenting on the fakir's apparition. In other words, in this feeling of astonishment and incredulity that she associates with the emergence of the lumpenproletariat, we can see an ideological *countermovement* of retreat, of denial, a pretense of separation in which she distances herself from that condition of suffering. This echoes the similar conclusion of the scene analyzed in the introduction, where we saw her overcome by anxiety, running away from her friend's house. To sum up, the ambiguity that, starting with the overcoming of the stiction process, the text continuously rearticulates in the various episodes is deeply rooted in the uncertainty of the narrator's social status, situated in that precarious condition exposed to the threatening abyss of the underclass. Yet it will be exactly through this double movement of attraction (or better, coincidence, revelation) and repulsion that she will channel the experience of the "contact" with the thin bodies that the upper classes of the city had long ago learned not to see. No doubt, we will need to interrogate further the "glass coffin" as both an optical and confining device.

Ascetic Images

> Temple of the spirit
> no longer bodies
> but pure, ascetic images
> compared to which mere thought seems flesh
> heavy, dim.[6]

These verses, spoken by Katherine Joyce while half asleep on a terrace on the slopes of Vesuvius (clearly visible in the background of figure 1.1), signify the revelation of a message from the past, a voice from a messenger who arrives to disrupt the apparent tranquility of a moment of intimacy between the woman and her husband during their siesta on this business vacation in the south.

As at the beginning of Ortese's childhood memory discussed at the start of this chapter, we find again in this key moment in Rossellini's *Journey*

Figure 1.1. Katherine and Alex on their terrace in Ercolano. *Source:* Roberto Rossellini, *Journey to Italy*, 1954.

to Italy the arrival of external forces knocking on the door of a private dimension, requiring the payment of a debt or the accomplishment of a task (finding the lost money, or making up a good story in lieu of it, in the case of Ortese), in any case expressing a compelling necessity to face a forgotten (or repressed) reality. Indeed, the erratic construction of the film pivots around this event, which ignites a crisis that will soon bring the spouses to the brink of divorce. We have seen in the scene analyzed in the introduction how the film's aesthetic-ideological mechanism is based on the emergence of a repressed historical content, working against the grain of the author's official intention. This secret drive will manifest itself primarily on a structural level, in the articulation of filmic space and time. However, on the surface of the film, it is immediately signaled by the omnipresence of signifiers of mysterious underground forces like volcanoes, caves, crypts, excavations, and so on. As we can see in figure 1.1, this function is fulfilled here by Vesuvius well visible in the background while Katherine recites the verses. It is important to note now, at the beginning of our analysis, that the attraction toward such places, one of the main directional forces guiding the action of the film, is a clear inversion of the pleasurable exposure to the sunlight, which was supposed to be central for a commonplace trip of northern people to "the region of the far South where the sun shines the brightest" (Ortese 2018, 122). Indeed, Katherine is lying in the sun, on her chaise longue on the terrace, while pronouncing the verses that begin her attraction to underground places, to which she will later undertake a series of expeditions.

Yet before attempting an interpretation of these verses it is necessary to interrogate the nature of the messenger. Who composed and spoke them first and who passed them along to Katherine, initiating a movement that will reemerge from the past on the sunlit terrace under the volcano to wreck her marriage? As she explains to her husband, the author was the young poet Charles Lewington, deceased two years before, who used to recite them to her; he had been in love with her before her marriage. As it is known (and immediately suggested by the couple's surname), the dead poet is here based on a character from James Joyce's short story "The Dead"[7] (1907, which closes the collection *Dubliners*, 1914), one of the two intertexts of Rossellini's film, the other being Colette's short novel *Duo* (1934). The stratification of the film's references to these two works is embedded in the intricate history of its development and realization, which included a screenplay, submitted to preliminary censorship in January 1953, that was rejected; a schematic, five-page outline of episodes and locations Rossellini wrote at the beginning of the shooting under pressure from a production executive; and finally a revised, detailed synopsis (what is usually called, in the Italian film industry, a *trattamento*) resubmitted two weeks after the rejection of the screenplay (at which point the shooting had already started) to amend the initial story according to the censorship's directions.[8] I will go back in more detail to this process in chapter 2; for now, it is necessary to understand the "function" of the character of the young poet, as it will reveal itself to be ambiguous—as is almost every element in the film.

Joyce's original character had been named Michael Furey, a seventeen-year-old young man ("a gentle boy"), who had died after standing in the rain to see the girl he was in love with one last time. The girl is now a grown woman, Gretta, married to Gabriel Conroy, who has been until this moment the protagonist of the story. They have attended a Christmas dinner at the house of some relatives and have now returned to the hotel in the cold night. Gabriel has noticed that Gretta is in a strange and dreamy mood after listening to the song "The Lass of Aughrim," which one of the guests had sung. In the hotel room, she reveals that Michael Furey (about whom she had never before told her husband) used to sing that song back in Galloway when they were kids. The two had to separate when she moved away from the town, and at that time Michael was already very ill with a lung disease. The night before her departure, she had heard a pebble hitting her window. She had rushed outside "and there was the poor fellow at the end of the garden, shivering." He had come to see her one last time: "I implored of him to go home at once and told him he would get his death in the rain. But he said he did not want to live" (Joyce 2014, 192). The husband, Gabriel, had at first been annoyed by the story, even jealous. But at this point, realizing this was a memory from a distant past, long before they knew each other, he is seized by "a vague terror" at the thought that this event, the most important in his wife's life, had been locked away from him in her memory, and that his perspective kept him from seeing his wife's reality. This is to say, she was a different person than he had imagined, as such an important part of her life was unknown to him, as was a peak of emotion like he had never known.[9]

In the film the story is adapted to a different context: Lewington had been a "thin, tall, fair, so pale and spiritual" young poet (instead of an employee "in the gasworks" and aspiring singer like Furey), whom Katherine had known since before she met Alex. He had been drafted into the army during World War II and dispatched to Naples ("actually right here," she says, making this sudden appearance of a ghost even more disquieting), where he had written the verses she recites and contracted the illness that killed him few years later. After the war, he had gone back to England where an episode similar to the one recollected by Gretta had happened the night before Katherine was leaving to get married in London. In some passages, Katherine's description of the night in which she sees the poet shivering in the cold rain in her garden is literally taken from Joyce's text (which demonstrates the strong presence of the intertext inside the film). But Lewington had not died immediately after, and the married couple had even met him later in London. Alex, who since the beginning of Katherine's recollection seems at first indifferent, then annoyed and jealous, malignantly comments on the sick poet's way of coughing, calling him "a fool." Yet he does not take this revelation ominously, like Gabriel, as a threat to his narcissistic illusions about his own person and life. For Alex this is rather the intrusion of an alien presence in the person of his own wife, an alien dimension that he had first felt creeping all around him as he entered this strange land of the south, yet one that he will constantly try to dismiss with annoyance without losing control.

There is one major difference between the functions of Lewington and Furey in the stories. The words Lewington utters through Katherine's mouth on the slopes of the volcano have a distinct historical context: They have been written during the war and in response to a specific situation he was then witnessing—Naples in those horrible years of hunger and destruction, which we have read about in Ortese's memories in the previous sections. While the Naples Rossellini and his crew were seeing in the first months of 1953 while shooting *Journey to Italy* was significantly different from that of a few years before, he had seen that Naples as well, while shooting the second episode of *Paisan* (*Paisà*) in the early months of 1946 (Gallagher 1998, 193–97), during the Allied occupation. He had worked among collapsed buildings still covering dead bodies, the camera capturing the thin figures of half-starved extras. Thus, similarly to the hunger artist in his glass coffin appearing in Ortese's book to reveal to bourgeois intellectuals an unbearable (and for them invisible) reality of suffering that survived unchanged from the years of the war and before, under the sunny surface of commonplace visions of Naples, Lewington's ghost speaks words that directly connect to that reality he had witnessed, and, against all preconceptions of the sunlit lands of the south, evoke "ascetic images."

It is important to note, at this point, that the film itself, on the surface level, seems to work against this interpretation. The day after the terrace scene in which Lewington is first named, Katherine drives to visit the Archaeological Museum in Naples, which was one of the many places Lewington talked about in his verses. The "ascetic images" he wrote about appear hard to reconcile with the carnal livelihood of the Greek and Roman sculpture Katherine sees, and, indeed, in commenting on her visit on the evening of the same day, the couple will joke that "poor Charles" did not understand at all that reality:

ALEX: Then they are not ascetic figures?

KATHERINE: No, not at all. Poor Charles! He had a way all his own of seeing things.

As we will see in chapter 5, my interpretation of the museum scene will reverse this irony and show a much closer connection to Lewington's verses, and to the repressed object of the film itself. The expression "ascetic images," here ironically dismissed by the protagonists, will come to signify, in my study, the inscription of the two works' historical content—the existence of the Neapolitan lower classes—whose traces I will reconstruct.

Joseph Luzzi, in his reading of *Journey to Italy*, writes that "Lewington's verses form part of [Rossellini's] critique of the romantic myth of Italy created by foreigners during the age of the Grand Tour and perpetrated for centuries afterward"(Luzzi 2014, 57).[10] As if to confirm this, Rossellini states in an interview from 1965: "The woman is always quoting a so-called poet who describes Italy as a country of death—imagine, Italy a country of death! This is absurd, because death becomes so much a living thing here that they put garlands on the heads of dead men. There is a different meaning to things here. To them death has an archaeological meaning, to us it is a living reality. It's a different kind of civilization" (Rossellini 1992, 155). Certainly, the initial impulse to include the dead poet's verses in the film had been to show the northern incomprehension of the southern reality, as Rossellini's intention had been (at least as he retrospectively framed it) to show the southern people *as they really are*, and not as they are seen by foreigners from northern Europe. In a television interview from 1962, he states, "In this movie I try to show what Mediterranean, Latin, people are like, how they are in fact and not as they are perceived by the Anglo-Saxons, or other Northerners, who always come to see us as if we were animals in a zoo" (Rossellini 1992, 120). In the revised synopsis included in Dagrada's book, the narrating voice says, "She [Katherine] must make a thousand efforts not to think that Charles was not a true poet, but rather a man of letters who, instead of seeing things in their force and reality, drapes over them the veil of his rhetoric" (Dagrada 2008, 516). And from Alex's perspective: "Upset, Alessandro says 'this is not the land of asceticism. It takes a man of letters who sees nothing to say such nonsense, even if in a poem . . . what an asceticism! One just needs to walk the streets; to look people in the eyes to realize that we are far from asceticism'" (517).

Yet a critical reading of the film, of its preparatory materials, and of paratextual interviews cannot fail to see how the stereotypical understanding of the south the author is claiming to debunk is really his own, whereas Lewington's verses seem, on the contrary, out of place in that same vision. What Rossellini and his collaborators in the project were proposing was simply the specular inversion of the centuries-old "Orientalist" idea of southern Europe as concocted in northern European modern political thought, as we have seen in the introduction. This vision conceives negatively of the south (and southern Italy in particular, or the whole of Italy, depending on the context) as the land of indolence and unfreedom, where the generous climate produces lazy people who do not need to work hard and cooperate to survive, thus weakening their instinct for freedom (Moe 2002, 1–9). What Rossellini has in mind, when he speaks of showing how the Mediterranean people "are in fact," is simply the positive side of this century-old commonplace conception, as the "truth" he wants to reveal is made of old clichés revolving around the southern picturesque:[11] The enjoyment of life in its simple contact with nature, the omnipresence of sex and desire, the religious inclusion of death in the balance of life, and so on. However, for a correct interpretation of Lewington's verses and their function, it is indispensable to read first a different poem this character was supposed to have composed, and which, present in the revised synopsis, did not make it to the final version of the film. In these verses, we will be able to observe an explicit thematization of the contradictory ideological process that we had noticed for the first time with the emergence of the "original emotion" in the car scene, where Katherine had pointed at the blood stain on the windshield.

This first poem was not an early version of the second one (the one effectively recited in the film), as they are both present in the early stage of the project, although the former is quoted in full and the latter is only hinted to with a reference to one of its verses,[12] and this is why I reference them as first and second poem, respectively.[13] Tag Gallagher's translation of the former is as follows: "Life is our only word. But the echo / of these places responds meekly: death. / People [are born here] infected with old age

/ and life is deprived of childhood. / Silence descends on every / thing like dust" (Gallagher 1998, 747n10).[14] Before proceeding with a textual analysis, it is important to note that this poem bears a direct reference to the final paragraph of Joyce's "The Dead," which lyrically closes on the image of snow falling all over Ireland: "Yes, the newspapers were right: snow was general all over Ireland. It was falling on every part of the dark central plain, on the treeless hills, falling softly upon the Bog of Allen and, farther westward, softly falling into the dark mutinous Shannon waves" (Joyce 2014, 194). This passage is echoed in the *silence covering everything like dust*, which in the Italian original, "il silenzio si adagia su tutte le cose," points more directly to Joyce's (original English) text,[15] where "adagiarsi" corresponds to "falling *softly*" and "su tutte le cose" to "on *every* part." Equally important is the presence of death, so strong in this "descent" of silence on everything, and Joyce's analogous imagery of death connected with this white burial of the whole country in the snow: "Like the descent of their last end, upon all the living and the dead" (Joyce 2014, 194). In this case, we can be fairly certain that the composition of the poem and its Joycean inspiration is mostly due to Brancati, as the final paragraph of *The Dead* had already struck his imagination. In a journalistic humoristic prose piece from 1938, titled "Joyce e la signorina,"[16] he had claimed to have heard a story from a woman from Trieste whom Joyce had taught English during his stay in the city. In one of the grotesque descriptions the woman gives of the writer, he looks through a glass paperweight, evidently one of those that can show snow falling on a landscape when properly agitated, and starts reciting lines from the final paragraph of *The Dead*, which are quoted in the English original:

> Joyce lifted the paperweight, squeezing it at the sides with his palms, and looked inside carefully. "Here is Ireland!" he said. "God, this is Ireland!" And he whispered, in the tone of someone repeating a poem from memory, these singular words: "Yes, the newspapers were right: snow was general all over Ireland. It was falling on every part of the dark central plain, on the treeless hills, falling softly upon the Bog of Allen and, farther westward, softly falling into the dark mutinous Shannon waves." (Brancati 2003a, 1324)

Let us now move to the analysis of the poem itself, which is built on a classic life/death dichotomy echoing in two more oppositive couples: childhood/old age, word/silence. Worth noting is the spatial connotation "these places," which seems to anchor, through the use of the deictic "these" (later strengthened with the other deictic "here"), the otherwise abstract meditation to a concrete situation, since the fictional author was supposed to have composed them with reference to Naples in the years of war and military occupation. In the revised synopsis, Katherine remembers these verses when she visits the Cave of the Sibyl in Cumae—where a strong echo effect will be present. In the film, when visiting that place—we will analyze this scene in detail in chapter 5—her inner voice will speak the first three verses of the second poem instead ("Temple of the spirit / no longer bodies / but pure, ascetic images"), while her close-ups looking at the ominous place will show her internal emotion. A clear reference to the war is present in that sequence, as immediately before entering the cave, her tour guide says: "In the last war, the British troops landed here," his voice coming from offscreen while an image of the beach and sea of Cumae is onscreen, prompting her memory of Lewington and the recollection of the verses. Kathrine replies: "Really? British troops landed here?—Yes, right here—And where did they stay?—All around here." The deictic insistence on the "here"—which is also present in the poem as we just saw—of an event that seems to converge, from the past, in the "now," refers to the materiality of an experience that contrasts with the idea that Lewington's words could refer to pure spiritual ideas without any contact with reality.

If we read the first poem in light of this scene, the initial impression of a vague meditation on life, death, time, and so on dissolves, and we can fairly easily place it in the context of the discourses on the disastrous situation of Naples in the final years of the war, even if the revised synopsis insists on the non-coincidence of Lewington's imagination with the reality of the south: "But precisely at this point a cry of children chasing each other, impressing the throb of their vitality in the air, and some shots with which, at the bottom of the valley, a wedding is celebrated, seem to strangely contradict to the poet's verses" (qtd. in Dagrada 2008, 516). When Lewington had landed, however, the omnipresence of death must have been much more than a poetic reflection, and the disappearance of such joyful impressions from the film's scene seems to acknowledge a similar awareness: The city and its surroundings had been largely destroyed by bombings, and for months the smell of dead bodies trapped in the rubble infested the air. This was one of the main elements that pushed Curzio Malaparte, who wrote one of the most famous descriptions of Naples in those days in his novel *The Skin*, to compare this situation with the plague of Florence narrated by Boccaccio (Malaparte 2013, 31). Not to mention there were also sickness, poverty, hunger, and the crowds of Allied soldiers populating the streets in cheerful desperation, before being shipped to deadly battles like those of Cassino and Anzio (Burns 1947, 3–17). Yet only a line-by-line analysis will clarify the historical content of the poem: "Life is our only word." What is this collective entity to which the subjective adjective "our" refers? What does it mean that life is a word (the only one)? The collective entity seems to put itself in the situation of uttering a word while staying in a certain place, then reflecting on the situation of this place. This is a subject who encounters and reflects on a place. It need not be a foreigner—a soldier who is sent to a certain place for military duties, a couple who arrives to sell an inheritance, a director and his collaborator who explore locations to write a film—but the fact that the word this entity pronounces is not in tune with the situation of the place itself (which responds with a different, opposite word "But the echo / of these places responds meekly: death"), nevertheless creates a discrepancy, an effect of distancing. In other words, the experience of the entity confronting the place could be described as that of somebody having a certain expectation, or seeking a confirmation, that is not matched by the place itself: "death" in the place of "life." If we think of other well-known literary witnesses of the war days in Naples, such as Norman Lewis landing on the shore of Paestum in his memoir *Naples '44*, or John Horne Burns and his characters from *The Gallery*, we can find a similar experience: the expectation of a certain classical atmosphere, we could even say of a picturesque land, which is constantly disproved by the violence of war.[17] This situation could then be considered typical of the disappointing encounter of military personnel with humanistic backgrounds arriving in southern Italy during or immediately after the war. Their "word," their discursive knowledge of those places had been one of *life*, one of the poetic imagination connected with the classical tradition and with the Orientalist myth of Naples, and their subsequent disappointment would have been that of a desolate, almost infernal landscape destroyed by bombs and misery, whose only response would have been "death" echoing in explosions and whose ubiquity was signaled by the stench of corpses trapped under the rubble. Yet for visitors arriving in later postwar years too, there must have lingered an "echo" of those painful months in hurt, deformed bodies and traumatized gazes, an echo that Rossellini probably felt while visiting the city in the early 1950s, and that he had already intercepted, much more intensely, in the early months of '46 while working on *Paisan*.

If we consider now the following verses: "People are born here infected with old age / and life is deprived of childhood," and connect them with canonical discourses (visual and literary) on the Neapolitan "disasters of war," among which are those of Malaparte, Ortese,[18] Lewis, Burns, and the same Rossellini in *Paisan*, we can identify a well-known motif, that of urchins forced by the harshness of street life to become adults, who are already "corrupted" by all the miseries of life as if they were old and experienced. This discourse, to be fair, had been present around Naples and its miseries since early modern accounts and had been rekindled in post-unification writings (notably by Matilde Serao) and would survive in the postwar period until the present moment, when it occasionally gains the spotlight of public attention each time a preadolescent is killed while attempting a street robbery or a film or TV show depicts "baby" street gangs.[19] Rossellini himself, as mentioned, had focused his Neapolitan episode in *Paisan* on this theme of "lost childhood" (a topic central to neorealist study of postwar misery outside Naples as well—one only needs to think of De Sica's *Sciuscià* and *Bicycle Thieves*), showing, in the first shots, children smoking, loudly talking street business while exchanging money,[20] and then stealing from the Americans. As for Brancati, in his novel from 1949 *Il bell'Antonio*, he too had observed the destiny of children hit by the disaster of war. In a passage describing his home town Catania, he writes: "On the piles of rubbish, naked and thin children, with their shoulder blades piercing their skin like wing tips, wandered in search of food" (Brancati 1964, 310).

In light of the previous considerations, the silence and dust of the final two verses, "silence descends on everything / like dust," will appear, on the one hand, as the immediate aftermath of the explosions of war, that is, the spectral absence of life's sounds, before the lamentations and cries start, and the fog produced by the collapsed buildings. On the other hand, silence and fog represent the impossibility of understanding—the *silence of reason*, as Ortese will put it—an obstruction, as deafness and blindness, of the senses that give us access to reality. In *Journey to Italy* that silence—the impossibility of a discourse able to rationalize the disaster of the Neapolitan condition—will be translated into the reverie through which Katherine will observe, from her car, the street crowds, whose sound dimension will appear muffled from the interior of the vehicle. This impression of a reduced, distanced sound through which the outside world manifests itself in the protected spaces inhabited by the couple will be a constant device employed throughout the film and will be a main object of analysis for this book. As for the obstructed sight—that produced by the dust and then by the perceptual fog signaling an "unpicturable" reality—the film, apart from the obvious reference we find in the Solfatara episode with its sulfuric vapors, always places a "screen" between Katherine's gaze and the Neapolitan crowds, which she will observe only through her car's windows (except, of course, in the final scene in Maiori). Not coincidentally, Katherine's first gesture toward the Neapolitan reality was to point her finger at that same type of screen (the car windshield), in the scene in which the "original emotion" had appeared for the first time.

To summarize the results of this preliminary analysis, far from being an abstract reflection on a land of "death and silence," the first poem seems to be traversed, under the surface of the superficial interpretation suggested by the narrating voice of the synopsis, by a double movement: On the one hand, the deixis ("these . . . here") points to the historically circumstantiated revelation of war in the places from which the poet would have instead expected a positive experience; on the other hand, after having concretized the disasters of war in the image of children deprived of childhood, it follows an opposite movement of distancing, of refusal, in which the presence of the destruction seems to dissolve in the fading of sound and vision. This structure echoes point by point the scene analyzed in the introduction, where the process of overcoming the ideological stiction was manifested and the "original emotion" was localized. The deictic reference to the concrete reality of the place was there visually represented by Katherine's finger pointing at the blood stain on the windshield. That single drop of blood, a synecdoche of the disturbing presence of violence and death, had evoked for a moment, in the quiet atmosphere of the beginning of the holidays, the crude reality of history. Finally, like the movement of retreat with which the poem ends (the fading of sound and vision), there too the presence of a protective screen (the windshield) and Alex's reassuring comment had dispelled the shadows of historical reality. However, the reference to the war and its consequences was so explicit in the poem that it ended up being excluded from the film. This does not diminish its symptomatic meaning, as shown by the symmetry with the analyzed scene, where the narrative articulation of the ideological contradiction becomes visible.

Yet what happens when the film substitutes the first poem with the full version of the second one (as we have seen, only an allusion to this latter was present in the synopsis)? Apparently, the very act of this substitution follows the same reverse movement of distancing from the initial deixis we have found at the core of the first poem, as the spatial reference "these places" disappears in exchange for a non-situated "temple of the spirit," a clear reference to the apostle Paul's First Letter to the Corinthians (6:19: "Your body is a temple of the Holy Spirit"). This cancels the deictic reference in exchange for an abstract reflection: The "temple" refers here to "bodies" that have ceased to be mere bodies, having mutated into "pure, ascetic images," making thought seem heavy and dim in comparison. The most evident shift is the disappearance of the life/death opposition, replaced by a different kind of antinomy, the one between bodies and images, which are then compared and opposed to "mere thought." Taken in this framework, "mere thought" is compared again to the bodily dimension ("pure, ascetic images, / compared to which mere thought seems flesh, / heavy, dim").[21]

Let us examine carefully the first part of the second poem. As mentioned, the deictic reference ("these places") to a precise historical situation has disappeared. Yet, if we look closer, we can find one strong semantic element that is preserved, the adversative conjunction "ma" ("but"). In the first poem, the adversative "but" reverses a positive element, "life," into a negative one, "death" (a response carried by the echo: "Life is our only word. *But* the echo / of these places responds meekly: death"). In the second one, the adversative conjunction confirms the positive nature of the first element, "temple of the spirit," which *no longer* coincides with the bodily dimension: "Temple of the spirit / no longer bodies / *but* pure, ascetic images." In other words, the reversal advanced by the adversative conjunction in the second poem in turn reverses that of the first one: The body as a temple of the spirit, carrying a transcendental element that goes beyond the mere bodily condition, is no longer a body, that is, something bound to death and destruction, of course, but also to the ideological machine of the picturesque—already implicit in the expectations of foreigners, as we have seen. Thus, as the other side of the antinomy, *pure, ascetic images* are the element capable of escaping this condition; moreover, this aesthetic turn, so to speak, on a religious trope evidently points to an overcoming of the impossibility of finding expression, on which the first poem closed. In other words, as a poem composed by a fictional foreigner facing war in Naples, the first one expressed the shock of that encounter, and the impossibility of understanding and picturing it ("silence descends on everything, like dust" is its conclusion). As a second version of that same poem, in a fictional context that has found full expression in the accomplished work, the second poem refers to the process through which bodies, by becoming "pure, ascetic images," can work as vessels of a transcendental element that is not destroyed by the heaviness of thought and bodily dimension, thus not sharing their destiny of destruction and irrepresentability.

By appropriating the expression "ascetic images" to define the inscription of the film's historical content—the existence of the lower classes, the "ascetic" bodies the poet encounters in this foreign land—I am making reference precisely to the function such a transcendental element seems to have in these enigmatic verses, as something able to escape both the destiny of bodies (invisible, uncommunicable suffering) and thought (lack of clarity, obfuscation: "Mere thought seems flesh, heavy, dim"). Indeed, in this context "thought" is to be interpreted in connection to the practical rationality of the foreign visitors (a typical northern trait according to Rossellini's stereotypical conception). This approach to reality corresponds to the "objectivist illusion" against which Merleau-Ponty would develop his reflections on the possibilities of aesthetic expression: "We are convinced that the expressive act in its normal or fundamental form consists, given a signification, in the construction of a system of signs such that, for each element of the signified, there corresponds a signifying element—in other words, in representation" (Merleau-Ponty 1973b, 148). While this simplistic conception would prevent us from understanding how a work can communicate an experience that the ideological machine makes invisible and even "unthinkable," such as the existence of the Neapolitan underclass, the "ascetic images" refer precisely to the capacity for communication opened up by the aesthetic gesture, to which we will return to in the next chapters. In sum, the mechanism alluded in the verses evidently anticipates the self-deconstructive movement the film sets in motion, through which its own ideological contradiction reaches the surface and affects the viewing experience. Why was this possible? Why did this film fail to focus solely on presenting the conventional perspective of the city's elite and foreign visitors—the picturesque—as Rossellini had planned?

In commenting on the difference between Rossellini and Antonioni, Tag Gallagher writes that, while the latter builds a cinematic world that irradiates his characters' subjectivity, "Rossellini's equally subjective characters always find themselves colliding with an objective reality that is stubbornly other than themselves and anything they can imagine" (Gallagher 1998, 406). Rossellini's first major directorial work was shot on a battleship, in a film hybridizing fiction and documentary, *The White Ship* (*La nave bianca*, 1941), which he codirected with Francesco De Robertis. In this work, the romantic fictional plot is overwhelmed by the scenes in which war action is documented with particular attention to the interaction between the fragility of bodies and the powerful presence of the machines[22]—and we will see how all this will leave a trace in *Journey to Italy*. Although simulated, these scenes were shot in a real environment and in a real situation of war—in 1941—with the real crew. In an interview with the *Cahiers du Cinéma* from 1953, the same year he shot *Journey to Italy*, in response to a generic question on *The White Ship*, Rossellini asks in turn: "Do you know what a battleship is?" He goes on:

> It's frightening: the ship must be saved at all costs. The men do not know what's going on, they are peasants who have been yanked away from their homes, their fields, and forced to operate all sorts of machines they do not understand . . . they are there nailed down to their posts, literally nailed down because if the ship is hit by a torpedo, even though part of it may be flooded, the rest has to be saved. . . . So, that's where they are, in the stagnating heat, behind steel armor, stuck, not just locked up but really stuck, and *deafened by a vague and incomprehensible noise*. (Roberto Rossellini 1992, 50; my emphasis)

We can observe two central things here: First, the last sentence of the quoted passage directly points to the same deafening effect that closes the poem analyzed above—thus suggesting once more its connection with a war environment. Second, the director's material participation in a situation in which a mass of bodies constantly risks a quick and brutal annihilation, like the one described here, effaces the privileged standpoint that allows the bourgeois individual not to *see* the horror of that and similar situations. Something similar happens in Naples in the first months of 1946, when he and his crew are shooting *Paisan*, and will happen again a year later, in Berlin, where he will go to shoot *Germany Year Zero*. As I already mentioned, in Naples they capture half-starved bodies in the crowd that fills their scenes, children in rags operating in the black market among the rubble where corpses are still trapped. They shoot the main sequence of the second episode in the cave of Mergellina, where a vast crowd of homeless people is living in inhuman conditions, trapped in a dark underground space deprived of any modern living standards. In *Journey to Italy*, that cave is absent,[23] as are the most evident signs of the war. Yet both will return, their traces inscribed in the articulation of space and time, in the bodies of the extras, in the narrative trajectory that only among those bodies can find its peace.

Chapter 2

Hidden Things

Ortese's Writing and Collective Trauma

TERROR EVERYWHERE

Experience, war, terror, limit, disorientation. These are some of the key terms in the short preface to *Neapolitan Chronicles* that Ortese added to the book for its reedition forty-one years after its first release, in 1994, titled "The 'Sea' as Disorientation" ("Il 'Mare' come spaesamento"). All five words point toward a traumatic source inscribed in Ortese's writing. Investigating the nature of this source and its implications for the ideological standpoint of the writer will be essential to understanding the nature of the literary experience her work opens up for us. Before analyzing the passage from which those words are extracted, it is important to recall briefly the story of the composition of the book, which is no less "disorienting" than the experiences the author will recall in the preface.[1] Published in June 1953 by Einaudi in the prestigious series *I gettoni*, directed by Elio Vittorini (both Vittorini and Italo Calvino collaborated on the editing process of the book), *Neapolitan Chronicles* collects two fictional short stories and three hybrid pieces, which Lucia Re has aptly defined as "racconti-inchiesta," that is, "a hybrid of the genres of the short story, the autobiographical essay, and the reportage"[2] (Re 2015, 35). Three out of five stories included in the book had already been published in the weekly journal *Il mondo*, the fictional "A Pair of Eyeglasses" ("Un paio d'occhiali"), the hybrid "The Gold of Forcella" ("Oro a Forcella"), and "The Involuntary City" ("La città involontaria"),[3] while the remaining two were composed specifically for this project: the fictional "Family Interior" ("Interno familiare") and the hybrid "The Silence of Reason." It was in particular "The Involuntary City"[4] that impressed Vittorini so much as to convince him to write to Ortese to offer to publish her book on Naples in his series.[5] When she received his proposal, she was in Palermo in the middle of one of her trips along the peninsula in search of occasions for journalistic collaborations (and in search of momentary hospitality). She arrived there in mid-November 1951 hoping to sell pieces to different journals, while planning a book on Naples to propose to Corrado De Vita, the director of Edizioni Milano Sera, which had published her collection of short stories *The Buried Princess* (*L'infanta sepolta*) in 1950. She planned to send him "A Pair of Eyeglasses," "The Gold of Forcella," and "The Involuntary City," although she sent this latter to *Il mondo* first, to collect immediately some money (letter to Prunas, December 11, 1951, in Ortese 2006, 105–9). Yet her proposal for Milano Sera would not be concretized, as Vittorini would jump in immediately with his own proposal from the more prestigious Einaudi. When she received his letter, she was once again deep in debt, had left the hotel and abandoned her belongings as collateral, and was living in a hospital, where a doctor she knew had offered to host her for free as a patient (her health was precarious anyway). Vittorini's letter came as a relief, yet for immediate help she asked, as usual, for Prunas's aid:

> To this day, I have only a package of nationals [the cheapest Italian cigarettes at the time], a box of Minerva [matches] and 100 lire, which I will probably no longer have tomorrow evening, Saturday. . . . I am a little disheartened, because without pocket money you cannot survive, and in Palermo, with so many friends, I cannot ask anyone for a glass of water. Flowers yes, bread no . . . it is sad not to be able to tell anyone that we are poor, without fear of suddenly feeling to be less esteemed. (Ortese 2006, 117–18)

She was soon able to leave Palermo and work on the book on Naples, although this was, logistically, a very complicated process, during which she mostly lived between Milan and Naples. In this latter, she did not have a home anymore, and she stayed for long periods at Prunas's apartment or was hosted by the journalist Franco Grassi (also a former collaborator of *Sud*). At some point in the summer '52 she even ended up in a convent of nuns in Bardonecchia (in the Susa Valley in the Piedmont's Alps), with the support granted by a writers' union of which she was a member (Ortese 2006, 124–26). Finally, after the completion of the last story of the book ("The Silence of Reason") in January '53, she was hosted in Ivrea, during the spring, with the financial support of the Italian tech magnate Adriano Olivetti[6] (who, in those decades, supported several writers and artists), and worked there to finish up the book revisions. This last lucky circumstance had been actually made possible by no less than the Italian President of the Republic Luigi Einaudi, who, like Vittorini, had been extremely impressed by her story on the Granili ("The Involuntary City") after which he resolved to fix the situation and shut down the place forever. He had pressured Olivetti to help Ortese, and after the book's release, he even invited her for a formal dinner at the Quirinale (the presidential residence). We know from the memories of Marcello Venturi reported by Clerici (Venturi had been Ortese's partner at some point in those years), that she had thought the food was "good but not abundant" (Clerici 2002, 232). Once experienced, hunger lasts forever.

These hectic months of '52 and '53 can be considered an integral part of the experience of mental and physical exhaustion she describes as the origin of the book in the introduction to *Neapolitan Chronicles*, where we find all the key terms mentioned at the start of this chapter: "I would add that my personal experience of the war (terror everywhere and four years of flight) had brought my irritation with the real to the limit. And the disorientation I suffered from was by now so acute—and was also nearly unmentionable, since it had no validation in the common experience—that it required an extraordinary occasion in order to reveal itself. That occasion was my encounter with postwar Naples" (Ortese 2018, 10). The author speaks here of an experience that brings her to the limit of an emotional turmoil provoked by the horror of war: the limit, that is, of what is sayable, of what here requires a split temporality to manifest itself, one of silence and one of discourse, none of which properly possesses the core of the experience itself. The horror of the years of war belongs to silence; only a second, deferred "extraordinary occasion" was able to trigger discursivity, to reinscribe the event of the war ("terror everywhere and four years of flight") within verbal discourse. The readers of *Neapolitan Chron- icles* will not fail to notice, however, that the disorientation expressed in the book is never directly linked to a specific experience, but rather works as a background radiation, as if it were made of the same substance as her *gaze* and as the translation of that gaze into writing. "Experience" prop- erly said remains unspoken ("unmentionable"). Given the way she frames events in the quoted passage, It could be tempting to try to interpret this book's relation to the traumatic experience from which it seems to originate through the "classical" framework of Cathy Caruth's understanding of the relation between trauma, narrative, and history.[7] Indeed, her definition of trauma as a shock that works as "a break in the mind's experience of time" (Caruth 1996, 61) seems to perfectly describe the split temporality of this passage, the double occasion to which Ortese refers when describing the composition of this book. Yet a closer look at the lines already quoted, a further consideration of the whole preface and, finally, a wider examination of the author's oeuvre in its biographical context, force us to question the validity, in her case, of the paradigm that understands trauma in terms of a "punctual" event (although a complex one, existing on two different levels of temporality), to use the definition of "punctual trauma" coined by Greg Forter, to which I will return.

When she writes that her experience of war "had brought [her] irritation with the real to the *limit*," rather than saying it had created that irritation, she is inviting us to consider more carefully her previous affirmation (from the same introduction) that the origin of the excessive and hallucinatory tone of the book's writing was in her neurosis: "Evident in it are all the signs of an authentic neurosis" (Ortese 2018, 10). She admits to not being able to trace the origin of this neurosis. It seems to go back to an unfathomable personal past: "It would take too long and would be impossible to say where its origin is" (10). Yet she does find a name for that origin, that is, "metaphysics" ("metafisica"): "For a very long time, I hated with all my might, almost without knowing it, so-called *reality*: that mechanism of things that arise in time and are destroyed by time. This reality for me was incomprehensible and ghastly" (10). Can "metaphysics" be the origin for a neurosis? The ambiguous way she uses this word, almost as a two-faced term indicating both a classic materialist vision of things[8] and the incapacity to accept it, suggests the possibility that it rather works here as a placeholder, an empty signifier standing for a reality she is not able to clearly define. In other words, if the origin of her neurosis is *metaphysics*, and this, in turn, refers to both physical reality and a refusal of it, she is not really offering a solution, but rather creating an enigma that needs to be interpreted. The refusal of reality, if we understand this latter as a discursive process of negation and distortion, coincides exactly with the aesthetic gesture as ideological production, as defined by Jameson, which we examined in the introduction. In other words, her neurosis, which had initially manifested itself as a refusal of reality in her early magic-realist short stories,[9] is here reactivated and worsened by the experience of the "limit," the terrible years of the war and of the postwar period, in which poverty, exhaustion, and hunger had de facto erased any safety barrier between her social position and that of the city's underclass, thus pushing her toward a condition that would open her capacity of vision onto this miserable reality while reactivating previous experiences of poverty and hunger with which she had struggled her all life: the "class confinement" in which she had always lived (Ortese 1991, 1). What is important to note is that this standpoint does not work, for her, as a momentary illumination, a space she enters briefly into contact with, as it would happen with a traumatic, "punctual" experience. It is rather a routine, an everydayness, and the "limit" she talks about is a social condition. As we have seen in the brief account of the months she worked on *Neapolitan Chronicles*, that book is not so much about that limit but was written from within it: "If that lacerated condition originated in the infinite blindness of life, then it was this life, and its obscure substance, that I accused. I myself was shut up in that dark seed of life, and thus—through my neurosis—I was crying out. That is, I cried out" (Ortese 2018, 10–11; translation modified). *I myself was shut up in that dark seed of life*: In this communal condition, in this same space Ortese's difference is generated, which made her able to write something that appeared completely alien to her colleagues and friends, so much so that they reacted as if they had never seen a reality that had always been in front of their eyes: the intolerable, incomprehensible poverty of the underclass, of course, but also the starving and exhaustion of a friend with whom one can discuss literature and politics while ignoring that she needs to eat—"Don't think I'm distracted, I'm *hungry*" (Ortese 2006, 57).

Thus, in considering the traumatic sources of her capacity of vision she hints at in this introduction, we need to look at the pervasive and enduring class violence through which the lower strata of society are kept in subjugation in daily life. As this subjugation produces an erasure of sub-jectivity through pure exhaustion (hunger, fatigue, anxiety, etc.), this process in turn creates a capacity of vision that might transgress the limits required by different ideological standpoints rooted in privilege (Jameson 2009a, 221). It goes without saying, given these premises, that a key task of this analysis will be to understand how this experience is embedded in Ortese's textual structure, where it first emerges, as we have seen in the introduction, with the textualization of the "original emotion." Following the subsequent articulations of the latter, I will show how the literary text is able to com-municate a specific capacity of vision rooted in class position.[10] Ortese's writing in "The Silence" will achieve this by creating a superimposition of two different dimensions—or layers of reality—of which the reader will clearly sense the contradictory coexistence in the narrative construction of space and time. With Merleau-Ponty's *Phenomenology of Perception*, we can consider this ambiguity as a fixation on a traumatic condition that, due to its destructive power, has become all-encompassing, while disappearing in the background of our relation to the world: "Traumatic experience does not subsist as a representation in the mode of objective consciousness and as a moment that has a date. Rather, its nature is to survive only as a style of being and only to a certain degree of generality" (Merleau-Ponty 2012, 85). Though removed from the surface of the narrated events, it is thus still able to act as a formative influence that makes itself felt through the presence of multiple signs of a different reality beyond the superficial one. Precisely this formative influence creates the "style of being" that Merleau-Ponty will investigate in his later lectures on aesthetic and literary expression. In Ortese's work (and, as we will see, in Rossellini's *Journey to Italy* as well), this style and the anxiety linked to it will communicate the traumatic form of life of the underclass, with its own specific relation to urban space and its own temporality, whose textual inscription I call "ascetic images." Of all the signs of this inscription, the first to be noted is the class anxiety narratively articulated through the "original emotion," which, as we will see, forces the narrative progression to be "distracted," that is, to go astray from its declared objectives. In chapter 3 I will show how this "distraction" will result in the inversion of the original narrative program of the story.

In order to better understand the nature of such class anxiety in view of the analysis of its formal influence on the functioning of the text, it is crucial to further clarify how its source is not in a singular, personal event but in a diffused, shared class oppression that can be historically contextualized as a form of "routine violence," that is, a social operation similar to the one defined by Gyanendra Pandey as the "unceasing, if partly unconscious and often disguised" (Pandey 2006, 14) ordinary violence used to exercise oppression in day to day existence, and to forge and "naturalize" the social formation of oppressed groups: "The routine violence involved in the construction of naturalized nations, of natural communities and histories, majorities and minorities" (8). While Pandey has developed this concept as a theoretical tool for the interpretation of Indian history (with specific reference to the Partition), its hermeneutic possibility can provide us with a helpful instrument to understand the "production," throughout the centuries, of the Neapolitan lumpenproletariat. Of course, it is also important to stress that the pervasiveness of such a routine oppression must be understood as something able to act beyond its physical manifestations, thus permeating every aspect of social discursivity, in both the public and the private sphere, as a symbolic form of violence. Bourdieu has described it as able to disappear and be "naturalized" in social relations, where it functions "in the obscurity of the dispositions of habitus, in which are embedded the schemes of perception and appreciation which, below the level of the decisions of the conscious mind and the controls of the will, are the basis of a relationship of practical knowledge and recognition that is profoundly obscure to itself" (2000b, 170–71). As we will see, it will be precisely this habitus that we will find inscribed in the two main objects of this analysis.

To conclude this section, it is worth briefly mentioning the strong, negative reactions produced by the release of *Neapolitan Chronicles*.[11] They had a decisive impact on Ortese's life, effectively cutting off her links with Naples and the Neapolitan intellectuals (with few exceptions) who, despite her nomadic life and unstable behavior, had until this point been her major support network. More importantly, the virulence of these reactions can make more visible the functioning of the ideological self-absolutory discourse of the Neapolitan intellectuals that Ortese diagnosed in "The Silence of Reason." Famously, the story, which is the narrativization of a journalistic reportage about young Neapolitan writers and intellectuals, included the real names of the people the narrator met in her two-day stay in Naples. These were her friends and colleagues from the journal *Sud*, which she exposes as the protagonists of the more classical of the narrative genres: the bourgeois bildungsroman.[12] From the youthful radical engagement of the early postwar years in which they had believed in the possibility of social change through intellectual and political activism (*Sud* had been the main symbol of this period) to the mature retreat into the comfort of the bourgeois condition finally acquired through success in intellectual professions, they are presented as middle-class people who had once been able to see the misery of the city's underclass yet now have accepted the "blindness device" provided by their class's ideology. However, the book, which reached a certain degree of national popularity and won the Premio Viareggio in 1953, was also attacked by the city's press for its crude depiction of the conditions of the city's lumpenproletariat, and created a general disappointment in the Neapolitan middle-class milieu. In an interview from the 1990s, Ortese thus described the consequences this story had on her life: "The Silence of Reason is the story that unleashed hell, so I never went back to Naples. I have had attacks from certain newspapers. And then personal insults. I have not dared to touch Naples anymore; it is a burning topic" (Clerici 2002, 240).

La Capria has already been mentioned in the introduction as the author of a reflection on the Neapolitan ideology as a tool to come to terms, for the city's bourgeoisie, with an unbearable reality (unsurprisingly, an imaginary resolution for unsolvable contradictions), and a way to "domesticate" the underclass. In the same collection of essays in which he develops these ideas, *The Lost Harmony* (*L'armonia perduta*, 1987), he discusses at length Ortese's book, whose accusation, evidently, was still "an open wound" (as suggested by Re 2015, 52) for him. Despite the self-absolutory scope of his discourse, his thoughts are nevertheless helpful for an analysis of "The Silence of Reason," as they attempt to locate its core element, its "hidden thing," in a typical phenomenon of the Neapolitan bourgeoisie (the very root of its ideology), that is, the "fear of the underclass [plebe]," in which he sees the origin of the typical Neapolitan ideology (which is produced, he concludes, as a reaction to that specific "fear"). As we will see in the next section, his argument is correct but needs to be turned upside down.

The "Fear of the Underclass" and the Neapolitan Ideology

The idea of a secret, all-encompassing fear inspired by the Neapolitan lumpenproletariat in the city's bourgeoisie is at the center of the essay in which La Capria discusses Ortese's book on Naples, titled "Does Not the Sea Bathe Naples?" ("Il mare non bagna Napoli?"):

> Let us be careful to seize the Hidden Thing ceaselessly squirming at the bottom of this book, with a deaf noise "like surf rustling on the sand after a hurricane."[13] This thing is again and always the fear of the underclass [plebe] that is once more generated, and here resurfaces, as a "condition of ontological insecurity," that is, as the risk of losing one's own ego . . . the hereditary fear felt by the Neapolitan petty bourgeoisie for the eventuality of being involved, perverted, submerged by the tide of the underclass. (La Capria 2003, 692–93)

The "hidden thing" La Capria mentions is not simply a generic petty bourgeois fear of the possibility of being "declassed" and absorbed into the lumpenproletariat, nor is it the vague psychoanalytical anxiety at which he hints—"to lose one's own ego." Rather, it is a more concrete and historically determined situation, one that he went on to explore in "The Fear of the Underclass" ("La paura della plebe") and in the other essays that follow the one devoted to Ortese. Here he largely follows and quotes at length *The Disquieting Siren* (*La sirena inquietante*) by Mozzillo in order to analyze the unique features of the Neapolitan lowest class. Mozzillo traces its historical origins to the policies implemented by the Spanish administration during the seventeenth and eighteenth centuries, which created a *monstrum* that was unparalleled in Europe at the time and that proved to be an unsolvable problem throughout the following centuries and changes in political sovereignty. The explosion of demographic pressure in Naples has been summarized as follows by Mozzillo, in particular with reference to the years 1663 and 1665 (a period of famine and plague, respectively):

> Famine and contagion surely were not unforeseeable and unforeseen accidents, but unavoidable outcomes of a process that for some time had been undermining the economic structures of the Kingdom. It now has been decades since the demographic pressure has negatively characterized the development of a capital that is about to become the monstrous head of a gracile and sick body. . . . Hordes of famished peasants enter the city. . . . A mob of derelicts that gradually grows bigger until they are forty thousand in a few months, and who are, moreover, as forgotten, confused in the already immense crowd of the beggars. (Mozzillo 1983, 18–20)

As we have seen in the introduction, this state of affairs (Sabatini 2013) ended up producing the "inhuman" situation Mozzillo describes[14] on the basis of accounts and letters by travelers from northern Europe who visited Naples in the eighteenth century, which give an idea of what must have been the disconcerting impression made by the Neapolitan reality on foreigners, and which explains the still unbearable conditions of that same population in the following centuries (Ghirelli 1976, x–xi).

According to La Capria's argument, the contact with the aggressive mass of the urban poor had always represented a higher threat and a source of anxiety especially for the lower strata of the bourgeoisie, who were weaker and deprived of the protections enjoyed by the upper classes. Indeed, the petty bourgeoisie had been the first victim of the popular fury that erupted in specific moments of crisis: the so-called "revolt of Masaniello" in 1647 and the bloody suppression of the Neapolitan republic in 1799, when the lumpenproletariat turned against the revolutionary bourgeoisie, and, manipulated by the king and the clergy, violently snuffed the revolutionary experience made initially possible by the help of the French army. La Capria maintains that the memory of such a traumatic event, together with the unsettling presence of the crowd of the poor, which suddenly becomes more visible in the most difficult moments, produced, as a compensatory reaction, a specific ideology, which, over the centuries, became the peculiar Neapolitan ideology: the "napoletanità." While he is not the first intellectual to analyze this ideology, his specific idea is that it was produced, in particular, as a compensation for an open "wound" that had never healed, as a result of the massacre of 1799: "In 1799 something irreparable happens: the Civil War—atrocious—and that image is traversed by a laceration that disfigures it. The 'napoletanità' was born to repair it. It was born after the genocide of the enlightened bourgeoisie who left the petty bourgeoisie alone in front of the immense mob, still seething with fury and *desire for robbery*. It was born as a reaction of the petty bourgeoisie to the fear of the underclass" (La Capria 2003, 730; my emphasis). According to La Capria, this ideology was not only a device used to domesticate an intimate fear but also a tool to domesticate the lower classes, providing them with a self-image in which their most unsettling features were blurred by the well-known positive side of the antinomy governing the traditional "Orientalist" perception of the southern populations (see the introduction)—vitality, passion, sensuality, love of music, and so on. He defines the effects of the napoletanità as "that work of seduction, so to speak, of the Neapolitan bourgeoisie tending to transform the *instinctive barbarity* of this part of the population [i.e., of the underclass] into something subtler and less dangerous, which is identified with that depth of sentiments common to every Neapolitan, and therefore abolishes all fearful diversity" (705; my emphasis). Yet what he calls a "seduction" can clearly be interpreted as a form of "epistemic violence," as defined by Gayatri Spivak (1988, 280–91), since this ideological self-understanding of the Neapolitan bourgeoisie is imposed on the whole society, and the subaltern, marginalized class is forced to fit into the framework. In this regard, it is worth noting an observation of Renato Fucini, who, in commenting on the docility of the Neapolitan poor toward the rich minority of the city in 1877, wrote in his travel account: "They tamed them, I tell you, they tamed them in a wonderfully wonderful way" (Fucini 1976, 30).

It is also important to specify that the way La Capria is framing the historical trauma suffered by the Neapolitan bourgeoisie, as "a tragedy, a defeat, which remained as an indelible mark in the psyche of the surviving . . . Neapolitan bourgeoisie" (La Capria 2003, 653), echoes a larger ideological operation through which this event became, in time, a "cultural trauma" in the sense that has been developed in recent trauma theory. In the essays collected in the volume *Toward a Theory of Cultural Trauma*, Jeffrey Alexander, Neil Smelser, and their coauthors have interpreted this kind of trauma as the product of a collective awareness that needs to be built over the years by an elite of cultural agents belonging to the social group that understands itself as the victim of a historical event able to mark its history: "A memory accepted and publicly given credence by a relevant membership group and evoking an event or situation which is (a) laden with negative affect, (b) represented as indelible, and (c) regarded as threatening a society's existence or violating one or more of its fundamental cultural presuppositions" (Smelser 2004, 44). Yet it is important to stress again that this cultural trauma has a class dimension only, as the Neapolitan lower classes have no active part in its elaboration. La Capria is not interested in exploring the other side of the story, where the traumatic "routine" experience of the underclass has no rhetorical force to become a "cultural trauma" in its own right, since, as stressed by Jeffrey Alexander, "for traumas to emerge at the level of the collectivity, social crises must become cultural crises. Events are one thing, representations of these events quite another" (Alexander 2004, 10).

In sum, what La Capria removes from his interpretive framework is a reckoning with the systemic social injustice that underpins the city's history, upheld through the centuries by both brutal repression and ordinary violence. A comparative perspective can be illuminating here: Regarding how political theory and social policies have addressed marginalized Black neighborhoods in American cities, Tommie Shelby (2016, 3) recently argued that only a *"systemic-injustice* [interpretive] framework" can lead to a correct understanding of the social position of their inhabitants. In other words, no coherent interpretation of the phenomenon of urban ghettos is possible without a serious reflection on the atavistic, structural conditions of injustice that have created them and that continue to take a toll on the life of their inhabitants. All historical differences notwithstanding, if we now look at the Neapolitan urban marginalization through this same framework, we can see that what is missing from La Capria's reflection is precisely the realization that no "pacification" (the resolution of "cultural trauma") is ever possible without a *rectification*—however partial, since the past cannot be simply erased—of the injustice on which the social order is built. Important in this regard is Shelby's consideration, which might seem obvious but remains challenging for intellectuals whose position is rooted in privilege, that "principles of *rectification* should guide attempts to remedy or make amends for the injuries and losses victims have suffered as a result of ongoing or past injustice" (Shelby 2016, 12).

Indeed, if we pay attention to La Capria's word choice—the "instinctive barbarism" in his last quoted passage or the "desire for robbery" in the previous one—it is clear that his historical analysis, formally accurate but incomplete, is in turn a classist, self-absolutory, ideological fable aimed at concealing the responsibilities of the Neapolitan bourgeoisie for the permanence of the abject condition of the lower strata.[15] Indeed, if it is true that the napoletanità functions as a psychological defense, a consolatory myth, it is also an alibi, the acceptance of a precise situation (one of privilege for the upper classes) as "natural" and therefore immutable.

It is helpful here to recall again Pandey's definition of "routine violence" as being present "in the construction and naturalization of particular categories of thought, in history and in politics" (2006, 15). This is exactly the ideology denounced by Ortese in her book, whose central function is revealed in its power to blind, to produce a narcotic indifference to the suffering of the surrounding lower classes. Not by chance, La Capria notes that it is exactly this refusal of the napoletanità that leaves Ortese defenseless in the face of the "fear of the underclass"—and here he comes closest to recognizing the apologetic nature of his own argument, when he defines the Neapolitan ideology as "a form of dizziness very similar to the *pietas* (and different from indifference) that all great civilizations have produced to oppose misery and horror when they were ineluctable. (But were they really ineluctable in Naples? Or would another bourgeoisie have found another way out?)" (La Capria 2003, 694). The response Ortese gives to the first "open question" is certainly negative, and this marks her unbridgeable distance from the Neapolitan intellectuals of her generation like La Capria, who needed to keep that question unanswered to avoid questioning their own role and responsibilities. After all, even if he had tried to give an answer to this question, he would not have been able to propose a solution that did not screen out the foundational injustice on which the Neapolitan social order is based. Indeed, his perspective on the bourgeoisie as the class that ought to have found "a way out" aligns with the interpretive framework that Shelby, in the aforementioned study, described as the "medical model." This paradigm implicitly views the ghetto's inhabitants as passive subjects to be "treated" as painful symptoms, without ever addressing the deeper roots that would naturally challenge the entire social order, while also denying their political agency.[16] Not coincidentally, in the Italian context the medical metaphor had been used to picture the north-south relationship since early post-unification discourses, as shown by Moe (2002, 236–49).

The importance of a comparative perspective that takes into account theoretical contributions from other contexts, such as Shelby's, becomes even more relevant when considering two typical elements of the reactionary discourse surrounding American ghettos: racialization and the essentialist culturalist approach.[17] Indeed, these elements consistently return, since the unification of Italy, in the rhetoric surrounding the so-called Southern Question, that is the political and historical discourse on the relationship between the north and south of the country, as noted by Jane Schneider: "By the end of the nineteenth century, Southern Italians were represented in Italy as racial or cultural others whose differences from northerners were intrinsic and for all time" (1998, 12). Schneider also makes reference to the discourses that have opposed, over the decades, this type of ideological approach, mentioning scholars, such as Sidney Tarrow, "who have focused on political economy as a counterweight to Southern Question essentialisms" (Schneider 1998, 12). In this regard, she recalls the "compelling argument that the difficulties of the South are rooted in a colonial or near-colonial past" (13), going back to the well-known analysis of the South in post-unification Italy sketched by Antonio Gramsci, who, as noted by Barbara Arneil, was the first, in his 1926 essay "Some Aspects of the Southern Question" (Gramsci 1957), to use the framework of internal colonization "to describe an intra-European power relationship" (Arneil 2017, 9).

However, it is important to clarify, in relation to this point and following Arneil, that the paradigm of "internal colonization," as used to study "ethnic minorities who were marginalized and oppressed by their own states through patterns of uneven economic development, exploitation, and cultural division of labour" (Arneil 2017, 9), must always be understood in the context of the political struggle in which it is used: "Internal and post-colonial scholars tend to use 'colonization' as a metaphor for domination in order to appropriate the rhetorical power that comes with calling any entity colonial at the same moment that the globe is engaged in decolonization" (228). Furthermore, this theoretical caution is required here by the uniqueness of the Neapolitan case, where, as is evident in La Capria's argument, the racial and cultural essentialism of the North-South discourse becomes implicit in shaping the class relationship within the city itself, for which the napoletanità functions as a sort of non-dialectical and illusory overcoming.

Despite this unacknowledged ideological knot, La Capria's intuition about Ortese is indeed profound but misses a crucial point about her "class position" in this historical traumatic confrontation about the two classes: "Ortese, however, has refused that kind of *pietas* . . . and finds herself, with all her sensibility uncovered, exactly in the condition of the bourgeoisie prior to the 'napoletanità.' She thus relives the unfinished story of that bourgeoisie in the face of the underclass [plebe]" (La Capria 2003, 694).

My own interpretation is that she does not find herself "in the condition of the bourgeoisie," as he says. Even if coming from a petty bourgeois family and thus being able to pass as such, the material misery of her condition, as we have seen, de facto pushes her far from that kind of standpoint. Therefore, the defensive apparatus of the napoletanità does not work for her. Her fear is not that "of the underclass," in the sense of an objective genitive, but rather the *underclass's fear*, in the sense of a subjective genitive. This is a fear that is certainly not punctual or linked to a specific circumstance, but is rather a low-intensity yet never-ceasing fear encysted in the smallest aspects of everydayness: the result of exploitation, exhaustion, malnutrition, the constant worry for the care of a larger family when no means of subsistence are available nor any comprehension and assistance are to be expected.

To sum up, it is certainly true that Ortese refused the reassuring protection of the Neapolitan ideology, but this happened not because of an excessive "feminine" sensibility (this is *au fond* La Capria's sexist argument),[18] but rather because her capacity of vision was not obfuscated by class privilege and by the necessity to preserve it (as was the case for La Capria and other intellectuals). Therefore, the core of her literary experience is not to be found, as La Capria argues, in the experience of the *encounter* of the bourgeois person with the crowd of the poor, but rather in a communal experience, a condition of misery the author had shared for years in her proximity with the underclass, and that she would continue to share, although in other forms, through the poverty and marginalization of the subsequent decades. We will see shortly how this translates in her writing. Yet what kind of traumatic experience is this? As already mentioned, illuminating in this case is the definition developed by Greg Forter in his study *Gender, Race, and Mourning in American Modernism*, where he works out a concept of trauma embedded in "the very mechanisms by which our societies reproduce themselves" (Forter 2011, 100). Forter echoes, I believe, the definition of "insidious trauma" earlier elaborated by Maria Root, whose effects she sees as being "cumulative and directed toward a community of people. In effect, it encompasses some very 'normative,' yet nevertheless traumatic, experiences of groups of people" (Root 1992, 240). In other words, we are not talking here of a punctual, overwhelming experience, able to pierce the conscious defenses of the person suspending the experience of time, opening a gap in the flow of the inner stream of consciousness. We have to think, rather, of a different paradigm, something of the order of the already mentioned "systemic traumatizations," which are employed by ruling classes to implement both "processes of patriarchal gender formation" and "the processes governing the production of class and racial identities" (Forter 2011, 100–1): "Insidious trauma incurred by minority groups usually starts early in life before one grasps the full psychological meaning of the maliciousness of the wounds" (Root 1992, 240–41). This is not the overwhelming event that explodes consciousness; this is instead the everyday instrument used to reproduce multiple dynamics of social oppression.

The "systemic traumatization" Ortese shared with the underclass[19] opens a second dimension under the surface of the text, as if her perception of the world was centered at each moment on a different "scene" than the one that is presented to us. Here, again, Merleau-Ponty can help us make sense of such perceptual-projective mechanism, as he reflects on a "second space permeating visible space," which "is the one that composes, at each moment, our own manner of projecting the world" (2012, 300). However, the textual analysis focusing on the traces of the emergence of this second layer of reality cannot be successful if it does not take into account the opposite ideological pressure that we will see traversing Ortese's work: that form of retreat—a recoil—the writer undergoes in the approximation with the "moment of truth" ("a more primary experience, namely that of collective fear and of vulnerability" Jameson 2009a, 220), when the aesthetic gesture manifests a painful historical reality by which the author's personal experience is directly touched. This is precisely the ideological contradiction inscribed in the scene analyzed in the introduction, where the "original emotion" is located. Overcoming the standstill that I metaphorically defined there as a stiction, the standpoint inscribed in the text has allowed a certain hidden content to be revealed; however, an opposite tendency toward wish-fulfillment (one that negates the personal participation in that same condition of misery) impacts the formal structure, thus complicating its interpretation. We will find time and again this complication in passages where the ideological contradiction is further articulated, and the narrator creates an effect of distancing from the reality of the suffering she faces. In these moments, that reality appears foreign and incomprehensible.

Rossellini from *Duo* to *Journey to Italy*, via Joyce

Colette's *Duo*: A Message from the South

Journey to Italy was initially conceived as an adaptation of Colette's novel *Duo*, published in 1934 by the Éditions Ferenczi, after a first appearance *en feuilleton*.[20] Rossellini had already directed a short episode for a collective film, in October 1951, adapted from the novel Colette wrote immediately before *Duo, La chatte* (1933). The episode was titled "Envy" ("L'invidia") and was included in the French-Italian collective coproduction *The Seven Deadly Sins* (*I sette peccati capitali*, 1952). A first mention of *Duo*'s adaptation project appears in a written communication between Rossellini and Lux Film in June 1952; in January '53, in a production document, *Duo* is used as a working title, although in previous documents the title *Viaggio in Italia* had occasionally already been used (Dagrada 2008, 290). The adaptation project was finally dropped, officially because the production discovered the rights had already been sold. As pointed out by Dagrada, there is no proof this was the true reason, besides an oral statement by the director of photography Enzo Serafin[21] and Gallagher's and other commentators' accounts not referencing any documentary proof (397). In any case, the screenplay sent to the Preliminary Censorship (Revisione Cinematografica Preventiva) in January '53, despite preserving some structural elements from Colette's novel, was not an adaptation properly said, so it is very likely that Rossellini and his collaborators already knew this latter would not happen way before it was officially acknowledged. As briefly mentioned in chapter 1, this manuscript submitted in January was titled *New Wine*,[22] and the only known surviving copy, which I examined, is in Antonio Pietrangeli's archive, today kept at the Biblioteca Malatestiana in Cesena. Pietrangeli, Brancati, and Rossellini had all worked on this screenplay,[23] although, as it is known, Pietrangeli was dropped from the official credits. I will analyze this screenplay in the next sections and formulate my own interpretation of the nature of the contributions of Brancati and Pietrangeli. Yet first it is important to analyze the structure of Colette's novel—the starting point of the whole process—in order to understand its relation with the subsequent steps of the film's realization. As my analysis will show, much more of what is usually maintained by critics passes from her novel into the film. I will then address the hybridization of this first intertext with the second one, represented by Joyce's "The Dead." This will be the focus, in particular, of the last section of this chapter, in which I will analyze the revised synopsis the authors submitted to the Censorship after the initial rejection of the screenplay, a key step for the final realization of *Journey to Italy* as we know it.

Duo is the story of a Parisian couple vacationing in the husband's family mansion in Cransac, in the south of France. Things fall apart when the husband, Michel, accidentally discovers that his wife, Alice, cheated on him a few months earlier with his business partner. Although that affair had ended and had been trivial for Alice, the crisis mounts for eight days, after which Michel commits suicide. Commentators of *Journey to Italy* have usually stressed how very little from the novel ended up in the film, that is, nothing but the vague plotline of a married couple's crisis during a vacation in the south: "The disintegration of a marriage owing to a crisis of intimacy," as summarized by Luzzi (2014, 55). Dagrada specifies further how this plotline interacted with the architecture of the film: "Around this nucleus, the screenplay bases a narrative framework that will flow entirely into the film, unlike the thematic nucleus that will instead be profoundly transfigured" (2008, 311). Yet, a careful analysis of the novel shows that much more of that "thematic nucleus"—however transfigured—survived in the film: If not its external appearance, we can find there two structural elements, two underground threads that run through its narrative, that is, (1) the story's environment (both natural and social) and (2) the plot's essential structure (once abstracted from its superficial manifestation).

As for the first one—the natural and social setting that surrounds the couple in crisis—Rossellini's idea of bringing the story to Naples at first seems to be the kind of twist that completely overturns its meaning. Gallagher, for example, comments as follows: "He retained Colette's conflict for his non-Colette film, adding a third character absent in Colette to draw out those subterranean emotions: the raw world of nature—Naples" (Gallagher 1998, 397). Brunette adds: "The focus of the novel, however, is very intensely on the couple, with no attention paid to their environment, and it is here that the film most strikingly departs from Colette's fiction" (1987, 156). But this is only apparently true. Probably what captured Rossellini and his collaborators' attention was exactly the ambiguous, subterranean yet powerful presence of the environment. First, the "raw nature" is not at all absent from the novel: The Parisian urban setting in which the couple's ordinary existence is supposed to unfold in non-vacation time gets completely obliterated by the exuberance of the countryside of Cransac, strongly present in the vivid descriptions, which do not have a merely decorative function but interact with the character's moods and ultimately with their decisions:

"The night, the water and the nightingale: here is the triad of a *décor* from which Colette, while describing, suggests correspondences with the drama experienced by her characters" (Mercier 1991, 1675). This presence of the natural landscape even ends up swallowing any remnant of "ordinary life" when Michel throws himself in the flooding river at the end of the story, while, with the intensity of its beauty, it seems to strengthen Alice's resistance to her husband's death drive. But even more importantly, this environment is populated by marginal "spectators" that somehow play an active role in the development of the crisis. Something similar will happen in Naples to the Joyces, their uneasiness mounting among a mysterious and strange population of a different class. Like the Joyces in their villa in Torre del Greco, Alice and Michel are not alone in the vast mansion, presented as the aristocratic seat of the local landowners of Cransac, from which Michel descends. By now the family's wealth has significantly decreased: The financial situation of the estate is in trouble, and the man's primary occupation is theatrical production. What intensifies the crisis and Michel's anguish is indeed the presence of the house's domestic workers, Maria and her husband and the property manager Chevestre, together with other, more obscure figures, which at a certain point, in Michel's obsession, coincide with the whole village. The man is afraid that these people might discover what is going on between himself and Alice. As noted by Joan Hinde Stewart, "Their anguish [the couple's] is intensified by his obsession with the gaze of others—servants, merchants, villagers. By trade a theatrical producer, he stages for the onlookers a display of conjugal entente, playing an elaborate role himself" (1980, 662). Yet Colette frames Michel's obsession as something more profound than a narcissistic wound to his "virile pride." His fear is more sinister and seems to connect him back to the ancestral class division on which the village community was built. This is just an impression at first, driven by the ominous reactions of Michel at the possibility other people listening to their quarreling:

> With a noiseless bound Michel jumped to the half-open door and closed it, taking care not to make a sound. "Are you out of your head?" he exclaimed. "They're down there in the kitchen, having lunch. Anybody'd think—really, now!—on my word! And the postman, too, probably just coming up the hill!" He stammered and talked excitedly, although he circumspectly kept his wrath under control and did not raise his voice. He gesticulated

vehemently toward the window, *opening his mouth in a squarish shape*, Alice noted, like the masks of classic tragedy. (Colette 1951, 390; my emphasis; translation modified)

Michel's open mouth, deprived of sound and frozen in an expression of horror, signals the outbreak of an affective intensity not easily interpretable in a conventional way. If at first Alice reads her husband's secrecy as petty, masculine pride (388), while observing him day by day she slowly understands something more profound is going on, also because his fear of the house workers becomes projected onto the whole village, thus opening the crisis onto a vaster line of ancestral class conflicts.[24] Then the novel seems to draw, in a subterranean way, this class conflict more to the center of the story, as we learn, through Michel's memories, of Alice's inferior class origin: "Alice, a child of chance, was one of a family loaded down with daughters who realized that they were a burden and struggled fiercely to exist" (405). Immediately after this revelation, even the relationships in the household start to shift. While the domestic worker, Maria, had until this moment shown a closer bond with Michel (though their relationship was of strict master-servant submission, however concealed in irony), she suddenly starts to develop a closer one—this time based on a form of solidarity—with Alice: "For the second time Alice thought she sensed, under Maria's impenetrable shell a warm wave of human feeling, an impulse which she likened to the solidarity that unites wife and concubine" (433). But this subterranean class conflict will soon prove to be something actually already concluded, a battle lost by the ancient master. The ominous character of Chevestre is revealed to be about to take over the property, as Michel is on the brink of failure: " 'I'll bet he's the one who put up the money for the mortgage on this place,' Michel thought. 'Seysset is only a dummy. If Alice knew! But she'll find out when I have to sell' " (423).

Thus, it becomes clear that this gradual widening of the story's main plot onto the emergence of class conflict will be preserved in the film, where it will subliminally emerge in the depiction of class relations, and in the appearance of the bodies of lower-class people: a process that will be powerfully signaled by the pressure of the subterranean dimension they inhabit—especially manifested by the complex soundscape (on all this we will focus in depth in the next chapters). However, as mentioned, this movement of revealing what is hidden under the surface of social relations is only the first structural element from *Duo* that ends up in the film. The second one constitutes the very core of the plot itself, and, via Joyce's short story, will have the same centrality for the film's architecture. We need to analyze the organization of the story in depth in order to bring it to the surface, although, in this case too we will discover it is hiding in plain sight.

Michel accidentally finds out about Alice's infidelity because he sees her handling a folder with a letter from her ex-lover; why she had kept (and momentarily retrieved) this and other letters, rather than destroying them, is not said, but it reveals the primacy of her own agency in the whole story. Moreover, the fact that for no apparent reason she awkwardly calls her husband's attention to the letter—we learn later that she does not care for the letter itself, its content, or her former lover—decisively locates in this place the "original emotion," signaling an ideological contradiction that here enters the story. There is a brief but unequivocal anonymous message in the letter, and Michel recognizes his business partner's handwriting: Ambrogio. In this context the southern connotation of the lover—the agent of disturbance, and finally of dissolution, of the bourgeois couple—cannot go unnoticed: "She pictured to herself quite coolly the face of the slender young man from Nice, whose black hair glistened like a bird's plumage" (Colette 1951, 447; translation modified). The southern man from Nice has an Italian name, and his hair is dark and shining, thus recalling the cliché image of Italian men with greasy hair.[25] Moreover, the comparison of the man's hair to plumage signals a closeness between this figure and the natural landscape that plays a role in the couple's dissolution (as we have seen, in both Alice's endurance and Michel's surrender).

Ambrogio's "message" will work in two different phases, as the first letter will be followed, at the end of the story, by the emergence of three more letters Alice will decide to reveal to Michel in a final attempt to placate him (something that will achieve the opposite effect). After the uncovering of the first, generic letter that reveals the affair, Alice tells Michel that it had been a brief mistake provoked by a moment of physical weakness (she had been ill), in which the two had developed a reciprocal sympathy based on common interests in culture and music (407). But Michel is not assuaged by this version of the story. On the contrary, he claims that he would have preferred, and could have easily forgiven, an affair solely provoked by an excess of physical desire. His is clearly a gendered framework: Alice's version of the affair is, according to Michel's worldview, feminine, based on sympathy, sensibility, "feelings," and so on. But the version he would have preferred is the masculine one:

"You don't even understand that the worst thing about it all is precisely that—er—friendship you gave the fellow, those hours you talked together, before sleeping together! By God! You even spoke of 'confidence'! And you said he liked the same things you do." . . .

"My dear child, you'll never understand a man in love and what a betrayal means to him. You'll never understand how a man can forgive and almost forget a mere matter of a woman's night with some other man, a temporary yielding to physical desire." . . .

"Anyone can lose his head or be swept off his feet by a wave of animal heat," he continued. "We men know what that means, by God! Let him cast the first stone—if he has the heart—who never . . ." (Colette 1951, 409–10)

It is very clear what is going on here, and what Michel is trying to do by gendering Alice's extramarital affair against his own conception of a masculine attitude toward the same issue: "Strong in his rights of man of quickly aroused desires" (409; translation modified), he regains self-confidence. Moreover, by implicitly acknowledging that he had extramarital affairs himself—certainly of the masculine, physical kind only ("let him cast the first stone—if he has the heart—who never . . .")—he is regaining control of the situation, reimposing a sexist framework on the husband-wife relationship, where the wife's infidelity is the result of feminine weakness. Moreover, the rival is in turn emasculated and framed as somebody who indulged in sentimental stuff, gentle talking, "confidence," and so on,[26] all things excluded by the virile conception of extramarital affairs: "a wave of animal heat." Yet he is not successful in this power struggle, probably also because, as we have seen, at the structural level the conflict is unfolding on another dimension too, that of socioeconomic relationships. But what precipitates the events is the fact that Alice ignores—or chooses not to understand—what he is trying to do to reaffirm his own male supremacy within the couple. She takes him literally, and after a few days of reflection, while he keeps on going back to this same argument, she reveals to him the truth. There are three more letters from Ambrogio. In these, the true nature of the affair is disclosed: It is precisely what Michel was invoking and his wife had initially denied—a mere physical affair ("a wave of animal heat"), which Ambrogio's words this time picture in full detail. This is what really kills Michel, what he cannot accept: the fact that Alice has escaped his sexist framework. She has cheated as he would have done it. No power imbalance remains, but absolute parity. It is precisely this message that arrives from the past, from the South (being delivered in a southern environment and by a southern character): that she is not the "character" he imagines, but a different, unknown person.

Thus, what has been considered by the majority of commentators of the film-novel relationship as the central event of the crisis described in the novel and what precipitates it, that is, the fact that the wife "refuses to feel apologetic" (Gallagher 1998, 397; a similar take in Dagrada 2008, 314n53) is really just a secondary consequence in the much more relevant "tectonic movement" in the couple's power balance. Precisely this shifting of power, with the narrative framework that provokes it—the advent of the messenger and his message from the past/South (Ambrogio and his letters, Lewington and his verses)—is indeed our second element, which will enter the film after being clarified through its confrontation with the second major intertext, that is, "The Dead."

Indeed, as we have seen in chapter 1 while analyzing Joyce's short story, a similar narrative mechanism connects Michael Furey with the Conroys: The wife, Gretta, whom the husband Gabriel believed he knew perfectly, whom he had framed in his own worldview, will be revealed to be—through the appearance of the young lover from the past—a different, completely unknown person. This event will be repeated in *Journey to Italy* with the recollection of Charles Lewington's verses: Their message from the past (and from the South), will reveal to Alex that Katherine is a different person than he had imagined, also opening the way for the emergence of a concealed, historical reality (de facto, this happens in *Duo* too, as the discovery of the affair also puts in motion the emergence of social tensions and a shift in class positions). Yet first, as we will see in detail in the next section, this narrative core, although heavily modified on the surface, will emerge in the screenplay too: Here, the husband, having been discovered in his infidelity, bluntly admits to having cheated on his wife. Yet, realizing she is not destroyed by the news, and not receiving any reply to his questions about whether she had cheated on him too, he assumes that she has and starts to become furiously jealous, exactly because, like in the novel, he realizes his wife escapes his implicit, sexist way of framing her.

New Wine, Old Clichés

No information is available on the circumstances and exact period of composition of the screenplay titled *New Wine*, kept in Pietrangeli's archive in Cesena. We only know that it had been submitted to the Preliminary Censorship before February 5, 1953, on which date a negative reply from that same office was signed. We also know that, in November '52, Rossellini was still undecided about his next film, as he traveled with Zavattini on the River Po delta in preparation for a different project that should have been made in collaboration between the two men, titled *Italia mia* (Dagrada 2008, 289–90). But the project was soon dropped to focus on *Duo*, as the *New Wine* screenplay that was received (although with the title modified to *Viaggio in Italia*) by the Censorship on January 24, 1953 (316n58) must have been in preparation for at least a few weeks. What has never been noted in any critical study so far, to my knowledge, is that two different versions of the first part (*primo tempo*) of the screenplay are present in the folder that contains it in the archive in Cesena, while the second part is only present in one single version. I will later briefly analyze the differences between the two versions and will propose an interpretation of their meaning. In any case, even taking into account those differences, the story told is technically already not an adaptation of *Duo*, as the jealousy crisis of the couple unfolds in a very different way than in Colette's novel; however, already at this stage, the important elements we have seen persist.

The plot is as follows: John and Isabella Joyce travel to Naples to sell the property inherited by John from his uncle, Horace Joyce (the uncle's name will become Homer in the next steps of the project). They are immediately impressed by the poverty and degradation of the local people (described vividly, something the Censorship would not appreciate) from the start of the story in Terracina, as they are driving south. In Naples, at the Hotel Excelsior, they meet by chance a group of English friends, who are living there as (wealthy) expatriates. Among them is Edith, a woman with whom John had an affair in the past and who is now in a relationship with a local young man. At dinner together Isabella notices some tension is present among Edith and John. The couple moves into the villa in Torre del Greco, and, while nonchalantly acknowledging his affair with Edith, John asks his wife whether she has cheated on him too. But she does not reply: He is disappointed, having expected that she would deny and declare her innocence. Thus, he assumes she has cheated too, and this will be the pivotal event in the story, because, on the basis of this assumption, John becomes increasingly jealous. At the villa they meet Uncle Horace's secretary, Charles, an Englishman who has stayed in Naples since the years of the war, when he had served there in the army, and his wife Adalgisa (Maria in the second version), a Neapolitan woman. The two have a disquieting effect on John and Isabella because of their strong and evident physical connection that manifests itself in many ways. But there are more disquieting presences at the villa: the young peasant Assunta and the construction worker Pasquale, who are about to get married but continuously and violently quarrel because of the young man's jealousy and unwillingness to wait until the wedding to sleep with his future wife. This works as a sort of secondary plotline in the screenplay: Assunta seeks refuge at the villa, and Isabella offers to host and protect her from her boyfriend. The two will finally marry and John and Isabella will attend the ceremony in the church, deeply moved emotionally—something that will help the denouement of the story. However, before this, many incidents punctuate the evolution of John's jealousy delirium, while tension in the couple increases. They visit Pompeii and witness the excavation of a cast created in the hollow space left by a couple, dead lovers buried in the debris since the eruption. The presence of this scripted episode already at this stage of the project demonstrates how the corresponding scene in the final version of the film (where it will be the culmination of an emotional climax) could not be the result of mere improvisation and lucky chance, contrary to what some critics have assumed.[27] This moment represents a pause in the couple's mounting tension as they are deeply moved (John especially), but then the fighting starts again. Finally, they decide to get a divorce, but first attend Assunta and Pasquale's wedding. The separation having been already decided and the lawyers involved, they decide to go for a final trip to Paestum. Here something has changed, probably as a result of the emotion both felt at the wedding, but they refuse to admit it. Yet something happens: A young man stares insistently at Isabella, and John becomes madly jealous again and assaults him. This final outbreak of his emotional turmoil also marks the reconciliation of the couple: They admit they still love each other and reconcile on their way back to the villa, which they will no longer sell.

This long summary was necessary to discuss the incoherent and strange nature of this preliminary phase of the story, where the pivotal role of jealousy is deeply ambiguous. On the one hand it is framed as clearly negative, as it drives John almost crazy, pushing him to persuade himself of his wife's infidelity and to almost end his marriage for no concrete reason other than his own fantasies. On the other hand, there are moments in which a clear, opposite point of view seems to emerge: Jealousy is in this case seen as something John has to learn to save his marriage. The contact with the South has shown him a totally different way to participate in romantic relationships. Indeed, if this mad jealousy almost kills their marriage, incoherently, it is exactly a violent outbreak of the same feeling (the physical assault on the young man in Paestum) that saves it. This unresolved ambiguity cannot be explained without acknowledging the presence of two different, even opposite ways of framing the duality of southern and northern elements, whose encounter, as we have seen in chapter 1, was the central motive Rossellini saw in his own film in all interviews and public reflections about it. The positive, "Orientalist" valorization of southern jealousy vis-à-vis northern "coldness" is perfectly in tune with Rossellini's stereotypical understanding of the South as expressed in interviews released about the film, like the one with the French radio from 1960 quoted in the introduction, where he used the analogy of the "draped" versus "sewn" civilization to exemplify the South-North divide. However, John's increasing jealousy, which seems to enter his soul upon contact with the southern environment, is also clearly presented as crazy and sick. This ambiguity signals conflicting authorial intentions at work on the project and points to the other major intertext—Joyce's "The Dead," whose presence was linked, as we have seen in chapter 1, with Brancati—which will replace *Duo* as the main influence in the next phase of the film's development.

Yet why does the use of "The Dead" as a way to interpret, so to speak, the inner meaning of *Duo* displace jealousy as a central element of the story? Simply because the two stories share an important element, one more evident in the former, less visible in the latter, compared to which jealousy in itself loses importance: The pivotal event around which the plots evolve is the fact that the husbands discover that they did not really know their wives. Both had tried to see them, throughout their lives in common, by imposing on them the framework of their patriarchal vision (Gabriel's romanticizing vision and Michel's infantilization of Alice[28]). Yet both women are really completely unknown to their husbands: They are *free* from that framework. In "The Dead," Gretta reveals that the most important and meaningful event of her life did not involve Gabriel in the slightest way and happened outside of their relationship. This makes him initially jealous, yet soon he realizes that this revelation has a meaning that goes far beyond jealousy. As for *Duo*, despite jealousy being apparently central, the pivotal event that precipitates the crisis and pushes the man to suicide is the recognition that Alice was very far from what he had taken for granted: She was instead a person able to act in what he considered to be a purely masculine way, only driven by a physical inclination. Indeed, starting with this common point, we can read, against the grain, the subtle structural affinities that connect the two stories: Both narrate a crisis that is initiated by a casual event—the discovery of an old letter in Colette's case; a song performed at the end of the dinner party, which evokes an old memory, in Joyce's case. In both cases what I have called "a message" delivered to the husband—that his wife is a free, unknown person—is entrusted to the words of a young man who does not embody the qualities of mature and performative masculinity the husband believes he possesses. We don't know Ambrogio's age, but he is called "this kid" ("ce garçon"), and Michel despises him as a non-virile figure ("this guy loved the same things you do"; "ce type aimait les mêmes choses que toi"[29]). As for the young and frail "virginal male" (Norris 2003, 225) Michael Furey, his "message" is not read or listened to directly but retold in Gretta's account; yet, beyond the song the adolescent used to sing to her, his reported words that he "did not wish to live" without her have the power to shatter all Gabriel's certainties and to precipitate that revelatory, near-death experience ("His soul had approached that region where dwell the vast hosts of the dead" [Joyce 2014, 194]) that closes the story.[30]

This structure would enter the adaptation project only once the Censorship forced the authors to deeply rework the screenplay, as we will see in a moment. Yet it is important to note that if carefully read, *New Wine* already bears a nascent element of the structure I just highlighted in "The Dead" and *Duo*, that is, the fact that the husband's jealousy crisis is provoked by his first consideration of the *possibility* that his wife has cheated on him as he has done, and with the same carelessness, as if it was something completely unimportant. His consideration of this mere possibility means indeed the realization of her unforeseen freedom, the possibility she could *escape* the sexist framework through which he had always looked at her. Yet, as it is evident, this aspect is not developed or explored in the story, and John's delirium unfolds as a typical jealousy crisis, in which he starts to become paranoid about her interactions with other men. As I have showed, however, the ambiguity with which such jealousy is treated, as if there were conflicting authorial agencies at play at the same time, plus the surname Joyce already used for the couple, proves, I believe, that Brancati had already envisioned the idea of avoiding the banality of the jealousy motive in favor of a more complex reflection on gender roles, which would result in the higher complexity of the relationship between the two in the film. Indeed, in the same months in which he was working on *Journey to Italy*, Brancati was writing his last and posthumous novel, *Paolo the Hot* (*Paolo il caldo*, 1955), where he deeply reflected on the darker sides of southern men's attitude toward jealousy (instead of indulging in his usual comedic take on the issue) and on their obsession with masculinity and sex. But he would have the possibility to move the project in this direction only after the Censorship paradoxically granted him an occasion in this sense.

The Role of the Censorship and the Contribution of Pietrangeli

In this section, I will present an original interpretive hypothesis regarding Pietrangeli's role in developing the script of *New Wine*, informed by my research at the Fondo Antonio Pietrangeli in Cesena. To support my argument, it will be necessary to closely examine quotations from the two versions of the original screenplay as well as journal articles written by Pietrangeli during that time and earlier. This will demonstrate Pietrangeli's involvement in the specific parts of the screenplay that were then removed from the second version (and from the subsequent steps of the project), which accounts—this my interpretation—for his exclusion from the film's credits.

As we know from the archival reconstruction carried out by Dagrada in her work on Rossellini's films with Ingrid Bergman, the screenplay we have discussed, yet with the title *Viaggio in Italia*, had been presented to the Precautionary Censorship (Censura Preventiva), an office of the Ministry of Tourism and Entertainment on January 24 (Dagrada 2008, 316n58). Yet on February 5 the production received a negative reply, with a refusal to approve the film unless the screenplay was deeply reworked. This document, kept in the Central State Archive in Rome (file 1616—Fondo del Ministero del Turismo e dello Spettacolo), and reproduced in the appendix of Dagrada's book (document 9, 506–510), offers a detailed summary of the plot, which allows us to identify the screenplay submitted, as noted by Dagrada (361n58), as *New Wine*. Yet, it is worth specifying, as this has not been noted before, that the quotations included in the summary demonstrate that the document submitted was the second version of that screenplay. As I already mentioned, in the folder kept at Pietrangeli's archive, two versions of the first part (*primo tempo*) of the film are present (in the next pages I will name them S1a and S1b, respectively), whereas the second part (*secondo tempo*) is in a single copy (from now on S2). S2 is a continuation of S1b, as shown by the page and scene numbering (a previous version of S2 is absent, and we don't know if it ever existed). Indeed, in the Censorship's reply, a line from Edith's Italian boyfriend Giovannino is quoted: "Are we going to lunch or not?," which corresponds to S1b, whereas S1a has "Well, so, are we going to eat that spaghetti at zi' Teresa or not?" The summary also describes the following scene (12) in S1b, which is substantially different than in S1a: "During lunch, we see this Giovannino who, while the others talk and joke, 'is mostly busy eating.'" The words quoted are absent in S1a. Also in this latter, Giovannino participates as a protagonist at the dinner, shows off his ability to eat a plate of spaghetti in just a few mouthfuls to "teach" foreigners, and then acts as a sort of judge when they later compete to see who can eat faster, whereas, in S1b, there is no competition and Giovannino is barely mentioned.[31] As we will see in a moment, all the differences between the two versions go in a precise direction. What is surprising, though, is that this direction seems to anticipate what the negative opinion of the Censorship would indicate. Or perhaps this should not surprise us, as well known were the "preferences" and caveat of the political regulation of the film industry led by the future prime minister, Giulio Andreotti, who was at the time the undersecretary to the Presidency of the Council of Ministers in charge of entertainment policies, whose objective was essentially hiding the conditions of poverty and subsequent "moral degradation" (Brunetta 2009, 81). In accordance with this vision, the remarks formulated by the Censorship lament the presentation of Italian (and Neapolitan in particular) living conditions in a bad light: "The Italy of the film is an Italy in which dirty people 'live on the streets as in their house,' it is an Italy of 'wild people,' of 'beasts.' . . . The city of Naples only gives a spectacle of mercenary servility, of frighteningly filthy and dirty 'bassi,' of pimps and 'honored' prostitutes" (qtd. in Dagrada 2008, 509).

This discourse is perfectly coherent with the political goals of the Christian Democrats in power, who on the one hand feared that communists could exploit the evidence of social misery in the country to gain consent, and on the other aimed at presenting a polished, "western European" image of the country. In this case the international scope of the production, with "the participation of a famous director and equally influential performers . . . destined to be broadcast on world screens," made things even worse: "This film, due to its content and its unilateral and sordid representation of a certain southern Italy, as well as harming the prestige and decorum of Italy, could harm the interests of our tourism" (qtd. in Dagrada 2008, 509). Yet there is another element we need to note in this document: Besides all the problematic details mentioned in the summary, the censor adds that what is disturbing is the bulky presence of "a crowd, or rather of an anonymous underclass [plebe], portrayed according to the abused clichés so dear to the Anglo-Saxons when they intend to vilify Italy and the Italians" (qtd. in Dagrada 2008, 509). Here the acute eye of the Censorship was able to spot two things not so easy to read in the screenplay (and then in the film), and which often go unnoticed. First, the point of view through which southern reality is presented is exactly the one typical of "foreign" (read: northern European) observers, which, as we have seen, goes contrary to Rossellini's claim that the central idea of the film was showing how Mediterranean people "are in fact and not as they are perceived by the Anglo-Saxons" (Rossellini 1992, 120). Second, there is the centrality of the representation of the "plebe" despite its lack of involvement in the main plot, and whose subterranean presence is so powerful to acquire a prominent role in the balance of the work.

Before considering how the authors follow these directions in the subsequent step of the production, that is, in the resubmission of a revised synopsis and then in the film, let us briefly see how they had actually already anticipated them in the shift between the two versions of the first half of the screenplay, which will help us understand, I will argue, the role of Pietrangeli in the project, as well as the reasons for which he was dismissed.

There are many divergences between S1a and S1b, but I will report here only a few meaningful examples to show how this reworking represents the mitigation of the tone and content of the negative presentation of the southern environment. The first evident case happens in the second scene, when the English couple stops at a bar in Terracina and has a first close encounter with the local crowd. While they sit, disgusted by the local tea, a group of street children gathers around their Jaguar and one of them climbs in the car honking the horn. In S1a the waiter yells at him with anger, "Get off kid! . . . Get off son of a bitch"[32] while in S1b the offense is omitted. Later, when John and Isabella finally enter Naples and, headed to the Hotel Excelsior in Mergellina, take the wrong road—Via Dei Tribunali instead of Corso Umberto—and thus are forced to pass through the heart of the poor neighborhoods of the city center, S1a describes vividly the misery of the spectacle and the disgusted reaction of the foreigners: "That fantastic look of fresh misery, moist and colorful, and yet, at least in the eyes of an Englishman, utterly indecent."[33] In S1b this simply becomes "that fantastic look of fresh, moist, colorful and extraordinarily alive misery."[34] When the sight of the road is defined as a "fantastic vision and at the same time perhaps a little repugnant,"[35] in S1b "a little repugnant" is omitted. The Joyces' reactions are again suppressed immediately after: "Isabella turns her gaze around and does not hide a sense of wonder and depression. John's grimaces clearly express repugnance and disgust."[36] This is reduced, in S1b, to "Isabella turns her gaze around and does not hide a sense of wonder." As in the whole of S1b, the effect of mitigation is often produced through the suppression of single adjectives, like in the case of "visions of horrific infantile nudities" (S1a, scene 7, 36), where "horrific" is omitted. A similar attenuation will invest the visit of John and Isabella at the mansion of the Marchesi of Gragnano (S1a, scene 20), where Isabella will be insistently courted by the local men. When they arrive in the inner court of the palace, they find it populated, as it was typical of Naples, with a crowd of people of lower social status, among which are the usual half-naked children who inhabit the *bassi* and the lower levels of the building. The couple reacts with shock as they try to communicate to receive information about how to reach the Marchese's apartment. The wife of the concierge does not understand John and is not very friendly. She is working on repairing her husband's trousers, and this latter suddenly arrives in underwear. While he tries to assist them, a kid interrupts them asking that the man go fix a toilet that has overflowed. In S1b (scene 19), beyond the usual work of attenuation in the use and omission of adjectives, the heavy materiality of that plebeian life is alleviated: The woman at the entrance is working on her husband's jacket, and this latter arrives in an undershirt but with his trousers on. When his assistance for the plumbing work is required, it is only to fix a water tank.

Many more examples would be possible. What matters the most for my argument, however, is to note that all this work of attenuating the signs of a harsh social reality brings us back to the issue of the presence of Pietrangeli in the project, and the intertwining of his creative influence with the other authors. Initially a film critic and a translator from French (Maraldi 1992, 10–22), since the second half of the 1940s he had been mostly active as a screenwriter, although his first creative collaboration as a film writer dates back to 1942 on the set of Visconti's *Ossessione*; he had already worked with Rossellini on *Europe '51* as a writer, assistant director, and actor in a small part; on *Where Is Liberty?* (*Dov'è la libertà*, 1952) as a writer (together with Brancati, among others); and on the adaptation of Colette's *The Cat* in the film episode "Envy," for which he wrote an initial version of the screenplay (Maraldi 1992, 25). Pietrangeli's career as a director started at the same time as his collaboration on *New Wine*, as in '53 his first film was released, *Empty Eyes* (*Il sole negli occhi*).

Yet, in order to formulate a hypothesis on the nature of his contribution to *New Wine*, it is important to look, in particular, at the texts he wrote as a film critic in the 1940s, when he regularly published in journals such as *Bianco e nero* and *Cinema*, and after the war in *Star* and *Fotogrammi*, to name just a few. In the articles published in this period he defined his political vision of cinema, presenting himself as one of the most uncompromising defenders of the practice of realism on screen, which before the end of the war was also a cryptic way of being against the regime and his Censorship, which had imposed an innocuous and clean way to represent reality (one only need to think of the so-called telefoni bianchi trend[37]) where all problematic elements were effaced (e.g., poverty and crime, not to mention sexuality). For example, in his article "Toward an Italian Cinema" ("Verso un cinema italiano"), published in *Bianco e nero* in 1942, he analyzed recent films that proposed, although not yet adequately in his view, a new way of representing reality, among which were Luigi Chiarini's *Sleeping Beauty* (*La bella addormentata*, 1942) and Mario Soldati's *Tragic Night* (*Tragica notte*, 1942). What he meant by "realism" in this context is something that brings us close to those same elements that the Censorship—the republican one at that point—would single out some years later in the rejection of *New Wine*, that is, the naked exposition of lower-class life, and in particular of poverty and its effects on society. In *Tragic Night* Pietrangeli appreciated the appearance on screen of the humble signs of working-class life, like the tools used by Tuscan peasants in their everydayness or the songs they sing while working in the fields.[38] In *Sleeping Beauty*, whose plot is even less remarkable than *Tragic Night*, he appreciated the unconventional (for the time) representation of "a humble and combative Sicily . . . a dry and hard land, violent like the men who, in contact with it, try to overcome it with violence: a Sicily, in short, a little unprecedented, and not at all touristic" (Detassis et al. 1987, 110). It is here, despite the familiar "orientalizing" picture of southern reality, that we see emerging an element of harshness (the violence necessary to survive in a violent land) that, under fascist rule, was already dangerously close to a social critique. Noteworthy is the reference to its "non-touristic" look—and we should also notice that Brancati was among the authors of the screenplay. What is even more interesting is that this realistic "stream" is traced back to two examples of pre-fascist Italian cinema. The first one is the historical epic *Cabiria* (1914), about which Pietrangeli appreciated "certain realistic elements" much more than the scenographic grandeur and lyricism: "At a certain point, the bunches of garlic and stockfish hanging in a cellar immediately reveal themselves more 'emotional' than the voluptuous D'Annunzio's captions" (Detassis et al. 1987, 107). Even more important for our case is his second genealogical example, directly connected with the representation of the Neapolitan reality, that is Nino Martoglio's *Lost in the Dark* (*Sperduti nel buio*, 1914), a film now lost but that was often quoted by critics and film historians, especially those interested in realism, before World War II (when all copies were destroyed): "Nino Martoglio gave us with *Lost in the Dark* the naked and cruel description of certain sordid environments of the Neapolitan *bassi* . . . the predilection, in short, for the real and true details of life and society" (Detassis et al. 1987, 107). We have here, in other words, "the frighteningly filthy and dirty 'bassi' " of Naples the Censorship will deprecate so much in *New Wine*, except that in Pietrangeli's argument their exhibition has a positive, progressive political value—even though, as it is obvious before the fall of the regime, the whole argument is limited here to its aesthetic and moral implications.

This was precisely the direction in which what was later called Neorealism would proceed: As affirmed by Luca Barattoni, Pietrangeli "can in fact be defined as a Neorealist before Neorealism, advocating a more intense bonding with Italian landscapes and social issues even before the actual advent of Visconti, Rossellini, and De Sica" (Barattoni 2012, 134). Indeed he was, as a critic, among the most resolute supporters of the emerging tendency toward the representation, or better, the exhibition of the postwar reality with all its signs of misery, suffering, and trauma inscribed in bodies, buildings, tools, landscapes, and so on: "Pietrangeli became the advocate of realist solutions that later would be almost prophetically adopted by the key figures of the Neorealist movement" (Barattoni 2012, 133). In a recent book Emma Katherine Van Ness has corroborated this interpretation of Pietrangeli's career as a film critic, showing his elaboration, in these years, of a film theory that he would later apply to his own films—although the resolute views of the critic would have in some cases to compromise with the film industry: "In many ways, Pietrangeli was the anti-Andreotti; as an early neorealist, he lobbied for politically and socially engaged Italian filmmaking from 1940 onward; rather than hide Italy's dirty laundry in their homes, as Andreotti famously requested filmmakers do, Pietrangeli called for a larger exposition of this so-called cultural 'dirty laundry' " (Van Ness 2020, 3). To sum up, at least in principle, Pietrangeli's outlook on realism was the symmetrical opposite of the political view of cinema expressed by the Censorship that rejected *New Wine*.

All this considered, I'm persuaded that Pietrangeli's contribution to the elaboration of *New Wine* was precisely his insistence on the crudest aspects of southern reality, the unmitigated and uncompromising representation of suffering bodies, "indecent" in their exhibited semi-nakedness, in their existence forced to unfold in the streets, even in the most private aspects. That the other collaborators had sensed that a limit had been pushed too far is proved by the existence of the second version of the first part of the film, where the harsh portrayal of the Neapolitan social reality is sensibly mitigated. That this work of attenuation could signify the erasure of Pietrangeli's specific contribution to the writing, would explain why his name is not credited among the authors of the text presented to the Censorship. Yet even if he had also collaborated on the second version of the screenplay, perhaps even personally implementing the changes aimed at mitigating the representation of social reality—after all, the second version is included in the manuscript held in his archive—his exclusion from the subsequent stages of the production, where many of the realistic elements concerning Neapolitan reality were completely removed (even in their attenuated form), illustrates how his collaboration was particularly tied to this aspect of the project.

The Revised Synopsis: Enter Ghost

At this point, before finally turning to an analysis of *Journey to Italy*, we must look at the intermediate step in its preparation, that is, the revised synopsis the production presented to the Censorship office after the initial refusal of the screenplay. As already mentioned, this refusal had been signed on February 5, 1953. On February 16 the revised synopsis was submitted (the credited authors, again, were Rossellini and Brancati), and the response to this latter was signed on February 18. Between these events stands the beginning of the shooting, that, although officially registered on February 14, started, according to Dagrada's calculations, on February 2 with the museum scenes (Dagrada 2008, 290n4). Shortly before this moment, the famous anecdote took place, reported by all commentators, that Rossellini wrote five schematic pages from scratch with a list of locations, actors, and timings of the film's scenes upon request from the desperate production manager Marcello D'Amico, who went to his hotel room to beg him for at least a shooting plan for the next day. These five pages, reproduced in Dagrada and other sources (Dagrada 2008, 504–5; Gallagher 1998, 398–99; Bergala 1990, 7–9), testify to a further transformation in the realization process between the screenplay and the synopsis, in which most of the elements of the former seem to survive, while the female protagonist's excursions to the touristic attractions are introduced, which, with the exception of the San Gennaro Chapel and the Church of the Annunziata (immediately discarded), will also appear in the synopsis and the film.

Compared to these five pages the synopsis represents a further step in the process of the elaboration of the film itself, whose shooting was already underway while Rossellini and Brancati prepared it. A thirteen-page manuscript (reproduced in the appendix of Dagrada's book), the synopsis offers a substantial innovation compared to the screenplay, that is, the introduction of the Joycean element we have seen, which fulfills, so to speak, the "prophecy" included in the protagonists' surname since the start. This probably means that Brancati's insight into the interpretation and transformation of *Duo* only here receives Rossellini's approval to enter the story. It happens after a quick summary of the beginning of the story with the car trip of the couple, whose first names have been updated to Alexander (sometimes Alessandro) and Caterina. There is no mention of the disquieting episodes that punctuate this journey in the screenplay, which were still present in the five-page working plan. In other words, there is no introduction to the archaic and brutal reality of the South, but only a vague reference to the fact that the forced intimacy of the journey immediately produces in the couple a revelation about the true nature of their relationship, at the beginning especially in Caterina, though soon enough Alexander will also be forced to undergo this process: "In truth, her relations with her husband have always been shallow, polite, perhaps elegant, but certainly conventional" (qtd. in Dagrada 2008, 514). At the Excelsior in Naples they meet their English friends, but there is no open revelation of Alexander's infidelity with Edith. About the two—the woman is now named Jackie—Caterina only notices that "there is a great confidence," which leaves things in ambiguity: probably a move to take completely out, as a form of precaution toward the Censorship, any reference to actually committed adultery. Something similar will happen with the original "doubt" regarding Caterina's own infidelity, which in the screenplay causes John's jealousy. After the arrival at the villa and a lunch with the uncle's secretary (renamed Tony) and his wife, the couple rests in the sun on the terrace, in a scene that is already the one we will see in the film. Here Caterina tells the story of the deceased poet (called Charles Lexington instead of Lewington) and recites his verses. At this point Alexander feels jealousy for the first time.

From this moment on, the events described anticipate quite exactly those of the film: Caterina's solitary excursions are mentioned, and so is Alexander's solitary and inconclusive trip to Capri to meet the English friends. Alexander's subsequent encounter with a prostitute upon his return to Naples is also sketched, in which the two only talk and he finds "comprehension." Finally, there is the visit to Pompeii with the unearthing of the cast of the dead lovers and the conclusive "entrapment" in the religious street parade (here happening in Pompeii and not in Maiori), which provokes the resolution of the crisis. Between these two events survives the scene in Paestum, in which Alexander's uncontrolled jealousy crisis ends with the beating of the Italian passerby (then excluded from the film). In this case, however, the outcome is completely reversed: If in the screenplay Isabella was convinced to reconcile by this event, as if it were a definitive proof of John's affection, Caterina is here disgusted and the two decide to get a divorce, only to change their mind shortly after in the middle of the procession. Almost completely gone is the "secondary plot" of Assunta and Pasqualino, who are now renamed Maria and Gennaro.

To sum up, the husband's jealousy crisis remains the central event of the story, yet now the southern setting in which the crisis unfolds loses any disquieting, uncanny character. As we have seen, the screenplay was essentially ambiguous on this matter: Jealousy was both a positive effect of the encounter with the passionate, picturesque southern dimension and a violent, abusive force, a form of oppression in gender relationships connected with the material oppression of a population showed in all its misery and "indecent" poverty. Here the ambiguity is resolved with the elimination of the political element: Both husband and wife had a problem in experiencing their own feelings, a problem originating in their northern character understood according to the commonplace vision of it as being cold, detached, too rational, fearful of the bodily dimension, and so on. Symmetrically, the contact with a picturesque South, equally seen through commonplace schemata, will be the antidote. Indeed, Alexander is incapable of experiencing his love for his wife with real passion, not able to feel and express jealousy. Caterina, in turn, is trapped in her romanticism and modesty, "always offended by the overly carnal expression of love" (qtd. in Dagrada 2008, 516), but soon enough she will ask herself: "Can a true love have a fully carnal expression, without, because of this, being indecent?" (517). The South has revealed this issue to them, who had never before been aware of the shallowness of their relations. The South, of course, will cure them at the end of the story:

> They are unaware that their humanity has matured.[39] It is useless to try to close themselves to each other. They have learned the art of expressing themselves fully. They know what it means to love each other completely, deeply, jealously. . . . They had tried to get home early [after the incident in Paestum] to escape themselves, not to admit the truth, driven by a residue of Anglo-Saxon modesty and pride, once again on the wrong path. (519)

And yet, things will not work this way in the film itself, which will propose a much more complex vision. To understand how this complexity unfolds, we must reflect again on the figure of the dead poet, in both the synopsis and the film. I suggested that the introduction of the Joycean motive had been Brancati's way of highlighting the central element of *Duo* as the discovery of the wife's autonomy and foreignness to the husband's sexist framework, thus displacing jealousy as a secondary side effect. In the film this element, the irruption of the "messenger" will both question gender roles and provoke the emergence—especially channeled by the aesthetic construction—of a historical content related to the sufferings of the recent war and the chronic conditions of misery in southern Italy, though tensions in class relations and social oppression were an underground stream already flowing in Colette's novel. In the synopsis the problematization of gender roles is completely absent, and the historical content is only implicitly present in the "first" poem I analyzed in chapter 1. Probably to avoid irritating the censors with anything less than conventional, the poet from the past here only plays a role in both sparking the husband's jealousy and introducing, through his verses, the theme of the northern misunderstanding of southern reality. An important point of the story narrated in the synopsis will be indeed to prove wrong the poet's interpretation of Naples (synecdoche for Italy and the South) as "a silent and dead land" (qtd. in Dagrada 2008, 515) and of his statues as "pure ascetic forms," (515) since Caterina needs to learn that the romantic vision of Italy is a distortion that she has to get rid of together with her fear of the physical dimension of love. According to this stereotypical and sexist framework, she also needs to learn how to enjoy Alexander's newly awakened jealousy, which he has learned from other men's gazes on her: "Suddenly a cyclist . . . turns to look at Caterina with a soft and sensual look. Alex notices it. This look brutally teaches him how desirable his wife is" (518).

"What if Italy, instead of being the land of silence and old age, is the land of vitality?" (517). The synopsis ends with a positive answer to this question, and with the couple reconciled with their inner feelings thanks to the old Mediterranean wisdom. And yet, in order to understand the film, we need to ask the opposite question: Is it possible that, instead of being the land of vitality, Italy is the land of silence and old age, or even a land of "ascetic" bodies, disfigured by hunger and poverty, which had been only exacerbated by the recent war, and whose roots went back to centuries of oppression?

Chapter 3

Voyaging in an Unknown Land

Idle Activities

"What the Young Writers of Naples Are Up To"[1] (Ortese 2018, 103): This is the title of the article that the self-diegetic narrator of "The Silence of Reason" is planning to write when she arrives on the Riviera di Chiaia, in Naples, "the evening of June 19" (101). The "activity" she is going to investigate is not particularly charged with high cultural value, although the objects of the investigation are young, promising authors. In fact, what she expects to obtain from Luigi Compagnone, the first person she visits, is "some particularly juicy bit of news, the kind that raises [so much] the tone of a piece of writing"[2] (102–3). There is nothing unusual in this form of cultural journalism declared from the outset of the story; readers might even take it with a certain relief after the tour de force she has imposed upon them in the previous two stories of the book.[3] Yet, as we will soon realize, this rather "fatuous"[4] idle activity (*what are they up to*) is contrasted to an opposite kind of activity: Compagnone and the other writers who will be the subjects of her piece had been the protagonists, only a few years earlier, of a "rebellion" (she will use this expression) against the atavistic injustice and misery Naples had been enduring for centuries. Guided by Prunas, these young intellectuals had founded the political-cultural magazine *Sud*, conceived as an engine of political engagement in the struggle to modernize and change Naples once and for all—a struggle Ortese would allegorize in these same pages as a battle between Reason and Nature, this latter pictured as an almighty, sinister entity who reigns over "the region of the far South where the sun shines brightest"[5] (122). She participated in the journal since its early days and published two stories in it. This experience had great importance for her personal and professional life, and, as she later recognized, was the first source of inspiration for blending her earlier magic-realist style with political engagement and ethical tension that would come to characterize her journalistic as well as her mature narrative style. It appears evident, therefore, that the idle activity that begins the story must be contrasted with this opposite, even tragic, failed endeavor of cultural and political revolution.

This situation shares a striking similarity with the one in which Rossellini's *Journey to Italy* originates, as the director goes back with his crew to Naples in 1953 (the film was shot between February and April, as we have seen) to make a bourgeois drama with international stars. He had already been there in 1946 to shoot an episode of *Paisan*, where he had worked among collapsed buildings still hiding forgotten corpses, the camera capturing the bodies of half-starved extras. This contrast is evidently replicated between the plots of the two films themselves, as the first had focused on the encounter between Allied troops and the defeated Italian people, attempting to capture a critical historical moment for the country, while the second followed an English couple and their marriage crisis, showing some of the most renowned touristic attractions of the bay. However, this opposition between what we have defined as "idle activity" and its "tragic" antecedent runs deeper in *Journey to Italy*, which inscribes it in its own structure: As we have seen in chapter 1, the Joyces' trip retraces the one the poet Charles Lewington had taken during the war with the Allied army. Thus, the contrast with *Paisan* returns in the sideral distance between what the couple sees in '53 and what the poet had seen during the war. A hiatus so vast it appears incomprehensible: The couple will interpret his verses—his talk of "ascetic images"—as the musings of a gentle soul, too sensible to grasp the carnal temper of the southern people, and scholars who have analyzed the film so far have also tended toward this interpretation. But the shadow of Lewington is undoubtedly not the only sign of the open wound of the war to punctuate the film.

In the analysis that follows, I will show how in both Ortese's story and Rossellini's film the structural mechanism of the texts constantly works to bring back to the surface the hidden dimension on which the past activity, in contrast with the "idleness" of the present, continues to happen, incessantly generating the emotional energy that signals an ideological resistance, and from which these works ultimately derive their vividness, their capacity to captivate the readers/viewers, magnetically attracting them toward a dimension behind the surface. To achieve—if only fleetingly—a transparence between the two dimensions, which both works strenuously deny (not surprisingly, a tendency emerges here, again, toward the recoil we have already discussed), and to show their deep, uncanny parallelism, I will use the tools of narrative semiotics, which, as shown by Jameson, have the power to bring us inside the "black box" of ideology, "through which narrative is somehow 'converted' into cognition and vice versa" (Jameson 1987, xiv). Merleau-Ponty's phenomenological analysis of the concept of expression—intended both as a "style of being" through which the world offers itself in perception and as the communication of it in the aesthetic gesture (which he later elaborated in the lectures of the early 1950s)—will pave the way for a possible interpretation, at the end of the chapter, of how the two dimensions of the text can be present at the same time.

The first sequences of "The Silence of Reason" and *Journey to Italy* share a similar narrative structure: The self-diegetic protagonist of Ortese's story has just arrived in Naples, after a few years of absence, to interview some young writers and intellectuals for a magazine article. When the story starts, she is in Piazza Vittoria, about to board a tram that will bring her to the other side of the Riviera di Chiaia, on via Galiani, to visit her old friend Compagnone for the first interview. There is a clear goal, a clear geographic itinerary. Analogously, in the opening sequence of *Journey to Italy*, Katherine and Alex Joyce are in their Bentley, driving south toward Naples. They are in the countryside of Lazio, in the territory of Latina, approaching the border with Campania. They have been summoned to Torre del Greco by the death of an uncle from whom they inherited a villa, which they intend to sell quickly while also enjoying a short holiday: a clear goal, a clear geographic itinerary.

It is also important to note that both sequences anticipate and summarize the structure and the basic plot of the whole story. In terms of Greimas's narrative semiotics, they both present a basic narrative program (Greimas and Courtés 1993, 297–98) which appears, on the surface, with the classic structure of the quest, where a subject (the protagonist-narrator in "The Silence" and the Joyce couple in *Journey*) seeks conjunction with an object of value (the information to be acquired in the interviews), or disjunction from it (the couple wants to get rid of the villa).[6] The impulse to start the enterprise comes from the "manipulation" operated by a "sender," which provides the ideological motivation and valorizes the object in one sense or the other: the "illustrated weekly magazine" (103), which pays for the reportage, in the first case, and what we could define as the ideology of financial good sense, which recommends getting rid of the villa, in the second. We know from the continuation of both works that this program is destined to fail, or at least to be compromised and indefinitely deferred beyond the limits of the story. What I intend to show is that a deeper parallelism between the two stories exists, beneath the surface of such apparent clarity, and its logic can be interpreted as the advancement of an "anti-program," which is always implied by the polemical dimension of narrative forms (Bertrand 2000, 182–84; Marrone 2021, 49–50). This oppositional narrative structure is put in motion by an anti-sender, which manipulates an anti-subject (which in both cases corresponds, on the surface of the text, to the same "actor"[7]: the character(s) representing the subject of the original program, ambiguously torn between the two opposite thrusts[8]), to invert the original desired outcome of the quest (conjunction or disjunction with the object). In both cases the pursuit of the anti-program will coincide with the attraction toward Naples' "underworld" and the experience of contemplation of (and immersion in) the lower classes. The surface composition of such structure will be clearly elucidated only with close readings of both texts. However, we can immediately note that, in the first case, an alternative ideological force, which the narrator will later identify with the personification of Reason ("Reason against Nature" is the allegory through which she interprets the failure of the Neapolitan intellectuals), will push her to deviate from her straightforward itinerary—to set aside her "object"—and, driven by the epiphanies of the crowd of the poor, to search for a mysterious and unclarified "truth" the city hides from both idle visitors and hypocritical inhabitants.

In the case of the film, this same role will be played by an entity personified at first by the enigmatic Uncle Homer, who, with his death, summons the couple to take possession[9] of the object, then later by the dead poet Lewington. However, as we will see, the narrative structure is here complicated by Katherine developing her own "secondary program," which, interfering with the quest mandated by Lewington, will focus on her private dimension, as she will try to revitalize and save her marriage. In any case, the anti-program, aiming at a deeper knowledge of the Neapolitan reality, will never cease to influence the development of the story and will guide the cinematic enunciation[10]—in its autonomous visual quest, so to speak—even when the protagonists will seem to ignore it, until the moment when, in the final sequence, it will reemerge to swallow the main narrative and to offer the unexpected denouement.

What is central for the understanding of both stories is that this anti-program represents the reemergence, in a diegetic form, of a political program that had marked for both authors the immediate postwar period, which I have identified above as the contrary of the "idle activities" on which both works seem to focus in their opening. It is, in the case of Ortese, the program of the journal *Sud*, that is, "to lay the foundations for that school or Reason which had already cleansed other towns, and whose absence here was due to the profound lethargy and dissipation of conscience"[11] (Ortese 2018, 117). Indeed, most of the young intellectuals the narrator wants to interview had been part, as we have already seen, of the *Sud* group, and that very program of foundation of a "school of reason" was nothing less than a project of studying the conditions of misery of the Neapolitan society, and especially of its most wretched part, the immense crowd of the lumpenproletariat: "We wanted to know everything, understand everything about this monstrosity that, in light of recent events, appeared to be Naples; we wanted to remove the finely carved tombstone that lay on its grave and find out if in that rot anything organic remained"[12] (117). In "The Silence," her narrative persona returns, against the grain of the apparent goal of her visit, to complete that task, although, at this point outside of any collective political effort, her enterprise will mutate in the construction of a literary experience in which the form of life of that miserable stratum of the population will emerge and "touch" the reader. At the same time, the reactivation of the original program of the group will bring a sort of terror to her ancient comrades, who will be forced by her sheer presence to face their own failure, implicitly accepted and embraced in exchange for personal success and integration into the ruling class, but never acknowledged as such. In this sense, at the structural level, in the interactions she will have with Compagnone and the other intellectuals she will meet, she will embody the avatar of the original sender of that very quest: Reason. She will thus appear to judge that collective subject (the *Sud* group), which had forsaken its original objectives: the investigation of the real condition of the population, political engagement, social justice, and so on.

All her comrades had—except Prunas—given in to the flatteries of the anti-sender of that program, which she allegorically depicts, in this story, as Nature. She will present them with a mirror in which they will observe this truth, and for this they will hate and despise her. The implicit condemnation of their treason and their failure constitutes what, in narrative semiotic terms, is called the "sanction," which the sender performs at the end of the story to evaluate the performance of the subject, which thus appears to be the dominant narrative function of the story. However, as we have anticipated, the secret contradiction to which the "original emotion" is linked lies elsewhere, in the ambiguous coincidence of the narrator with the lumpenproletariat, which she compels her comrades (and us readers with them) to see, against her own apparent, superficial intentions.

In the case of *Journey to Italy*, the anti-program surreptitiously mandated by Homer/Lewington, the taking possession of the villa as a figure of the knowledge of the Neapolitan reality that culminates in the encounter with its lower classes, can be read as a return to the program that had animated the making of *Paisan*, and, on a diegetic level, its Neapolitan episode in particular. Not coincidentally, the itinerary of the Joyces along the peninsula toward the south is precisely the reverse itinerary followed by the episodes of that film, which follows the advancement of the Allied army from south to north. The attempt at representing an intellectual and emotional encounter between the Anglo-Saxon liberators and the wretched, defeated Italian people had been the core of that experience. In the Neapolitan episode, this schema had taken its clearest—and less melodramatic—form in the encounter between the African American soldier and the urchin. Shooting between the ruins of a destroyed city in the early months of 1946, the encounter with the suffering bodies of the city's poor, where the signs of the war were deeply carved, had represented the core of an enigmatic experience to which Rossellini could not help returning. The bodies of the humble crowd in the streets of Naples will again play a central role in *Journey to Italy* and will produce its denouement, the miracle in the Corso of Maiori in the final scene, with the sheer pressure of their physical presence. This replicates the similar conclusion in the Neapolitan episode of *Paisan*, where the vision (again, the pressure of the physical presence) of the homeless crowd in the cave in Mergellina had provoked the final understanding and emotional breakdown of the American soldier. Differently than in Ortese's story, in Rossellini's work the irresistible impulse toward the knowledge of the miserable conditions of the lower strata of the population is never thematized as such: No mythical personification of Reason appears to call the protagonists to fulfill a destiny. Only elusive figures like Homer and Lewington appear to secretly mandate the "anti-program" that makes the protagonists go astray from their reasonable goals.

The opposition between the two programs and the suspension of the principal one marks the most recognizable feature of both works, that is, their erratic rhythm, their tendency toward the interruption, the distraction from the original task (from any recognizable, practical task), which ultimately produces the impression that what really matters lays between the fragments of the sequential narrative, in the contemplative attitude of the characters and of the point of view offered to the reader/viewer. What I will show with the close readings that follow is the persistence of a second, underground dimension—an underworld—with its own spatiality and temporality,[13] which emerges each time the narrating impulse abandons its primary task to indulge in the contemplation of the form of life of the popular classes, and whose first appearance can be traced back to the scene where we located the "original emotion."

"Evening in a Manner of Speaking": The Opening of "The Silence of Reason"

When I discussed, in chapter 2, the nature of Ortese's traumatic experience, I noted, with Merleau-Ponty, how such a form of life can become a "style of being" that informs the way the subject connects to the world, which in turn can be translated into a *communicable* subjective experience. In Merleau-Ponty's reflections developed in the lectures of the early 1950s in particular, literary style, like the pictorial one and the aesthetic gesture in general, can encompass and communicate the form of our relation to the world[14]—the habitus, in Bourdieu's terms. Thus, the hunger discussed in chapter 1, not as a momentary, painful incident but as a form of life Ortese experienced for many years in the postwar periods—as a way of structuring daily routines and interpersonal relations—not only produced her peculiar social standpoint that ultimately allowed her capacity of vision to include and understand the existence of the underclass; it also informed her literary style in a way that incorporates the spatial and temporal relationship to the world of that specific form of life, "the 'personal' style, the particular stamp marking all the products of the same habitus" (Bourdieu 1977, 86). This is why, while reading "The Silence," we perceive, beneath the surface of a linear, task-oriented narrative (interviewing some persons to write an article) within the limits of a precise temporal framework (two calendar days in June), the pressure of a different, never-ending, always identical day that never passes: the eternal present of the lumpenproletariat, the nightmarish temporality of those who survive in the informal economy, for whom every day everything starts over, together with the inescapable necessity of finding the means of daily survival again and again. As we have seen in

Clerici's reconstruction of Ortese's life in those years and from her letters, this experience was well known to her.

If mental and physical exhaustion, characterized by onsets of anxiety that continuously interrupt the rational coping with daily routine and the capacity to linearly narrativize events, are part of this experience, it is no coincidence that "The Silence" begins with a sign of distraction, as the anxiety to correct one's own thoughts emerges in the middle of the first line, even before the principal verb is pronounced: "On the evening of June 19 (evening in a manner of speaking, since the sky was bright and the sun was still high over the sea, its glare intense), I boarded the #3 tram, which runs along the Riviera di Chiaia to Mergellina"[15] (101). When the first parenthetical sentence interrupts the narrative discourse, the reader has just had the chance to assimilate a time notation. It is important to note that the narrative gesture that establishes here the voice of the self-diegetic narrator coincides with the parenthetical notation itself, with this first contradictory, distracting affirmation that immediately doubts the validity of the temporal marker "evening." The narrator is thus established as a mere semantic subject, just a voice before we readers get to know anything else. Yet, the metanarrative reflection on the exactness of the term just used, with the exercise of a "directing function" ("function the régie") in the terms of Gérard Genette's narratology (1972, 262), has a capital importance, as it dictates one of the most important features of the story: the constant erosion of the solidity of the narrated reality, which hints at an underground dimension always on the brink of emerging. If we now look closely at the content of the parenthetical affirmation, meant to justify the doubt of the possibility of using the definition "evening," we immediately recognize a further element destined to distract the attention of the reader from the straightforward proceeding of the story: in the Italian original the sun is not just unremarkably "high over the sea," intensely glaring. The sun is "a mezzo il mare," a rare and archaic sounding expression in Italian literature,[16] and its personification is not just ambiguous but straightforward: Contrary to the English translation, where "intense glare" can rightly refer to both a source of light and a living, gazing being, the "sguardo intento" of the Italian original only pertains to living beings, and thus arrives as a violent trope, immediately putting in motion the personification of cosmic entities on which the allegorical structure of the story is based. It also creates a foreboding sensation of being observed by a superior force, whose positive or negative meaning it is impossible to establish, for now.

Only after the end of the parenthetical meta-reflection does the first principal verb of the sentence properly establish a self-diegetic narrator, together with the spatial dimension of the story, which, in contrast to the preceding past participle "fisso," ("intent," but also "immobile") starts a horizontal movement across the geographical space: from Piazza Vittoria, the beginning of the Riviera di Chiaia, to Piazza Principe di Napoli (today Piazza della Repubblica), where she will get off the tram. The translators decided to break the sentence here, but in the original it continues unabridged with a description of the tram, which immediately introduces another figure destined to strongly put in motion the allegorical invention of the story: "I sat in a corner seat next to a woman without a nose, who had an enormous plant in her lap, and I began to think about what I would say to justify my visit to Luigi Compagnone, who worked in the cultural department of Radio Naples and whom I hadn't seen in quite some time, and to whose home, in fact, I was now going"[17] (101–2). The woman without a nose, with her skull-like image, immediately suggests a second personification after the sun: death. Andrea Baldi has called the abrupt apparition of this first character in the story "an aberrant detail, sign of the visionary capacity of Ortese," and has commented as follows on the absence of the nose: "The presumed injury is an imaginative *transfert* of the blows inflicted by existence, a scar opened by every day humiliations" (Baldi 2010, 60). Besides the vaster symbolic function here noted by Baldi, the absence of a nose also carries a more circumscribed historical reference, that is, syphilis and prostitution (an association widespread in Italian culture since the early modern period), which immediately connects the Neapolitan underclass with its peculiar historical dimension, in which atavistic sufferings continue to inscribe the archaic in the modern. It is also possible to go further with the interpretation, given the importance of allegorical personifications for the structure of the whole story, where Nature and Reason appear as primordial divinities fighting over the destiny of the city and its population. If the sun as a source of light that looks down "intently" on the movement of the protagonist could be seen as a first occurrence of Reason—although a perverted, sinister version of it as we will see—the skull-like woman, with the hole at the center of her face, suggests darkness, and thus an inversion of that figure. That this could be seen as an image of anti-Reason is further corroborated by what immediately follows: Her gesture of carrying in her lap "an enormous plant" is conveyed in the Italian original with the expression "portava in grembo," which is usually associated with childbearing. It thus evokes the idea of maternity, clearly associated, in Western tradition and in this story in particular, with Nature, the "ancient mother" (Ortese 2018, 183) ("l'antica madre" [Ortese 1994, 169]). As I will propose, the noseless woman, besides being a first personification of Nature, will also have a narrative function similar to the one the Neapolitan intellectuals (all but one under the spell of Nature) will have in the rest of the story. This allows the opening sequence to replicate, on a smaller scale, the same narrative structure of which it is a part.

For now, it is important to note that the same sentence in which the noseless woman is introduced continues with the first mention of the reasons for the narrator's trip, that is, the visit to see Compagnone to start the interviews, which we partly examined in the introduction. In the second paragraph she goes back to the tram and to the present of the story, and starts with another metanarrative hesitation: "No one could have said that the tram was in a hurry"[18] (103). This immediately recalls that "evening in a manner of speaking" of the first line with its "directing function." Thus the negative, metanarrative notation about the tram's motion inaugurates a description of the space she is in and the one she is traversing (the tram and the street, Riviera di Chiaia), rendered in extremely vivid terms, clearly establishing a figurative dimension in which an abstract, ideological discourse is embedded, which anticipates the unfolding of the whole story.

By looking closely at the expressions used for the description, it is possible to note the emergence of two opposite figurative isotopies, one referring to energetic movement (inchoative and durative) and the other to declining movement (terminative tending to immobility), which, at a more abstract level, refer to ideas of vitality and dying respectively, as we will see in detail. The tram the narrator is riding proceeds extremely slowly as construction works on the road are underway, and this image already suggests a contrast between a powerful mechanical movement and the friction that impedes it and slows it down. When the narrator notices the slowing pace, she has the irrational suspicion that the driver might have fallen asleep or even be wounded—although she in fact mentions this as if it were a normal deduction given the situation: "One might reasonably suspect the driver had fallen asleep, or was lying wounded in his seat"[19] (103). This extravagant suspicion inaugurates a visionary contemplation of the material landscape she is traversing, which must lead us to the hypothesis that the metanarrative negations that punctuate these paragraphs communicate the contrary of a detached, rational reflection on terminology and work rather as markers of a mounting anxiety the narrator tries to dominate by interrupting the mimetic identification with the narrated past, thus pointing back to the present of the enunciation. These are common traits of metanarrative negation in the narrative context, as remarked by Marion Colas-Blaise in her reflection on negative textuality: "The negation is more than ever linked to a strong intensity, which is coupled with an *embrayage* on a staged instance of enunciation; the negative force is 'indexical,' that is to say, refers to the instance of enunciation and to the situation of enunciation by contiguity" (Colas-Blaise 2014). The negation insistently returns in the second paragraph devoted to this description, where the narrator focuses her attention on the street and on a possible—or rather impossible, as it turns out to be—definition of it, which she concludes as follows:

> But here something was different, which soon made it necessary to reject those two descriptive adjectives. No, one could speak neither of *distressed* or of *destitute*; this street was, instead, smiling and terrible, much like the expression of intelligence and generosity that the faces of the dead have. It was a *dead* street, or at least that's how I defined it to myself, hoping to be able to find later a less vehement and irrational description, something that turned out to be impossible.[20] (103)

This provisional conclusion is relevant for our analysis, as both abstract isotopies I mentioned (vitality and dying), are transcended toward an obscure middle ground, a semantic zone that subsumes and *negates* both of them: Death is negated by intelligence and generosity, and vice versa. Similarly, the conclusion that the street is dead is immediately suspended by the hope of finding a better definition. Yet this mechanism extends to the whole description, and, as we will see, is central to the whole story. The figurative dimension of movement connected at the abstract level with vitality is anchored to terms describing the movement of the tram and the activity of the construction works, while the opposite dimension, the one approaching immobility connected to death, is communicated through the terms describing the "fantasy" of the wounded driver and the dead appearance of the street itself. However, as shown by her metanarrative hesitations (the negations we have seen), none of the two poles seems to be able to define the impression she receives from the traversed space, which proves to be in fact participating in—or rather negating—both. The street seems "dead," and yet is not. The driver might be dying, and yet is not. This spectral, intermediate dimension between life and death is indeed referred to by definitions that participate in both isotopies, at the figurative and abstract level: The movement of the workers is defined with a term that implies both movement and immobility (movement *sur place*), use of energy and pointless dispersion of it—"formicolio" (rendered in the translation as "swarm"). The street appears as a petrified torrent, communicating both the strength of movement and a spectral immobility: "The paving stones were all dislodged, so that the street resembled a raging torrent whose turbulent waters, once rushing obliquely, were suddenly straightened out and petrified"[21] (103). Finally, the plain reference to death in "it was a *dead* street" (subsequently again declassed to provisional definition, as we have seen), is preceded by two couples of adjectives, the first couple negated in favor of the second. The first term of each couple can be referred to the dimension of ongoing movement and vitality (proceeding from the figurative level in the first couple to the abstract level in the second), while the second term of each couple to that of ceasing of movement and death: "distressed . . . destitute" ("agitato . . . squallido"), and "smiling and terrible" ("ridente e terribile").[22] Moreover, the second couple introduces the key image of a facial expression in which life and death are ominously reunited: "The expression of intelligence and generosity that the faces of the dead have." We will need to look for the key of the ideological interpretation of this text precisely in this ambiguous condition between life and death, which is not life and yet not death either, and which the lively expression on the face of the dead exemplifies at the figurative level.

The contemplation of the spectacle of the Riviera di Chiaia disfigured by renovation works subsequently incites a historical excursus about the appearance of this same street when it was devastated by the bombings during the war. This historical recollection plays a pivotal role in the interpretation of the ideological structure of this work: In these lines, the semantic zone that subsumes and negates both the oppositive isotopies we have seen (vitality and dying), that middle ground which is not life nor death, is revealed to be the fundamental form of life of the "plebe," the crowd of the underclass that populates the street, and, at the same time, to be the inversion of a different existential dimension open to possibility and meaning, which has now been lost. The narrator visualizes the condition of the underclass through the image of a theriomorphic creature that fidgets under the sun: "The thing both dark and brightly colored, that interminable procession [ribbon] of the working class[23] [plebe] incessantly stirring at the foundations of the buildings"[24] (104). A few lines later this same description is repeated and clarified by resorting to the figure of the agonizing snake:

"The eternal Neapolitan crowd that moved on its own, like a snake struck by the sun but not yet dead"[25] (104). However, in the passage between the two figurations of the crowd something important happens, which marks the shifting between the two historical moments, that is, the years immediately after the war and the present of the narration: The first manifestation of the "crowd-creature," despite being very similar to the second one, and having been announced in similar terms to those used to describe the people on the street a few lines earlier (the "swarming human elements," "gli elementi umani formicolanti"), exits the schema of the pointless activity, of the mere agitation that is not life or death. If the semantic definition of that spectral condition is the neutralization of any possible meaning, like "the expression of intelligence and generosity" on the faces of the dead (the irrationality of such a definition is admitted by the narrator as is the impossibility of finding any other way to put it), the painful agitation of the "creature," after "the savage years between 1940 and '45"[26] (104), for the first times seemed to produce a meaningful act, one able to initiate a change: "The thing . . . had, for the first time in those years following the tempest of war, emitted a new sound, unexpected and enchanting, like surf rustling on the sand after the hurricane"[27] (104). First of all we notice here a different temporality than the one that has been used throughout the book (and will be prevalent in the continuation of this same story) to describe the city and its population; that is, instead of the references to circularity, eternity, immutability—"eternal Neapolitan crowd" the creature will be named a few lines later, when the narrator will go back to the present—we have here something "new" and "unexpected."[28] Although the third adjective in the series ("enchanted") seems to anticipate the semantic field of the fairy-tale that will structure the allegorical discourse of the story—Nature as a magic power able to freeze time and any human capacity for change—what immediately follows clarifies that the temporality opened in postwar years by this "new sound' was qualitatively different: "In that dull, continuous sound was anxiety, but also, even more, hope"[29] (104).

"Hope," as the opening toward the future and a general availability for change, is precisely what will be absent from the rest of the story, what has proved impossible in the previous stories of the book. Not coincidentally, the abstract isotopy referring to the human capacity for positive change (ultimately a reference to history itself), connected to the terms "nuovo . . . imprevedibile . . . inquietudine . . . speranza," is immediately after reflected at the figurative level in a description that plainly borders on the allegorical construction: "That was why the windows of the houses glistened, and the pink and yellow façades were given new vitality when struck by another sun"[30] (104). The "other sun" that had shone in response to the new hope of the people is thus different from the one that has been "intensely glaring" over the narrator since the beginning of the story. Differently than this latter, the "other sun" had been able to bring to life colors, the pink and the yellow of the buildings, with their vitality for once not infected by the sinister presence of death and decay. This, then, is the figuration of Reason, the "anti-sender" that will oppose Nature[31] in the allegorical construction the story will propose, and of which the initial sun seems to be only a dead remnant, sinister proof of Nature's victory. Yet that brief opening onto a new historical possibility of change did not last, and the excursus immediately closes with a fading away of the colors,[32] with the gray dust that covers all surfaces and brings the population back to its perennial hypnotic slumber: "A patina, a mysterious concoction of rain, dust, and above all boredom, had spread across the façades, covering their wounds, and returning the landscape to that rarefied immobility, that expressive, ambiguous smile that appears on the faces of the dead"[33] (104).

This second return of the smiling face of the dead precedes a vivid description of—or rather an abrupt zooming in on—the crowd previously mentioned as a dark entity, then as an agonizing serpent. The long period heavily relies on anaphors and accumulations of adjectives and nouns (usually in triple sequences), and renders in metonymic detail what had been previously allegorically pictured in the meaningless agitation of the beast. The abstract isotopy that finds expression in the figurative level of the description seems to refer to the idea of a general indistinction, a blurring of limits in which forms and actions lose any sense. Humans are first confused with non-human animals, then their shapes lose any recognizable trait: "Those half naked men and women and children, those dogs and cats and birds, all those dark, weary, empty forms"[34] (104). Their actions are in turn deprived of meaning, as if they do not even keep the basic directionality of need satisfaction, but only express a fragmented agitation and vain dispersion of energy: "All those throats barely emitting a dry sound, all those eyes full of an obsessive light, of an unspoken plea; all those living creatures who dragged themselves along in a continuous motion resembling the actions of someone with a fever, or the nervous mania that possesses certain beings before dying, through a gesture that seems crucial but is never final"[35] (104–5). This vertigo of meaninglessness is then mitigated by a new set of actions that seem to follow a pattern of basic human behaviors, as if the blurring of the image at the peak of anxiety during the first contact provoked by such a violent zooming would then be followed by a focusing able to interpret the apparent chaos as a set of rational actions. Yet, even framed in the reassuring limits of recognizable human behaviors, the actions of the crowd appear imbued in the same sorrowful dismay: "That great husk of a crowd, those people who cooked, combed their hair, conducted business, made love, slept (though never really slept) in the open air, was always stirring, always disturbing the archaic calm of the landscape"[36] (105). It is worth noting that the translation here loses the anaphoric repetition of the disjunctive conjunction "o," which rhythmically separates and connects the crowd's actions, as if they were a rapid sequence of unrelated still pictures. We must also note that, despite the human reality expressed by these actions, they are nevertheless connected with the same abstract isotopy of the previous set—indistinction, blurring of limits, meaningless dispersion of energy—some in themselves, like "conducted business" ("trafficava" in Italian, which implies an unclear accumulation of actions), "stirring," and "disturbing," others because of the abrupt juxtaposition with each other ("cooked . . . combed hair . . . made love . . . slept").

To sum up, while the story had initially presented human behavior inside the framework of an opposition between a meaningful, ethically charged activity (the original program of the *Sud* group), and the "fatuous," idle task of the journalistic inquiry on the (equally frivolous) activity of the Neapolitan young writers ("what they are up to"), only with the passage we just analyzed does this opposition become explicit, as its first term is at last concretized in the lost postwar "anxiety"[37] and "hope" of the Neapolitan people, presented in the historical excursus. If we construct these oppositive kind of activities as the two contrary terms of a semiotic square (figure 3.1), we notice how the two sets of actions presented in the first "zooming" onto the crowd could work as subcontraries (i.e., each as the negation of one of the two contrary terms), as the meaningful, ethically charged kind of action is negated by the sheer meaninglessness of the first set of formless movements of the crowd ("dragged themselves . . . continuous motion"), while the idle, fatuous activity is negated by the desperately vital and important set of basic actions of physical survival ("cooked . . . combed hair . . . made love . . . slept"), which appear nevertheless to be equally futile as they are folded into the meaningless agitation of the underclass' existence. It is important to note, here, that a hypothetical reconciliation of the contrary terms (meaningful and idle activity) would point to an ideal state of society, in which human action could include both serious and unserious components in one single behavior.

Figure 3.1. Human activities in "The Silence of Reason." *Source:* Created by the author.

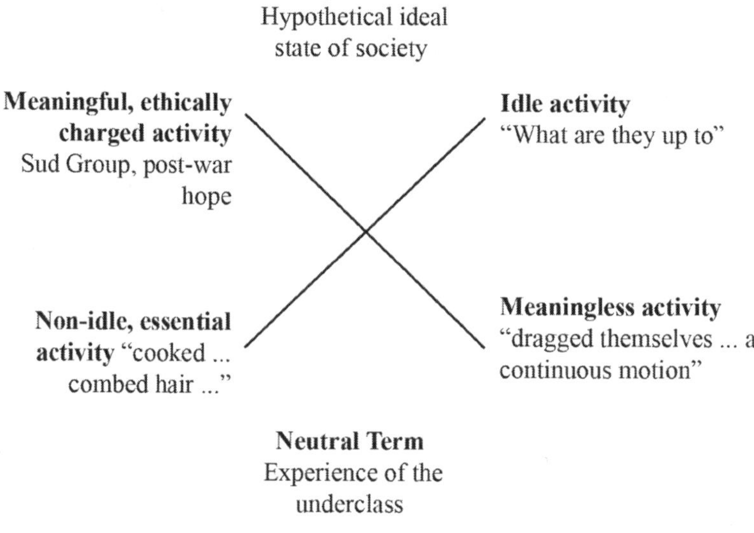

In other words, what is called in semiotic jargon the "complex term," reuniting both contraries, would imply here a reconciled social condition in which human action would not need to be "tragic" to be meaningful, and could indulge in idle playfulness without compromising to oppressive power. On the other hand, the union of the subcontraries, the "neutral term" (Greimas and Courtés 1993, 251–52) of semiotics ("non-idle, essential activity" and "meaningless activity"), is presented in the story as the inscription of the habitus of the underclass' existence—what I call "ascetic images"—and which, as we have seen, is signaled by the presence of two sets of actions, both referring to an abstract isotopy consisting of the blurring of differences, of the abolition of meaning, a concept that Greimas considered to be intrinsically linked to the effacing of the differences thanks to which meaning is generated in the first place (Greimas 1976, 36–37). Such abolition of signification is obviously more than mere meaninglessness, and can be produced, as a limit never fully reached unless in absurd reasoning, only where sheer meaninglessness is undistinguishable from something that is of vital importance for survival.[38] As we have seen, the poor are busy surviving (with the most vital of actions) while also dragging themselves in a continuous, meaningless motion.

The existence of the lumpenproletariat—its habitus pictured at the visual level by two contrary sets of actions—is the experience this story attempts to communicate. Hidden below the astonished gaze of the visitor from the north (the preferred mask of the narrator, her typical form of recoil), the continuous emergence of this condition always bordering on the abolition of meaning is what connects Ortese's story to Rossellini's film. In light of the author's experience of poverty, hunger, and exhaustion we have seen in the previous chapters, it is easy to understand how such an unbearable historical reality could mutate in the "second space permeating visible space" (Merleau-Ponty 2012, 300) of her literary imagination, something that, despite her own *fantasm*[39] of picturing herself as the northern, compassionate visitor, always transpires through the layers of her narrative constructions, as we have seen since analyzing the scene where the "original emotion" emerged. In *Phenomenology of Perception* Merleau-Ponty reflected on those situations in which, beyond the interchangeable present moments of everydayness, a traumatic "eternal" present has been fixed and cannot be dislodged (Merleau-Ponty 2012, 86). That this is the case here, and that the experience communicated by the text goes far beyond that of the projected avatar (the visitor from the north), is confirmed, beyond the emotional intensity generated by the rhetorical means we have seen, by the visual perspective through which the crowd scenes are visualized. As is clear from a simple examination of the text, what in semiotic terms is defined as the actantial role of the observer (i.e., a cognitive role inscribed in the text) extends here far beyond the implied coincidence with the actorial position of a character who actually observes and participates (an "assistant-participant" better specified as "witness-protagonist" in Fontanille's terminology [1989, 20, 48]), that is, in this case, the self-diegetic narrator describing the figural appearance of the fictional world; her descriptions, in theory performed from the point of view of the voyager on the tram traversing the Riviera di Chiaia, immediately make visible a sort of optical unconscious,[40] a perspective not reconcilable with that of the intradiegetic narrator, who certainly could not have observed the missing buttons of the driver's jacket ("In reality the man, in a faded jacket with its buttons missing, was sitting in a normal fashion"[41]), nor distinguished "all those throats barely emitting a dry sound," or defined with precision the other pointless actions of the crowd (who "cooked . . . combed their hair . . . made love . . . slept"). To sum up, this vivid, "unrealistic" point of view—as the optical unconscious always is—presenting the lumpenproletariat's existence is the way this historical experience accesses representation in Ortese's text. Masked by the protective layer of the *fantasm*, through this gesture of recoil she is able to foreground the experience of hunger and exhaustion through which her book was shaped. It is not surprising, indeed, that bourgeois readers of the book like La Capria, whose ideological standpoint would not allow for the same capacity for vision, could not interpret her visual potency as anything but an emotional incapacity to face reality. About the passages quoted above, La Capria will talk about the "unreliability to which an overly offended sensibility can arrive" (2003, 692).

The conclusion of the descriptive sequence in which the lumpenproletariat emerges carries a third repetition of the figure of the smiling dead: "That ambiguous smile, that sense of death taking place, of life on a plane different from life, arising from corruption alone" (105). We can now interpret it as yet another threat of the abolition of meaning: On a semiotic square representing the abstract level of the axiological systematization of human activity implied by this story (figure 3.2), it constitutes the neutral term, which allegorically pictures the middle ground emerging between the negations of both the isotopies of vitality and dying in the first description of the Riviera di Chiaia, and which, not coincidentally, had culminated in the same image of a dead, smiling face.

Thus, the existence of the lumpenproletariat, the hidden dimension communicated by the text, appears as a nightmarish condition in which humans are not truly alive nor dead, consumed, as they are, by an activity that is both absolutely necessary (finding the daily supply of money and food to survive) and absolutely meaningless (the nervous, irrational wave of movement that seems to possess them). That the communication of this experience from within is made possible by an ideological point of view

Figure 3.2. Abstract isotopies connected with human activities in the story. *Source:* Created by the author.

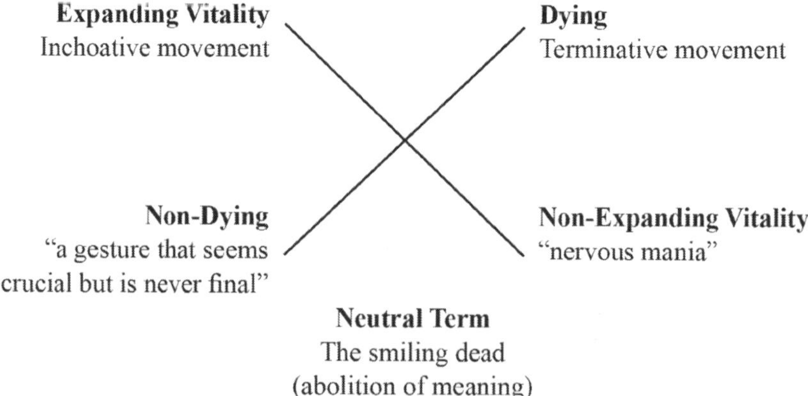

irreconcilable with that of the visitor from the north, and obviously with that of the intellectuals the narrator will interview, is further demonstrated by the following sequence, which, following closely the model of the scene analyzed in the introduction (although it precedes it in the story's diegesis), where the overcoming of the stiction process is captured and the "original emotion" located, demonstrates how the ideological contradiction traverses the text and is continuously rearticulated in narrative form.

The noseless woman becomes the center of the story for the next paragraph: "The sun, shining through a windowpane, momentarily reddened the knees of the woman sitting next to me"[42] (105). The sun—this sun, in a June in the early 1950s,[43] after the hopes fleetingly illuminated by the postwar *other* sun had faded—touches the woman as if to invest her with the power of this perverted Reason, or anti-Reason, which has fallen under the spell of its ancient enemy: Nature. The woman smiles while looking out of the window at the spectacle of the crowd in the street. It is this same spectacle that has just astonished the narrator, and yet the woman smiles, and the smile that now "dances" on her face cannot help but recall the one that appears on the face of the dead, and signifies, in the axiological system we are sketching, the abolition of meaning ("life on a plane different from life" [105]) coinciding with the experience of the underclass: "A very slight, self-satisfied smile danced in her black eyes above the scar"[44] (105). Yet she is not part of that same crowd: in the structure of this sequence, she is spatially separated from the "snake" of the crowd agonizing in the street. She shares the same privileged point of view of the narrator and possesses that special capacity of *not seeing* the poor, which will be the peculiar ideological standpoint of the Neapolitan privileged classes. Like the intellectuals the narrator wants to interview, who have given up their original political struggle, the woman *shares* the discourse of power, the dominant discourse that cancels the horrors of poverty and only sees in Naples the commonplace splendor. She starts explaining that the renovation works will be completed by the Festival of Piedigrotta, thanks to the new mayor who has promised "extraordinary" lighting. For readers of the time of the release of the book, this mayor figure could not be anyone other than the newly elected (in the administrative elections at the end of May 1952) Achille Lauro, the local politician who became known for dominating and imposing the corrupt postwar political climate of the city. At this point another passenger exits anonymity and utters something indistinct to echo the woman's discourse: "A skinny man . . . who looked truly ill . . . whispered . . . *Lassa fa' a Dio*—Leave it to god"[45] (105). Thus, the discourse in praise of political power is joined by the fatalistic, superstitious discourse that de-historicizes Neapolitan reality, excluding any possibility of change.

Yet now something new happens, the narrative mechanism we have seen in the introduction, and that will be replicated each time the narrator will be in the presence of one of the intellectuals who betrayed their original, meaningful task (of whom the two passengers she has mentioned are anticipatory avatars): Her presence will evoke a forward movement of the lumpenproletariat itself, which, through some figure that singles itself out—that is, showing agency, not just being singled out by a foreign gaze—will force itself against the ideological blindness of the onlookers. This alone, however, would not be enough to break this barrier: What is really able to overcome it, thus exposing the existence of the lower classes in full visibility, is the gaze of the narrator herself. Reflected in her gaze, evoked in full presence by her emotional reaction, it will cease to be invisible to the others as well. In this visualizing mechanism, the physical barrier, which like the window brought to visibility by the girl's spit is always present in these scenes, the screen that normally works as a means of protection and concealment, will become a device of vision and revelation, and this will be, as we have seen, a common element with Rossellini's film. In this case, the screen is the tram's window. Looking at the opposite side of the road, the narrator now explores with her gaze the Villa Comunale, the public gardens, and describes them as a space enforcing a strict class separation between the outer section (closer to via Caracciolo and the sea) reserved for the aristocracy, the middle part populated by the bourgeoisie, and the last one, bordering the route of the tram, left to the lower classes—it is worth noting the absence of a proper working class in this classification: "The children of the working class[46] [plebe], from the ages of five to fifteen, happily occupy, instead, the shadiest spots; they go there to pee or to torture animals or to sit around dreaming of love, seduction, and songs. Tuberculosis sufferers are brought there by their relatives on doctors' orders and fade away on the flagstones like white butterfly wings"[47] (106). We find here again the spectrum of activities we can place on the lower side of figure 3.1, at the same time belonging to the physical needs, and to the irrational meaningless actions, here introducing for the first time its most cruel side, represented by the torture of animals. To be sure, this is not so different from what she described earlier while looking at the other side of the street. Yet something more happens now, as usual initiated by the sinister presence of the setting sun "faintly gilding the decapitated statues and busts"[48] (106), which again appears as a figure of the inversion of Reason, an emissary of Nature showing its presence in the place where the defeat of Reason is manifested in the absent heads of the statues. The underclass this time imposes itself, demands to be seen by those who were blind to their presence, precisely like the beggar girl will do in front of Compagnone's house: A group of kids "of an indeterminate age"[49] (106) unbutton their trousers and expose their sex, starting to follow the tram to be seen by the passengers. "They began to run along the wall, in an attempt to follow the tram, with shrill, sad, passionate cries, wanting to draw our attention to all they possessed"[50] (106). Yet not even now do the passengers of the tram (the two who have been singled out over all the others) seem to notice or to pay any attention to the kids on the other side of the screen. More kids appear, and even if they are not posing to be seen by the passengers, their actions trouble the narrator, as they are engaged in the kind of activities anticipated at the beginning of the description (torturing animals and urinating), here described in more detail. That these actions seem to exemplify again the semantic zone of the abolition of sense, the eclipse of meaning already signaled from the start of the story in the descriptions of the crowd of the poor, is clearly stated by the narrator: "They had no legitimate occupation"—but the adjective used in the original is "ragionevoli" (reasonable), with a direct reference to Reason—"and were buoyed by a childish madness"[51] (107). "Buoy" here translates the verb "sollevare," whose semantic connection with the sentence is figurative and not immediately clear, as if the kids were empty forms literally lifted up and sustained by madness, or hypnotized bodies possessed by a force that keeps them existing in a zone suspended between life and death, foreign to both. That this again borders on the eclipse of meaning itself is demonstrated by the fact that the distinctions between subject and object vanish: One of the tortures they perform is on a butterfly ("others were intent on skewering a butterfly"[52] [107]). This shows a precise symmetry with the first theriomorphic comparison the narrator had used to define these same kids a few lines earlier, who had been observed while "fad[ing] away on the flagstones like white butterfly wings."

Only now, reading the scene as reflected in the emotional reactions in the narrator's eyes, are the noseless woman and the sick man forced to react in turn. Their reaction mirrors that of Compagnone in the scene we analyzed in the introduction: sudden hostility toward the narrator, as if discovering that she is not "one of them," as if seeing her coincidence with the bodies outside of the barrier, the secret contradiction of this text where the "original emotion" is located. She has forced them to *look*: "The noseless woman was observing me quietly, and observing the street, and observing me and the street together; she must have thought something about what I was thinking, because the smile with which she mentioned the upcoming festival had disappeared, replaced by a fleeting gleam of suspicion . . . her stare was vacant, and yet her intensity and curiosity made me uncomfortable. The man, too, was now staring me right in the face"[53] (107). The narrator feels so uncomfortable that she gets off the tram earlier and continues on foot, and here the first sequence ends with a first deviation from the main narrative program. Of course, she continues to head to Compagnone for the first task of her "mission." However, the pressure of the environment has already managed to slow her down, to make her deviate from the fastest route.

Before closing this section, it is important to examine the visualizing mechanism that the actantial observer of this story (embodied on the surface of the text by the self-diegetic narrator, although not in all circumstances, as we have seen) has activated, as this will be the way in which the underclass' existence is communicated by the aesthetic mechanism of this work. In the last description of the lower class kids, we have seen one more example of what I earlier defined with a reference to Walter Benjamin's concept of an "optical unconscious," that is, the process through which the cognitive position of the observer shifts from that of a witness-protagonist, coherent with that of the narrator on the tram observing the Villa Comunale through the window, to that of a spectator immersed in the crowd, lost among the kids "buoyed by a childish madness," thus able to perceive details like the skewering of a butterfly's wing. This sudden proximity, equivalent to an extreme close-up not justified or prepared by any fictionalized point of view, generates an emotional intensity that is thematized in the story by the effect it has on the other passengers, who are forced to perceive it in the triangulation between that spectacle and its reflex in the eyes of the narrator ("and observing the street, and observing me and the street together"). But it also affects the reading experience produced by the text. Not coincidentally, it is exactly this one example that La Capria chooses to demonstrate what he considers Ortese's incapacity for realism:

> Another example of the unreliability to which an overly offended, and therefore at times prejudiced, sensibility can arrive can also be gathered from some small and I would say insignificant clues. That from a moving tram one can see on the wall of the Villa Comunale a row of street urchins mockingly showing their sex to the travelers, I am willing to believe. But how do you, always

from the same moving tram, see others further on who "were
intent on skewering a butterfly," I really do not understand this.
(La Capria 2003, 692)

This lack of understanding is really the symptom of a defensive refusal to
engage, as a reader, in the anamorphosis of the role of the observer, which,
from the privileged position of the separate spectator with a dominant van-
tage point, gets suddenly dispersed in the middle of the crowd, deprived of
any protection. We need to remember here that the ideological position of
the privileged classes consisted in their capacity not to see what is in plain
sight before them. Building on Fontanille's schematization of the modalization of space[54] we saw in the introduction, we can now follow the itinerary
that produces the "complex term"—the "picturesque" vision—where the
underclass becomes invisible in plain sight (figure 3.3). This is an "exposure"
perfectly dominated by an ideological mechanism able to negate it by producing an obstruction through which the actualizing modality linked to the
exposure (not-being-able-not-to-see) is mastered and inverted in the "being-
able-not-to-see" (the ideological *capacity not to see*), which then reaches its
final and perfected stage of inaccessibility, where the underclass is definitely
eliminated from the picture—although remaining in plain sight—and the
subject is granted the privilege not to see what is there in front of them.

We can now understand that the operation performed by Ortese's
text consists in inverting that inaccessibility toward the fourth position of
the square, the one where the obliterated object suddenly becomes visible

Figure 3.3. The itinerary of cognitive modalization of space. *Source:* Created by the
author, based on Fontanille 1988, 120.

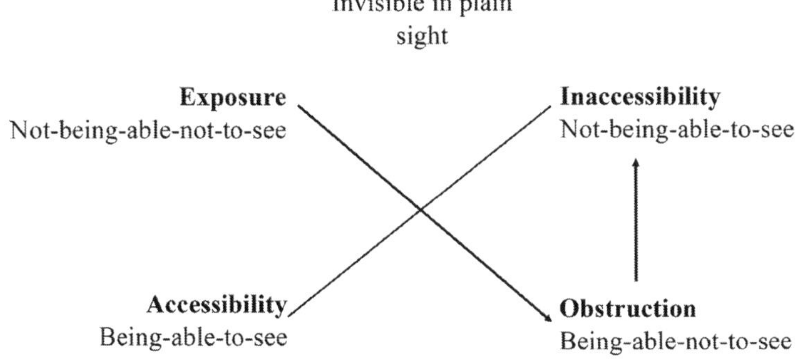

again, or rather flashes out as that which had always been there,[55] and only a maleficent spell (the enchantment of Nature, with its magical-ideological power) had been able to obscure. "Accessibility" is different than "exposure," as it is never a vision that can be taken for granted: It needs engagement, the assumption of responsibility, as it is the result of the embracing of a possibility (*"being-able-*to-see"): "Accessibility characterizes everything that can be seen, glimpsed, any flaw in the obstacle, which pushes back the limits of the visual field (mirrors, reflections, open doors or curtains, etc.)" (Fontanille 1989, 55). This is the effort that the protagonist-narrator of "The Silence" requires of the bystanders and that they refuse grudgingly, as if her offer of a different capacity to see, which has appeared on the very screen that was protecting them (the window) and in the emotional intensity of her own reaction (her eyes are here a device of direct *and* indirect vision), could reveal the fallacy and the artificiality of their own position. At the same time, this is the effort that the text requires of the reader, equally demystifying, equally intense and tiring, and remains a fleeting possibility, as it is so easy to refuse. This is demonstrated in the previous quote by La Capria, who, immediately after, while praising her as an *artist* ("Ortese is such an artist that she's right even when she's wrong" [La Capria 2003, 692]), refuses to consider her narrative as a credible depiction of the Neapolitan reality, thus de facto refusing to engage fully in the experience of the text, which would force him to renegotiate his own ideological position of privilege.

"Where Are We?": The First Sequence of *Journey to Italy*

The viewers of Rossellini's film can already imagine the answer to this question when Alex Joyce wakes up (figure 3.4) and utters these words (the first of the film) to his wife in the third shot of *Journey to Italy*. Katherine is driving, her eyes fixed on the road, and she replies that she does not know where they are.

While the diegetic itinerary opens on this sensation of being lost, with one character emerging from sleep and the other from reverie, the very first element of the film, the song on the opening credits performed by Giacomo Rondinella, the Neapolitan classic "O paese d'o sole," immediately foreshadowed the setting of the story, restricting it from the broad and generic "Italy" of the title to a familiar southern location, so often connected in Italian cinema to its popular music. However, this is not the

Figure 3.4. Katherine and Alex in their car. *Source:* Roberto Rossellini, *Journey to Italy*, 1954.

only information communicated by the song, which also conveys a certain pathetic intensity, full of joy and sorrow at the same time, that becomes more evident for those who understand the lyrics: "Today I am so joyful / that I would almost start crying / for this happiness."[56] Joy and tears are here motivated by the realization of being in Naples again: The lyric subject is a returning emigrant who has renounced making his fortune abroad to go back to his little house and his dear ones.[57] There is joy, but clearly there are sorrows too, painful memories, failure, broken dreams. The cathartic refrain, "This is the land of the sun, this is the land of the sea," despite being often quoted as the epitome of stereotypes on Naples,[58] is in itself permeated by the same bittersweet feeling, as it is followed by this further specification: "Where all the words are sweet or bitter, but they are always about love."[59] This ambiguity of meaning where love transcends both sweetness and bitterness, this thin balance between an appearance of joy and a deeper, unknown dimension where suffering is also concealed, will be embedded in the whole film, starting with the relaxed first appearance of the Joyces intent on a leisurely trip, which immediately starts to show signs of disquiet, of an *unknown* below the surface. However, we should also notice, from the outset, how the song also shows a similar situation to Ortese's story: Somebody who had left long ago now returns to Naples, and presumably from the north. His voice does not mention any negative element of the Neapolitan reality, yet there is a pain hidden in plain sight, in the light of the sun and its reflections on the sea.

When the opening credits fade on the first diegetic images—a wide shot of a street unfolding in daylight, as seen from the front of a speeding car—Rondinella's voice is at the peak of its intensity for the refrain, and it is not mingled with the diegetic sound, which only starts once the song is over. Yet when it does, it will not be the car's engine that we hear, but rather the loud and bothersome whistling of a train (offscreen), which only appears, rushing away in the opposite direction, in the next shot, this time seen from the left side of the car. The train had been mentioned in the song as well, but from there the returning emigrant had heard mandolins playing: another contrast between two dimensions, the sweetness of returning and the bitterness of departure (the train we see in the film is going north), or rather the harmony of ideological timelessness (Naples and its eternal mandolins) and the cacophony of historical reality. This latter had indeed immediately manifested itself, already in the first shot, with the omnipresence, at the side of the road, of commercial billboards, which punctuate the otherwise idyllic landscape that we will immediately be able to identify with the countryside between Latina and Terracina. Rossellini is going back to Naples to make another film there, after *Paisan*,[60] yet this is already a different historical landscape, where, in the early 1950s, the economic development and the wealth of a nascent consumerist society are starting to leave visible marks.

Nothing significant happens in this first sequence that shows the couple on their way to Naples and ends the moment they enter the Hotel Excelsior on the seafront on Via Partenope (on the other side of the lungomare with respect to the destination of the narrator in "The Silence"). We come to learn why they are on the road, that Alex is annoyed they did not just come by plane to save time, and that he wishes to get rid as soon as possible of the villa inherited by Uncle Homer. We also learn that this is the first time they are "really alone" since their marriage—and that Katherine starts to resent that Alex feels bored in this situation and still thinks of his London business. What really matters for this analysis is how this brief sequence contains *in nuce* the structure of the whole film, how the emotional intensity produced by the encounter with a foreign reality—that Rossellini carefully attempted to elicit from his actors in the disorienting and extenuating experience of the shooting—is able to bend the space and time of the story, to consume the narrative program on the surface, to expand the merely instrumental encounter with the southern reality until nothing else matters. At the formal level, this mechanism is produced by the triangulation of medium shots of the couple in the car, their close-ups, and the views from the car, constructed as subjective shots, following the codes of the point of view. In this analysis I will refer to the formal reading of this film performed by Adriano Aprà and Luigi Martelli in "Syntagmatic Premises for an Analysis of *Journey to Italy*" ("Premesse sintagmatiche ad un'analisi di *Viaggio in Italia*"), published in the second issue of the short-lived journal *Cinema e Film* in 1967, in which the authors examine the structure of the film's diegesis with a methodology based on Christian Metz's "grand syntagmatic" as elaborated in those years (Metz 1968). I will occasionally also reference another useful essay from that same issue of *Cinema and Film*, that is, the "grammatical" analysis of the same film performed by three young critics who followed Pasolini's own idiosyncratic version of film semiology (Albano et al. 1967).

According to Aprà and Martelli, the structure of the first (of two) segments of this sequence can be considered an "ordinary sequence" in Metz's terminology, that is, a series of events chronologically ordered and with a narrative unity, where some portions of the action are eliminated. This is a very common type of syntagm in fictional films, yet something peculiar happens here. While this kind of sequence typically excludes elements that lack interest for the plot—and this is usually done for the sake of rhythm and flow[61]—Rossellini seems to use it to accentuate the boredom of dead time, which forces the characters to contemplate the landscape and to look into themselves. Thus, the temporal discontinuity produces a paradoxical effect, that is, it loosens the impression of the very linearity and measurability of time, which is thus forced, even if not to disappear completely, to be replaced by the full frequentative, that is, by a time in which it is not so much the logical succession of actions that counts, but their repetition and, in some way, their simultaneity (here not diegetic but rather subjective: The frequentative translates the set of sensations experienced by Katherine and Alex, rather than these sensations in their singularity, that is, as elements of a narrative progression) (Aprà and Martelli 1967, 199).

My hypothesis is that the film experience communicates here the pressure of an emotional intensity evoked by the encounter with a foreign reality, which we will soon be able to localize in the contact between the streak of blood and the car windshield, as we have seen in the scene analyzed in the introduction, where the ideological contradiction properly enters the text: such pressure prevents the narrative from organizing itself in the regular "vectorial" temporal succession, thus generating an impression of mystery, of suspension of meaning, given that no object has appeared yet, at such an early stage, which could possess the force to provoke a similar phenomenon. In the terms of Fontanille, we could say that, even before any thematic encounter with the object, the cognitive perception of the environment as shown by the film is modified by the influx of a passional—thymic—intensity, which creates the atmosphere, the *Stimmung* of suspension and unease in which the film immerses us, what he calls a "projection" of the thymic on the cognitive (Fontanille 1989, 132), and which, following Merleau-Ponty's reflections discussed in the previous sections, we could consider the sign of the emergence of a traumatic reality concealed under the surface, which does not let itself be displaced. Indeed, the encounter with such reality is soon foreshadowed in two successive episodes where the couple is confronted by enigmatic objects, which immediately precede the appearance of the streak of blood: first in the sudden arrival of a speeding car that scares Alex when the couple stops to change positions (Alex wants to drive in order not to fall asleep), then, when they are forced to stop and proceed slowly as a herd of buffaloes invades the street. In the first case, the two are perfectly able to interpret and thus *neutralize* the encounter: Alex by resorting to negative stereotypes about southerners ("What noisy people: I've never seen noise and boredom go so well together"), Katherine by going with more positive ones (they drive like madmen and are amusing). Yet in the second case, things go differently. This time no word is uttered by the couple as the buffaloes fill the space and engulf them, a scene that the final sequence of the film will mirror, when the physical pressure of the crowd on the Corso in Maiori will stop their car. Indeed, it is not improbable that—precisely for the sake of this symmetry—Rossellini considered the encounter with these animals essential, as it was already present in the five-page sketch (Dagrada 2008, 504–5) I mentioned in chapter 2, where it is the subject of the very first paragraph (with a precise indication of the kilometer on the Domiziana road where the buffaloes can be met). At the formal level, this scene culminates with a canonical point-of-view shot of Katherine, with the camera panning on the animals from the inside of the car to follow the axis of her gaze then cutting on a close-up reaction shot of her face slightly frowning, as if being struck by an uncomfortable emotion we cannot clarify (figure 3.5).[62]

Thus the object, incomprehensible in its exposure—what appears here is just a herd of buffaloes—is attracted toward a space of revelation by an emotional reaction not yet understandable. The mechanism will be repli-

Figure 3.5. Katherine's reaction shot. *Source:* Roberto Rossellini, *Journey to Italy,* 1954.

cated multiple times, during the sequences in which Katherine will drive through the city, and will find its culmination in the final scene, where that mass of bodies (human this time, yet no less mysterious and disconcerting) will provoke the story's resolution. Like in Ortese's tram scene we have just analyzed, this mechanism will produce the indirect revelation of an object otherwise made invisible in its own exposure by the influence of ideological blindness. At this point it is not yet clear what this object might be. But Katherine's reaction alerts us that something more than "just" a herd of buffaloes might be involved here.

Merleau-Ponty has reflected on the power of close-ups to evoke the presence of the "irrepresentable" in his preparatory notes to the lecture course *The Sensible World and the World of Expression*: "Extraordinarily intense presence of what is not made explicit here: glance toward . . . [a] {horrible} scene, that isn't seen—When it is presented, [it's through] its influence on facial expression—Thus soldering over the gaps, indirect presentation, i.e., indication of what is absent by what is present = gearing together of the one in the other, pregnance of the one in the other"[63] (Merleau-Ponty 2020b, 127). This evocation of the invisible in the visible is central to the mechanism of the film, which will use it to communicate its historical content.

It is also central to Rossellini's method, for his own way of interpreting and showing reality through the body of his actors, that cruel mechanism that has so much fascinated and puzzled critics: "Rossellini wanted both of them [Bergman and Sanders] to be as confused and troubled during the process of production as their characters would be on screen . . . [their] off-screen situations are relevant to, or rather, are part of, the *Journey to Italy* aesthetic, on a fundamental level that goes beyond naturalistic characterization or a director's megalomania" (Mulvey 2000, 100), which means, in Alain Bergala's words that summarize Rossellini's method "[t]o make the other suffer in order to capture on his face and body the revealing effects of this suffering" (Bergala 1990, 28). But this was not a generic "suffering" Rossellini was trying to capture here. By his own admission, he wanted to show the interaction of his characters (and of his actors) with Naples, with the southern environment. Despite the stereotypes he always talked about in interviews (his own form of retreating from a painful reality), this was also meant to force the process of filmmaking to react with a concrete historical element, the Neapolitan reality and the sufferings of its underclass, ancestral and yet made more acute by the recent war. These sufferings, and the bodies that endure them, will creep into the filmic text to create the inscription that I call "ascetic images." For this to be possible, Rossellini needed to abandon the actors and crew without instruction, and thus have them come into contact with the city for several weeks, anguished by inaction, lack of plans, lack of scripts with which they could prepare, and so on. Their bodily reactions are thus not specific responses to given situations—as obviously the reaction shots of Katherine are only edited together with her subjective shots, often shot in her absence—but the result of the immersion in a condition exhausting enough for the reassuring cover of ideological discourses to start dissolving.

Concerning Merleau-Ponty's reflection quoted previously, Orna Raviv has commented as follows on this kind of aesthetic mechanism: "The intensity created by withholding what the character sees is more than a narrative device to create suspension; by showing what the characters see only as it is expressed by their bodies and facial expressions the presence of the invisible in the visible is invoked" (2016, 174n40). As we will see, such "invocation" is reinforced, in *Journey to Italy*, with a triangulation between bodily reactions, the evocatory power of Lewington's enigmatic verses—pointing to a hidden historical reality—and the shots in which the bodily presence of the Neapolitan crowd is directly shown. Yet it should be clear by now that the mere presence of those bodies is not enough for them to become truly visible, onscreen or in everyday reality: This is why an aesthetic mechanism like the one at play here and in Ortese's story has to work to reverse the operations of ideological blindness, thus opening a space for the revelation of their existence. It is also important to note that the mentioned triangulation is not the only device through which this revelation is performed. As we will see in detail in chapter 5, the soundscape of *Journey to Italy* plays a vital role in evoking the underground dimension of the popular classes, as a discrepant and often puzzling use of ambient, "active offscreen sounds"[64] connected with the invisible crowd will constantly contradict the private unfolding of the bourgeois drama of the couple (Bruno 2002, 383–84). This is a cinematic device commonly used to suggest the presence of a different layer of reality (temporal or of any other kind). Rossellini's continuous use of it, however, transforms its scope into a core element of the film experience itself. Such centrality—although not with reference to this film—has been stressed by Vivian Sobchack in her reflections on the pivotal role of the invisible in the experience of vision, developed in engagement with Merleau-Ponty's philosophy:

> We must acknowledge subjective experience and the invisible as part of vision—that part which does not "appear" in it or to us, but which grounds vision and gives the visible within it a substantial thickness and dimension. . . . By their very delimitation [visible and invisible] implicate other modalities of access to the world and experience. For example, what is invisible or "absent" in vision might be audible or "present" in perception to inform the act and significance of seeing. (Sobchack 2009, 290–91)

The soundscape does not yet have such a revelatory function in the first sequence, and yet its importance is anticipated in the encounter with the buffaloes, which are announced by the atmospheric ringing of their bells, heard in silence by the couple lost in the contemplation of their black, silent shapes. From this moment, the pressure of the thymic on the cognitive element increases; the objects of external reality seem to become only projections of an affective force, mysterious signs of a meaning not yet understandable. This is the mechanism that is clearly formulated in the scene analyzed in the introduction, where we located the "original emotion" on the streak of blood that Katherine notices on the windshield, and that closely follows the "epiphany" of the buffaloes. Meanwhile, punctuated by silence, the couple's stunted dialogue only expresses their unease; yet is this "unease" what we see projected over the landscape? This is partially the case, but the aesthetic mechanism will soon override the diegetic importance of the marriage crisis, which in the final scene will be solved precisely by its irrelevance in the pathetic motion of the crowd—and this will be their salvation, the *miracle* of the dissolution of the individual into the historical element.

The Sleeping Spell: Sleep as a Figure of Ideological Blindness

"I must say one sleeps well in this country." These are the first words Alex utters as he wakes up in the hotel room in Naples on the morning of the Joyces' first day in town. A montage of all the allusions to sleep, both verbal and visual, would reveal the consistency of this topic throughout the film. We have seen how the first picture of the couple, in the prologue, had already shown Alex waking up in the car, his gaze disoriented at finding himself in the middle of an unknown territory. Two days later in the film's diegesis, during the visit to the Archaeological Museum, the local guide will show Katherine the statue of the Drunken Faun, who "is about to fall asleep." "Sleep is a wonderful habit," he comments. While showing her the statue of the Farnese Hercules reclining on his club, he will also joke that "everybody seems to get rest around here," except himself. These are just some of the remarks about sleep throughout the film. What then is this soporific force that the Joyces discover from their first entrance into this country? Is it just the relaxation automatically associated with a place where hardworking, wealthy people exclusively go on vacation, the *dolce far niente* the aristocratic friends of Uncle Homer talk about with Katherine at the party where the two will be soon invited? If this is the most visible layer of an unknown reality, another is certainly hidden below. After all, in the middle of such relaxation and rest, the Joyces will only find their own crisis, their common void, and even hatred for each other: "I despise you" will be the last words Katherine tells Alex before the final denouement in the miracle. And there is even more: When Alex will descend into the kitchen of the inherited villa, after their first lunch there, to ask for more wine, he will find the two domestic workers sleeping on the chairs, with their heads resting on a table for ironing, as if they had fallen asleep because of exhaustion in the middle of work, their bodies expressing signs of discomfort (figure 3.6).[65]

Figure 3.6. The beginning of the "comic scene." *Source:* Roberto Rossellini, *Journey to Italy*, 1954.

This same image of a person reclining their head on a table because of exhaustion will be recalled, again, in the scene of Alex with the unnamed prostitute. The woman (Anna Proclemer) tells the story of her friend who had died in a nightclub two days before: "She put her head on the table . . . and she died." Immediately after, while reclining her own head on Alex's shoulder, she confesses she would have killed herself had he not called to her a few minutes earlier. Like her friend who had died, whose heart had simply failed on a night like all others—a night of work, we can imagine, given the place where it had happened—she seems exhausted. The reversal of the *dolce far niente*, this exhaustion that runs below the surface of leisurely appearances, is one of the signs of the underground dimension that permeates the film, and one of those more closely related to death: "I think I would have thrown myself into the sea," she had said, thus evoking the main figuration of death, as noted by Rancière, in Rossellini's films: the falling body—from Anna Magnani collapsing on the street of *Rome Open City* to the Sicilian girl thrown down onto the rocks by the German soldiers in the first episode of *Paisan* (who also throw partisans in the water in the last episode) to the suicide kids of *Germany Year Zero* and *Europe '51* (Rancière 2001, 165–85). Thus, even if unwittingly, Alex has prevented here the happening of what is inevitable par excellence in Rossellini's ill-fated destinies. And this should probably be interpreted as already belonging to the sphere of the final "miracle," a happy ending the author himself will seem unable to make sense of in later interviews.[66] Although, as we will see, there will be much more to interpret in the final sequence than a simple form of reward for an involuntary good action.

Let us go back to Alex waking up in the hotel room on the morning of the first day, where the other layer of this "reversal" of the *dolce far niente*, of the film's obsession with sleep, is soon suggested. The scene opens on a typical "postcard" panoramic shot that shows the Gulf of Naples in the bright morning light, from Capri to Vesuvius, taken approximately from the position of the Hotel Excelsior where the Joyces are staying. Already on the black screen, while the film was fading from the previous scene at the restaurant, an ambient sound had started that continues on the panoramic: voices of fishermen shouting while performing some work (the profession can be identified by a few comprehensible words), then starting to sing a typical Neapolitan song ("O Marenariello," Gambardella, Ottaviano). This offscreen sound continues—with no variations in volume, which already signals a certain distance from what is expected from diegetic ambient sounds—in the next shot, showing the interior of Katherine's hotel room. The camera is placed on the open window and shows the interior in full shot, while the woman prepares her stuff to leave. In theory, this camera's position could be the continuation of the panoramic movement of the previous shot. At this point, while the voices have started singing, and could thus quietly start functioning as a non-diegetic musical score (something similar will happen at another, crucial moment of the film, as we will see), we notice that Katherine is interacting with this sound. She approaches the window and looks outside, beyond the camera, as if looking for something. Her point of view follows, and we see in low angle Via Partenope, the Fontana del Gigante, the sea (thus, retrospectively, the initial panoramic could be imagined as a previous point of view of hers[67]). There are two distant boats in the water, but no clearly identifiable source for the voices is visible, and the volume, compared to the distance, does not invite the spectator to imagine it to be placed in one of the two boats. Indeed, in Katherine's reaction shot we see her still looking around, even above in a final attempt to make sense of the voices' source: Maybe they could come from another room on a higher floor? her interrogative gaze seems to ask (figure 3.7).

In the terminology of Michel Chion, these offscreen, ambient sounds could be defined as "active," as they have an effect on the character, which

Figure 3.7. Katherine looks for the source of the sounds she hears. *Source:* Roberto Rossellini, *Journey to Italy*, 1954.

in turn elicits the viewer's attention toward them. In sum, they are not only there to give a realistic sense of the environment: "I give the name *active offscreen sound* to acousmatic[68] sound that raises questions—What is this? What is happening?—and that incites the gaze (and the camera) to go find out. Such sound arouses curiosity, which propels the film forward and engages the spectator's anticipation" (Chion 2019, 83). Throughout the film, these ambient sounds will be pervasive. As Bruno has noted, "Sound is everywhere in the film: from the credit sequence on, it is a continuous presence that has an existence of its own, even outside of narrative motivations" (2002, 384). Indeed, ambient sounds will not always be "active" in the sense we have seen, yet their obsessive insistence will create a split-reality effect, as if the space we see—often closed, dignified bourgeois interiors—had a deeper, invisible layer populated by a crowd from the lower classes of the city. This crowd, though a source for these sounds, will never be shown, aside from Katherine's point-of-view shots during her itineraries through the city (only fleetingly) and in the last scene with the procession and the miracle. This particular use of the soundscape will have a dramatic effect in itself, as "a sound or voice that remains acousmatic creates a mystery of the nature of its source, its properties, and its powers, given that causal listening cannot supply complete information about the sound's nature and the events taking place" (Chion 2019, 73). This mystery will have a haunting nature, immediately manifested by the film in the following shot. Katherine passes to the next room to wake Alex up. Here she opens the curtains but the windows remain closed, yet the voices of the singing fishermen have followed her with unchanged volume. This is a presence one cannot simply ignore by seeking the protection of closed spaces: It is an entity not shut out by doors or windows. Or rather, the "counter-spell" produced by the aesthetic mechanism of the film is able to make this presence real exactly because it chooses to *reveal* it instead of placing it in full sight, where the ideological blindness is perfectly able to make it disappear, having transformed that full presence in its favorite device of concealment. We must recall, here, the semiotic square of the cognitive modalization of spaces proposed by Fontanille and examined in the last section (figure 3.3), where we can visualize the ideological operation of concealment, able to negate the full exposure of the object of knowledge in its obstruction (where the subject of ideology becomes *able not to see*), to push it toward complete inaccessibility, and, finally, to make it coincide with the complex term, where ideological blindness—as the inaccessibility of something exposed in full sight—is fully acquired.

Thus, for the middle-upper-class Neapolitans as for the northern tourists, being awake de facto coincides with dreaming, a waking dream where the underclass disappears from the magnificent landscape of the gulf, where the paradise is finally deprived of its devils, under the benevolent safeguard of an entity that keeps unwelcome nightmares away. Yet in real sleep sinister presences cannot be controlled. As Alex wakes up, he says he cannot remember what he was dreaming. Katherine bitterly jokes that he might have been dreaming of his friend Judy they met the previous night. Here the relics of the jealousy plot on which the screenplay was originally based (as we have seen in chapter 2) directly collide with the pressure of other underground forces, this time emerging from the political unconscious of the city. The film alludes to such forces here through this moment of superimposition of the mysterious ambient sounds with the declared void, the "unknown" of Alex's dream ("I was dreaming of something, but I cannot remember what it was"), as it had done in the previous sequence with the Joyces' reactions to mysterious "signs" along the road. We can here sense how the aesthetic mechanism is starting to reverse—through these signs of a mysterious presence—the ideological blindness device, to drag the object toward the square's fourth position of revelation, where one might become again *able to see.*

In other words, the filmic text creates at least the possibility of a "contact" with its historical content. However, we must recall that such content can only be approximated but never fully possessed, as the position of "exposure"—in my hypothesis—always coincides again with ideological falsification: the existence of the underclass as historical phenomenon, its physical presence and the totality of the material circumstances that incessantly produce it within the socioeconomic structure that makes it possible, like history itself can only be grasped as "rather an asymptotic phenomenon, an outer limit, which the subject approaches in the anxiety of the moment of truth"[69] (Jameson 1979, 13). That Rossellini's film could be able to approach such a moment of truth is arguably due to both a series of contextual circumstances (the historical situation in which the film was created and the personal experiences of the people involved) and textual elements (the aesthetic strategies to capture and communicate the emotional reaction of the actors to a precise historical environment).

A similar mechanism of revelation of a historical content is also at work in "The Silence of Reason," where, not coincidentally, an obsessive preoccupation with sleep also punctuates the unfolding of the story. On the last page, the narrator looks out of the window of her hotel room, her gaze performing a panoramic of the whole city formally similar to the one of Katherine we have just seen: "In the immense light, delicate as that of a seashell, from the green hills of the Vomero and Capodimonte to the dark promontory of Posillipo, all was united in sleep, a marvel without consciousness"[70] (Ortese 2018, 187). The sleep that envelops the whole city is the central allegory, throughout the story, for the ideological capture that makes any political change impossible, thus depriving the population of a clear consciousness of its own material conditions. We need to remember Althusser's definition of ideology as the imaginary picturing of one's own material relations with society, "imaginary relation to real relations" (Althusser 2001, 167), as a dreamlike, fantasmatic grasping of the social environment one lives in, "the imaginary representation of the world" (164). Noteworthy also is how this "magic" sleep appears to be protected by a sort of underwater environment, as the light in which the city is immersed is compared to that of a "seashell," that is, to the fleeting reflection of sunlight on shells on the bottom of the sea. The story opens under the "intense glare" of a sinister sun representing a defeated Reason, a perverted remnant of it acting under the spell of Nature, which is also signified by its reflections on the noseless woman and on the beheaded statues; here, again, the whole city appears in a light that is literally inverted, as it has been transformed in a reflection coming from below, signifying, once more, a perversion of Reason.

Indeed this fantasy, placed right at the conclusion, responds to and completes the allegorical structure of the story, developed in the recurrent passages that we could call "allegorical meditations" where the social structure of the city is depicted in mythical, fairytale terms. For instance, while sketching the character of Compagnone in the second section ("Story of Luigi the Bureaucrat" or "Storia del funzionario Luigi"), immediately following the opening sequence, the narrator had depicted the city as the battleground of two elementary forces, Nature and Reason (both gendered as feminine in Italian); the first one, always victorious, has entrapped the whole population in what in fairytales would have been called a "sleeping spell."[71] Her permanent triumph is secured by the help of a "secret ministry" adumbrating the city's intellectual class, as appears obvious from the continuation of the story. It is also worth noting that, in the very title of the chapter, Compagnone, the paradigmatic example of a once rebel intellectual who has now turned to Nature's service, is defined as a "bureaucrat," "funzionario" in Italian, which is the generic definition for those who work in the public administration with an intermediary status (a lower ranking executive), thus signaling his "employment" in the ministry of nature: "In the region of the far South where the sun shines brightest, a secret ministry exists for the defense of nature from reason: a maternal genius of limitless power to whose perpetual and jealous care the sleeping populations of the place are entrusted. If this defense were to slacken for only a moment, if the cool, gentle voices of human reason were to get through to nature, it would be destroyed"[72] (122). If the Neapolitan intellectuals are thus pictured as a mysterious bureaucracy (we must not forget that the story will end under the influence of Kafkian imagination), they also appear to be completely under a spell of influence performed by Nature, deeply asleep in their own ideological dream: "And all the young writers I had known, were they not singing the praises of their ancient mother? Was there even one who would cast the light of human reason on nature? All, all of them were sleeping now near the sea, they were sleeping from Torre del Greco to Cuma"[73] (183).

This big sleep is essentially a defense from the possibility of becoming aware that keeping one's own privilege ultimately depends on preserving the lower classes in their condition of oppression. The Neapolitan lumpenproletariat cannot even hope to transform itself into a "working class" properly said: It must remain the ancient *plebe*, "the eternal crowd of Naples," so that everything remains as it is, and the centuries-old social balance stays untouched. Yet this is no easy task, given the uneven proportions of the two classes and the peculiar urbanistic structure of the city, where the presence of the lower class is ubiquitous, and the upper classes cannot simply physically isolate themselves from it. This is why they developed the peculiar Neapolitan Ideology we discussed in chapter 2, which, far from supporting the enforcement of a separation—a strategy that could not work because of both the socioeconomic and the urbanistic structure of the city—fantasized instead about the exceptional "Neapolitan spirit," thanks to which all material problems, even the harshest, like starvation and homelessness, were all sublated in the stereotypical instinct to endure and enjoy life no matter what, everything being finally obliterated in music, in passion, in the material pleasure of being exposed to the sun. This was the "Gold of Naples," about which Giuseppe Marotta wrote a successful book and which he defined as "a remote, hereditary, intelligent, superior patience" (Marotta 1964, 18). This, in his opinion, was rooted in "the convulsions of the soil, in the puffs of deadly steam that suddenly erupted, in the waves that climbed over the hills, in all the dangers that threatened human life here" (18), that is, in the timeless, nonhistorical influence of Nature, rather than in centuries of political oppression and ruthless policies that transformed the larger part of the population into a lumpenproletariat confined in the informal economy. What the narrator of "The Silence" seems to suggest is that under the fantastic image of such "patience" imagined as the universal Neapolitan virtue, the "indifference" of the upper classes is rather to be seen—which is really *their* gold, allowing them to preserve their privilege while still feeling like decent people: "I knew this indifference was a form of control. Everyone was indifferent here, everyone who wished to survive. To become emotional would be like falling asleep in the snow"[74] (168). Yet this *other* sleep that leads toward death is completely different from the ideological sleep that is everyone's normal condition. This sleep, like the one from which Alex has woken up in the hotel room on the morning of the first day, is rather a figuration of the contact with something unknown (outside of the familiar layers of ideological vision), the space where the horrible reality of the underclass can be revealed, and where the aesthetic experience of the two works we are examining eventually leads readers/ viewers. Not coincidentally, this particular kind of "becoming emotional" ("commuoversi") in front of a normally invisible object—which the narrator likens to this other, deeper kind of slumber leading to death—could be seen as the main structural operator able to make the initial narrative program of the two stories (to conduct a few interviews, write the piece, and go back north; to sell the villa while doing a little vacation, and then, for Katherine, to find a way to save her marriage) deviate toward the "anti-program" of the contemplation of the miserable—unthinkable—existence of the poor, the hidden dimension of both works whose pressure feeds the emotional intensity that punctuates the story. We move from the idle to the tragic activity, from the present work to a past one that still needs fulfillment: "The reason I had gone there—to obtain information and gossip about the Neapolitan writers—had vanished, making way for a deeper interest that was not without a certain undefined *fear*"[75] (115). This fear, which the Italian "spavento" defines more precisely as the reaction to a sudden event, is the emotional outburst that brings about the revelation of the duplicity of reality, which only ideological blindness can present as unified and unproblematic. Indeed, immediately after acknowledging the "fear" she feels at approaching Compagnone, the same she had felt in observing the crowd from the tram, she adds: "I had to admit that Luigi was not merely a bureaucrat, nor was he entirely a Neapolitan, just as those around him weren't, either, in the same way that the grim route I'd taken a little earlier in the tram revealed more than a Naples of mere color and recklessness. Naples wasn't just an onrush of antiquity, it was also the anguished concerns of youth flowing beneath that antiquity"[76] (115). The "concerns of youth," literally the "young things" that flow ("with a lot of anguish") beneath an ancient, apparently unbreakable surface ("the archaic calm of the landscape" [105]), coincide here with the effort to access that second layer of reality we have been discussing, and directly refer to the attempt of the Neapolitan youth—the *Sud* group—to dissipate the ideological incantation and act on historical reality to produce a change. This effort had long ended, for which the anti-narrative program of this story is a form of late, compensatory fulfillment. It is important to understand that what is at play here is not just an operation of demystification, coinciding with describing the miserable social reality that ideology conceals. Of course, *describing* is also part of the mechanism, but the aesthetic experience afforded by the text goes further. As ideology's effect is precisely to occlude what is exposed in plain sight, what the text does is to produce an experience of revelation: This is often thematized in the narrator's reflections, like in the last quotation, but it is also played out in the moments in which the condition of the poor—their habitus—emerges with the highest pathetic intensity through a violent use of rhetorical tools and the manipulation of the actantial role of the observer, or when the solidity of narrated reality is eroded by the "directing function" of the narrator. Something comparable happens, as we have seen, in Rossellini's film, where a second layer of reality is revealed through the specific use of the soundscape and the rise of emotional intensity reflected by the physical reactions of Katherine at the appearance of the signs of the city's hidden dimension. In both cases, the experience of the text makes us access an object that transcends what is ordinarily visible on the surface, and this explains the deeply disturbing effect the works we are studying can have.

The Text and Its Historical Content

"Writing is always a response to the *transcendence*, which is bursting and pain" (Merleau-Ponty 2020a, 186; my emphasis), Merleau-Ponty suggests in the preparatory notes for his lecture course at the Collège de France, *The Problem of Speech* (*Le problème de la parole*, 1954), whose last part is devoted, following a lengthy examination of Saussure's conception of language, to the revelatory potential of literature, and is based on a reading of Proust. The "transcendence" he names here corresponds precisely to the opening toward a layer of reality that is painfully removed from visibility (any contact with it results in "bursting and pain"), which the ordinary, social projection occludes and makes it impossible to decrypt and translate in theoretical discourse. Although he does not talk of the duplicity of reality (of its opaqueness) in terms of ideology, his notes for the lecture courses in the years 1953 to '54 reassess perception in terms of a projective and ambiguous conscience susceptible to social mystification. In the working notes for the lecture course *The Sensible World and the World of Expression* (1953), he had reflected on "the institutional or cultural element of all perception"[77] (Merleau-Ponty 2020b, 134), endeavoring to "produce [a] new analysis of perceptual consciousness (or of the consciousness of illusion) as essentially *projective* consciousness (in the Freudian sense): how we see on things what is obviously [an] expression of the subject. In this sense perceptual consciousness is essentially expression" (133; my emphasis). That this perceptual ambiguity should be read not only in connection with the *Gestalt* theory's figure-background contrast,[78] but also in light of a political understanding of the institutional element of perception, is demonstrated by the reference the author makes, in the same notes, to a Marxist interpretation of consciousness (we will see in a moment that Marxism was at the center of his reflections in these same months): "Polymorphism of consciousness, ambivalence, indirect or inverted consciousness: psychoanalysis, Marxism and the mystification of consciousness. Consciousness as divergence [écart]"[79] (131).

To sum up, the "polymorphism" of consciousness, like the sleeping spell to which the Neapolitan intellectuals have surrendered, risks working as an incantation transforming social relations in a natural landscape. Such an interpretation remains largely implicit here; and yet, as mentioned, around the same months Merleau-Ponty was reflecting on a more radical political version of the same polymorphism, as elaborated by Lukács in *History and Class Consciousness* (the very point of departure for the understanding of ideology I am following in this book), about which he wrote the essay " 'Western' Marxism" ("Le marxisme 'occidental' ") published in *Adventures of the Dialectics* (*Les aventures de la dialectique*) in 1955.[80] Here he thinks of Lukács's dialectical materialism as "a way of saying that the relations among men are not the sum of personal acts or personal decisions, but pass through things, the anonymous roles, the common situations, and the institutions where men have *projected* so much of themselves that their fate is now played out outside them" (Merleau-Ponty 1973a, 32; my emphasis). We find here again the expressive act of *projecting* (what he also calls "anthropological projection" [Merleau-Ponty 2020b, 139]) as defining the mystifying power of (social) consciousness, which makes appear as objective and immutable the relations that are really produced by social conflicts. What becomes evident when reading the lecture notes I have mentioned against the background of *Adventures of the Dialectics* is that for the philosopher this expressive power has a dialectical potential: Its projective, "expressive" function, when taken up in the aesthetic gesture, can also acquire the power to disrupt and unmask those same ideological contents it had placed into things in the first place, thus clearing the opening in which the historical content can finally appear. The aforementioned quote from the 1953 course continues as follows: "The problem of the understanding is thus to understand how this polymorphism can be taken up in a way that transforms equivocation into signification, ambivalence into ambiguity" (Merleau-Ponty 2020b, 131).

It is precisely this liberatory function the aesthetic gesture can have, which in *The Problem of Speech* he tries to better clarify using the concept of "style," defined, quoting Proust, as "a question, not of technique, but of vision"[81] (Merleau-Ponty 2020a, 181), that is, "the set of means by which one makes things and others appear—as opposed to means of defining them." We can see here, in this simple opposition between "definition" and "apparition," something comparable to the dichotomy I traced above, between what could be considered as an "objective" description of a given social situation—whose "objectivist illusion" (Merleau-Ponty 1973b, 148) could have satisfied La Capria's sense of realism—and an aesthetic device able to manipulate emotional intensity and the actantial role of the observer, through which the concealed object can be suggested and communicated to the reader/viewer in an indirect way. We need only think here of the violent approximation to the bodily existence of the crowd of the poor performed by the narrator at the beginning of "The Silence," or of its haunting presence in the soundscape of *Journey to Italy*. Both strategies attempt to escape the power of concealment of ideology—which, again, works precisely by occluding what is offered in full sight. In her essay on *The Problem of Speech*, Lovisa Andén has noted: "In the act of expressing the world we already experience, literature brings us closer to the being that reveals itself in our perception. It brings us closer to the being that we otherwise over-write with conventional significations, and that thus requires an interruptive labour to write forth" (2019, 217). Although in the following years Merleau-Ponty will develop this insight toward his ontological project, in these months the dialectical potential of the expressive gesture is equally close to an understanding of the aesthetic dimension as the opening of a *transcendence* where ordinarily foreclosed experiential contents might emerge. In short, the idea of "consciousness as divergence" offers a pattern to interpret the oblique strategies through which Ortese's and Rossellini's works actualize their historical content, and completes an important stage in the itinerary the philosopher had started with his reflections on the reemergence of traumatic experiences in *Phenomenology of Perception*.

There, Merleau-Ponty had defined "transcendence" in Heideggerian terms, as the being-in-the-world that structures individual experience (Merleau-Ponty 2005, 493), and had linked the concept to Husserl's "operative intentionality" (*fungierende Intentionalität*), a pre-personal, non-thetic connection to the environment that constitutes the foundation for the personal, subjective one.[82] It is precisely the reference to operative intentionality that allows Merleau-Ponty to think the relationship between bodily perception and environment as founded on an "openness" where the natural and the cultural cannot be separated,[83] and the affective element is already free to circulate (in a way reminiscent of Heidegger's conception of Stimmung [Jameson 2013, 38]), producing a pre-personal experience that is a form of knowledge non-codified by verbal, rational thinking.[84] As we have seen in chapter 2, this "openness" on a "formless existence that precedes my history and that will draw it to a close" (Merleau-Ponty 2012, 362) had been the gateway, in *Phenomenology of Perception*, for the traumatic experience to become—below any conscious control—a "style of being" (Merleau-Ponty 2005, 112) expressed by individual existence, a mechanism the philosopher had also linked to the incapacity, in certain mental illnesses, to control the mental projection of a second (private) space over the common space of shared experience (339–40). This paradigm had offered a model to understand why, in the works we are studying, a second layer of reality normally removed from visibility can make its presence felt under the apparent surface of the story, and be revealed by the aesthetic mechanisms we are exploring, thus escaping ideological blindness.

With reference to this same topic, the importance of Merleau-Ponty's reflections from the lectures at the Collège de France in the early 1950s—and from *The Problem of Speech* in particular—consists in the fact that we find here an attempt to articulate the process through which certain kinds of experiences—those whose removal and resurfacing provokes "bursting and pain"—can be communicated in the aesthetic gesture and the literary work in particular. In this chapter we already saw a meaningful example of this "evocative" power of aesthetic gesture from the 1953 course *The Sensible World and the World of Expression*, in the indirect presentation of a "horrible scene" by the cinematic close-up's reaction—"pregnance of the one in the other" (Merleau-Ponty 2020b, 127). Indeed, what interests the philosopher is not so much the generic capacity of the aesthetic gesture to "describe" experience, to code certain events in visual or verbal language, but the way it is able to communicate, to *express* (this, together with *style*, is the keyword in this context) precisely those contents that are not definable in ordinary language and in logical terms, what he calls, starting with the "musical ideas" explored by Proust,[85] "the sorts of ideas, of alogical essences that cannot be translated into the terms of the ideas of the intelligence" (Merleau-Ponty 2020a, 162). We could think of these "ideas" as sort of unknown variables that the literary (and more generically artistic) work is able to reveal, to which a quantum of pathetic intensity is necessarily attached, and that it is possible to link to the emergence or the revelation—in the transcendence to which expression responds (173)—of the *historical content* hidden under the surface of a story. In the case of Merleau-Ponty's analysis of Proust's *Recherche*, Mauro Carbone has shown how the "sensible ideas"[86]—as Merleau-Ponty will later define them in *Visible and Invisible* (Merleau-Ponty 1964, 196)—are generated through the "operative intentionality,"[87] originally linked to "transcendence" in *Phenomenology of Perception* (Carbone 2020b). As we have seen, it is because of such "operative intentionality" that experiential contents access bodily perception without being thematized by consciousness, and can then reappear in the moments of revelation—in involuntary memory—as a reality experienced for the first time, able to mobilize a pathetic intensity unknown to ordinary, everyday experience.[88]

However, it seems to me that an understanding of Merleau-Ponty's concept of "alogical essences" emerging in the work of art, at the time of *The Problem of Speech*, can be enhanced by taking into consideration his contemporary political reflections from *Adventures of the Dialectics*, where he defines the concept of proletarian praxis, as sketched by Lukács in *History and Class Consciousness*,[89] in surprisingly close terms. Like the non-logical, almost unthinkable experiential contents expressed by literature in its privileged moments, Lukács's idea of praxis, as the indistinguishable unity of action and knowledge of the proletariat—where the classic subject-object dichotomy has collapsed[90]—is not communicable in discursive terms, and is only understandable as a being-in-the-world, "a vector, an attraction, a possible state, a principle of historical selection, and a diagram of existence"[91] (Merleau-Ponty 1973a, 49). In turn, the alogical contents of literature are "things that are categories, dimensions, structures of time, space, life. The quality of a world = such organizing principles, included in a concrete fabric."[92] The difficulty here lies in the fact that the communication of experience is understood as inseparable from the totality of the relations of its material—historical—being-in-the-world[93] ("a diagram of existence," "structures of time, space, life"). This is never fully representable, and when it appears, in our terms, in full exposure, must be already coated in ideological obfuscation. In other words, communication of experience as representation, as coding/decoding of discursive information, is impossible, and can only be imagined as the sharing of a standpoint.[94] Therefore, like the privileged moments in which art is able to recreate the "place" from which an experience can be shared, "the profound philosophical meaning of the notion of praxis is to place us in an order which is not that of knowledge but rather that of communication, exchange, and association [fréquentation]" (Merleau-Ponty 1973a, 50). In other words, if the experiential core of literature consists of "a linguistic whole [ensemble langagier] of the same form as the prelogical unity of our life," (Merleau-Ponty 2020a, 166) which "cannot be translated into the terms of the ideas of the intelligence" (162), and is rather to be placed "above the 'idea of intelligence'" (163), "for a philosophy of praxis, knowledge itself is not the intellectual possession of a signification, of a mental object; and the proletarians are able to carry the meaning of history, even though this meaning is not in the form of an 'I think'" (Merleau-Ponty 1973a, 50).

In the years that followed, Merleau-Ponty would develop these ideas in an ontological direction, particularly in *Eye and Mind* (*L'œil et l'esprit*, 1960) and in the manuscript of *The Visible and the Invisible* (which would be published only posthumously). At this stage, the alogical content accessed in aesthetic experience, through which the sense of being-in-the-world can be communicated, is rethought as a fundamental structure of vision itself: "The hallmark of the visible is to have a lining of invisibility [une doublure d'invisible] in the strict sense, which it makes present as a certain absence" (Merleau-Ponty 1993, 147). In *Eye and Mind*, he develops this reflection starting from painting, which becomes a model of vision itself: What is at stake is much more than a simple cognitive relationship with an object (the access to a specific content). Rather, it concerns the communication—beyond any authorial intention—of an impersonal experience that is much broader than what is intentionally codified and decoded in the process: "For I do not look at it [the painting] as one looks at a thing, fixing it in its place. My gaze wanders within it as in the halos of Being. Rather than seeing it, I see according to, or with it [selon lui ou avec lui]" (Merleau-Ponty 1993, 126). It is precisely because of this way of thinking about communication that these late reflections can help us further clarify the narratological value of Merleau-Ponty's understanding of the aesthetic gesture.

While the ideological machine functions through the strict regulation of the possibilities of vision ascribed to a subject based on their standpoint, the inscription in the aesthetic object of an experience that extends beyond the individual, and carries within it the historical coordinates of a being-in-the-world, can push individual vision beyond its own limits. We have seen, in this sense, how the manipulation of the actantial role of the observer, in the first sequence of "The Silence," with its recourse to what we defined, with Benjamin, as an optical unconscious, reveals the depth of a historical experience that would otherwise have remained inaccessible to the point of view of the bourgeois comfortably seated in the streetcar. A similar phenomenon occurs, as we will see, in the analysis of *Journey to Italy*: The communication of the historical content sedimented at the core of its experience, that is, the habitus of the lower strata of the population, will be conveyed through the historical concreteness of a being-in-the-world, articulated as a "style of being" enhanced through emotional intensity.

In *The Visible and the Invisible*, this process is exemplified by an image that had already appeared in Merleau-Ponty's work (Merleau-Ponty 2005, 467)—namely that of two people pointing something out to each other in the landscape. What should be the most banal of communicative gestures here becomes the sign of an ontological leap: "It is not I who sees, not he who sees, because an anonymous visibility inhabits both of us, a vision in general": "Then, through the concordant operation of his body and my own, what I see passes into him, this individual green of the meadow under my eyes invades his vision without quitting my own, I recognize in my green his green, as the customs officer recognizes suddenly in a traveler the man whose description he had been given" (Merleau-Ponty 1968, 142). If in the late work this "anonymous visibility" becomes the place where contact with Being as visible occurs, with its "thickness" (135), in our "window of opportunity," shortly before the mid-1950s, the thickness of vision, its excess over the strictly individual perspective, coincides with its historicity. In other words, it is history that inhabits us and passes through us, striking us beyond the manipulations of the ideological machine, where we are most exposed, in that non-thetic, impersonal attention that is the *fungierende Intentionalität*. Here, our experience opens up to the world ever anew as original ("pre-personal adhesion to the general form of the world, as an anonymous and general existence" [Merleau-Ponty 2012, 86]: Thus he defined our embodied connection to the world in *Phenomenology of Perception*). This is where access to the historical content of the works we are studying becomes possible.

To conclude these reflections, it is important to note that this potential of literature and of the aesthetic gesture in general can never be taken for granted and might be only fulfilled when the author—and possibly the receiver, as effects are never granted either—are able to come into contact with the reality that manifests itself in the "transcendence," to which a work is responding, with its own quantum of suffering, which is always involved when something pushed away from the surface of reality has the emotional intensity to pierce through ideological barriers. Hence the many references, in Merleau-Ponty's lectures, to the suffering implied in the creative process: not only the "bursting and pain" already evoked, but also sorrow as "the mode of appearance of the idea" (Merleau-Ponty 2020a, 186), which echoes a passage from the *Recherche* he quotes immediately after: " 'Sorrows are . . . atrocious servants, impossible to replace, and which, by subterranean ways, lead us to truth and death' "[95] (186). Not by chance, this aesthetic reflection proceeds in parallel with the one on proletarian praxis, that is, a form of life where awareness about the material conditions of society—class consciousness as conceived by Lukács—is produced by the utmost degree of reification, in which workers must know themselves as commodities:[96]

The fading of ideological obfuscation is only made possible by the highest degree of suffering imaginable in a given society, in the position where no privilege to defend, no possession to lose, remains. This is deeply related to what Ortese and Rossellini had perceived in the Neapolitan underclass, to their capacity to communicate its habitus. However, it is important to stress that this capacity to see (the being-able-to-see of the fourth position on the square of the cognitive modalization of space) does not coincide with the acquisition or the communication of a discursive knowledge of the object at the core of the work itself. Granted, there are different degrees of awareness, from Rossellini's incapacity to talk about his own film outside of orientalizing stereotypes to Ortese's lucid accusation of the Neapolitan intellectuals and their ideology. Yet even in her case, the communication of the experience out of which both works had grown—the un-concealment of the habitus of the underclass—can only happen in the absorption in the aesthetic gesture: "There is no knowledge, by the writer, of his [*sic*] book, for that would be to believe that the book is made up of available meanings, while it is the advent as language or organization of the universe of a mental landscape, which only takes on its full relief when confronted with others, that is to say for the reader" (Merleau-Ponty 2020a, 184).

Chapter 4

Dead and Restless

"The Silence of Reason"

The Crypt

"The Silence of Reason" is based on an aesthetic mechanism of visualization, which constantly attracts on the surface of the visible a reality that had been concealed in the dark by an ideological arrangement of blindness and vision. The scene analyzed in the introduction, where the "original emotion" is located, and the brief sequence of the tram we saw in chapter 3 both had offered a model of how this mechanism works throughout the story: Those who are protected by privilege inhabit and traverse the city shielded by screens; the people inside comfortable houses and those on the tram are separated by the crowd of the poor, hence the windows are a device of vision and concealment at the same time, as ideological blindness is produced precisely at the core of a vision offered in plain sight. The arrival of the narrator in the place of privilege momentarily short-circuits this schema: Her presence "provokes" a coming forward of the bodies of the underclass (the beggar girl, the poor kids that expose their bodies to the travelers and attempt to follow the tram). At the same time, this vision, reflected and amplified in her own gaze and through her emotional reaction, forces the other onlookers to react, to *see* the bodies of the poor. Here the structural level of the text mirrors the thematic one: The emotional wave generated at the contact with the existence of the crowd of the poor by the use of rhetorical tools and by the manipulation of the actantial role of the observer reveals to readers a reality whose intensity is normally obfuscated—which provokes, for example, the refusal to engage in the text's experience from interpreters like La Capria, who thinks the story lacks "realism."

At the end of the first section the narrator arrives in front of Compagnone's house, situated on the ground floor of an apartment building and accessible through a door-window giving onto a small terrace, through which the living room is visible from the street (the logistics of the house are important for the story). Nobody seems to be at home; she rings the bell and puts her face to the glass of the door to peer inside: "I . . . pressed the porcelain buzzer . . . I put my face to the window"[1] (Ortese 2018, 110). The whole second section of the story, where the character of Compagnone is introduced, together with the other Neapolitan intellectuals of the *Sud* group and the story of the journal, takes place during this hesitation on the threshold of the house. Indeed, the recollection of the past, the entire background story, occurs in the time of the ringing of the doorbell,[2] and it is not presented as an intermission but as an act of remembering happening in the diegetic time as a sort of vision, during which the narrator's memory projects different scenes from the past on the empty room she is observing: "I thought I glimpsed some figures, and heard, perhaps, the sound of familiar voices. . . . These figures lingered there for a few moments . . . then, like the digits on a taxi meter, they were replaced"[3] (112). However, this intense concentration of time and history in a few brief moments hides another important element. The pressure of her hand and forehead on the surface of the screen represents more than a cognitive activity (checking if anyone is there), as it also signals a pragmatic one: an infraction toward the internal protected space, thus replicating the gesture of approximation of the bodies of the poor on protecting barriers, while exactly anticipating what the beggar girl will do on that same surface a few minutes later.

Compagnone enters the present of the story at the beginning of the third section, titled "Chiaia: Dead and Restless" ("Chiaia morta e inquieta"). The title sounds perplexing, at least at the beginning, as the *dead and restless* Riviera di Chiaia had been the focus of the first section, while the present one begins with the appearance, at the center of the previously empty living room, of the person the narrator has come to visit. The interaction between the two will be complex, and, as usual in this story, the narrator's gaze will play a pivotal role. The scene can be divided into three parts based on the "states" of Compagnone in relation to the Neapolitan reality—that is, allegorically, his variable degrees of servitude toward his master Nature. First of all, the apartment, described in great detail, is pictured as a sinister place where life and death are strangely intertwined. Upon entering, she immediately feels "a horrifying atmosphere of cellars and graveyards"[4] (132); and yet, immediately after, we learn that Compagnone lives there with his wife and their infant child—a place where human life seems to be ending also harbors its beginning. He himself seems to be existing in the same paradoxical terms. When she first notices him, he shows signs of liveliness and intelligence: "His thin face bowed . . . looking at the door in bewilderment . . . he had recognized and observed me"[5] (131–32). Yet the vital energy expressed in such recognition of the old friend long absent is immediately contrasted by an opposite message: "Nothing, absolutely nothing, indicated the least interest or pleasure"[6] (132). Then comes a bizarre simile to explain this state: "A deadly coldness—the coldness of those who, rather than flee the world, watch it shrink and fade, and, turned to stone, do not dare to raise even a lament"[7] (132).

All this considered, Compagnone's presentation evidently recalls, at the abstract level, the opposition between vitality and dying, the inchoative movement of attention toward the novelty (signaled at the figurative level by the inclination of the head and the spark of recognition), and the terminative fading of any emotion, compared to the situation of a being progressively turning to stone, so scared that the whole world seems to fade. It is evident at this point that Compagnone mirrors the Riviera di Chiaia as presented in the first section of the story. That street, taken as a figuration of the Neapolitan reality tout court, had been defined by proposing—and then negating—terms connected to inchoative, energetic movement together with others recalling terminative movement bordering on immobility. We had seen how, at the abstract level (figure 3.2), they were linked to ideas of vitality (intended as an expanding impulse) and dying respectively (intended as a diminishing effort approaching its own ending). The final image used to picture this double negation had been the smile on the face of the dead, repeated, with variations, three times in a few pages: "That expressive, ambiguous smile that appears on the faces of the dead" (104). Not by chance then, immediately after Compagnone's initial description we have read above, the narrator continues: "A smile crossed that face, which was more detached and dead than that of Chiaia"[8] (132). Indeed, Compagnone coincides here with the neutral term of the square where we represented Neapolitan reality (figure 3.2), the final definition of the city as being neither alive nor dead. This state perfectly fits the sleeping spell performed by Nature, which, in the previous section, was told to keep her children in the state of "sleepwalker[s]" (123) ("sonnambul[i]" 117). We also need to recall that Compagnone had been, during the years of the journal *Sud*, the more representative person of the city's brief period of hope, described in the historical excursus in the first section, when Neapolitan reality had briefly coincided with a meaningful—although tragic—activity open to hope and possibility. Like Naples itself, he seems indeed to have decayed into an abyss of meaninglessness.

At this point we can ask what is the object that scares Compagnone so much as to make his world vanish. " 'Please, come in,' he said, continuing to smile in *that way*, his gaze everywhere but on me, as he held out a sweaty hand"[9] (132). The narrator immediately realizes that she herself is the origin of such a fright, or, more precisely, she understands that it is *her gaze* that frightens him so much. Hence, a complex series of movements in the room begins, as she is taken by a sort of pity and attempts not to include him in her visual field: "I sat down near the large table, and I thought I shouldn't look at him, so I turned my back"[10] (132). While not looking at him, she describes the feeling of his presence in terms that confirm his position in the neutral term of the square: "I couldn't see him but I felt him . . . it was as if behind my back there were an abyss, a chasm full of hands clapping, which created a desolate sound, an endless sigh"[11] (132). In other words, his existence is a privation of life, an abyss, a void (she also says, immediately before, "an absence") that is nevertheless alive, but a life that is pointless agitation, like hands clapping in the dark for no reason, producing a sound that should be full of energy and yet contains the desperation of a sigh with no end. Yet all her efforts not to scare him fail. As noted in the analysis of the first sequence, in the anti-narrative program that runs under the surface of the story the narrator, as an avatar of Reason herself, has come to judge her old comrades, to sanction their treason, their abandonment of the struggle to change Naples, their passing on the side of Nature in exchange for peace and bourgeois stability: "I thought it would be best to minimize my thoughts and my energy, to banish from my mind, or at least relegate to a tiny corner, *any words* related to the living world, which could only upset him. I would calm him by showing him that, owing to life's exigencies, I, too, had been intellectually humiliated and conquered"[12] (133). If we translate the original Italian more closely, those "words" the narrator wants to "banish" from her mind become "those voices" ("quelle voci"), which directly recall "the cool, gentle voices of human reason" (122) ("le voci dolci e fredde della ragione umana" 117) she had earlier mentioned as the only counter spell able to destroy Nature and its enchantments, which confirms once more her role as an avatar of Reason. When she finally looks at him directly ("I . . . cautiously turned to look at him"[13] 134), everything dramatically changes, and he is not the sleepwalker anymore, neither alive nor dead, forgetful of his own failure and of the desperation of his present situation. The sleeping spell momentarily breaks, and Reason's sanction, coinciding here with the narrator's gaze, is being pronounced, or at least felt by the one who is being judged:

> Although it seemed impossible, in just a few minutes something had drastically changed in him. The statue who had opened the door to me was now alive and trembling. It was as if he were seeing something of enormous magnitude right in front of him. . . . He was behaving just like a child who sees a tiger in his room, or a huge spider on his rocking horse, but, for some deep reason (an even greater terror, perhaps), he *can't* reveal that he has seen the object of his fear.[14] (134–35)

This return to life also alters the terms of their conversation. In the previous phase of their encounter, when she had declared the purpose of her visit—to collect information about the Neapolitan writers—and asked for his help, he had replied with indifference; however, she had noticed a reaction contradicting such an impression and that could in fact explain it with resentment and envy: "In the mirror, I saw his thin, sweating face quiver and his eyes open greedily, like someone who sees something glitter in front of him"[15] (133). In other words, consequently to his role as a servant of Nature, and corrupted by the search for success and social stability, he is greedy for literary fame—which however he is unable to achieve, unlike some former companions of the same lost endeavor (this, *au fond*, is the root of his desperation). Yet not surprisingly, once he is brought back to life by the narrator's gaze, once he momentarily escapes the spell of Nature, he seems to realize the abjection of his situation. Sure, he is at this point beyond salvation, and behaves "as if . . . he were hearing the sound of bells coming up from the floor"[16] (135), as if he were now inhabiting a different world, an upside-down dimension (another figure of the perversion of Reason perhaps, like Naples' lights coming from the bottom of the sea at the end of the story). Yet despite his fear and even his hatred for having been forced to see and know his real condition, he does not only declare himself incapable of helping the narrator (which is already a profession of humility for someone who had been described as the center of the cultural world of the youth of Naples), but he even refuses to give her information about himself, genuinely showing astonishment at the fact that she would like to include him in the article. This surely sounds like a form of atonement. But Nature does not so easily allow her "son" to escape the enchantment. Something happens that brings him back to his initial state of living dead. His wife Anita enters, greets the guest, inquires about the reason of her visit, and immediately urges her husband to help with the article, and the narrator to write about *him* too, adding that he had started to write a novel. She plainly shows frustration at his lack of effort to reach success in his profession ("He doesn't know how to promote himself. . . . He cares nothing for money, as if he didn't have a family. And he writes no worse than others"[17] 136). Essentially, she reminds him of the reasons for which he had forsaken the "camp" of Reason in the first place, lying bare the bildungsroman paradigm that the young intellectuals of the *Sud* group, like any new generation from the middle class, were supposed to follow: from the radical excess of youth to bourgeois respectability, from idealism and "bohemian" poverty to pragmatism and financial stability.[18] Moreover, a careful analysis of the way her character is sketched shows an evident connection to the allegory of Nature—of this Nature that is nothing else than a perverted Reason—in terms similar to those used for the noseless woman on the tram, Nature's first human avatar in the story. Like this latter, Anita is marked by simultaneous signs of death and motherhood:[19] When she enters the room, the narrator immediately notes that she must have left the child in the other room, and she soon leaves when the screams of the child call her back. But there is also something directly inscribed on her face, like the skull-like scare of the noseless woman: "She had about her a look of calm that revealed neither mirth nor thought. Her hair was so thin you could see her cranium"[20] (135; translation modified). Absence of thought and of joy, the image of the skull looming through: Nature has emerged from the bottom of the crypt to reclaim her servant. As she exits, Compagnone mutates again, and his momentary return to the laceration of life and intelligence fades: "Something had shattered inside him, the anxiety of a moment before had fractured, and silence had returned to dominate his memory. Even my presence had ceased to disturb him; he had become perfectly indifferent"[21] (137).

Yet indifference is not sufficient protection, not for the mechanism the story has put in motion. Like the poor kids in the Villa Comunale who had assailed the tram's passengers with their own image, a group of ragged, barefoot children now makes its presence felt in the street outside of the house, and this leads to the scene we have analyzed in the introduction, where the city's ideological infrastructure is brought to visibility by the girl's spit, and the "original emotion" of this story is located on the imaginary organic matter landed on the head of the bourgeois intellectual. What remains to be said about this scene, in light of the textual analysis of chapter 3, is that the vivid and detailed description that precedes it, borders on the optical unconscious we have discussed and produces what in rhetorical terms is known as hypotyposis, in particular when it focuses on the seven-year-old girl who leads the group, who had "her head closely cropped, and [was] wearing a gray rag that, leaving her chest bare, came down to her feet in the manner of a lady"[22] (139; translation modified). The figurative level of the text is here evidently connected with a thematic isotopy pointing to deprivation of childhood, insisting on the forced adulthood of street kids, which, as we saw in chapter 1, is one of the main topoi connected with the representation of the horrors of the war in Naples. The vividness of the description once again forces the reader to accept the point of view of an observer who is no longer separate from the scene (like, theoretically, the diegetic narrator).

The resulting emotional intensity seems to be even thematized by the kids, who, "as they walked, and begged, they let out cries of laughter, their pleas at once clownish and desolate, as they paraphrased in dialect one of the many hymns to the Virgin: Heavenly Virgin / have pity on us . . . and they emphasized the word *pity* by doubling over with laughter every time they said it"[23] (139). Despite the playful appearance—which nevertheless is kept in connection to the said abstract isotopy by the presence of terms like "desolate"—the children insist on the word "pity," which directly asks for emotional participation, while also mocking it with their laughter. As we have seen, Compagnone refuses to engage in any compassion and immediately shields himself behind the screen of the "picturesque," calling the narrator to the window to participate in the appreciation for the colorful scene ("So colorful, so perfect"). Thus the object is neutralized at the core of plain visibility, and suffering becomes a pictorial motive, an occasion for aesthetic enjoyment. When, however, the feared contact between classes happens, and Compagnone irrationally starts fearing that the girl's spit may have somehow reached his head, what we have identified as the "original emotion" immediately spreads as a wave of anxiety that will affect the entire story, and will be rearticulated in all subsequent episodes: "His voice was a combination of infinite patience and infinite terror, as he struggled to achieve a calm that was completely unnatural 'Is there something . . . something wet?' "[24] (140). This anxiety does not have a clearly defined content—as History itself, the totality of material relations, is never fully representable, "at the same time that it is omnipresent and inescapable" (Jameson 2009b, 341). Therefore, Compagnone's dismay evokes the questioning of the naturalness of the structure that keeps him safe: The "infinite patience" deriving from the trust in the solidity of the social structure gets fractured by the "infinite terror" at glimpsing the possibility that that same structure might not hold, that the children of the lumpenproletariat might be free to spit on the head of bourgeois intellectuals. We also need to recall that the text might here point to something we know from letters and witnesses of the time, that is, like the seven-year-old girl, many times Ortese had come to this door to beg for food or money.[25] And we will see how this allusion will be repeated several times throughout the story. In this case, as Compagnone realizes the obvious complicity—this is the hidden contradiction associated with the "original emotion"—between the narrator and the lumpenproletariat outside his window, he unkindly sends her away: "Now go away. Go away" (140) ("Ora vattene, vattene" 133).

Once outside, the narrator literally runs away into the descending night. She traverses the Riviera di Chiaia backward, this time on foot, and again meets the crowd of the poor. The description sequence that follows—which starts with visual elements and culminates with a focus on sounds, in accordance with the advancing night and the fading of visibility—confirms and completes the similar description from which the story had started: "It was the hour when Naples lights up and swells like a jellyfish, and the city's wounds shine, and its rags are covered with flowers, and the people reel"[26] (141). While the comparison with the jellyfish marks a metamorphosis of the classic siren, which nevertheless preserves the dangerous trait, and the reference to wounds and rags accentuates the impression of hurt and misery, the reeling people display a collective action that encompasses both poles of activities earlier assigned to this crowd, that is, the essential and the meaningless, as the act of *stumbling* expresses both a basic human action (walking), and the uncontrollable, eccentric movement produced by lack of bodily control. This same coalescence of movement and pointless dispersion of energy is confirmed by the next notation: "In the streets there was a sensation of movement and excitement, which on closer examination was nothing"[27] (141). Before delving into a more detailed description of singular beings, which will raise the tone and emotional intensity of the meditation, the narrator contrasts her own role of observer (and therefore the point of view offered to the reader) with a different cognitive subject, that is, "the bourgeoisie and the aristocrats, who displayed no irritation or disgust" at the appearance of the poor overflowing the main street from the allays, "because they didn't even notice them"[28] (141). Such ideological blindness is shuttered by a series of images introduced by the anaphoric repetition of the indefinite pronoun "chi" (the translation preserves the repetition but loses some of its rhythmic intensity): "Some fanned themselves with a piece of cardboard, others slept on the sidewalks with their mouths open, some ate, some sang sad lullabies. In the rooms, next to the beds, some were cooking, and some, at times even young men, lay on the beds thinking"[29] (141). We see here a series of essential human activities, which, like in the crowd description from the first section analyzed in chapter 3, are attracted toward the sphere of the meaningless agitation because of their flashing nature, their mere juxtaposition: "Everything was chaos and dark fascination"[30] (141). Not by chance, the closing of the passage ends on a restless, non-conscious movement: "You would not have said that they were awake, but rather that they were moving about restlessly in a bad dream"[31] (142). Also noteworthy is the return of the metanarrative negation. As we have seen in the first sequence, by pointing to the separate dimension of the enunciation, it signals the rising of an intolerable anxiety that forces the narrator to step back from the present of the mimesis; in this case, despite the movement of pulling back, the use of the second person seems to attract more closely readers in the presence of the object, as if to place them in direct contradiction with the indifferent—blind—upper-class crowd.

The final part of the passage keeps raising the emotional tone through the thickness of its rhetorical fabric, thus producing a climactic effect culminating in the description of the noise in which the city seems to drown itself in order not to feel its misery, sealed with a triple negation "that noise . . . was not happy or serene or good,"[32] and a further specification composed of three more elements: "A horrible silence lay beneath it, a paralyzed memory, and a frenzy of hope"[33] (142). This final consideration on the hidden nature of the soundscape seems to negate the two temporal ecstasies on which properly human experience is based, as the past fades within the paralysis of memory and the future is blurred in the chaotic agitation of hope (again a pointless movement). Thus, the experience of the lumpenproletariat is once more suggested as a superimposition of vital actions and pointless agitation, where the essential and the meaningless collapse on each other in what here feels like an eternal present with no past or future, no memory, or hope, which coincides with the neutral term of the semiotic square of human activities inside the social reality of Naples (figure 4.1), which can be updated as follows.

Figure 4.1. The experience of the lumpenproletariat in "The Silence of Reason." *Source:* Created by the author.

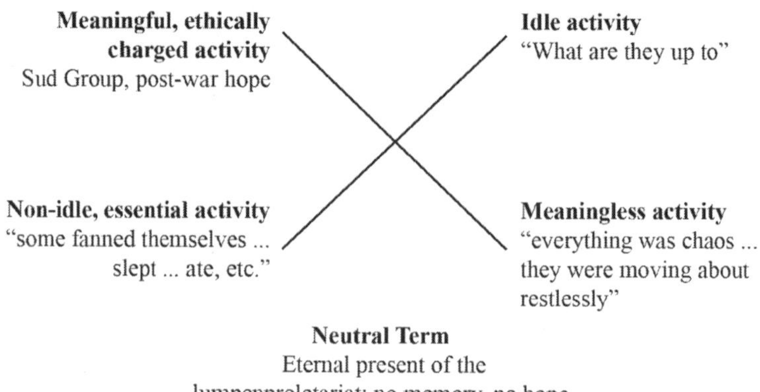

It is no coincidence that, as in the first sequence, this organization of human activities corresponds, at a more abstract level, to that in which vitality and dying oppose each other (figure 3.2). Thus, the experience of the crowd of the poor coincides with the image of the smiling dead, where meaning approaches its own abolition. What is striking is that, as we have noticed, in that same position the text had placed Compagnone too, whose smile, "dead and restless," mirrors—in a figurative sense—that of all Chiaia. This shows that, in the allegorical structure of the story, the intellectual who has abandoned the political struggle, and thus abandoned the poor to their destiny, has been punished by being relegated to the same dimension of meaninglessness, to the same eternal present made of "chaos and dark fascination." This is further confirmed by the fact that the first image of the crowd in the passage we have analyzed was one of stumbling ("and the people reel"), and this same gesture introduced the figure of Compagnone, which the narrator had imagined, in a sort of hallucination, once she had stepped out of the tram, "with his usual unhurried, slightly weary, limping gait"[34] (109).

The Stage

Throughout the story, the crowd of the poor's emergence into visibility is presented at first as an event with no spectators, except for the *one* spectator who is the narrator herself, who, in some episodes, seems to *incite*, by her mere presence, a coming forward of some individuals from that crowd, who demonstrate in these cases their own will to be seen, like the kids who ran after the tram and the young girl outside of Compagnone's house. They thus also become visible to other onlookers, which leads to a dramatic climax. More similar episodes are to come, in which, as we will see, such "coming forward" will assume the form of a stepping onto a stage, as if, at the structural level of the story, the crowd-entity, on its own quest for recognition—and in parallel with the anti-narrative program, which seeks contemplation of this same entity—would be constantly emboldened to access a wider form of visibility. The meaning of the coincidence of the specular movements of contemplation and self-disclosure is obviously linked to the central contradiction of the story, from which we saw the "original emotion" emerge. Indeed, the narrator's "staging" of the plebeian existence, despite the purported astonishment of the foreigner, must be linked to the social standpoint expressed by the literary gesture. If the text is able to communicate a precise experience with its own temporality, thus escaping the filter of the picturesque, which neutralizes the visibility of the object in its full exposure, it is because at its root lies the sharing of that same existential condition—this is why the girl who spat and the narrator are presented as doubles, fundamentally performing the same gesture of intrusion and "sanction." Precisely here we must locate the connection between writing and hunger, from which this analysis started. That experience, accompanied by homelessness, exhaustion, and the resulting humiliation, neutralized, for long periods, any class difference between Ortese and the mass of the urban poor, as she was forced to endure that same "eternal present" we have seen emerging at the core of the existence of the underclass, where meaning is abolished in the coincidence of pointless dispersion of energy and vital gestures of survival. In that existence the temporal ecstasies toward future and past fade, and this is exactly the point where hunger incessantly drives one back, to that inner—material—void that absorbs all energy, all thoughts. This specific temporality, lived in everydayness as itself a form of systemic traumatization, enters aesthetic expression not as a decodified-recodified object of knowledge, but precisely as those "alogical essences" or ideas that Merleau-Ponty linked to Husserl's operative intentionality, the pre-personal and anonymous bodily openness onto the world (Merleau-Ponty 2005, 113, 410–11). Through this dimension the individual is connected with the totality of the social order, where the "irrepresentable" of history is somehow present in "the thickness of the pre-objective present, where we find our corporeality, our sociality, and the preexistence of the world" (Merleau-Ponty

2012, 457). However, if the expression of the existence of the lumpenproletariat, of its habitus, is the historical content readers might access through
these pages, not as rational knowledge, and not as "just the statistical and
common aspects of the world, but [as] its very manner of touching and
inserting itself into the individual's experience" (Merleau-Ponty 1970, 24),
traces of the narrator's belonging to that same wretched dimension are dis-
seminated throughout the text, which is continuously fractured by signs of
anxiety manifesting this hidden dimension below the surface of the story
and its apparent narrative program, its task-oriented temporality.

At the thematic level, this belonging of the narrator to the infernal
existence of the underclass is made evident by references to hunger itself,
to her traumatic need to rely on friends and acquaintances to provide for
material sustenance. This becomes especially evident in the fourth section
of the story, where she visits the apartment of the writer Rea. When she
arrives, she suddenly realizes that it is lunch time: "I had the feeling that
the family was having lunch and that my visit would be awkward. I even
wondered if I should come back later"[35] (149). Indeed, she finds Rea, his
wife Annamaria, and the writer Pratolini about to start lunch, and she
(awkwardly[36]) joins them. This reminds us that when she had arrived at
Compagnone's house it was dinner time, and this was probably the reason
why nobody opened the door for a while; and even when Compagnone
finally joined her in the living room, his wife was in the kitchen giving
dinner to their son. In short, the hours she chooses for her visits adumbrate
an old habit, an old anxiety, forced by necessity, of relying on friends for
daily meals. This is further demonstrated by the uncomfortable reactions of
her friends at seeing her. Rea's is particularly meaningful: " 'You are here.'
He said, with the same coldness as Compagnone, *concealing his alarm*. And
he continued to stare at me without smiling"[37] (150). Not coincidentally,
her last meaningful encounter, the one with Franco Grassi, who will lead
her to the Caffè Gambrinus when they will meet Prunas and Gaedkens, will
involve her friend buying her a coffee. In other words, again, here, behind
the surface of a linear, task-oriented time (visiting people to interview), we
witness the emergence of a different, circular temporality revolving around
the dark seed of hunger, organizing daily routine around the satisfaction
of the most basic of needs, while everything else is a pointless dispersion
of energy.

The encounter with Rea will be substantially different from the one
with Compagnone, as these two figures play different roles in the structure
of the story. Rea is not framed as one of the Neapolitan intellectuals who

had first attempted to work progressively to change society, only to betray this juvenile radicalism later; he is an emerging writer who had recently won an important literary prize, and, in his short stories, has never problematized the structural injustice of the Neapolitan reality. In the narrator's view, his Neapolitan characters do not escape the picturesque, and in his pages the tragic effects of poverty and oppression are blurred by stereotypes; in fact, she summarizes Rea's work as the "resurrection of the Neapolitan myth"[38] (128). Indeed, in the story Rea claims to be part of the "people": "I love the people. I, in fact, am the people"[39] (153). Although the narrator seems to agree (141, 151),[40] in her opinion Rea appears to be somebody who, coming from the lower class—however, his social origin is in the provincial working class and not in the urban popular classes—has betrayed his own class, and is actually profiting from depicting its conditions in accordance with the usual stereotypes, which, not by chance, are very much appreciated by the public. Therefore, at the structural level of the story, Rea does not share the role of the other intellectuals, and the sanction the narrator performs on him is due to a different kind of betrayal. Indeed, he seems to *mimic*, from his privileged position, the role played by the underclass throughout the story—that is, exposing themselves, seeking visibility and recognition. He will profit from the narrator and the other guest's visit to literally perform, to stage his "plebeian" existence. Although in a perverted and fetishized form, his "performance" will coincide with the other form of the coming forward of the underclass we will witness in the central part of the story: not anymore as the pushing against a protective screen (the tram's windows, Compagnone's door-window), but as a form of representation, enacted from a place able to function like a stage. This enhanced form of visibility is meant to break through the usual device of ideological concealment to which these people are subjected: The stage, as a space of presentation, includes both concealment and un-concealment, thus, like the visibility of the screen within vision itself, points to the structural mechanism of exclusion and problematizes it. Not by chance, on her way to Rea's house, the narrator meets a first form of such a representation, at the same time recalling what had happened at Compagnone's house and anticipating events yet to come.

As she is walking among apartment buildings, "from a balcony, a woman called out to a younger woman dressed in yellow and red who was hanging out laundry in the garden. She responded, almost singing, 'I'll be right up.' After a moment, from the balcony, the woman shouted back unexpectedly and in dialect: 'Here's hoping you spit blood.' I looked at the woman who had tossed off this omen and she was calm and collected"[41] (148). The sudden and gratuitous nature of this curse, together with the immediately regained calm of the woman, which makes it seem almost unreal, reveals an underground stream of violence bursting above the surface, and, with its sudden disappearance, points to the precarity of the apparent calm. That this episode should be linked to the one of the girl's "assault" on Compagnone's window is suggested not only by the comparable gratuitous and unexpected modality of the gesture (again referring to a release of organic matter), but also by the notation that immediately follows: "I saw a row of white balconies with clotheslines strung between them, as I'd seen at Luigi's, and hanging from them were socks and underwear. A drop of water, which was not rain, fell on my hand"[42] (148–49). Besides the explicit reference to Compagnone himself ("Luigi"), the water drop falling on the narrator's hand directly recalls the event that had closed that first episode, signaling the pressure of the "original emotion" almost stalking the narrator throughout the narrative diegesis. Thus it does not come as a surprise when, at the peak of a conversation over lunch, the reference to that wet drop returns once again as Rea expresses all his contempt for Compagnone and states, "I spit on a man like that"[43] (153). If in this last case the recurrence of this gesture seems to signal Rea as yet another manifestation of the coming forward of the underclass toward visibility, sanctioning Compagnone's betrayal of the progressive cause, Rea's self-representation only stages a fetishized plebeian experience, in which he attempts to identify himself with his own literary representation of Naples. However, the pressure of the "original emotion," obsessively rearticulated in the narrative structure of the episode, should alert us that Rea's role might be directly linked to the main ideological contradiction around which the story is built. He appears indeed as the specular opposite of the narrator, her inverted double: He pretends to belong to the underclass while being at this point a (relatively) wealthy, middle-class intellectual. The narrator, on the contrary, while presenting herself in turn as an intellectual astonished by the city's poverty, secretly coincides with the lumpenproletariat. This peculiar position occupied by Rea is confirmed by signs that characterize him as a further avatar of Nature, that is, in the allegorical structure of the story, of perverted Reason. Indeed, his path to personal success has been the use of literary expression not to reveal the conditions of misery of the lower classes from which he came, but to produce one more contribution to the orientalizing discourse that has been growing around the city for centuries, that is, the exact opposite of the political program of the *Sud* group. Moreover, as in the first sequence the presence of Nature had been signaled by the light coming from the perverted sun (lighting up the noseless woman and the headless statues in the park), at the peak of his performance Rea appears in turn illuminated by a kind of inverted light, coming from below: "Suddenly the young man became wildly cheerful. His small pockmarked face lit up like the stones of Naples, when, in the night sky, fireworks explode, first in silence, and then with whistles and loud bangs"[44] (156). It is important to note that the rhetorical sophistication (through the use of a hyperbaton) of the Italian sentence creates a peculiarly powerful effect not possible to replicate in translation, since, until the appearance of the grammatical subject at the end (the fireworks) clarifies the meaning, the reader of the original text expects the stones to be the subject rising toward the sky, which implies something like a volcanic eruption. Nevertheless, the force of this image, abruptly corrected by the more ordinary one of the fireworks, is preserved in the reflections flashing on the stones, which will return in the light reflected by shells from the bottom of the sea in the final lines of the story.

Finally, Rea's mystifying attempt to present himself as being part of the "people" inaugurates the central topic of the next section of the story, where the lower classes' own attempts at self-representation will be absorbed and neutralized by the mystification promoted by the upper classes' dominant discourse. The section's title, "Literal Translation: 'What Is the Meaning of this Night?,'"[45] has a complex structure, hinting at the people's interrogation about the meaning of their condition and at the translation of this interrogation into a comprehensible discourse. The term "translation" refers here to both the passage from dialect to standard Italian and to the one from the obscurity of everydayness to literary expression. As we will see, the question posed in the title is the translation from the dialect of the desperate exclamation of the mother of a young suicidal woman, who thus tries to make sense of the obscurity that has fallen around her despite the clear light of the day. Yet before arriving at the place where the suicide has happened, the narrator relates her bus trip from the Vomero to Via Roma, as she reflects on the possibility of meeting the writers Prisco and La Capria for her interviews, whom she "knew well"[46] (162), but she dismisses this possibility; the first she considers not to be appropriate if one is looking for truth (150, 162), and the other "did not seem relevant for an identification of Naples"[47] (162–63; translation modified). In both cases the issue is their belonging to the middle-upper class—that is, their substantial foreignness to the reality of the urban underclass. This is an important passage, since it quietly signals that the narrative program of the story has officially changed, from "idle" interviews of young writers ("What are they up to") to a "tragic" compulsion to investigate the truth of Naples, that is, from the narrative program mandated by a perverted Reason (whose first avatar is the illustrated weekly magazine for which the narrator has to write an article) to the anti-narrative program mandated by Reason. This reflection culminates in another vision, or hallucination ("I told myself that I had been hallucinating"[48] 163): From the bus window the narrator sees, through a building's window (yet another example of the multiplication of devices of vision and concealment), Gianni Gaedkens, "one of the most renowned members of the *Sud* group" (163), whom she considers to embody in a more authentic way the contradictions of Naples. "I was looking for something that was Naples, Vesuvius and the counter-Vesuvius, the mystery and the hatred of mystery"[49] (163). Indeed, Gaedkens's special status in the structure of the narration is demonstrated by the fact that he is the only character whose name has been fictionalized, at least partly: Gaedkens was his mother's surname (Clerici 2002, 258), while his real name was Scognamiglio. This tactful, special consideration probably expresses a sense of closeness deriving from a long friendship and a similarity of existential conditions, since, like Ortese, Scognamiglio led a miserable existence in those years, troubled by poverty and unemployment,[50] and for several months in 1951, Ortese shared an apartment with him and his wife in Rome—"days of hunger," according to Clerici (2002, 198–99). Moreover, it is possible (Clerici 2002, 239) that the very title "Il mare non bagna Napoli" was inspired by a poem Scognamiglio published in the same issue and page of *Sud* where Ortese's story "Suffering Splendor of the Alley" ("Dolente splendore del vicolo" 1946) appeared: "I am forever leaving this city / where the sea has disappeared."[51] Thus, unsure whether she has really seen him, the narrator gets off the bus in Via Roma (today Via Toledo) with the purpose of seeing Prunas to ask for information about Gaedkens, whom she knows has moved to Milan to look for a job.

The spectacle of the crowd of the poor here is structured similarly to the one she observed the night before in Chiaia, as we find all the elements used for that description. It is introduced by relating an impression of a frantic movement that is proved to be nothing upon closer inspection: "Here too, there was a great commotion, a feeling of extraordinary excitement . . . but then drawing nearer I saw it was nothing"[52] (164)—a situation that recalls the superimposition of vital movement and pointless dispersion of energy that marks the underclass' existence. Subsequently, the ideological blindness of the bourgeois is signaled: "There was no acknowledgment of the presence of these lower classes on the faces of the bourgeoisie"[53]

(164). Finally, as if to pierce through this protective barrier, the detailed description raises the emotional tone through rhetorical intensification, from the combination of the negative construction of sentences with the hyperbolic use of numbers ("It wasn't just two or three old mothers . . . there were a hundred, two hundred. There weren't five or six men with concave chests and shifty eyes . . . but at least a thousand"[54] [164]), to the abrupt juxtaposition of trivial images ("scratch their heads, dragging a lame foot"[55] 164) with the high tone of a clause like "eyes dulled by memories"[56] (164). Moreover, while a simulacrum of the reader is directly called to coincide with the actantial role of the observer, which, at the surface level, emerges as an observer-participant in a series of hypotheses about the possibility of seeing certain things, surprisingly a plural of courtesy is used (the "voi"), which is completely out of place in a context like this, where one would expect either the informal singular or the ordinary plural (obviously this is not reproducible in translation): "If you had been looking for . . . you would have been abundantly satisfied. . . . If then you had the desire to find . . . you would have been terrified"[57] (164–65). Thus, this sort of rhetorical contortion draws our attention back to the instance of enunciation, as if an excess of anxiety had forced the enunciator to momentarily destroy the diegetic mimesis—something similar to what had happened, in the first section, with the insistent use of the negation and the directing function. One important element of novelty differentiates this crowd description from the previous one in Chiaia, though, as the crowd's will to perform their own visibility follows the pattern opened by the woman who had violently cursed another from a balcony before the visit at Rea's, taking advantage of an elevated device of visibility and concealment like a building's window—a "stage"—to escape the invisibility of exposure, to reveal itself while at the same time making the device of visibility and concealment visible: "The faceless throng filled up that marvelous street and poured in from the surrounding alleys *and looked out all the windows*"[58] (164; my emphasis).

Immediately after the description, at the peak of emotional intensity, an allegorical meditation follows, the device used by the narrator to channel the pathos of her text toward a rational reflection on the historical conditions of Naples based on the use of cosmic figures like Nature and Reason. In this case, since the object of the meditation is the ideological blindness of the bourgeoisie, she proposes a hypothesis about the mythical origin of the two classes: "Either the people [plebe] had, like the volcano, opened up and vomited forth these more refined people, who, just like something *natural*, cannot see something else that is *natural*"[59] (165). This is immediately negated, however, by the materialist observation that the upper class's blindness is due to the will to preserve its own condition of privilege, which could be put at risk by any change in the social structure: "Or this category of humans, which was, by the way, rather limited, had, in order to save themselves, renounced the ability to see the common people [plebe] as living beings who were a part of themselves"[60] (165).

The second part of the episode focuses on a suicide completed from a balcony—a stage, again—and is the occasion to "sanction" the Neapolitan journalists, pictured in a sort of collective fresco. The guiding figure here is Franco Grassi, a journalist and an aspiring writer, who calls the narrator from a building window and is probably the only character in the story to show her real kindness. While she waits for him to descend, she notices a little crowd in front of a building entrance, from which "a loud weeping" could be heard. "Something had actually happened here" (165), she observes, a notation that sharply contrasts with the usual formula that precedes the descriptions we have examined of the crowd of the poor, where a first impression of something meaningful going on is contrasted by the conclusion that nothing has actually happened. She can only see a "bright red stain surrounded by other, smaller stains"[61] (165–66). An eighteen-year-old housemaid has completed suicide by throwing herself off the balcony,[62] and the chatter of the crowd immediately relates three different versions of the story: The girl's reasons to complete the tragic gesture vary from the plausible mistreatment by her mistress to the most incredible political motivations (the nostalgia for the exiled king of Italy). In sum, the simultaneous disappearance of the girl's body (only a stain of blood remains) and of the motivations of her gesture testify, again, to the ruthless presence of a device of invisibility that contrasts all the attempts of the underclass to "come forward," from the most playful to the most tragic. These attempts have always involved the presence of windows or balconies, used as both barriers and devices of visibility. While previous cases, from the seven-year-old girl to the generic "formless face" of the crowd looking through the windows, had focused on the visual aspects of the device of concealment, the suicide of the housemaid directs our attention to the verbal, discursive power of the ideological machine. As the people's chatter immediately erases any possibility to understand the girl's gesture and the material conditions that provoked it, it adumbrates the journalistic discourse on which the narrator focuses immediately after, as she introduces the journalistic milieu of Naples, including Grassi himself. This latter looks perfectly indifferent to what has just happened and prefers to talk about a novel he is writing.

However, as we learn soon after, he will have to write an article about the event. This lack of interest for the object of his work, this incapacity for emotional participation from the very person whose job consists in the "official" storytelling of the event, demonstrates the direct involvement of the city's intellectual professions in the machine that perpetuates privilege and oppression. Only the stain of blood, yet another articulation of the "original emotion," remains to signal the physical presence of the routine violence that the discourse constantly erases.

As Grassi and the narrator walk together in front of a building where many local journals have their editorial office, she has a vision in which many of the Neapolitan journalists of the time are visualized in a sort of diorama, "one of the many hallucinatory moments of Naples,"[63] which, with its effect of unreality, forces her "to look for the director of this exquisite work"[64] (170), as if everyone had been part of a theatrical mise en scène. Just as Compagnone had paid for his betrayal of the progressive political cause by being absorbed into the same meaninglessness of the existence of the underclass (his "dead and restless" smile is the same of Chiaia), so the journalists seem to be destined to the same fate they are preparing for the girl who has taken her own life: to disappear into the unreality of chatter, absorbed in a darkness where the light of reason cannot reach them, the "meaningless night" interrogated by the mother of the girl who had dared to ask "Why isn't it daytime? What is the meaning of this night?"[65] (167).

The Glass Coffin

As the narrator enters the Caffè Gambrinus with Grassi, the last section of the story starts: "The Boy from Monte di Dio" ("Il ragazzo di Monte di Dio"). The title immediately presents us with two enigmatic elements we will meet in the final pages: the "boy"—not the man or the young man—who will soon be revealed to be Pasquale Prunas (he has already been defined as "boy"—"ragazzo"—in several occasions throughout the story), and Monte di Dio, which is of course a neighborhood in Naples, where they will walk during this last encounter. However it also means, in Italian, "Mountain of God," thus evoking a solemn atmosphere that marks the climax of the allegorical structure of the story. The man she was looking for, Gaedkens, is there with Prunas, so she will have the possibility of meeting the final two people she had thought of, not for the original interviews but for this new and mysterious quest for the truth of Naples, in which *Sud*'s program continues and its old members are judged. The difference between the two men and the other she has previously met is already signaled by their gesture of greeting, as when they shake hands, theirs are "dry and a little cold, not sweating like Luigi's, or burning like Rea's"[66] (175). This element is not in itself immediately meaningful: the final two comrades from the *Sud* group are certainly different, but of what does this difference consist? The whole final section of the story is about explaining this difference, formulating a judgment, the sanction of Reason.

Prunas's story had already been told together with that of the journal *Sud* in the section devoted to Compagnone. In those pages he had been defined as somebody who, despite not being a Neapolitan himself (he was from Sardinia), was genuinely engaged in the political cause of changing the terrible conditions of the postwar city. Unlike everyone else, he was not interested in his own career, in personal success. Moreover, although a leftist, his liberal ideas about the independence of culture were at odds with the Stalinism of the Communist Party of the time, which left him isolated among the intellectual milieu of the city once the *Sud* group had dissolved. However, although he clearly did not betray *Sud's* political agenda, he seems to nevertheless expect and anticipate the narrator's sanction, as she reads, in his sorrowful gaze, a silent plea: " 'You must have pity,' said those dull eyes. 'You must try not to look. Is it true that we are dead?' he asked. 'Is it true that we've been absorbed by the city and now are at peace?' "[67] (176). And later, while they are taking a walk in via Chiaia:[68] "Reason's friend hated me, because of the memories I brought back in him, because of the mirror I held up to him"[69] (177). Yet the definition of "friend of Reason" already signals that this judgment will not be negative; moreover, the elevated lyrical tone of the sentence (enhanced by the isocolon structuring the two subordinates), habitual for the meditations involving the allegorical structure of the story, foreshadows the importance of this issue for the balance of the story. However, the sanction will take a long time to be defined and will ultimately have a dialectical structure.

As is usual in "The Silence," the reflections about Prunas will revolve around the opposition between the abstract isotopies of expanding and declining vitality, with different manifestations at the figurative level. Although the young man is immediately presented as someone who is dangerously close to the dimension of the fading of vitality (his face is "downward tilting . . . thin and quiet, of a brownish yellow"), behind this appearance he shows signs of a strong livelihood: "His lips were animated by an imperceptible smile, full of hostility." In sum, "He seemed dead, dead on his feet," and yet "instead, he was listening"[70] (173). His face is "pale" ("pallido"), but "alert" (176) ("attento," 161). Unlike Compagnone, who, like the whole Riviera di Chiaia, cannot be defined as dead or alive, and ends up being placed in an intermediate condition that negates both—the sleepwalker, the smiling dead, the neutral term where meaning is abolished (figure 3.2)—we find here, in this first stage of the sanction, a clear negation of death and an affirmation of life: "In Naples, the Sardinian youth had immersed himself in misery, but he hadn't died; he was old but not yet dead, because he was unable to conceive of the word death"[71] (178). This preserved vitality is immediately clarified in its political dimension. All the other intellectuals had accepted to become *indifferent* in order to survive ("Everyone was indifferent here, everyone who wished to survive" [168]); and yet, in the allegorical structure of the story, they had all been deceived by Nature, since, through this indifference, they had been absorbed in the perennial sleep, in a crepuscular condition that, paradoxically and despite being far removed from poverty, coincides with that of the underclass: *neither life nor death*. We have seen this for Compagnone, but it ultimately applies to all of them: "All, all of them were sleeping now near the sea, they were sleeping from Torre del Greco to Cuma" (183). This indifference had been reached by renouncing all capacity of emotional participation in the condition of misery once at the center of their political preoccupation: "To become emotional would be like falling asleep in the snow"[72] (168). Now, Prunas's difference lies exactly here: "He was incapable of emotion, of being sad, except at moments, and they were soon forgotten. His thirst for life, his capacity to build life, were both suffocated and immense"[73] (178). His resistance to emotion (again, the term translates *commuoversi*) *except at moments* means that he is actually able to feel the emotional participation in the misery of the people. However, his political instinct and his capability to forget quickly (and to forget himself too) allow him to avoid being completely absorbed in misery, so that he might remain able to "build life." Not by chance, in the afterward written for the Adelphi reedition of the book in 1994, the author will unequivocally define him as a leader, "the boss, the commander"[74] (191). Even here, when she depicts him at the lowest point of his intellectual career, she sometimes refers to him as "the son of the colonel," which points to his father's rank but still confers upon his figure a martial aura of leadership. This difference ultimately offers a possible explanation for—and is in turn clarified by—the frequent use of the apposition "boy" (not young man, or youth, like in the English translation, but "boy," "ragazzo"), which seems at first to be a way to belittle him. In the opening of the first section, he is even compared to a girl: "His shoes were black and small as a girl's, as were his dark hands, and in fact everything about this minute person suggested an adolescent rather than a man"[75] (173); and this same comparison had already appeared at the very first mention of him, "as small in stature as a little girl"[76] (112; translation modified). Indeed, at the figurative level of the story, Prunas's appearance seems to position him on the side of the girls who had collided, in different ways, with the surface of the devices of invisibility (the seven-year-old outside of Compagnone's house and the dead housemaid), rather than with the other men of the group, all of whom had selfishly betrayed the cause of political justice to pursue some form of professional realization. Thus, this perennial adolescence seems to refer to his capacity to participate in both sides of reality, exactly like the narrator: in that of the intellectuals, foreign to the misery of the underclass, and in that very misery, although only in the brief moments of emotional participation ("incapable of emotions . . . except at moments").

At first, Gaedkens, who we must not forget was the one the narrator had decided to look for while leaving Rea's house, seems to be in a similar position to that of Prunas. He resembles "a dying eagle and a flower. He had the same bloodless ferocity and the grace"[77] (174): again, an expansion of vitality, growth, and decay simultaneously. Yet, his importance for the final part of the story will soon fade, as if the narrator will find something terribly disappointing in him. Like Prunas, he has not betrayed the original political cause in exchange for success, and yet, incapable of the same strength as Prunas, of his capacity to "build life," he has succumbed to desperation, embracing indifference, foregoing his own capacity for empathy. He has "the smile of one who will never be surprised by anything again, or suffer or rejoice, except mechanically"[78] (175). Not by chance, while Prunas has been superimposed onto the girls of the story, Gaedkens comments ironically on the girl's suicide: " 'Here they're always killing themselves the same way,' Gaedkens said ironically. 'The balcony. The balconies and the windows of our city don't seem to have any other function' "[79] (175). Hence, it will not be a surprise that he will be absorbed into that same tangle of vital actions and meaningless dispersion of energy that the Neapolitan intellectuals of the story must in the end share with the underclass. In fact, as the four friends start walking, they are all taken into this dimension: "But once in the streets of Naples, you can't help moving in this direction and then that, without any purpose. . . . You walk aimlessly, you talk for no reason, you're silent without motive"[80] (177). However, while the narrator and Prunas will engage in a meaningful dialogue, Gaedkens has completely surrendered to the enchantment of the city: "He was speaking yet his voice resembled silence. It was the voice of someone who loved form . . . not the voice of a man but an echo"[81] (179). The content of his speech is not reported.

The idle walk suddenly stops when they arrive at a place that, contrary to what had been said a few lines earlier, proves their itinerary to have been meaningful after all. It is the former cinema club we met in chapter 1, where the four friends find the ominous "fakir," the hunger artist who seems to have migrated here from Kafka's short story: the final narrative articulation of the itinerary of the original emotion, which repeats here for the last time a pattern that has now become familiar. The hunger artist is briefly glimpsed through a complex device of visibility and concealment, separated from the viewers by multiple screens: "A dark curtain hiding a door to another room. . . . At a certain point, behind the curtain, which remained open for an instant, something clear sparkled, and in that thing—a simple glass coffin—one could see a long form"[82] (181). Although here there is no physical movement of "coming forward," like in the case of the kids in the Villa Comunale, the girl out of Compagnone's house, the woman shouting from the balcony, and the suicidal girl in Via Roma, the theatrical self-exposure of the artist nevertheless manifests the same intention to be seen (also, the definition of the seven-year-old girl as a "sideshow freak" had already anticipated a link between the two figures). Moreover, like in those previous cases, the screen is included in the vision itself, which here assumes the standard mechanism of "revelation" as presented, for instance, in Western art: the opening of a curtain. Finally, what we see inside the glass coffin immediately recalls the by-now habitual image of the smiling dead: "It was a man in black, smiling, who looked around patiently, smoking a cigarette"[83] (181). Yet that figure, which, as we have seen, had come to allegorize the abolition of meaning associated with the crowd of the poor, shared by the intellectuals who had surrendered to the spell of nature, had only been framed negatively, among many hesitations, through the exercise of the "directing function" of the narrator endlessly pointing back, through verbal negations, to the text's enunciation and to the anxiety produced at the contact with its historical content. In other words, if in previous apparitions the smiling dead had coincided with the neutral term of the semiotic square where the opposition of the two main isotopies underlying the story had been visualized, in this case there is no hesitation or negation on the part of the narrator. The hunger artist affirms, on the one hand, the proximity with death, as his performance, taking place inside a glass coffin, is a diminishing of vital energy asymptotically approaching its own extinction; on the other hand, and simultaneously, his smile, the agency that frames this event as an artistic act, manifests an affirmative vitality, an expression of a personal, meaningful intention. In other words, the smiling artist inside the glass coffin is an inversion of previous appearances of the smiling dead, and we can situate him on the complex term of the square (figure 4.2), where life and death, meaningful and idle activity, are paradoxically reunited.

As all previous manifestations of the underclass' agency had revealed, to different degrees, the complicity and even the identification with the narrator (let us recall Compagnone's reaction to the girl's gesture), whose connection with the experience of hunger is adumbrated by the signs we have seen, we can consider the appearance of the hunger artist as the climax of the whole story, in which the structural identity of the narrator with the suffering crowd flashes in full sight and the "original emotion" finds its last articulation. However, while the inextricable link between art and hunger becomes visible in this figure, it also offers the image of a utopic redemption, in which suffering is sublated into the meaningful artistic expression. Of course, this cannot cancel the pressure of the contradictory ideological thrust belonging to the "original emotion," constantly visualized in the movement of retreat of the narrator, in the anxiety generated at the proximity with the crowd. Not by chance, her reaction to the appearance of the fakir is astonishment, a violent sense of disorientation: "I wondered if I had had

Figure 4.2. The hunger artist as the positive inversion of the smiling dead. *Source:* Created by the author.

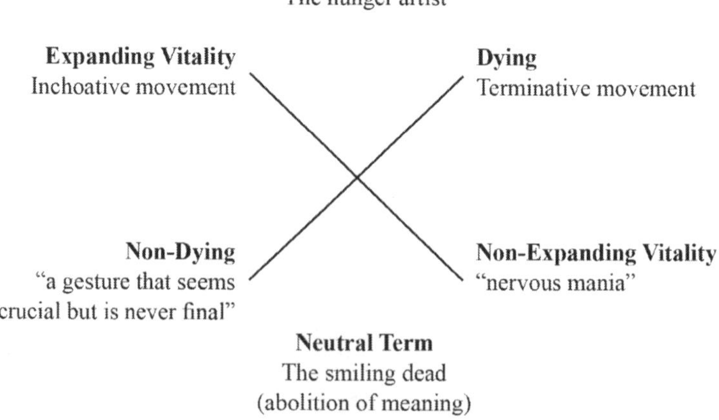

a drink of something strong while wandering anxiously around Naples"[84] (181). It is not difficult to read, in this excess of anxiety, something more than the surprise at seeing something unexpected.

The complexity produced by this double movement of revelation and concealment pushes the narrator to look at Prunas again, as if the presence of the fakir had produced a new element she might use to interpret his enigmatic figure. Thus, we witness a second movement in the dialectic of her judgment of the young man: "I wondered if he was extremely alive or only extremely dead"[85] (181). While she had concluded earlier that he was still alive, still not a sleepwalker in the service of Nature, still able to use reason, she completely changes her mind now. After asking him some questions about his current life, to which he does not respond, she concludes:

> So I was certain that he was truly dead, finished. . . . None of those whom I had met so far had hidden from me his death. I had seen the declaration of the end, of failure written in fairly clear characters on each face, like an eviction notice on a shabby door. . . . The city had destroyed him. And why shouldn't it have destroyed him? They had all fallen here, those who had wanted to think or act, all talk had become confused and only augmented the painful human vegetation. This nature could no longer tolerate human reason. . . . And this boy too, had fallen.[86] (182–83; translation modified)

What appears clearly in this passage is the awareness that what the narrator has called "death" throughout the story, as a collective, historical condition, is not something that can be simply ignored by anyone. No one who lives within the city's social reality can be spared by it and avoid contact with it. This "death," this negative element, the pressure of the material misery on which the little wealth of the city is built, if not experienced directly in everyday routine, is nevertheless present in the minds of those who do not see it due to their own ideological blindness; this is why Compagnone must participate, despite his privilege, in the abolition of meaning that stands at the core of the existence of the poor. The mark left from this blind spot, impeding the capacity of reason to process a complete picture of their reality, has hypnotized all the intellectuals whose critical thinking was once employed to find ways to change the structure of society. This slumber is the price they paid to be free to forget. Still, if this darkness needs to be acknowledged, this does not mean it cannot again be sublated through reason's dialectical process, that is, through the very mechanism of concealment and revelation the text has put in motion, showing and hiding, at the same time, its historical content—the existence of the urban lumpenproletariat. Thus, the moment the narrator recognizes in Prunas the necessity to face the negative, the progression of the story does not stop. On the contrary, only now is it free to go toward its conclusion.

This third and final movement is initiated by a new discourse by Gaedkens, which seems to demonstrate the pleasure of the mere contemplation of the negative: "Speaking of Naples as a phenomenal terrain, he delighted in the transience of the land, which was continuously changing shape, where nothing was stable and everything generated deception and fear"[87] (183). Yet surprisingly, Prunas interrupts his friend: " 'And so?' Prunas asked abruptly, but calmly. . . . Such a lively and incredulous smile once again lit up Prunas's face, so inadequate to the hour and to Gaedkens's words, that I was still surprised. But he said not a word more"[88] (184; translation modified). At this point, a last walk through the city, in which Prunas and the narrator leave the other two behind, shows them in a sort of hallucination, all the Neapolitan intellectuals whom she had met or mentioned until this point, as if to mark the profound difference between these latter and the last two remaining beings who have not forsaken Reason. Indeed—and this is the moment the sanction is finally pronounced about Prunas—she recognizes that, despite "being dead" (we have seen the necessity to accept and incorporate the negative), he is nevertheless still alive. He thinks, and his thoughts are aimed at *doing things*, in fact, they are still fixated on the old political program of *Sud*: "I remembered that he was always like this, in the years of *Sud*, when he was on his way to the printer: taking these small rapid steps without seeing anything, cold, his thoughts intent on what needed to be done"[89] (185). The point here is again the capacity of the "boy" to experience emotional participation without being overwhelmed by it, and even more than this, his ability to *use* emotions, to put them in the service of reason—a process in which we can start to recognize what the text we have just read has kept on doing, by manipulating the emotional intensity continuously generated by the presentation of its historical content: "I seemed to understand with immense wonder that he had neither imagination nor emotion, at least not in the normal sense, or if he did he considered them a kind of energy that had to be continuously controlled, and this allowed him not to be afraid of Naples"[90] (185).

A few pages earlier, the narrator had said of Prunas, "He was truly dead, finished . . . this boy too, had fallen." However, the last mention of him, in the final lines, will say that while "all was united in sleep . . . the Sardinian boy . . . was perhaps at this hour still thinking"[91] (187). It is important to note that this last notation of the enduring intellectual livelihood of Prunas is not a retractation of the previous conclusion—that he is dead, that he has deeply experienced the dimension the text calls here "death." If we think back to Compagnone, we realize that his coincidence with the "dead and restless" appearance of Chiaia, with the figure of the smiling dead, had been the result of his refusal of that "death," which had required, as a prize, the renunciation of life too. Hence the crepuscular condition, neither life nor death, the neutral term where meaning is abolished, and where the bourgeois intellectual, having saved his privileged position and his privilege *not to see* the misery on which that privilege is based, must share, in a paradoxical way, the meaningless existence of the poor, their eternal present where the future is a shadow and the past a torment, the "sleep" in which the whole city is united. But Prunas's case is completely different, and, as it starts to become clear, coincides with the narrator's own implicit self-understanding inside the story's structure, as it had flashed out in the hunger artist as a mirror image of herself. In the semiotic square where we have visualized the opposition of the abstract isotopies on which the story is based (figure 4.2), he too must occupy the "complex term," the one in which expanding and fading vitality, life and death, are present simultaneously. If we agree that what we here call death is a historical condition, we realize that the resistance in this position implies a renunciation to the ideological blindness that protects privilege from seeing its own roots in injustice. Therefore, the acceptance of the historical element in full awareness must coincide with the refusal of the selfish impulse at self-preservation (of the other intellectuals it was said, "Everyone was indifferent . . . who wished to survive" 168).

Not by chance, in the last exchange with Prunas, when asked what he would do if he had the money, he replied he would buy "machines, a print shop" (186) ("Macchine, una tipografia" [171]). In this synecdochic reference to the engagement in cultural activism, the "boy" (and he is a boy here precisely because, differently than grown men, he does not think of his own career first) thinks of himself as just an operator of political activity, not as an author, a personality, a martyr even. The "free machines" (186) ("Macchine libere" [171]) he desires are those able to "cure" humans, to act politically. In order to be free, they must be self-produced but also not subordinated to personal ambition. Yet this reference to a personal choice, to the ethical coherence of the individual, could in itself sound here like a simplification of the complex fresco that has been traced throughout the story. In fact, a closer analysis of this last section reveals that this ethical element appears to be *only one* of the two necessary components of Prunas's ability to stand his ground, to remain alive in the assumption of historical misery. If we think of the hunger artist as the first allegorical occurrence of the position of the complex term of the square, we must realize, by going back to its origin in Kafka's story, that the reason for the personal heroism of the artist who stands his ground well into death, without renouncing his performance against all odds of the historical moment that has made his art obsolete, is revealed to be rooted in his own way of being, in the materiality of his body rather than in a free choice: "I couldn't find the food I liked. If I had found it, believe me, I should have made no fuss and stuffed myself like you or anyone else" (Kafka 1971, 250). Similarly, Ortese's text has presented Prunas as somebody whose unique way of behaving is deeply rooted in his character rather than in his rational "free will." The multiple notations about his small body, resembling a child or an adolescent, are only a first step here. References to his being "cold" are present several times (170–72, 185–87), and in one case this is even linked with his being *barely human*: "Like all monstrosities, Naples had no effect on people who were barely human, and its boundless charms could leave no trace on a cold heart"[92] (185). In sum, Prunas's capacity not to fall prey to emotions, and to manipulate them instead, is rooted in his character as determined by contingent, historical circumstances, and cannot be reduced to a sort of nonhistorical ethical heroism that would distinguish him from all other intellectuals.

We can see here one of the most important passages in the political reflections developed by this text. If we connect it with the narrator's own participation in the existence of the crowd of the poor, with her complicity with some of the figures who had "come forward" and the hunger artist in particular, it appears evident that what allows some to escape ideological blindness, making them capable of incorporating the negative and performing an ethical choice, is a material, contingent situation. In Ortese's case, this is the sharing of a social condition, the traumatic experience of hunger that has put her, for long periods, in the same standpoint of the Neapolitan lumpenproletariat, experiencing the same underworld. This is why her text was able to do more than just "describe" the horrible condition of the poor. As is evident from La Capria's comments we have examined, and from the scandal produced by the book, her style did not comply with the accepted, domesticated, stereotypical "realism" of other habitual depictions of Naples.

On the contrary, her text strove to recreate the existential coordinates of that existence—its habitus—even before any thematization and rational reflection—a move her text carried out only subsequently in the passages I have called allegorical meditations. As suggested by Merleau-Ponty's reflections on literature's possibility to communicate experience, such communication can only happen when a text is able to "produce a system of signs whose internal articulation reproduces the contours of experience"[93] (Merleau-Ponty 1970, 25). This can be done, as shown by his contemporary reflection on Lukács's *History and Class Consciousness*, only when expression coincides with praxis, when it is indistinguishable from the sharing of a social, material standpoint. Only in this case do "the reliefs and sweeping lines of these contours [of the experience to be communicated] in turn generate a deep syntax, a mode of composition and recital which breaks the mold of the world and everyday language and refashions it"[94] (Merleau-Ponty 1970, 25). The "deep syntax" has been precisely what we have investigated through the means of semiotics, the structures that allow the undefinable, literary ideas—literary experience—to touch the reader to reveal the historical content of the text, a textual inscription I have called "ascetic images." But this is not enough. The text does more than that, as it attempts to use the emotional energy generated by this contact for its own ideological purpose, for its evident political goal—the continuation of *Sud*'s original program. Not by chance, this ruthless, *cold* manipulation of emotions is said to be the main feature of Prunas, founder and director of that journal.

The closing of the story replicates once again this rhetorical mechanism of "manipulation" that had sustained it throughout. While in the city "all was united in sleep, a marvel without consciousness," illuminated by the light of a perverted reason coming from the bottom of the sea ("the immense light, delicate as that of a seashell"), the narrator looks "toward the red walls of Monte di Dio, where the boy from Sardinia, so simple and cold, was perhaps at this hour still thinking"[95] (187; translation modified). At this point, while this image of political resistance still echoes, the text produces a final outburst of lyrical intensity destined to reinforce its political argument. This is done through the thickening of the rhetorical fabric, where a parallelism of disposition—an isocolon ("only the calm wash of the sea over the rocks could be heard, only the hills could be seen, increasingly vivid and victorious in the light"[96]), a partial chiasmatic structure played on the repetition of the figure of the alley (not rendered in the translation: "and farther down, the buildings and gray alleys, the miserable, diseased alleys"[97]), and finally a hyperbaton, so common in Ortese's prose (not rendered in the translation:

"where among the piles of garbage some lights still shone"[98])—create a crescendo culminating in the fading of the night's light in the overwhelming clarity of the day: "but the day was rising ever higher and more brilliant, and gradually even those last lights went out"[99] (187). Light on light, as if the rising sun of Reason would finally reabsorb the distortion imposed on it by human machinations.

Chapter 5

The City and Its Depths

Journey to Italy

Blood on the Screen

In the analysis of the scene where the "original emotion" first appears in the film, we have seen how Katherine is alarmed by the streak of blood on the windshield and fears the possibility of malaria: a threat that must seem to her—and certainly to a part of the audience—as exotic and archaic. In other words, her verbal discourse, like her finger, points here to an unknown, disquieting dimension at the center of this southern reality the couple is accessing. The emergence of verbal discourse completes, so to speak, the catalog the film's first sequence has displayed of cinematic tools it will use to attract to the surface its hidden content. This has included, until now, a peculiar construction of the point-of-view shots, in which an absent or incomprehensible object is evoked by the emotional projection fueled by the close-up, the disruption of linear time (the ordinary sequence's tendency toward the "full frequentative"), and the active offscreen sounds. In this specific case, the verbal allusion articulates a doubt, a hypothesis alternative to the discourse defining the south as the exotic, revitalizing, exciting but ultimately safe touristic destination (we find this perspective in Alex's reassuring response). It is here "just" the fear about the dangers of malaria, expressed with a simple question, but it will soon mutate, and again because of Katherine's initiative and voiced by her, in the verses of the deceased poet Lewington, which will question the positive vitality of this place and will evoke "ascetic images." Is it possible that this is the land of silence and old age? We had asked this question at the end of our analysis of the film's synopsis written by Rossellini and Brancati (see chapter 2). Yet before further investigating the function of the verses against the background of Katherine's and Alex's exploration in the central part of the film, it is important to discuss the key role of protective screens throughout the film, at both the formal and thematic level, and whose presence has been directly made evident by the dead bug. Indeed, all sorts of barriers, material and immaterial, split the reality explored by the film into two different dimensions. The first one is the touristic, picturesque image of Naples, the one endlessly sung by the Neapolitan ideology, the carnal vitality, the "opposite of asceticism," which Rossellini was eager to show to the world while claiming to vindicate the "real" Naples from stereotypes. The second level is the historical reality of Naples in the year 1953, that of a population whose vast majority was living in poverty, heavily exploited, surviving in the informal economy, and still bearing traces of the shock of war and military occupation: in sum, "the plebeian Naples (which is all of Naples)" (Ortese 2018, 108), the one described in socioeconomic terms by Allum, the same Thomas Belmonte will meet, almost unchanged in its suffocating misery and endemic violence, for his fieldwork in the 1970s (Belmonte 2012; also see chapter 2).

If the initial narrative program of the Joyce couple, explained in narrative semiotic terms in chapter 3, mandated by the logic of capitalist efficiency, consists of selling the inherited villa as quickly as possible, and Katherine's own secondary program consists of saving their marriage, the anti-narrative program—which opposes the first and will "solve" the second—seems to be directed precisely at the encounter with this second layer of reality, mandated by the soldier-poet Lewington, with his verses describing a land populated by "ascetic images." Of course, the authorial interpretation of the film as it can be deduced from the screenplay, the synopsis, and the interviews we have previously examined seems to envision this anti-program as the simple expansion of the "touristic" purpose of the visit: The two northern travelers, too embroiled in the rationality of their bourgeois status, should "take their time" and learn to enjoy life, to appreciate the carnal, passionate side of it (these are, after all, the kinds of stereotypes through which most vacation trips to southern destinations are still sold). Yet how is this picturesque reality of the South communicated visually? For the whole film—excluding the significant, final exception we will see—the camera follows the Joyces, together or individually. They are almost always separated from the environment by protective barriers that limit what spectators can see in the external world.

The action begins in the car, and, from this secluded space, the first subjective shots through which we access the external world only show the mysterious and disquieting signs discussed in chapter 3. From the car the Joyces pass directly into the hotel, a restaurant, and finally, after another brief commute in the car, the villa. This situation will only change with Katherine's first solitary expedition, after roughly one-third of the film. Starting with their arrival at the hotel, we are only presented with sporadic external views that are perfectly touristic and conventional: the generic images of a nocturnal urban scenario that immediately precede it, a static shot from the entrance of the hotel, showing Fontana del Gigante as they arrive, the panoramic shot from the hotel room with the whole gulf followed (or continued, depending on the interpretation—see chapter 3) by Katherine's point of view glance (again showing the Fontana del Gigante), a brief image of the exterior of the villa as they approach by car, then some background images of the gulf from the villa's terrace, alternated with static postcard views of it. All these exteriors are never constructed as subjective "projections," in Fontanille's terms we have used to describe those in the first sequence (Fontanille 1989, 131–40), and the thymic element is completely neglected in favor of the purely cognitive, informational value of situating the story in a precise geographic environment (not by chance, except for the villa, they show immediately recognizable views), and of the pragmatic function of advancing its development (the Joyces reach the hotel, then the villa). In other words, these exteriors have no subjective value whatsoever, as they do not enter into dramatic interaction with the characters, thus not eliciting any emotional response, contrary to, for instance, the buffaloes and the whole sinister Pontine landscape in the prologue. Therefore, until this moment, the famous Neapolitan picturesque is limited to postcard visions of the gulf with no emotional connection to the story, while mysterious signs of a "different," for now invisible, reality have already signaled their presence: the active, offscreen sounds of (likely) the fishermen outside of the hotel room on the morning of the second day. The same voices will resume their singing as soon as the Joyces arrive at the villa, and, in a haunting way, they follow them as they are guided by Tony and his wife Natalia to explore the villa's rooms.

Aprà and Martelli (1967) have defined this brief sequence as a "scene" in the terms of Metz's "grand syntagmatic," that is, a continuous and linear depiction of events, with a strong tendency to the long take, which enforces the impression of "objectivity" (201). This strongly contrasts with the unlikely capacity of the singing voices to "follow" the characters and be equally heard on all sides of the building, in interior and exterior spaces alike (the garden, the terrace), regardless of open or closed windows. The continuity of this presence, which will be constantly proposed by the film and had been already mentioned as a key element since the early, rejected screenplay, constitutes what Michel Chion defines as an "acousmêtre": "A neologism meaning an 'acousmatic being' (*acousmatique* + *être*, also playing on *maître* or master, because this figure is often powerful). Designates the invisible character created in cinema by hearing an *acousmatic* voice . . . when this voice has enough coherence and continuity to constitute a full-blown character" (Chion 2019, 201).

A "full-blown" collective character, the Neapolitan crowd, this almost invisible underclass, will have enough coherence and power when it appears at last to literally bring about, with its sheer physical presence, the denouement of the story. Yet before that moment, we get several glimpses of it, the first of which takes place at the arrival at the villa, when three domestic workers come to take care of the Joyces' luggage. They appear at first on just three occasions: the long shot depicting the arrival of the car, in which their bodies, evidently different in size and health from those of the "masters," hasten in the background to reach the rear of the car, moving subserviently to pick up the luggage. We see them more clearly only when they finally carry the baggage, reaching the group in one of the bedrooms, evidently struggling to carry the heavy weight (figure 5.1).

Figure 5.1. The maids carrying the Joyces' suitcases. *Source:* Roberto Rossellini, *Journey to Italy*, 1954.

This image would have certainly communicated more clearly sensations of discomfort to an audience of a few decades ago, still acquainted with the habit of carrying a pre-rolling suitcase—that is, an audience made of bodies who had inscribed in their sensory-motor schemas the sensation of carrying such heavy, unpractical loads.[1] Yet even today, their distress is evident to us, as evident is their physical difference from the wealthy visitors. Their bodies *speak*, as those of the poor had done so often in Neorealist films, telling stories often more effectively than awkward plots.[2] In the next scene, the woman stands silently in the background by the table at which the four masters have lunch, and soon after Alex will again find her, together with the man (likely her husband), uncomfortably sleeping in the kitchen with their heads on the table (see figure 3.6), when he will try to refill his wine, in a scene cut from the Italian version. This scene, usually referred to by critics as the "comic scene," was post-synchronized in Italian too but finally excluded from the Italian version, as explained by Dagrada (293). Nevertheless, it is central to my interpretation, as I read the fact that it was eliminated as a sign of discomfort Rossellini and his editor must have felt about it, especially in relation to a potential Italian audience (the scene is included in the international version). Of course, the main reason for the exclusion is that, dubbed in Italian, it does not make much sense (but Italian audiences of the time were used to seeing worse—one need only think of the Italian version of Godard's *Contempt*, released just a few years later). Immediately before, Alex and Katherine are shown lying in the sun on the terrace, after lunch, finally alone (see figure 1.1). Alex goes downstairs with his empty pitcher, and he knows where to go. Indeed, since their first entrance into the villa, they had been shown the precise location of the kitchen and pantry, in the first and longest shot of those inside the house: The camera watches them enter, then pans left and follows them into the drawing room, while Natalia explains the function of this beautiful space full of artworks. As the camera pulls back, they exit and proceed toward the stairs, always admiring the ambiance, while Alex says he did not know his uncle had "such good taste" and Katherine softly passes her hand over the beautiful inlaid wood panels of a piece of furniture. As they start climbing the elegant curvilinear staircase, Natalia stops to point to an offscreen space below the staircase, which she explains is the kitchen and pantry. The presence of this space, even if not shown and solely existing in the form of an allusion, starts to establish an architectural geography charged with opposite values, as it subtly contrasts with the brightly lit white spaces they are traversing, completely free of any sign of work, which is evidently relegated to the lower, dark part of the building, in a blind spot the camera does not move to include (for now). It is precisely there that Alex heads to ask for more wine and finds the sleeping servants.

We see him redescending the same stairs and hesitating in front of a small door, which this time is shown. He opens it and must slightly bow his head to enter, a first physical sign of an uncomfortable reality. Unsurprisingly, the room he accesses is dimly lit, which immediately establishes a strong contrast with the sunny terrace from which he just descended. Also, the chairs and tables (an ironing table) on which the domestic workers are uncomfortably sleeping visually oppose the beautiful chaises longues on the terrace (see again figure 3.6 and figure 1.1). At first Alex tries to explain himself cordially, but the woman does not understand his English. Her way of speaking is aggressive, and Alex quickly gets upset. Even considering that the meaning of the woman's speech was not intended to be understood by international audiences, it is unclear how this could be perceived as comical in any way. The husband's intervention, urging the maid, in strict Neapolitan, to bring Alex to Tony for an explanation, must also sound aggressive and unfriendly regardless of the precise meaning. Alex is offended and disgusted when she gestures resolutely to follow her and finally takes him by the hand, literally dragging him out. At this point he wears his black sunglasses, as if to "interpose a barrier between him and the woman," as noted by Dagrada (2008, 322), who also notices how the scene, especially in its second part, goes way beyond what could be considered as "comic" in this context.[3] Dagrada's interpretation is that this scene "certainly lingers amusedly on the physical and character exuberance of the maid, but at the same time records a very harsh X-ray of what Alex Joyce perceives of the 'draped' peoples; X-ray that adds to the equally harsh one of prejudice (*Stromboli*), conformism (*Europe '51*) and egocentrism (*Ingrid Bergman*)" (322). Here Dagrada is making reference to the difference, already mentioned in the introduction, between "draped" and "sewn" people, the favorite allegory Rossellini used to talk about the North-South opposition in this film. Yet what seems evident to me is that the difference between Alex and the woman goes far beyond the linguistic/cultural incomprehension. This opposition is inscribed not only in the already noted difference of their bodies—which speaks to the abyss separating privilege from exploitation along the generations—but also in the structure of the house itself, which, like most buildings of this kind, enforces class differences, in this case by separating master and servants between the upper sunlight of the terrace and the lower darkness of the kitchen/pantry. This contrast is repeated not only in the striking opposition between comfortable and uncomfortable physical positions but also in the spatial-temporal dimension inhabited by the two couples: The open space where the Joyces are resting signals an opening of possibilities, which the two will take advantage of, exploring the region freely in the subsequent days. This also implies an "open" temporality the two will enjoy: the idle time of the wealthy's vacation, their freedom to use it as they like. On the contrary, the space the domestic workers inhabit is tight, the dark wood that covers the walls makes it seem even more oppressive, and the only window is closed. They are resting too, but they are doing it with their head on the tools of toil, a reminder that this break is limited, and they will need to return to their labor soon. Thus, this cramped, dimly lit underworld, an upside-down image of the world of the masters, signals a lack of existential possibilities, the inescapable temporal circularity of survival and toil.

We are now in the position to evaluate the dichotomy produced by the "comic scene" through the same semiotic square we have used to analyze the contrast between the activity of the intellectuals and that of the crowd of the poor in Ortese's story. In this case (figure 5.2), the Joyces resting on the terrace occupy the second position on the upper side, that of the "idle activity," while the two domestic workers are situated on the lower side. They occupy the neutral term, reuniting both the fourth spot of "essential activities" as they "steal" their necessary moment of rest from the daily toil and the third position, that of "meaningless activity," when the woman starts behaving aggressively with Alex, showing an erratic excess of energy in the

Figure 5.2. The activities of the masters and those of the servants. *Source:* Created by the author.

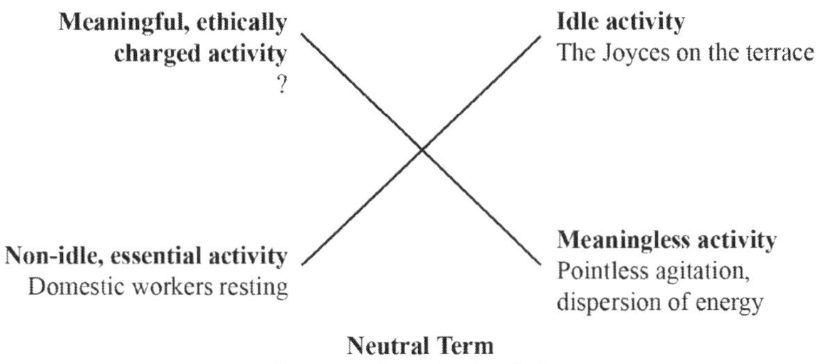

interaction. But this dispersion of energy can be seen in previous scenes as well, for instance when they first approach the car to pick the luggage up and their bodies weirdly move with agitation as if to express a solicitude that is not really needed for the practical success of the task, and which therefore ends up only expressing anxiety.

Not surprisingly, the first position of the square remains void here. However, the empty space left by the absence of the meaningful activity, the one that investigates and directly addresses social injustice, will soon reach the surface of the film once Lewington's poetic riddle initiates the quest for the "ascetic images." Indeed, as soon as Alex returns to the terrace with his wine, the medium shot that shows the couple finally lying in peace in the sun this time also includes Vesuvius in the background (figure 1.1). They cannot see it from their position: We see them standing still, their skins glaring white in the sunlight, as if dreaming of something, while the volcano lurks behind them, creating a sense of looming menace—something Rossellini had learned well how to capture on the island of Stromboli—signaling the presence of an enormous, repressed, underground force, which directly connects this bright space with the underground dimension into which we have been allowed to peer. Here on the terrace the singing of the *acousmêtre* resumes, while it had been silent in the lower room.

From that depth (from the past, from the dark, from death), something now emerges, precisely in this shot. Katherine suddenly recites the verses of a deceased poet we have not been prepared to meet, Charles Lewington: "Temple of the Spirit / [here the film cuts on a close-up of Alex's surprised face] no longer bodies / [and here on her close-up, whose somber expression contrasts with a brightness of the lighting that almost blurs the contours of her face] but pure ascetic images." To these verses, Alex reacts first with indifference, then with discomfort, exactly as he had done a few minutes earlier with the maid. *Pure ascetic images.* The next day Katherine will search for them in the Archaeological Museum, after which both will joke about the sensible poet who did not understand the sensuality of this land (and of its people). How are they not able to associate this expression with the people who have carried their luggage, who attend to their domestic needs, with the crowds of the poor they will soon see in the street? However, the pressure of this underground dimension will gradually force its way to the surface and will even save their marriage in the final scene. Yet, again, how is this blindness possible? The ideological mechanism we have analyzed while exploring Ortese's text provides an answer: The force of the dominant discourse about Naples is able to neutralize the unpleasant reality by keeping it in full sight. At the visual level, the film manifests this mechanism by showing the constant seclusion of the protagonists' bodies between protective barriers, through which the historical reality of the environment is allowed to appear only as "framed," like in the case of the car's windows or the domestic structure. At the same time, it also shows how the ideological discourse is enforced through the presence of the "filters" through which Katherine approaches this foreign reality: the guide book in her hand at the very beginning, soon replaced, as noted by Bergala, by the many human guides she will hire or accept as a companion for her excursions.[4] Nevertheless, the sudden emergence of the verses has an effect on her. As a form of manipulation operated by the anti-sender (Lewington), they have the effect of pushing her to embark on a series of itineraries to find and understand the emotion she feels in them, and that she cannot explain, in the places that have supposedly inspired it for the poet. However, as I have hypothesized from the beginning, the "performance" these verses really demand of her is an itinerary in search of a different kind of historical knowledge: the encounter with the hidden object of the Neapolitan reality, the existence of its underclass, occluded on the very surface of the city. Not by chance, Katherine's itineraries of exploration in the following days will force her to cross paths, again, with this strangely invisible kind of people she has been able to ignore at home, as we will see in the next section. Yet she will only go halfway on this route: In the middle of her itinerary of discovery, she will refuse the burden implied in accepting this task and retreat to the idle touristic explorations, where she will paradoxically look for inspiration to save her failing marriage. As for Alex, he has immediately refused the riddle proposed by the verses, and he will only venture into protected, lofty spaces, like the aristocratic house of Uncle Homer's friends, or the island of Capri—a secluded, touristic paradise itself—to meet his idle friends. His only encounter with the harsh, invisible reality of the city will happen in his brief adventure with the suicidal prostitute we have discussed, which will only provoke a starker refusal to see. Thus, in this very refusal, the couple will meet again, until the moment in which they will be forced to accept the challenge offered by the poet.

The Surface of Everydayness and the Wounds of History

Besides its narrative organization, at the level of its discursive structure *Journey to Italy* can be interpreted as an itinerary leading from the invisibility to the full visibility of a hidden object, in four progressive stages. The first one, the first sequence analyzed in the introduction and chapter 3, only indirectly evokes its presence through the means we have analyzed. The second one, which starts on the first morning in the hotel, introduces the presence of what is invisible in the form of an *acousmêtre*, and then presents it for the first time as a visible, diegetic element with the arrival at the villa and the appearance of the domestic workers, before clearly delineating a structural opposition between their existence and that of the masters in what has been called the "comic scene." The third stage begins with Katherine's first—of four—excursions to local tourist destinations. Each of her visits is preceded by a car trip in which she drives through the streets of Naples, alone the first three times and with Natalia for the last one. All driving sequences follow—although at times only loosely—the structure of the point of view, alternating close-ups of the woman with subjective views of the street and its crowd. I will focus here on the way the object is revealed in these sequences, and on their role in the narrative structure of the film, while the fourth stage of this itinerary will be analyzed in the next and final section. Before starting my analysis, it is important to clarify how it relates to, and diverges from, Bergala's reading. He maintains that this film encapsulates two separate dimensions, one visible on the surface—the characters and the plot—and one running deeper, consisting of mysterious signs pointing to the emergence of something not clearly definable, which will only appear in the end and which he considers to be a "transcendence" he also names "grace" and "revealed reality." Rossellini's film, he claims, succeeds in keeping structurally together two heterogeneous dimensions, that is "the characters and their imaginary journeys (what they believe themselves to be, and what they believe to be seeking, 'their' scenario)" on the one side, and on the other, "the Real as what signals something, but in an enigmatic way (this concerns me, but how, by what end?), and let us say the Transcendence (grace, revealed truth)" (Bergala 1990, 49). The waiting for this final revelation imbues the film with its peculiar emotional tension, he claims, and gives it its revelatory force.

Although it is certainly correct that Rossellini's method consisted in creating the expectation for a revelatory, epiphanic moment that would appear in the end as the impact of a form of (non-defined) "transcendence" over the ordinary narrative of life—something that is particularly evident in *Stromboli* and *Europe '51*—my own interpretation, as I clarified in previous chapters, is that the transcendental content the film accesses here is *not* indefinable. What the "original emotion" articulates, at the border between protective spaces and external reality, is the ideological contradiction between a stereotypical understanding of the South as a touristic cure for the northern malaise and a precise historical dimension of violence and suffering, that is, the condition of the Neapolitan lower classes. This is the historical content whose textual inscription I call, taking a clue from Lewington's verses, "ascetic images." In other words, well beyond clear authorial intentions—we have seen Rossellini's hesitations—the act of aesthetic expression, as theorized by Merleau-Ponty (2020a, 173), *responds* here to the encounter with that transcendence, where it is possible to come into contact with the repressed content of society's political unconscious. Therefore, I argue that what Bergala refers to as "grace" is an emotional side effect resulting from this contact, produced by the successive rearticulations of what we have seen emerging as "original emotion." For instance, Bergala clearly states that the reality beyond the protective screens, during Katherine's car trips, alludes to a "transcendental" content; yet my interpretation is that "visible" and "transcendental" here *coincide*. As we will see in a moment, the transcendental is out there, invisible in full sight, transubstantiated in the picturesque, even when nothing "picturesque" really appears.

With the first car trip sequence, as noted by Aprà and Martelli, the two dominant motives of the film, already introduced in the first sequence, are isolated and juxtaposed: the relationship of the characters with the surrounding reality and their own marital relationships. Indeed, as Katherine leaves the villa, Alex sarcastically asks her if the destination of her visit—the Archaeological Museum in Naples—is the object of Lewington's poem she had recited. This dictates her emotional state during the drive, protected by black sunglasses (which work here as additional protective screens), almost not paying any attention to the urban landscape she is traversing, while talking to herself with resentment about Alex's meanness (her first words are "I hate him"). This soliloquy, or rather the intermittent emergence of her inner speech, reinforces the barrier already established by the ideological discourse covering the external reality of Naples, which thus results in being almost invisible to her. On one occasion, however, this reality elicits an emotional reaction visible in her close-up: a smile, which we can interpret as a sign of availability, an opening toward the object the poet has secretly asked her to meet. Indeed, despite her lack of participation, the images we are shown already bear some connections with the reality of the lower classes that has been introduced with the appearance of the domestic workers at the villa: The buildings and the streets have a squalid appearance, the first human to be singled out by a panning movement integrated into the structure or the point of view is a "shoe-shine" man sitting in front of his tools laying on the sidewalk. The next element to catch Katherine's attention is a group, one man and three women, hastening to cross the street, at whom she honks impatiently, apparently not noticing that one of them, an elderly woman, is struggling to carry some heavy bags, an action that directly recalls the one performed in front of her by the servants the day before (figure 5.3).

At this point, and for the rest of the trip, the images shown do not communicate the impression of a random, authentic encounter with urban misery, but seem rather to convey a precise authorial intention, as they show two nuns walking in front of a shop with a big, visible "lotto" sign, then a priest between a poster of the communist party and one of the Christian democrats, followed, in the same panoramic shot, by workers renovating the street in Piazza Garibaldi. The selection of these precise images seems intended to signify the social contradictions of the city between the survival of the archaic and modernity, official religion together with profane superstition and political struggle. Although the content of these scenes was not orchestrated,[5] the editing charges them with an ideological intention that dissipates the previous impression of authentic encounters. Not by chance, these two shots are not perfectly harmonized in the structure of the point of view, as they

Figure 5.3. Katherine's point-of-view shot from the car. *Source:* Roberto Rossellini, *Journey to Italy*, 1954.

do not match Katherine's eyelines, and, in the second case, the position of the camera does not even coincide with the driver's seat, as if Rossellini and his editor (Jolanda Benvenuti) were suggesting that such an intentional presentation of the city could not bear the mark of Katherine's subjectivity. As for the diegetic, ambient sound, so important for the encounter between the protagonists and the local environment, it is rather discreet throughout the scene, perfectly matching the expected urban soundscape, without marking its presence through some unrealistic discrepancy, as we had noted on previous occasions. Only when she arrives at the museum does something of the sort happen: A feminine voice is distinctly heard inviting another woman to hang the clothes to dry as the sun has come out, to which a masculine voice responds by singing "O sole mio." This offscreen singing continues into the next scene, in which Katherine is already inside the museum, heading for the entrance, thus replicating the kind of ambiguous pervasiveness ambient sounds had already demonstrated at the hotel and the villa.

At this point it is important to anticipate an overall interpretation of the four touristic sites Katherine visits in the central part of the film. They are all places where the surface of everyday reality is put in contact with a dimension that transcends it, that shows how its reassuring appearance—the careless, vital existence of a sunlit, touristic paradise—is really excavated by uncharted passages extending in the darkness of a temporal and geological abyss, which, as we will see, always proves to be in connection with the wounds of history, as if it was a mirror image of a haunting past, recent and remote at once: World War II as the last figure of a series of horrors, which, like tormented ghosts, are not allowed to fade. The Archaeological Museum immediately proves to be a palimpsest of references to an abysmal past, historical scars, and modern military history. The sequence is based on a subjective structure more complex and ambiguous than the one used for Katherine's car trips. Although formally preserving the point-of-view structure, the statues shown in reverse shots are allowed to manifest their own "subjectivity" through their looks to the camera, which complicates our reception of the subject–object (human–statue) interaction, creating the impression that Katherine is observed as much as she observes. This ambiguity has been carefully described by Albano, Del Bosco, and Faccini in their "grammatical" analysis of the scene: "The shots of the statues and objects in the museum normally precede the medium or close-up shots of Katherine; the shot-reverse-shot of the previous sequences is reversed, but reality continues to act as a stimulus. But it involves her, precedes her, surpasses her. One could say, at first glance, that the subjectivation of the reverse shot is missing. After all, this is precisely the most ambiguous sequence of the film" (Albano et al. 1967, 193).

With a similar interpretation, but specifically about the bronze of the athlete called by the guide a "discus thrower,"[6] who is at the center of the longer and more intense "exchange" with Katherine, Bergala has stated that "it is no longer a banally transitive look at an object that Rossellini films at that moment, but a face-to-face, a real shot/reverse shot where it is at least as much the young discus thrower who looks at the woman as the opposite" (1990, 59–60). This sort of "resistance" of the statues to submit to the objectification of a one-way subjective structure is highlighted by the further contrast created by the emotional musical score of Renzo Rossellini, which now enters the film for the first time, against the verbal commentary of the guide, both informative and ironic, which is mostly heard offscreen and seems to work as a containment of the *unheimlich* vitality of the statues, absorbing it back in the armless order of an antiquarian and picturesque discourse. But what is this subjective force, this appellative impetus that emanates from the statues? To understand this, we need to pay attention to the overall structure of the sequence, which is neatly divided into two parts, an element to which commentators have not paid enough attention. The first part of the visit is devoted to bronze statues, and the second to marbles, while the caesura is marked by a wipe transition. The bronze statues are all full bodies captured in expressive, dynamic gestures: the sitting young man, the drunken satyr and faun, the dancers, the athlete. They have bright, expressive eyes made of glass paste so that the vivid iris and pupils create the effect of an alive, appellative gaze, which emerges in all its power in the case of the athlete, whose close-up is created by a frontal tracking movement of the camera that approaches him swiftly, thus mimicking an onrush of emotion, a sudden empathic connection (figure 5.4).

This is accentuated by the cut on a medium shot in which he and Katherine are both visible in profile, and the young man's outstretched hand seems to be attempting to hold her at the precise moment in which she turns to follow the guide, whose voice we hear moving away (figure 5.5).

At this point, after the wipe transition, we are shown a series of marbles, first the busts of Roman emperors, then, after the significant intermission of a mutilated bust of Venus, the famous Farnese Hercules and Farnese Bull. While the bronze statues had portrayed young, anonymous bodies petrified in the midst of complex movements, expressing tormented anguish fully channeled by the final, mute invocation of the athlete, the series of three emperors conveys an impression of ruthless force (figure 5.6), as their impassionate, blank stares (their marble eyes are deprived of expression) are

Figure 5.4. A bronze statue gazes intensely at Katherine. *Source:* Roberto Rossellini, *Journey to Italy*, 1954.

Figure 5.5. A bronze statue appears to beckon Katherine. *Source:* Roberto Rossellini, *Journey to Italy*, 1954.

unveiled by circling movements of the camera arriving to frontal close-ups from lateral perspectives or vice versa, while the guide's speech enumerates their cruel deeds and the musical score proceeds with dismayed solemnity.

Figure 5.6. Emperor Tiberius. In Roberto Rossellini, *Journey to Italy*, 1954.

The opposition between the three emperors and the bronze statues is thus reinforced by the discourse, as the nameless bodies of the latter give way to historical figures of powerful men (Caracalla, Nero, Tiberius). We can now read this opposition as responding to the one we have already noticed in the villa in Ercolano: named and defined characters versus anonymous ones, clarity versus darkness (the glaring white of the marble against dark-skinned bronzes), serene immobility versus twisted movement, self-assurance versus anguish, rest versus fatigue.

Here the semiotic square used to interpret human activity inside Naples' social reality (figure 5.2) would see the marble emperors on the second position of idleness, and the bronzes divided between the third (dispersion of energy) and the fourth (essential, basic activities), with the sole exception of the group dancers, who, nevertheless, rapidly filmed between the reclining drunk faun and the quivering athlete with a sweeping, horizontal tracking movement, seem to be entangled in the same incomprehensible feverishness we perceive in their intent, lively gazes. Finally, the topological opposition inscribed in the villa, the one between upper and lower positions, also appears with the much-admired crane shot that shows the Farnese Hercules through an expansive, circling movement that ends behind the massive shoulders of the hero. At this point, by retreating and tilting downward, the camera reveals the high position from which the shot is taken (figure 5.7), as the small bodies of Katherine and the guide appear far below, while farther in the background, at the opposite side of the vast room, we spot the equally massive shape of the next and last object of the visit: the group of the Farnese Bull.

Bergala has based much of his reading of the film on this sudden appearance of the crane shot perspective I just described. In his opinion, this exception to the human-height position adopted by the camera throughout the film (which will be used again only for the subsequent Farnese Bull and for the final sequence in Maiori) signals the irruption of an alien agency ("une autre instance" 57), the presence of the "mystery," the "grace" that will wait for the characters at the end (Bergala 1990, 60–61). Without intending to deny the evident connection of this shot with the penultimate one of the film in Maiori, my own interpretation is that the uplifted vision showing the Hercules fulfills two structural functions. First and foremost, with its topological position of absolute control and dominance (mirrored by the powerful body of the statue), it climactically reinforces the opposition between the series of impassionate and static portraits of powerful men and the previous, frantic and submissive appearance of the bronzes. In other words, it completes a plastic itinerary from bodily postures tending to horizontal abandonment

Figure 5.7. The Farnese Hercules. *Source:* Roberto Rossellini, *Journey to Italy*, 1954.

(the reclining, sitting, or squatting gestures) to heightened verticality, thus symmetrically replicating the villa's dichotomic topology of master-servant relationships. This same climax is maintained in the crane shot that shows the marble group with the Farnese Bull, where the violence of domination and the misery of submission are reunited in the pyramidal construction. In sum, the figural itinerary designed by the museum visit foreshadows the historical dichotomy between a nameless mass of oppressed bodies lying in a dark underworld and a few powerful individuals enjoying dominance in full light: a dichotomy in which the social landscape of Naples—which the Joyces are traversing without seeing—can be inscribed. Not coincidentally, with his first words the guide had mentioned that the rooms now populated by the statues were once cavalry barracks of the army: The supposedly timeless dimension of art is thus included in the material signs of military history.

As for the second, structural function performed by the sudden appearance of the uplifted, high-angle crane shot, we can read in it a return to the dimension of filmic enunciation—an *embrayage* in semiotic terms—no different from the disquieting effect of the subjective shots of the bronze statues, which, as Mulvey has stated, seem to shutter the fictional dimension built by the story until this point.[7] In other words, more than the emergence of a generic spiritual presence, I read here a climactic progression in the series of aesthetic events that have punctuated the film since the beginning, each time one of the mysterious signs we have analyzed created a ripple on the mimetic unfolding of the plot, thus pointing to a repressed social landscape slowly gaining access to visibility despite the thick texture of ideological vision. Therefore, in this itinerary of reemergence toward visibility, we could consider the museum sequence as a sort of allegorical fable, in which the opposition between dark bronzes and white marbles reenacts the horrors of historical oppression, a material epiphany that completes and fulfills the early appearance of the servants at the villa and of the first specimen of the street crowd.

About *Journey to Italy*, Antoine De Baecque has noted that it is one of the first films of the postwar period to bear traces of the reemergence of the repressed memory of the horrors of World War II. Although he has specifically in mind the unearthing of the plaster couple in Pompeii in the penultimate sequence (De Baecque 2008, 93–98), which he connects to foreclosed images of the holocaust, I want to highlight how the emotional looks-to-camera of the bronze statues echo the equally disturbing, similar shots of the women secluded in the asylum at the end of *Europe '51*,[8] which De Baecque links to the repressed memory of the first looks-to-camera of the prisoners of death camps filmed at the moment of liberation. Although I will not follow his hypothesis of a connection with the memory of the camps, I second his interpretation of an entanglement of form and history produced by the horrors of the war.[9] However, I widen it to include the connection with the centuries-old oppression of the Neapolitan underclass that the war has worsened and briefly made visible, as had periodically happened in moments of particular crisis. Thus, I read here the outbreak of the statues' subjective perspectives inside the fictional unfolding of the story as the trace of the historical oppression of the vast mass of the Neapolitan poor: a legion of invisible bodies erased from the surface of a touristic paradise by the blinding ideological discourse. This is a discourse that nevertheless can vacillate, momentarily deactivated by the opening produced by the aesthetic gesture, able to create a connection with repressed historical contents, which are thus allowed to "return, as a hallucination of history and a vibration of mise-en-scène" (De Baecque 2012, 3).

To conclude the analysis of the museum sequence, it is worth mentioning the frontal, single-shot presentation of the mutilated (no head and no arms) Venus Katherine contemplates after the emperors, immediately before the Hercules, as a sort of caesura between the historical and the mythical (figure 5.8).

This is the spot when the guide's "humor" succeeds in teasing her the most, as he confesses that this statue is the one he prefers, as she "is not young as the others, she is more mature," thus offering an oblique appreciation to the tourist, who reacts with irritation. This moment is revealing of

Figure 5.8. A marble Venus. *Source:* Roberto Rossellini, *Journey to Italy*, 1954.

the functioning of the aesthetic machine of the film: the moment of tension between Katherine and the guide, directly connected with the Orientalist topic of the sensuality of southern men, manages to occlude a deeper layer of meaning embedded in the apparition of the statue, and in Katherine's emotional reaction to it. The marble statue is perfectly centered against a background equally divided between a dark space immersed in shadow and a white wall. But the body itself loses its margins on the side bordering with the white surface, as they appear to be feathered by shadow, thus creating a second contrast (a sinuous line of shadow between the white marble and the white wall), which is also mirrored by the object's own shadow situated at the other side of the white wall. In sum, this deeply ambiguous image, with its rhythmic articulation of light and darkness, of vertical and horizontal lines—the standing posture against the horizontal sketching of the falling drapery—encompasses the contrast we have seen at play between the marble and the bronze sections, offering in plain sight a picture in which both serenity and suffering seem to be reunited. To be sure, the mutilated statue's potential disquieting effect is attenuated by the strength of the iconographic tradition, which has transformed it into an innocuous vector of classical, archaeological beauty. Yet, after the deep contrast built in this sequence, and especially after the stories of carnage the guide has just related about the emperors, even this Venus assumes a sinister look, where harmony and massacre converge, thus creating a contradictory icon similar to the one where we first observed the emergence of the "original emotion": the *Venus of Milo* in Ingarden's text.

Moreover, the Venus's "mature" beauty, stressed by the guide, offers a mirror image for Katherine, who is now for the first time put in close proximity with a possible empathic contact with the "ascetic images": the invisible dimension of suffering she has just experienced in the exchange of looks with the bronze athlete, but has so far failed to see in the reality of the city. Such empathic contact will be strongly reestablished at the end of Katherine's next driving sequence, before being abruptly dismissed during the visit to the Cave of the Sibyl in Cumae. But this will only take place after the situation with Alex has significantly deteriorated.

On the day after her visit to the museum, the couple attended a party held by Uncle Homer's aristocratic friends, where the men's exaggerated courting of Katherine increased Alex's jealousy, already ignited by his wife's planned "pilgrimages"—this is the ironic term he uses—at the sites sung by Lewington in his poems. Thus, he leaves for Capri to meet his romantic interest Judy, who resides there with the other British friends the Joyces had met on their first night at the Excelsior. On the same morning of his departure, after reading the cold, bitter letter he has left, Katherine drives to the archaeological site of Cumae. As noted by Bergala, of all her drives, this is the one when Katherine is more open to the encounter with the city's foreign reality: "She hasn't put on her sunglasses, her face is a little worn out and wrinkled, like after a sleepless night, we immediately feel her more fragile, more exposed than usual" (Bergala 1990, 52). This is probably because her inner suffering, the sudden disappointment at discovering that her husband has really left her behind, has momentarily broken her ideological defenses against a reality that she is in principle not interested in understanding outside of a touristic framework, but that she has nevertheless been manipulated into exploring by the emotional power of Lewington's verses. Indeed, at the departure of the sequence we see her in close-up speaking to herself about Alex with bitter irony. She seems completely uninterested in the spectacle outside of the car, and yet it is precisely through this absentmindedness that the environment comes to meet her. The first subjective view, taken frontally from the car, seems to be connected to the last shots of the previous drive sequence, as it conveys a scene that appears to have been edited precisely in this point as an ominous sign: In front of the Basilica of Santa Maria della Sanità, where the entrance to one of the catacombs of the city is located, Katherine stops to give way to a black funeral carriage drawn by black horses, while we hear the voices of the bystanders speak about the deceased. Yet this allegorical vision is situated in one of the poorest neighborhoods of Naples (completely outside any reasonable itinerary Katherine may have followed to reach Cumae from Ercolano), and thus offers a coherent opening to the two subsequent subjective visions, where the underclass of the city will look directly into the camera, like the bronze statues had done in the museum. After the first stop, the woman resumes her soliloquy, but one of her bitter smiles is cut short by something she sees on the left side, and the following eyeline match shows, with a panning movement, two poorly dressed women walking in the opposite direction of the car, one of whom briefly looks into the camera, her expression concealed in shadow. This vision has a tensive relation with the subsequent one, with which it creates a climactic crescendo: If here the thymic element projected on the images by the "contact" with the previous facial expression of Katherine had communicated a sense of unease that seemed to connect it to the gloomy vision of the funeral, the second one singles out a woman with deliberate intention, and the panning movement that keeps her in focus as the car drives by is mirrored by her head slightly turning back to follow the camera (figure 5.9).

This fleeting and yet prolonged look (doubled by that of a young man in the background who also turns back to look at us) increases the emotional intensity, also because the body of the woman—a street vendor standing on the sidewalk among other people intent in similar humble occupations—closely resembles the one of the maid at the villa, thus connecting the geography of the city with that of the house. It is important at this point to reflect on the fact that the author had here deliberately decided to stage a non-orchestrated encounter (the most intimate one in cinema: an exchange of looks in shot-counter-shot) between a wealthy tourist and a (real) street vendor captured on camera, something that had never happened in the dozens of films produced in these years around the Orientalist motif of the visit to Naples, a taboo enforced in all discourses about Naples, as the reactions to Ortese's story eloquently demonstrated.

In his classic theoretical reflections on the novelty brought to human experience by the introduction of cinematic close-up, Béla Balázs notes how this tool allowed the communication of a sort of "aesthetic essence" of the social class: "Behind the external, conventional characteristics, the close-up revealed the hidden, impersonal class traits in individual faces. These class characteristics are often more obvious than national or racial characteristics" (1953, 82). These "class traits," where the habitus of the Neapolitan underclass is inscribed, which had already briefly emerged in *Paisan*, were the repressed content of the many Neapolitan films of the time, often musicals (as mentioned, in 1954 alone *seven* such films with Giacomo Rondinella

Figure 5.9. A street vendor in Naples. *Source:* Roberto Rossellini, *Journey to Italy*, 1954.

were released). This is why this brief encounter went almost unnoticed in the critical discourse around the film, or at best was considered to be an index of an incomprehensible reality, the scar left by a Lacanian Real. Following Jameson's model, I will instead read it as the trace of the centuries-old history of oppression communicated by the bodies of passersby in the Sanità neighborhood in early spring 1953. The significance of this encounter is not coincidentally signified by its "wrong" insertion in the structure of the point of view, as the tracking movement is not coherent with the car's direction. As highlighted by Aprà and Martelli, this lack of coherence transforms the aspectual linearity of time of the "ordinary sequence" into a "frequentative" time (202), where the overwhelming emotional tone of the encounter bends, as we have already seen happening in the first sequence and in the museum scene, the rational narrative order. The climactic effect of this encounter is then stressed by the subsequent reaction shot of Katherine, her longest close-up in the film (ten seconds), in which she moves her head and lips as if searching for a word that could explain the incomprehensible vision she is experiencing, for once completely forgetful of the "marriage crisis plot" her character is living through (figure 5.10).

Thus, a single body looking back at us through the camera brings to the surface the reality ideology has erased, responding to the first sign that emerged, against that same car's windows, in the scene where the "original

Figure 5.10. Katherine reacts to something she sees in the street. *Source:* Roberto Rossellini, *Journey to Italy*, 1954.

emotion" was located on the streak of blood left by the squashed bug. This happens precisely because we visualize these "signs" not only *through* but also *together with* the screen that is supposed to keep them at a safe distance while presenting them as picturesque (the luxurious car of the tourist), and because the editing puts them in direct contact with the emotion of the subsequent reaction close-ups, thus establishing a crescendo between the one that responded to the mosquito, in the first sequence, and this latter, more intense reaction to the street vendor's body.[10] Furthermore, the structure of the point of view in this last scene mirrors the one through which Katherine observed the buffaloes, just before noticing the streak of blood, in the first sequence. In both cases the subjective structure is comparable to the type of point of view termed by Fontanille as "suspension," in which the object of subjective vision is not directly shown, but only indirectly evoked by the emotional reaction of the observer.[11] Indeed, even if the street vendor is shown, the object invoked by the magnitude of Katherine's reaction is only metonymically actualized by what is visible, a phenomenon also discussed by Merleau-Ponty in *The Sensible World and the World of Expression*. In the working notes that close the preparatory materials to that course, he adds that in "the universe of expression" knowledge is not produced by the positive presentation of an object—as we have seen, direct presentation is the place where ideology is able to obfuscate reality—but by the production of a standpoint through which contact with the repressed contents of history can be experienced: "Consciousness always aims, not at being, but at gaps in being (glances, etc.) through which it grasps significations" (132). Here the reference to the "glances" ("regards") directly connects this reflection with the quoted passage on the potentiality of close-ups (Merleau-Ponty 2020b, 127), where the specific power of cinema was defined as precisely this capacity to produce the experience of something invisible at the core of visibility.[12] As already mentioned, Torlasco (2008, 70) has reflected on this same phenomenon in Pasolini's *Oedipus Rex*, noting how it can "immers[e] character and spectator alike into a depth that cannot be contained within the spatial and temporal parameters of any individual existence." It is precisely through cinematic moments like this that a fissure is produced, through which the historical content can access the cinematic experience. Not by chance, the exchange of looks Katherine has with the street vendor also represents the moment in which the invisibility of the *acousmêtre* is made to inhabit a single, visible object, as if the soundscape that until this moment had signaled the disquieting presence of this social class beyond the screen of the domesticated presentation of the city had the possibility to flash for a moment in the eyes of this woman randomly encountered by the camera. Could we read in this aesthetic event an example of that "vibration of the *mise-en-scène*" that signals, according to De Baecque, the resurgence of history from the depths of its repression?

This will be for now the climax of Katherine's encounter with the reality of the underclass, which will be overcome only by the final scene of the procession in Maiori. As Gilles Deleuze also noted in his remarks on the film in the opening pages of his second book on cinema, she seems to have spotted here something intolerable: "*Journey to Italy* follows a female tourist struck to the core by the simple unfolding of images or visual clichés in which she discovers something unbearable, beyond the limit of what she can personally bear" (Deleuze 1989, 2). From this point she pulls back, as appears evident from the subsequent episode of the visit to the Cave of the Sibyl in Cumae, where she will refuse to continue on the path demanded by Lewington and will go back to focus solely on her marriage crisis. Yet before this turning point, a strong continuity is established between Katherine's emotional state at the end of the driving scene and the beginning of the visit to Cumae, as the close-up shot slowly cross-fades on her close-up while walking together with an old guide—whose voice we hear, before being allowed to see him in the next shot—along the foot of the hill of Cumae, toward the entrance of the cave. Not surprisingly, as had happened during the visit to the museum, the guide begins by remarking on the place's link to military history, as he explains how, "after the Greeks and the Romans, this place was transformed into a fortress." However, in this case, the connection with more recent historical events is not merely allegorical and is immediately established: After mentioning that Aeneas had landed there after the fall of Troy, he adds that "during the last war, British troops landed here," and this part of his speech is heard offscreen while we see a long shot of the path in front of them, where the stone walls of the hill, the woods of Cumae, and finally the beach and the sea are gradually shown in what looks like a sustained (twelve-second) subjective shot of Katherine with the camera slowly advancing. In this same shot, Katherine's voice is heard asking offscreen: "Really, they landed here?" and he replies: "Yes right here." This insistence on the deictic "here" strongly reinforces the connection between the recent events of the war and the place, which is thus abruptly subtracted from the fog of a mythical past to be reinscribed in the historical present. Moreover, the repetition of "here" echoes the same deictic adverb that we encountered in the first poem attributed to Lewington in the film synopsis, which we analyzed in chapter 1, where another "here" reinforced the concrete presence of the place: "People are born *here* infected with old age." It is also worth noting that the ambient sound during this shot becomes almost inaudible, which makes the man's voice resound against the tree branches moved by the wind, as if this were a series of silent images. This creates an effect that resembles filmic representations of dreams or memory images, as if we were about to be shown a flashback of the British landing. Katherine is surprised by this information, which evidently brings her back to Lewington, to his first arrival in this land. When the film cuts back to a medium shot of her and the guide (we see him pointing the finger toward the beach as he finishes his sentence, "Yes right here," which reinforces the deictic effect), she asks where the troops had stayed after the landing, as if attempting to mentally follow the sudden appearance of the ghost of the poet. But the man simply replies by inverting the direction of his pointing finger, "all around here." However, although this deictic insistence seems to bring us back to Katherine's finger pointing at the streak of blood, she will refuse to accept the emergence of the historical content that is clearly rising to the surface of the story.

Their entrance to the cave is shown with a long take from within the depths of the tunnel carved in the tuff, where we see them entering in the distance and advancing toward the camera, while the guide demonstrates the echo effect with his voice and by clapping his hands. The particular lighting of the place created by regularly repeated openings situated on the external wall creates an alternation of light and shadows, a rhythm of black and white zones that directly recalls the same opposition in the Archaeological Museum, a connection reinforced by the guide's remark about the walls of the cave once being completely covered in bronze. At the symbolic level, the entrance into this chthonic dimension seems to establish a direct connection with a past—both mythical and historical—that keeps returning to the present, like a haunting echo effect. As they reach the point where the camera is positioned, this pans to follow them entering a lateral ambient, which the guide says were the Sibyl's baths, then turned by Christians into catacombs. A cut on what again looks like a subjective shot of Katherine shows us the ruin of the ambient and signals that we are entering a more intimate dimension, where we will be able to experience the woman's emotional reaction, something that is made evident by the start of Renzo Rossellini's eerie music, which continues the theme of the museum visit. Indeed, as we see the man exit to guide her further into the cave, the film cuts to a medium shot of her advancing toward the camera until appearing in close-up: The guide has just said that lovers in ancient times would come to the Sibyl to ask about the destiny of their love. Katherine is visibly moved, and we hear her inner voice repeating Lewington's verses ("Temple of the spirit / no longer bodies / but pure ascetic images") while her face shows an internal turmoil that strongly resembles, and overcomes in intensity, the close-up that had closed the previous driving sequence. The trembling of her lips marks the emotional climax of the story until this point, signaling the endpoint (for now) of the itinerary started with the first appearance of the "original emotion."

One could be tempted to conclude that the affinity of these emotional outbursts could describe a progression of knowledge toward the hidden meaning of Lewington's verses, as if she was finally able to clarify the emotion she had felt in them. First the appearance of the Neapolitan underclass, then the ghostly presence of the war had opened up the possibility of unveiling the hidden object of the quest, of this anti-narrative program secretly mandated by the poet. And yet, as anticipated, we soon realize that at this very moment the quest has been—at least momentarily—abandoned, at both the narrative and the discursive level of the film. Katherine's emotion in hearing about lovers visiting the Sibyl's Cave was not due to Lewington but to her own marriage crisis: the reference to the lovers' destiny and what follows clarify that much. She refuses to continue the visit and renounces to see the very core of the site, the rooms of the Sibyl. Instead, she climbs the hill and visits the temple of Jupiter, from which she emotionally looks at Capri (obviously a geographical fabrication, as the island is not visible from that point), directing all her attention to Alex. It is evident then that this moment marks a movement of retreat from a deeper dimension of knowledge (the Sibyl's rooms were the place where a transcendent truth could be revealed) toward a well-known tangle of personal, private interests. In sum, Katherine has at this point confirmed her refusal to continue the quest mandated by the poet's verses and has gone back to her original program.

This appears evident from her next two driving sequences, which are very different from the previous two. On these occasions, her encounters with the local reality will not even be determined by the authorial intention to present some specific aspects of the city, which had emerged in some moments of her previous itineraries. As Bergala has noted, at this point she has stopped being receptive and has started superimposing her own preoccupation with the landscape outside the car: "She has chosen to see, in the reality she encounters, only what she preselects, that is to say what speaks to her about her marital concerns and what mirrors her envy of a wife in crisis" (Bergala 1990, 53). Not by chance, on her route to the Solfatara in

Pozzuoli, first she only sees couples walking hand in hand, then only women pushing strollers: Her facial reactions show something between amusement and astonishment, as if she was aware of projecting her own fantasies and obsessions onto the landscape. Here Rossellini's intention of using the stereotypical image of the South as the land of romantic and physical love (the "opposite of asceticism") appears to coincide completely with the vision of the protagonist. At this moment, *Journey to Italy* bears the most resemblance to the myriad of musical comedies or dramas produced in Naples at the time, where the ambient images shown at the various touristic attractions seem to be solely populated by couples in love. For this segment it is thus necessary to disagree with Aprà and Martelli, who consider it to be one more example of Katherine's receptivity toward external reality, a sign of which they consider to be the presence of extra-diegetic music (Aprà and Martelli 1967, 203). One need only consider the nature of Renzo Rossellini's musical score in this segment to be persuaded that its function cannot be likened to the one exercised in the museum or in the Cumae scene. Evidently more lighthearted, the score channels here emotional distention instead of increasing tension: It is the relief deriving from the abandoned confrontation with reality, which has given way to a return to the familiar landscape (which is literally projected on the real landscape) of one's own imagination.

The fourth driving scene, toward the cemetery of the Fontanelle, reinforces this schema, as Natalia's presence efficiently works as an ideological filter that selects and presents only the aspects of reality that serve its cause. In the usual structure of these sequences made of close-ups of Katherine reacting to subjective views of the external world, close-ups of Natalia are inserted, in which she points with her finger at all the pregnant women in the street, some of which are then shown. The pointing finger clearly offers here a domesticated replica of the gesture that had first appeared with the "original emotion," as if to signal that the ideological contradiction on which the film is based has been definitely solved. Indeed, the reassuring mechanism of the previous drive is here even strengthened by the explicit discourse about the prolific nature of the local people, whose principal occupations seem to be sleep, food, sex, and procreation (these are the topics touched upon in the two women's conversation). We will also later discover that Natalia too is obsessed with the desire to have a child, and this is one of the reasons why she goes to pray at the Fontanelle. Yet, exactly at the end of this driving scene, the hidden object, the historical existence of the Neapolitan underclass, again reaches the surface of the discourse, and its presence is even more evident as it clashes with the discourse that tries to tame it, thus practically demonstrating, once again, the functioning of the ideological machine we have been exploring throughout this work, which hides what is visible on the surface. Katherine notices a little donkey pulling a cart with three persons on it and pities it for its cruel effort,[13] but Natalia immediately mitigates her dismay, together with any possibility of a resurgent empathic connection: "But they are very strong: it's a tough breed." This affirmation seems to work perfectly to appease her, since, after a distracted comment about how spicy local foods are, she smiles and says, "How beautiful the children are here," while we are shown three children pulling a heavily loaded cart (one of them looks into the camera) (figure 5.11).

If the donkey had been able to elicit her compassion, Natalia's discourse seems to have succeeded in bringing about a complete anesthesia: Children are beautiful; it does not matter if they are performing hard work (and exactly the same the donkey was doing a few seconds earlier!), which is after all completely normal for children of the urban lumpenproletariat. As the two women reach their destination and walk toward the Church of Maria Santissima del Carmine in Materdei, entrance to the Fontanelle cemetery, they go through a crowd of children playing in a muddy street, to whom they do not pay any attention.

Figure 5.11. Street children in Naples. *Source:* Roberto Rossellini, *Journey to Italy*, 1954.

The tourist visits subsequent to these two car trips follow a pattern consistent with what precedes them. The Solfatara in Pozzuoli is certainly the most successful of all of Katherine's excursions: The city's historical reality seems not to disturb her enjoyment carefully directed by a guide for once completely serious and professional—and yet, even here an attentive examination shows how ideological obfuscation undergoes a self-deconstructive process. Similarly, the visit to the Fontanelle cemetery, although carried out under Natalia's supervision, ends up bringing to light that same historical reality initially hidden under stereotypes and folklore, just as had happened with the donkey and the children at the end of the preceding trip.

The visual construction of the Solfatara episode is based on a loose symmetry between the two shots that open and close it, which contributes to the impression that this might be the sequence in which the dominance of the formal construction on the shown reality reaches its highest point. The camera initially shows one of the pits with boiling mud that punctuate the crater. On this indistinct matter we see the guide and Katherine's shadows advance, and we hear the guide's voice, while the camera starts tilting upward. At the end of the movement, we see both standing on the border of the pit, where we also see a pole with an explanatory sign, while the man continues his introduction. Still in the same long take, the camera pans right to follow them advancing to the side of the pit to reach a point where the guide will demonstrate the phenomenon of ionization. In the entire sequence—the only one of the four without music—we never see a close-up of Katherine: Her closest proximity consists of a medium shot in which she is taking a photo with her Rolleiflex; we also see some close-ups of the boiling mud, which can be interpreted as subjective views of Katherine, although no element of movement or sound, no emotional reaction (outside of some conventional verbal expressions of approval or amusement) gives them any emotional intensity, which makes this excursion the only one in which the thymic element is completely absent.[14] This absence contributes to the impression that this outlandish landscape with its white surfaces, its boiling pits, and its ubiquitous smoke appears as completely domesticated by the human discourse that encapsulates it: the guide's speech of course, but also the explanatory sign, the photographic gear, the newspaper rolls used to demonstrate ionization, the two human bodies that awkwardly squat and bend to perform the actions required for a full "enjoyment" of the demonstrations. Even so, we perceive how the nature of the place points to a dimension beyond the surface, inhabited by uncontrollable forces. Sure, in this case there is no evident reference to the recent war, and yet the obfuscation of visibility due to smoke and vapors directly recalls a similar image in the first of Lewington's poems ("Silence falls on everything / like dust"), which we had interpreted as a reference to a double muffling of sensations (sound and vision) due to the effects of bombing. If we proceed in this line of thought, we must also realize that the images in the Solfatara are the closest, at the visual level, to combat scenes Rossellini had shot for *The White Ship*, where the main visual element used to convey the feeling of danger, despair, and entrapment had been the smoke—but the moment in which Katherine squats with a cigarette in her hands to ignite the ionization also bears a mnestic trace of the American agent Dale squatting with a cigarette to fuse a mine to cover up for a partisan operation in the last episode of *Paisan* (figures 5.12–5.13).

Figure 5.12. Katherine in the Solfatara in Pozzuoli. *Source:* Roberto Rossellini, *Journey to Italy*, 1954.

Figure 5.13. Dale lights the fuse of a bomb. *Source:* Roberto Rossellini, *Paisan*, 1946.

Furthermore, the guide's mention of the destruction of Pompeii while showing Katherine the small crater called "pocket Vesuvius" (further evidence of the domesticating effect of the explanatory discourse) completes the picture with a reference to the classical archaeological past, which had accompanied the previous two visits.

Particularly meaningful is the last segment of the visit. First of all, as anticipated, it mirrors the first one, reinforcing a sense of orderly closure (an impression immediately contradicted, as we will see), as it is introduced by an image of volcanic activity with no human figures, before the camera tilts downward to include Katherine and the guide who are gazing into the crater from its border, as they had initially done (but from the opposite side). Yet here a new element intrudes into the picture: To demonstrate the effect of the eruption of lapillus that destroyed Pompei, the guide suddenly calls a young assistant who was evidently standing right there just out of frame ("Giovanotto, ragazzo!" in Italian in the English version too) to move the soil with a shovel. Thus we discover that a third human presence, completely ignored by the two, had been there alongside for all the time of the visit. We barely see a piece of his head from behind Katherine (in a shot that becomes a whole palimpsest of occluding surfaces: Katherine's back hides the young man's back while both cover the object they are observing, the place of the "eruption," which is also shielded by a heavy cloud of smoke) before observing the act of his labor, as finally a subjective shot shows us a close-up of the shovel moving the lapillus. The film then cuts back to the previous shot with Katherine and the guide commenting and enjoying the phenomenon, but now the young worker has disappeared. Thus, here too the construction of the filmic space demonstrates how the ideological discourse is able to obstruct the presence of the human element on whose labor the social edifice is based. Like the destructive forces of the underground are domesticated and transformed into a tourist attraction by the discourse (the guide replies with an authoritative "No" to Katherine's initial question about the potential danger of the place), similarly the lower-class mass that makes up the vast majority of the population is either excluded from visibility or domesticated through the picturesque. Yet the filmic construction manages to bring it to the surface, and, while showing the mechanism of visual occlusion itself, also offers a demonstration of the possibility of its deconstruction. Not by chance, as Katherine and the guide exit the shot, we finally see the young man fully enter the frame to follow them quickly. This fragment is completely unnecessary to the construction of the story; it thus destroys the initial impression of symmetry that had to encompass the episode and reopens the quest for the hidden object that had been apparently dropped at Cumae (the anti-narrative program mandated by Lewington), which is now clearly configured as a task for the actantial role of the observer, not necessarily coinciding with one of the characters, and that will be fulfilled in the final scene, when the camera intentionally leaves the protagonists and moves away to frame the crowd. The film will end with the crowd passing through the shot from one side to the other, like the young worker of the Solfatara, but in the opposite direction.

Finally, Katherine's attempt to abandon the anti-program to flee the overwhelming anxiety that derives from it and return to her original quest is shown to fail definitively with the last of the four excursions, the visit to the Fontanelle cemetery accompanied by Natalia. The most striking feature of this episode, the shortest of the four, is the way it contradicts its premises. The day before, Natalia had proposed this excursion to Katherine as a tourist must-see, entirely focused on the picturesque aspects of the city. The car trip the next morning, as we have seen, had displayed the control of the ideological discourse over the city's reality. However, the beginning of the visit immediately overturns these premises. As we see the two women enter the church from the street, Natalia leads Katherine, and right before stepping inside slightly turns back to give her a reassuring look (carved skulls on the door already loom ominously) as if to show that she is in full control. Yet when we see them enter the catacomb itself (one must pass through the church first, exit from the back, and access another door leading inside the flank of the hill), things have already radically changed. The camera is inside a vast space immersed in darkness as we see the women's shadows entering against the external light. Katherine comes first, Natalia hesitantly follows and even stops to kneel and make the sign of the cross, while Katherine slows down and turns back, surprised by this behavior. As they proceed—Natalia no longer appears reassuring and in control—ominous music starts with slow and heavy percussions. As they reach the camera, this latter pulls back to track them in a medium shot, thus not revealing the structure of this vast dark chamber, which is never shown with an establishing shot, so that we are forced to share the women's disorientation. The shot is only briefly interrupted by a subjective segment in which we see a funereal statue lying behind a protective net. Its tormented posture and the previous and following expressions of Katherine, intensified by the music, here forcefully repropose the thymic element that had disappeared from the subjective shots at the Solfatara. Moreover, Natalia appears not to know where to go; Katherine leads, hesitates to find the way, while the former humbly follows her. As they access the next chamber, another subjective segment, with a tracking movement in close-up, finally shows us the main "attraction" of the catacombs: the long rows of skulls stacked on top of each other above a sort of low wall made of bones, lighted by candles. At this point we see the reaction of the two women in medium full shot: As Katherine appears dazed, for two times Natalia turns to look at her at length, as if trying to measure the magnitude of her dismay. As they proceed further in the chamber and the camera pans to observe them move away, we finally get an establishing shot displaying the vastness of this huge subterranean chamber, with high vaults of tuff, whose walls are surrounded at the bottom by the piles of skulls.

As we see the two women at a distance, belittled by the vastness of the ambient punctuated by the undistinguishable shadows of sporadic other visitors, Natalia quietly leaves Katherine to go kneel in front of what appears like an altar (also made of bones) and pray. Even from this distance, with her face not clearly distinguishable, Katherine seems lost until she realizes where Natalia is and what she is doing. We then observe her frontally in medium shot, advancing toward the other woman, not knowing what to do or say. When this latter finally turns around to talk to her, what she says has nothing to do with the picturesque discourse about Neapolitan folklore she had used to "sell" her the trip: "My brother died in Greece during the war." She comes here to pray because his body was never returned: Praying in front of the unknown dead offers a form of consolation. Katherine does not say a word. All ideological control over the narrative matter and the visual field has completely disappeared. No discourse can tame these kinds of images, and no diegesis can be asserted over them. The vastness of the dark subterranean space makes the human bodies of the living insignificant like their discourses. To such an impression that we could define as "mathematical sublime" in the sense of Kant, the huge mass of ancient human remains responds in turn by producing a "dynamical sublime," as it encompasses in one glance the annihilation of generations through the eras. The Fontanelle had been used during the many catastrophes of the city since the seventeenth century as a mass grave for the Neapolitan underclass,[15] of which it offers a ghostly, collective representation. Its uncanny impression is only apparently mitigated by the rigorous order imposed on the bones by the nineteenth-century restoration, before which heavy rains were able to flood the place and push the human remains into the city's main sewer, thus clogging it (Scotto di Santolo et al. 2013, 643): a material demonstration of the psychanalytical concept of "return of the repressed" in political terms. In sum, the visit to the real underground of the city, where the material signs of its history of oppression are clearly visible, overlaps with the memories of the recent war evoked by Natalia—an association that is also reinforced by the fact that Rossellini had captured on camera a similar Neapolitan cave at the end of the second episode of *Paisan*, to show the conditions of the people displaced by the bombings. If we superimpose the two sequences, which could have been shot in the same place (although we know that the cave in *Paisan* is the one in Mergellina), we obtain a palimpsest of the history of the Neapolitan underclass from past centuries to the present, the living and the dead united by the same destiny of suffering under the same dark vaults.

Miracles

The last two sequences of the film—the visit to Pompeii and the procession in Maiori—summarize and subvert the formal and thematic structure on which the relationship between the Joyces and the local reality of Naples had been arranged throughout the film. Although fleetingly, the couple is here forced to live through the experience of the hidden object of the quest mandated by the dead poet: the existence of the lower classes. The main element of continuity and symmetry between the two scenes consists in their focal center of attention, in both cases a sculptural object: the plaster cast of a couple in Pompeii and the statue of the Madonna Addolorata (the Virgin Mary according to the iconography known as Our Lady of Sorrows) in Maiori. The two objects are located at the end of opposing vectorial directions: The cast is slowly unearthed, thus drawing the onlookers' attention downwards; the statue is carried in procession on the men's shoulders, as is customary, and thus attracts the gazes of the crowd upward. The formal framing of the opposition is not symmetrical, though, as the first scene follows, in its first part centered around the excavation, the subjective structure prevalent in Katherine's previous expeditions, thus mostly consisting in a shot-reverse-shot of the Joyces looking down and of their point of view; on the contrary, the second part of the following sequence where the statue appears shows the procession through objective crane shots—although the full shot of the Madonna is taken from a low angle, which symmetrically inverts the way the cast was framed. This lack of formal symmetry in the use of subjective and objective structure results from the necessity to represent a break in the way the ideological mechanism is portrayed in the story. If the Pompeii episode still shows ideology's power to impose meaning on the surface of reality, thus occluding its content while in full sight, the procession's scene halts the mechanisms to let the object finally emerge.

For a correct interpretation of the Pompeii scene, it is important to note that this latter is ambiguously connected with both dimensions on which the film has unfolded until this moment, thus representing a climax for both main narrative programs. For Katherine's original program, which we summarized as a quest to revitalize and save her marriage, the emergence of the effigy of the dead couple represents an image of failure however we read it. It matters little whether it shows eternal love in opposition to the already decided end of their marriage or a macabre allusion to that same end; for Katherine it means the dissolution of all hope to which she had clung in the previous days. As such, charged by her increasingly expressive facial reactions in the subjective structure in which it is inserted, the scene reads as a perfect example of the moment in which the passional itinerary of expectation (patience) implodes, turning into its contrary, according to the description Greimas gave of the culmination of this process: "The instance in which tension, which characterizes patient expectation and is overdetermined by the category of intensity, becomes excessive, even intolerable, and brings about knowledge of the nonrealization of the NP [narrative program] of the doing subject" (Greimas 1987, 154). At the same time, if we reflect on the anti-narrative program Katherine had failed to follow but which nevertheless continued to haunt the film, as a secret task for the actantial role of the observer even when not in conjunction with the subjectivity of the character, we must place this image of excavated bodies with all the other signs of the emergence of a repressed object from the city's depths, with which Katherine had come into contact throughout her tourist excursions. Moreover, the event of reemergence itself is in this case performed amidst a group of almost faceless laboring bodies squatting on the ground (the nameless workers of the archaeological enterprise), which thus completes the analogy of this with the past excursions, where the reference to a further dimension beyond the surface of reality (historical, mythical, or geological) had been at times accompanied by the appearance of the bodies of a laboring population, although filtered through the lens of the picturesque. To these common elements, we should also add Tony's explanatory discourse, almost a live chronicle of the excavation we hear over the subjective segments, which mirrors the functions of the previous guides, and the tense musical score, which, like in all previous excursions except Solfatara, had highlighted the rising pathetic intensity evoked by the visit. However, the double meaning taken over by the cast also signals the capital moment in the story in which the Joyces are forced to take the first step toward a real knowledge of the mysterious object they have previously refused to see. If we think of the first moment in which their structural relation to the Neapolitan reality clearly appeared, that is, taking possession of the villa, which instated them into the role of local masters, we see how they are now observing an inverted mirror image of themselves in an object that clearly overlaps with the position of the underclass in that exemplary structure. If on that occasion they had been comfortably lying in a heightened place in the sun, in a brightly lit and open space that demonstrated a full—unlimited—availability of existential possibilities, they now project themselves over two anonymous bodies buried in a deep, dark underworld, entrapped in the anguish of a twisted position that excludes any existential possibility, exactly like the nameless servants in the low and dim ambient of the kitchen, surprised in the middle of an uncomfortable and fleeting moment of rest among the impending tools of toil (figure 3.6). It is also important to note that the symmetrical opposition between the two moments is highlighted by a major element of the landscape, placed in the background on both occasions, that is, Vesuvius, looming beyond them on the terrace of the villa and here again as they observe the excavation of the cast. As we have seen, it functions as a signifier of underground forces on the verge of exploding onto the apparent tranquility of the surface. Thus, for the first time they are forced to come closer to the insight of the social position we visualized on the neutral term of the semiotic square of the activities of privileged and oppressed classes (figure 5.2), where we find an existence trapped in a condition encapsulating the basic, forced gestures of survival and the pointless dispersion of energy due to the excess of anxiety, where all meaning seems to be abolished.

This will only be a first step of course, and will not be fulfilled until the final sequence. Before that moment, though, the experience of that position will be once more reinforced in the second part of the sequence, in which the camera follows the Joyces as they traverse, alone, the ruins of Pompeii to reach their car. This solitary flight from the place of revelation had happened as a consequence of Katherine's emotional breakdown at seeing the plaster bodies completely freed from the ground. Their exit from the archaeological site offers a striking visual materialization of the desert-ified inner landscape of the exhaustion of hope, which for Katherine has been just consumed; as for Alex, he has refused to see that hope in the first place, so he does not possess any awareness of the situation. However, the connection of this with the previous half-sequence does not relate solely to the failure of Katherine's "marriage salvation" program but also to the story's main anti-program, for which it constitutes a painful development toward fulfillment. The itinerary is shown through seven shots repeating the same structure: The Joyces enter the frame from the left and walk toward the camera, usually until the moment in which they are framed in a medium shot, then the camera pans to follow them until they exit on the right. Each time, except the last when they have nothing more to say to each other, as they approach the camera they initiate a conversation connected to their previous argument, which then abruptly ends. This repetitive structure of both formal and thematic levels reflects here a presentation of the skeletal urban space, which, despite appearing open and brightly lit (most of the shots begin and end as long shots), again signals a lack of possibilities, as all the visible passages, except the one the couple ends up taking, are blocked with some sort of barrier (figure 5.14).

This reinforces the impression of the dead end reached by their marriage, but also continues to place them inside an experience materially similar to the one belonging to the lower classes, where the lack of existential possibilities—which had been, at the start of the Joyces' adventure in Naples, the opposite of the vast opening they had experienced from the villa's ter-

Figure 5.14. The Joyces among the ruins of Pompeii. *Source:* Roberto Rossellini, *Journey to Italy*, 1954.

race—is coupled with the necessity to perform certain basic actions (going home via the most direct route) and with the pointless dispersion of energy (the outburst of discomfort and even desperation that each time aborts their conversation). This is why I disagree with Bergala's suggestive interpretation of this passage, that the ghostly landscape of Pompeii could represent "a city in negative, a void of space-time through which they must pass before being reborn" (Bergala 1990, 63). This is precisely not a void, but a space completely saturated and exhausted, where the apparent multiplicity of viable directions is only an illusion, and the only possible itinerary is strictly enforced by the material construction of space itself.[16]

With the next driving scene—the first part of the last sequence—we finally see the couple alone again in the Bentley like in the first sequence, while the film goes back to a subjective structure based on the alternation of medium shots of the Joyces inside the car and subjective views of the external world, until the moment in which, on the Corso in Maiori, in the middle of the procession, their car is stopped by a guard, they exit, and the film definitively shifts to the objective structure. Yet we could say that the possibility of subjectivity ended, for the Joyces, when they looked at the plaster cast. Too evident is their disinterest in the chaos unfolding around them, which is shown through the absence of any thymic element in the presentation of the external world, as their thoughts and emotions, and Katherine's in particular, are completely focused on their sentimental situation. The fact that their entrance into the crowd, with the car forced to slow down, completely encapsulated by it, directly reconnects to the ominous encounter with the buffaloes in the first sequence, clearly signals that we have reached a point in which a promise of revelation must be fulfilled. This revelation will not happen *thanks to* the Joyces, though: It will not be motivated, in other words, by a choice or a gesture, conscious or unconscious. The external world interests them only for the obstacles it poses to their advancement, a fact that is materialized by the insistent sound of the car's horn, whose cacophony covers both the ambient sounds and the typical festive music played somewhere by a popular concert band for the procession. As their discussion about the technicalities of the divorce eliminates even their initial, practical interest in the event around them, we witness an exchange, portrayed in a shot-reverse-shot alternation of close-ups inside the car, in which, clearly visible in the background, are the lateral back windows, which thus frame the passing crowd as a sort of screen. This pivotal moment brings to closure a main stream that had been traversing the film. On the one hand, it demonstrates the film's occasional allegorical use of street crowds during Katherine's drives, when, after her refusal to open her attention to the existence of the lower classes, she had started to project her own desires and expectations onto the external world, thus "evoking" all the couples of lovers, the pregnant women, or those with strollers. In this case, as she bitterly comments that the origin of their relationship problems had been the lack of children and he retorts that she had been the one not wanting them in the first place, we see, several times, children appearing framed by the window, unseen by Katherine but clearly visible: not a visualization of her hopes in this case, but of her regrets. Yet, exactly because in this case the most evident subjective projection is brought inside the objective part of the subjective structure, the film is also clarifying the functioning of ideological vision as it had been suggested until this moment: The screen through which vision happens, at the same time a protective barrier enforcing a separation, is able to erase the content of vision while framing it in full sight, transforming it in a picturesque ornament of the landscape or in an allegorical element. We cannot avoid noticing here how the particular frame in which a young girl is included in the window in the background of Katherine's close-up directly recalls the scene in Ortese's story—analyzed in the introduction—in which another young girl suddenly made the screen visible, and thus initiated the narrativization of the "original emotion." Here too she interacts with the screen, both the diegetic and extradiegetic one, as she fleetingly looks into the camera (figure 5.15).

Figure 5.15. Katherine in the car during the miracle sequence in Maiori. *Source:* Roberto Rossellini, *Journey to Italy*, 1954.

It is certainly not an accident that shortly after this series of images the subjective structure definitively fades. As they have been stopped on the side of the road by the guard, twice we see them looking outside, moving their heads trying to spot the crowd's center of attention to finally understand what is going on. On both occasions, however, the shot that follows, which we would expect to be subjective, is taken from the heightened perspective of a crane, showing, from above their position, a high-angle long shot of the crowd with the statue of the Madonna advancing far away in the background. Objective vision of the crowd has thus definitely expelled their subjectivity from the formal structuring of reality, something that also reflects their mental focus still being placed on their own situation, as, after these fruitless attempts at seeing, Katherine tries to move physically closer to Alex, a gesture he refuses, and after which they exit the car. At this point, for the first time in the film, except for the two moments in which the guide in the Sibyl's Cave had touched Katherine's wrists and a prostitute in the car had placed her head on Alex's shoulder, they are touched by local common people,[17] as the presence of the pressing crowd does not allow them to move without touching or being touched. Their presence inside the crowd is portrayed through medium shots first of Alex exiting the car, then of Katherine doing the same to try to go around the car to reach him. This action is interrupted four times by crane shots showing, from four different perspectives, the crowd orderly moving in the different "streams" of the procession. It is important to note, in addition to the physical contact with the crowd portrayed in the medium shots of the Joyces, that these shots display a multilayered space, in which, beside the main focus on the protagonists, bodies are able to pass in front of the camera at different distances from it, and even to look into it, thus rendering tangible the actantial role of the observer as it has separated from the character and has been taken up by anonymous focalization. Before the fifth return to the medium shot of the Joyces in which they will be reunited, a full shot of the statue of the Madonna is inserted, in which her iconography is finally visible, together with the dagger that typically pierces her heart. As the focus of the complex lines of forces traversing the crowd, at first the climactic appearance of this image of pathos does not bring about any effect on the Joyces, thus confirming that it is not to be interpreted as seen through their own subjective view. Yet it somehow ends the separation between the private story of the couple and the public event, as the subsequent medium shot continues with a camera movement that reveals it as being taken from a crane, as the camera "slides" away while casting its visible shadow on the people below[18] and ends on a wide vision of the crowd. Finally, after two close-ups in which Katherine will for the last time try to push Alex to reconsider the decision, only to end the discussion on the expression "I despise you," a long shot shows the occurrence of the miracle: In the chaotic crowd's movement we spot a man at a distance, seen from behind, raising his arms, while a woman in the foreground, looking offscreen, screams "'O miracle!" A frantic sequence of shots follows. Katherine is carried away by a stream of people as she turns back to call Alex. We see her in close-up, while the camera quickly pans to follow her; a reaction of Alex follows, then for two shots the two have completely disappeared. We see chaotic movements of the crowd, people screaming, kneeling, gesturing toward the sky, the center of attention being the elderly man that has started walking again—but we will only understand this later as we see somebody carrying his crutches behind him and parading them as trophies. Then Katherine reappears, but only as a distant, distressed, screaming face at the end of a stream of bodies pushing her away; next we see Alex entering the flux of the crowd trying to reach her, until they again disappear inside the mass traversed by incomprehensible forces. What is the meaning of these frantic moments? If, until the last image before the "miracle," we had received further confirmation that Katherine's quest to save her marriage had definitely ended with the contempt she expressed for Alex, what is the significance of what comes next for the anti-program, *the other quest*, the one for the object hidden below the surface of this mysterious reality, the existence of the underclass, the "ascetic images"?

Writing about *Europe '51*, Jacques Rancière notes how that film included an attempt to find a peculiar, formal technique to portray the inhabitants of Rome's slums, as if the director had understood that a specific form was needed to communicate the experience of being inside that crowd—something that was (and is) by no means common for upper-class individuals and about which the "fear of the underclass," from which this work started, offers an evident proof: "The people are first of all a way of framing. There is a rectangular frame that the camera cuts out; inside this frame there are lots of people. And that is enough. We have here a necessary and sufficient structure of representation: the people are represented by a frame that encloses a lot of people—a fundamental structure that pays off in sensible qualities that become moral ones" (Rancière 2003, 113). Interesting for the present argument are not so much the "moral qualities" he mentions as the "sensible" ones produced by this way of framing the popular crowd. As this film has abundantly shown, privilege and material wealth first and foremost translate into the availability of space, and into the possibility of preventing other people from accessing that space. The Joyces have been shown in the private comfort of their car, on their vast and empty terrace, in the beautiful, silent rooms of their villa—although, the insistence of the diegetic *acousmêtre* had constantly reminded them—and us—of the presence of an alien being forcibly removed from those spaces, pressing on their borders. Indeed, being poor has meant at all times inhabiting crowded spaces and not being able to afford room and privacy. The way this final sequence gradually constructs the invasion of the couple's private, proxemic space by the common people, until the point in which they are violently forced into brutal contact with them, enhances the experience communicated by the presentation of the crowded space of the poor, as described by Rancière, until the point in which that experience is channeled into the spectators, not through a simple decoding of intellectual information but through the "cinesthetic subject" theorized by Sobchack, which I referenced to explain the effect of the first appearance of the city's lower class as the servants carrying the heavy luggage for their masters. If in that case the impression could have been perceived by viewers as just a fleeting sense of discomfort, almost below conscious awareness, it must be felt much more clearly and strongly here because of "the way we are in some carnal modality able to touch and be touched by the substance and texture of images; to feel a visual atmosphere envelop us; *to experience weight, suffocation, and the need for air*; to take flights in kinetic exhilaration and freedom even as we are relatively bound to our theater seats . . . and sometimes even *smell and taste* the worlds we see on the screen" (Sobchack 2004, 65; my emphasis).

What Katherine and Alex are experiencing here, not just fictionally but as Bergman and Sanders in the materiality of their bodies, is precisely the "weight, suffocation, and the need for air," the heat and the smell that being trapped in the crowd must have implied. Thus their disappearance and reemergence inside that human flux for the first time places them and us in a condition we had witnessed without being able to understand: the complete lack of possibility, the material exhaustion of any possibility implied by the saturation of the space with bodies. What remains, no differently than during the long walk to exit the ruins of Pompeii—although the effect is reached here in a diametrically opposite way—is the only viable activity in this situation, that is, the one that allows one to survive: going forward with the crowd to avoid being crushed while turning back to ask for help. Indeed, in the previous analysis and while reading Ortese's story, we have seen this category of actions emerging again and again, as the basic gestures one performs to survive—from material labor to the care for one's own body—are the gestures that the poor are forced to perform as the only form of action accessible to them, which we have placed on the fourth position of the semiotic square of the privileged and oppressed classes' activity. Differently than in Pompeii, though, where the long way out had been only a momentary, bleak deviation from a normally leisurely routine, also self-imposed by the situation, as Alex had even asked Katherine if she didn't want to "look around for a moment" before they go, here in the procession they are absorbed in the totalizing experience of physical danger, where any other horizon of possibility fades. If we now reflect on the fact that, together with the imposed gestures of survival, they also discharge their fear and anxiety through the frantic, pointless agitation of the visible parts of their bodies, we can finally conclude that they have been swallowed up in the position of the neutral term (figure 5.2), in which meaning is abolished and where possibilities end: the normal condition of the dispossessed, where we find the "ascetic images" spotted by the poet during the war.

The quest, therefore, is here fulfilled. The Joyces have reached the knowledge of the mysterious object, and it is now clear that there was no other way. No merely intellectual, external knowledge of it was possible, as the function of ideological blindness is precisely that of hiding what is visible in plain sight—that is, in the case of Naples, through the picturesque and the ancient stereotypes that fuel the "Neapolitan ideology," which are only a local version of the master discourse of Orientalism in this Southern-European declination. Not by chance, instead of showing the Joyces understanding the form of life of the lower classes, or worst of all acknowledging it through some form of empathic connection, the film has created for them a standpoint through which that existence might be experienced.[19] However, as this was also the object of the quest whose subject had coincided with the actantial role of the observer, the communication of such an experience has not simply been thematized but also assumed by the aesthetic mechanism whose goal has been, to go back to Merleau-Ponty's formula from which this reflection started, to create "the set of means by which one makes things and others appear—as opposed to means of defining them" (Merleau-Ponty 2020a, 181). In other words, with a violent stimulation of the cinesthetic subject in this final sequence, prepared by the climactic structure of the whole film, viewers not only visualize an experience but become able to access a standpoint through which the existence of the underclass, as that form of life where necessary and pointless action coincide, is communicated as a series of experiential coordinates, a "non-logical content" that can only be lived through but not really decoded through a rational description, as Merleau-

Ponty noted while defining "alogical essences" accessible through the artistic experience as those "things that are categories, dimensions, structures of time, space, life. The quality of a world = such organizing principles, included in a concrete fabric" (Merleau-Ponty 2020a, 164).

In other words, for the experience of others to be communicated, bodies must become the "ascetic images" of the aesthetic experience, that is, images inhabiting the coordinates of their own life-world, channeling their own habitus. However, with the disappearance of the Joyces inside the experience of the underclass, the aesthetic mechanism of the film has performed one more inversion: If for the two protagonists the event of the miracle coincides with the absorption in necessity and meaninglessness, what animates the crowd around them is the exact opposite. In that saturated space, by breaking the lines and fluxes prescribed by the procession, they have accessed the condition in which activity is freely chosen and effective: the first position of the square, the "meaningful activity." This has been inscribed in the filmic space since the beginning of the sequence, as the medium shots of the Joyces outside of the car already demonstrated a multiplicity of spatial layers, which people could freely access to move in all directions. Moreover, the pointless gestures through which anxiety is discharged had been replaced, or at least subsumed, inside the festive celebration of joy caused by the miracle, which the crowd of Maiori has clearly embraced with irony while complying with the indications of the director they all knew well, without failing to enjoy the empowerment of being the protagonists of the performance, as appears evident from the many looks to the camera and from the relaxed attitudes of those who simply decide to stand and enjoy the spectacle. Thus for once the humble crowd of the commoners occupies the privileged—utopic—space of the complex term, in which meaningful activity is reunited with the idleness of the pure enjoyment of life, a condition not even the masters are allowed to inhabit because of the burden of oppression—at the other side of which they stand—that prevents them from accessing a truly meaningful form of action, let alone reconciling it with an idle use of time (figure 5.16).

It is not a coincidence that once the Joyces reemerge from the dangerous embrace of the crowd to be finally reunited in their own, private embrace, "miraculously" reconciled, they are nevertheless excluded from this privileged, fleeting condition—something plastically visualized in the isolation they inhabit, as the crowd has suddenly made room for them, and some are even *enjoying them as spectacle*, smiling at the performance, standing all around them. What has happened is simply that the experience of the

Figure 5.16. Semiotic square of the miracle sequence. *Source:* Created by the author.

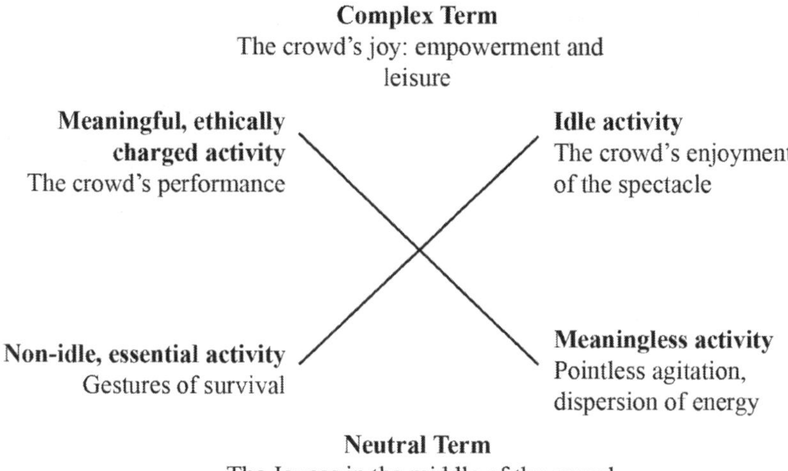

abolition of meaning, of the dangerous existence of the poor, has momentarily purged Alex from the drive to pursue his own original program, the one that began the story: going *there* to sell the villa, enjoying a brief vacation and then going back home, in compliance with the ideology of business and efficiency, the ideological sender of this quest. As Katherine's search for a meaning that could rebuild the foundation of their relationship interfered with this ideology, their marriage, as a "business enterprise,"[20] had ceased to be profitable to him and she had become a burden he had to cut loose. Yet now, still from within the place where absolute raw precarity cancels the efficient administration of life, Alex's previous concerns do not make sense anymore. The only thing that makes sense in this condition, as many know well, is simply the fulfillment of the immediate task of daily survival. For those who survive in the informal economy, each day has its own, fully concluded task—survival—beyond which the mind does not dare go. This is why, in the pure present, the only temporality conceded to the underclass, the Joyces can be happy again, and Katherine's quest is also, miraculously, fulfilled. But this is only natural given the dimension they have accessed. This is why the camera leaves them with a crane movement that once again only shows the crowd from above, followed by a fixed, medium shot of some members of the concert band (their music had never ceased, although it had been overshadowed by the cries during the confusion of the "miracle"). In front of them, in one of the layers of space the film has liberated for the free movement of the people, the crowd now passes framed in close-up, too close and fast for many details to be grasped, except for some amused, fleeting looks-to-camera. Thus, the originally hidden object points back to the surface of enunciation, as the girl had done with the window in Ortese's story, as the trace of blood on the car windshield had suggested in the beginning: The film circles back to its original source of anxiety and, beyond itself, to the looks-to-camera of the refugees in the cave that close the Neapolitan episode in *Paisan*. However, just as the emotional quantum evoked by Bergman's physical reaction to the surrounding reality could only be defined as something "unbearable" (in Deleuze's words), what emerges here is the "irrepresentable" consistency of the historical process. Fleetingly expressed by the permanence within the condition in which all privilege is abolished, the film has here already retreated from it toward the utopic staging of popular joy, thus replicating the original movement of revelation and refusal that founds the secret rhythm of both Ortese's and Rossellini's creative gestures.

Epilogue

Ars Moriendi

To conclude this analysis, let us return once again to that archetypical place in the text where we located the emergence of the "original emotion." In both works, the latter is initially conveyed by the anxiety of a physical contact, which occurs in a phantasmatic way (in "The Silence of Reason") or is only feared (in *Journey to Italy*). This is a common experience in that historical context, which is still ours: the fear, felt by the privileged, of being touched by the poor, who inevitably seem—almost ontologically—to represent a threat to those who live sheltered from social precariousness in its various possible forms. However, the ideological contradiction to which this anxiety of contact is linked is fundamentally different for Ortese and Rossellini. While Rossellini's film demonstrates the functioning of the ideological machine of the picturesque, thanks to which the privileged can enjoy a pleasant and "safe" vision of southern reality—which is thus exposed and denied at the same time—Ortese goes beyond this, as her way of framing this contradiction has its roots in the ambivalence of the self-diegetic narrator's identification with that situation of misery that the narrative mechanism at once denies and reveals.

At the same time, both works communicate the fundamental traits of the existence of the poorest strata of the urban population, that habitus in which the essential gestures of survival cease to be distinguishable from the meaningless ones through which anxiety is expressed. As we have seen, this condition enters the text as an "inscription"—which I have called here "ascetic images"—partly involuntary, or in any case capable of going beyond the conscious will of the authors, capturing elements of the historical context within which the work takes place. The context thus becomes a latent content (the "historical content" I have defined with reference to

Jameson's work), with which the texts themselves put us in contact in a way that is immediate and subliminal at the same time, and that only textual analysis can reconstruct. The inscription, in other words, is what testifies to a direct contact—in this case, the contact with the reality of Neapolitan misery, in which Ortese and Rossellini participated in different ways—and becomes accessible, in the work, through the coordinates of a standpoint, of a point of view. My aim has been here to develop a reading method able to follow the articulations of social invisibility and to decrypt the traces of a political violence that the text registers and communicates beyond its surface—although it is often the surface itself, as we have seen, that becomes the perfect hiding place.

To understand the foundations of this type of interpretation philosophically, I referred to the writings of Merleau-Ponty from the same years as the works analyzed and therefore participating in that same "window of opportunity" for historical knowledge of the early 1950s, compressed as those years are between the trauma of the war and the oblivion brought by economic development. By bringing together Lukács's writings on the praxis of the proletariat and his own reflection on artistic expression, Merleau-Ponty offered us a way to think about how it is possible to communicate an experience that the ideological machine makes invisible and even "unthinkable." Such is the existence of the lumpenproletariat, and more generally, of the lower classes in the two works we have analyzed. According to Merleau-Ponty, the expressive gesture has the possibility of virtually making our senses "vibrate":[1] It is the action of the invisible in the visible—so important for his subsequent philosophy—that has oriented our analysis of the visual dimension of literary and filmic texts.

If the "original emotion" marks the opening of a contradiction, which I have explained, with a metaphor taken from mechanics, as the overcoming of a stiction (static friction) that "holds back" the onset of textualization, it is not possible to say that the texts analyzed show us its closure. In fact, what we have ideally identified as the conclusion of the itinerary of the ideological contradiction, already from the first chapter—the epiphany of the hunger artist in "The Silence of Reason," the verses in which the touristic reality disappears in the disaster of war in *Journey to Italy*—is nothing other than a further confirmation of its terms, a more plastic and explicit representation of it, which does not in any way hint at a possibility of overcoming it. On the contrary, it would seem that the process of textualization is fueled by the impulse to hide its own historical content at least as much as it responds to the need to escape the sway of the ideological machine. It is no coincidence that the separation, the gesture of withdrawing, of refusing contact with the rejected "creature" returns in the conclusion of both works. It is not surprising, then, that the persistence of this contradictory impulse continued to haunt the two authors for years to come, throughout their long careers. Of course, it is not possible to follow these developments here, but it will be useful to note a possible closure, whose symmetrical correspondence to the archetypal moments we have identified will serve as confirmation of the initial hypothesis. If at the origin of both narrative paths there is the anguish of a rejected contact, which is followed by a separation, at its conclusion there must be an opposite impulse, hinting at the possibility of mending that separation.

In the final sequence of the biographical television film *Blaise Pascal*, made by Rossellini in 1971, in the last period of his career, marked by his abandonment of cinema in favor of television, we witness an inversion of the aesthetic mechanism most typical of *Journey to Italy*. As death approaches, Pascal (Pierre Arditi) asks his sister Gilberte (Teresa Ricci) to take him to the hospice (Les incurables) to die there within the crowd of the poor. This wish is verbalized as the sick man is shown lying on a luxurious bed covered in embroidered fabrics. The medium shot that signals the quiet intimacy of this moment is entirely occupied by his body and that of the woman surrounded by soft materials (the brocade of the tapestries, the bed covers): a representation of death "muffled" by the comfort of material luxury reserved for the privileged individual. This representation is perfectly consistent with the image of the isolated individual of genius, to whom we owe the advancement of civilization according to the paradigm followed here by Rossellini, the classical one of the lives of illustrious men—one of the possible declinations of Monumental History in the Nietzschean sense. It is no coincidence that the desire to be reunited with the crowd of poor, which seems to deny the strict class division implicit in this paradigm (and, of course, in the historical moment being recounted), seems at first to be little more than a rhetorical ruffle, immediately canceled out by the invasiveness of the décor, and in fact never mentioned again in this final sequence, which will see the protagonist die in the comfort of his bed. At most, the only visual element that seems to confirm (and communicate) the anguish of this request is the sweat covering Arditi's face, combined with the low and breathless tone of his voice. However, shortly after, something happens that becomes fully understandable only in light of the analysis just carried out with *Journey to Italy*: The film's soundscape stops functioning coherently with the images, pushing us to question its meaning.

When Pascal asks his sister to receive the Viaticum (the Extreme Unction), the sound of his breathing detaches itself from diegetic coherence, acquiring autonomy with respect to the body to which it was originally tied. Moreover, in the subsequent long take, which culminates in the protagonist's death, this breathing gradually transforms into a death rattle of increasing intensity. As if to accentuate the incoherence, the camera moves away from the bed, retreating until it creates a full shot in which we see the entire environment, with the bystanders in tears, while the volume of breathing becomes disproportionately loud compared to the spatial coordinates and the other sounds (figure E.1).

We also see the protagonist speaking, and his voice (coherent, unlike his breathing, with the position of his source) does not interrupt his death rattle. Thus, with the human bodies shrunk by the distance, the (growing) power of the death rattle becomes a sort of sonic close-up of an entity that is not completely present. What is its meaning? One cannot help but notice how the individual's breathing, even though linked to a visible source, acquires an acousmatic ambiguity. Not completely acousmatic, in fact, since its source is visible, but at the same time no longer certainly tied to it (the overlapping of words and breathing), the breath occupies in this sequence a role that is specular in relation to what I have called,

Figure E.1. Blaise Pascal on his deathbed. *Source:* Roberto Rossellini, *Blaise Pascal,* 1972.

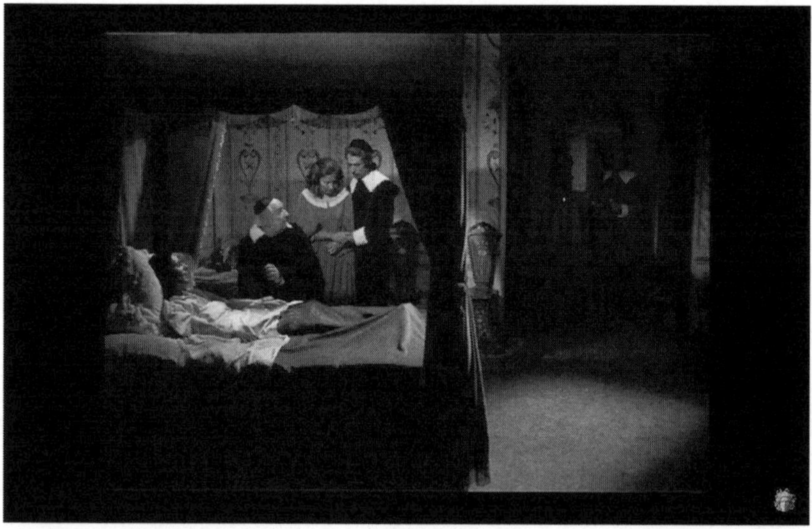

following Chion's definition, the *acousmêtre* of *Journey to Italy*, that is, the invisible crowd that haunts the solitary comfort of the protagonists. While in the 1954 film the incoherent soundscape signaled a presence obscured by the ideological machine, almost twenty years later that separate dimension shows us its reverse side—the now irremediable isolation of the individual—precisely at the moment in which the latter has expressed a desire to reunite with that crowd that has remained invisible. This desire explicitly expressed and immediately forgotten, ignored by the progress of the story, can in fact only produce the impression of a disappointed expectation, of an uncompleted task.

In *Journey to Italy* the diegetic program of the protagonists aimed to escape contact with the invisible crowd, while a contrary agency expressed by the cinematic enunciation made it nevertheless present in its soundscape. Finally, the protagonists could be reunited with this presence through the "miracle," unwittingly realizing a historical knowledge in which their private aspirations lost their meaning (and only in this way could they access a paradoxical salvation). On the contrary, in *Blaise Pascal*, the desire to reunite with the crowd of the poor remains unfulfilled, thus signaling—*e contrario*—the importance of a need for historical knowledge that has now been aborted, even though until that moment knowledge itself, scientific and spiritual, had been the center of the protagonist's life. Therefore, the incoherent isolation of the death rattle calls into question the entire meaning of the film, suggesting that the only thing that really matters remains open, unresolved. To sum up, the impulse to escape physical contact, which is the starting point of the '54 film, is reversed into the opposite desire in the '72 film, where it remains embedded like a void to be filled, almost echoing, therefore the mold in which the lovers of Pompeii are cast: an admission of failure, a late palinode that clarifies the meaning of both works.

A few days before dying, in March 1998, Ortese wrote a short introduction to the reedition of one of her works from about two decades earlier, *The Port of Toledo* (*Il porto di Toledo*, 1975),[2] a delirious,[3] "false autobiography" (Ortese 1998, 14). Between the roman à clef and the prosimetrum, in this work Ortese transfigures Naples into an imaginary marine Toledo, dressing her language with Hispanic oddities. Initially published without any success, *The Port of Toledo* was initially conceived as a way to reuse and vary the short stories and poems of the early years of her career, for which the biographical passages—later expanded beyond the initial intentions—were originally intended to serve as an introduction and explanation.[4] As we saw in chapter 1, this recycling of already published writings was a real obsession of her practice as a writer tormented by poverty and the need for money, always looking for ways to elude physical and mental exhaustion by refurbishing old works.[5] It is no coincidence that *The Port of Toledo* was dedicated, since its first edition, to a woman named Anne Hurdle, executed as a forger.[6] But who Anne was, and how Ortese had learned about her, we only get to know in the 1998 introduction to the book.

Briefly mentioned by Benjamin Constant in an entry of his diary on April 20, 1804, Anne Hurdle was convicted of forgery and executed in London at the beginning of the nineteenth century, at age twenty-three: "Speaking of pain, two months ago I read the story of a young girl of twenty-three, hanged in England for forgery, which impressed me greatly" (Constant 1895, 28). He goes on to describe how the woman remained silent throughout the trial, and only screamed at the moment of the execution, when she felt the trapdoor open under her feet.

For more than twenty years, Ortese's imagination remains fixed on this miserable figure. When she talks about her in 1998, reconstructing Constant's brief notes in her own way, we cannot help but notice the return of a character we have now come to know: the social outcast who refuses the fate of the "creatures" condemned to darkness. These figures, like Elena Adelaide Shelley with whom we began, are briefly "extracted" from darkness and exposed to the light of the "picturesque" for the amusement of the privileged, only to be then plunged back into obscurity. But the beggar girl from "The Silence of Reason," like the kids chasing the tram and the girl who jumps from the balcony, all reject the darkness and bring to the light of the visible, beyond themselves, the entire mechanism that oppresses them, advancing the narrative itinerary of the ideological contradiction. All this we find in Ortese's Anne Hurdle: "Anne lived in *blind*, infinite poverty. That one was her part of the world. One day, her mind, perhaps weakened by the *dark*, sought salvation. It was the money. She didn't have it, she worked hard to forge it. At the trial, she never defended herself. She knew she had irremediably offended the Law who wanted her in the *dark*, which was her natural place" (Ortese 1998, 13; my emphasis).

It is certainly no coincidence that the material poverty, the "class confinement" (Ortese 1991, 1) to which Anne is destined, is here indicated through the visual metaphor of light and darkness: Once again we see the functioning of the ideological machine emerge as an instrument of blindness and vision, which renders Anne and her poverty invisible. And just as the beggar girl had sabotaged that mechanism by bringing to light, with her spit, the screen of ideology, here Anne—who had already attempted to escape that mechanism through forgery—on the point of death lets out a cry, refuses silence, breaks the machine of invisibility by resorting to another sensorial field, making her existence inevitable, inescapable: "She always remained silent. Only when she saw it—the monument to the purity of life—she threw out a long cry, the only one of her life. Thus, she fell asleep" (Ortese 1998, 13). Against all odds, that cry is effective. From the pages of a London gazette it haunts Constant, only to reemerge at the culmination of the work of another "forger" who has rejected her own destiny, and who, in another late introduction, that of the reedition of *Neapolitan Chronicles* in 1994 (which we briefly examined in chapter 2), describes her entire creative process for that book as a scream: "I myself was shut up in that dark seed of life, and thus—through my neurosis—I was crying out. That is, I cried out" (Ortese 2018, 10–11). In this case, the scream signals a direct connection between the beggar girl's act of sabotage (central to that book) and the process of textualization. With one fundamental difference, however: If in the scene in which the "original emotion" had emerged, as in each of its reiterations throughout "The Silence of Reason," the impulse to reveal misery had coincided with the narrator's withdrawal, who had contradictorily affirmed her own difference, avoiding contact with the poorest stratum of the population just as she was revealing her identity with it, here Anne's proximity is declared and invoked: "From the very beginning this book was dedicated to Anne. I wrote it with Anne. Anne has always been with me. . . . I thought, perhaps just felt, that it was necessary to be close to her, to carry her load" (Ortese 1998, 13).

Thus, at the point of death, proximity, even identity ("I wrote it *with* Anne") is finally affirmed, and with it the contradiction linked to the "original emotion" can truly fade. We can now finally observe how the closure of the contradiction to which the most intimate root of an author's creativity is linked is conceivable, at most, only as an *ars moriendi* (real or symbolic), as the art of *dying well* that closes a life's work in its entirety, as a late awareness that can no longer be followed by any work, since the contradiction that is here sublated is precisely the impulse from which every work began. If in Rossellini's case the extreme moment that leads to awareness is a momentary and imperfect accident, and can therefore flash by without actually interrupting the work, in the case of Ortese, whose experience of social knowledge is much more extreme and totalizing, the end of the contradiction coincides with the final silence, which puts an end to the impulse to withdraw, to the need to wear a mask. And while Pascal can only dream of overcoming his isolation to access a communal death, Ortese's self-diegetic narrator finally reunites with Anne, when the onerous need to write has ceased. Thus, in this extreme figure we observe one last time the crowd of beings who refused to accept the darkness, opening, with their defiant gestures, new possibilities of the visible.

Notes

Introduction

1. The Shelleys stayed in Naples from December 1818 to the end of February 1819, lodged at No. 250 of the Riviera di Chiaia (Seymour 2000, 220–31).

2. "History has lost sight of how commonly children were abandoned and adopted in Italy at that time" (Seymour 2000, 227).

3. The expression "ascetic images" will appear in quotation marks when used in this technical sense.

4. Their positions are discussed by Joseph Luzzi, who further reflects on the topic (2014, 65–67).

5. Elena Adelaide Shelley died in Naples in the summer of 1820, while in the care of unknown persons (Seymour 2000, 221).

6. The city was part of the Republic of Poland at the time.

7. While I write, war is upon the city again.

8. This work had previously appeared in Polish (*O poznawaniu dzieła literackiego*) in 1937. However, as Ingarden personally worked on the German translation for the 1968 new, expanded edition, I will reference the latter as the original text, also because the footnotes on which I will closely focus appear for the first time in this edition. The English translation has also been made from this edition.

9. Titled *Das ästhetische Erlebnis*, this paper can be read in Ingarden 1969, 3–7.

10. A technical term in semiotics, I will use "isotopy" in the sense of "semantic isotopy" as defined by Denis Bertrand (2000, 262): "Recurrence of a semantic element in the syntagmatic unfolding of an utterance, producing an effect of continuity and permanence of an effect of meaning along the chain of discourse. It can thus concern the establishment of a figurative universe . . . but also the thematization of this universe" (unless otherwise noted, all translations are my own).

11. "Die Qualität fällt uns . . . auf, drängt sich auf, ergreift uns," (Ingarden 1968, 196). Unless otherwise noted, for this section all subsequent citations in English refer to Ingarden 1973, while all citations in German refer to Ingarden 1968.

12. ". . . Fühlen wir nur, sie locke uns an, sie wolle uns dazu bewegen, uns ihr zuzuwenden, um sie in einem direkten anschaulichen Kontakt (wie durch Berührung) zu besitzen. . . . Um das zunächst auf übertragene Weise auszudrücken, berührt, weckt oder erregt sie uns eher auf eine eigentümliche Weise, als daß sie uns gegeben wäre" (196).

13. "Ein wachsendes Streben nach Sättigung mit dieser Qualität, nach ihrem dauernden Besitz" (196).

14. As they are not relevant to my argument, I will not discuss them here.

15. Precisely such "all-pervading norms of polyphonic harmony and classical aesthetics to which Ingarden's theory is so deeply committed" (Iser 1980, 178) constitute one of the main differences between Wolfgang Iser's theory of the "aesthetic response" and Ingarden's one, which nevertheless provided a foundation to the former. Notably, Ingarden's conception of the work of art has been compared to Johann Winckelmann's: "They used similar terminology in their appraisals of aesthetic experience and even demonstrated similar limitations and blind spots" (Morrison 1996, 36).

16. "Most famously, Albert Speer's neoclassical tower for Germany, with its National Socialist eagle perching atop a swastika, faced off against Vera Mukhina's enormous Worker and Collective Farm Woman, striding forth in the name of the Soviet Union" (Herbert 1998, 14).

17. "Nothing is spared in order to persuade the passerby that each country is the greatest in the universe. . . . From the two sides of the Champ de Mars, the gesticulating colossi of the Soviets defy the eagle of Germany that lies in wait for them." Pierre d'Espezel, "L'exposition internationale des arts et des techniques dans la vie moderne," *Revue de Paris* 44 (August 15, 1937); qtd. in Herbert 1998, 36. "Opposite or almost the flag of Red Russia, to our left, that of Germany with the swastika is surmounted by a golden eagle, which does not spread its wings, but seems to hunker down and wait." Albert Flament, "Tableaux de l'exposition," *Revue de Paris* 44, (June 15, 1937); qtd. in Herbert 1995, 112.

18. "The aesthetic act is itself ideological, and the production of aesthetic or narrative form is to be seen as an ideological act in its own right, with the function of inventing imaginary or formal 'solutions' to unresolvable social contradictions" (Jameson 2002, 63). Here Jameson alludes to Althusser's foundational definition of ideology as "the imaginary relationship of individuals to their real conditions of existence" (Althusser 2001, 162). "Le rapport imaginaire des individus à leurs conditions réelles d'existence" (Althusser 1976, 114). On this point, see also Jameson's preface to his *Allegory and Ideology* (2019).

19. "The idea of a perceptual standpoint is of course everywhere in the air in this period, from experimental psychology to phenomenology, from notions of Weltanschauung to Henry James's practice of 'point of view' in the narrative organization of the novel. Lukács's version has its family likeness with all of these" (Jameson 2015, 13). In this essay, Jameson analyzes the connection between Lukács's

pre-Marxist aesthetic manuscripts from the years of Heidelberg (*Heidelberger Philosophie der Kunst*, 1912–14, *Heidelberger Ästhetik*, 1916–18) and the conception of ideology from *History and Class Consciousness*—about the latter, of course, he has written since the early 1970s.

20. I will put the expression in quotation marks when used in this sense.

21. "The combination of fiscal pressures from the new Spanish state, the rapacity of local feudal lords and widespread famine in the countryside drove many of the rural poor into the City of Naples in the early sixteenth century. . . . If we trace the dramatic population growth of Naples in the sixteenth century alongside a series of severe famines and attendant epidemics, we can see the connection between hunger and urban population growth. Throughout the second half of the sixteenth century, southern Italy as a whole suffered through several famine cycles, while the population of urban Naples continued to grow dramatically" (Selwyn 2004, 32).

22. "Naples also made its mark on the rapidly expanding Society of Jesus, serving as a training ground for members, as an internal frontier that shaped the Jesuits' missionary praxis, and as a place from which to recruit leading members of the Society of Jesus, including those destined for far-off mission fields beyond Europe" (Selwyn 2004, 3). Historian Jennifer Selwyn's book, specifically devoted to the Jesuits' mission in Naples, also offers a wide-ranging reconstruction of the historical debate on the origin of the abnormal conditions of the kingdom in the Early Modern period.

23. All these characteristics also appear in the director's other Neapolitan films, from *Metropolitan Blues* (*Blues Metropolitano*, 1985)—although it does not focus directly on the themes of poverty or marginalization—to *Baby Gang* (1992), which explicitly revisits them. Antonio Capuano should also be compared to Piscicelli; in his work *Vito and the Others* (*Vito e gli altri*, 1991) he effectively explored the intersection of proletarian marginalization and organized crime, using a genealogical perspective—mixing documentary and fiction, obsessively presenting images from TV and video games—that underscores the "inevitable" criminal trajectory of street children, doomed to be discarded by society and exploited by the Camorra. This theme will reappear in *Gomorrah*, both the film and the series.

24. Infamous single-room dwellings located on the ground floor, with the only opening being a door-window facing the street.

25. Countless travel narratives and collections of letters on the topic were published in French, German, or English in the eighteenth and nineteenth centuries (Mozzillo 1993; Moe 2002, 13–81; Colletta 2015).

26. The complete passage Charles de Brosses wrote in a letter from Naples on November 24, 1739, continues as follows: "And, unfortunately, what is corrupt abounds, the city is populated to the point of overflowing. All the bandits and layabouts from the provinces have flowed into the capital. They are called *lazzarielli*; these people have no homes; they spend their lives in the middle of the streets doing nothing and living on the distributions made by the convents. Every morning

they crowd the stairs and the entire square of Monte-Oliveto, so much so that it is impossible to pass through: it is a horrible sight that will make you vomit" (de Brosses 1858, 375–76). In 1776 even the Marquise de Sade wrote that the horror of the Neapolitan poor was "physically impossible to imagine" (qtd. in Moe 2002, 63).

27. "An appreciation of the primitive, natural, less civilized aspects of Naples and the south will become increasingly common from the 1780s on" (Moe 2002, 64).

28. "In the same eighteenth century in which the idea of Europe seems to solidify, and in which Orientalism, as Said has discussed, is established as an academic discipline, Europe starts conceiving a *new* logic for self-definition that renders the Other superfluous. . . . In order for European theory to dispense of the absolute Other, a different rhetoric of antithesis between what Europe is (identity) and what it is not (difference) must, nonetheless, be organized" (Dainotto 2007, 53–54).

29. "The picturesque corresponded to the taste of the sentimental traveller, the *connoisseur* on the Grand Tour, the refined and cultivated intellectual, the painter capable of discovering the various beauties of the landscapes, and the nature-loving philosopher" (Milani 2009, 93).

30. "Yet in Rousseau as in Montesquieu, the south remained a distant fantasy of primitivism against which modern and northern Europe, with nostalgia or with pride, could still theorize itself. It remained the antithesis—nature; the past—posited by the spirit of a modern north eager not only to define itself but also to overcome its own discontents in some superior synthesis, or in a return to a hypothetical origin" (Dainotto 2007, 101).

31. The original title is translatable as *Naples Has No Sea*.

32. In chapter 2 I will treat in detail the creation of both Ortese's book and Rossellini's film.

33. To this figure must be added around 30,000 refugees who arrived in the city in 1943 (Laffin 2019, 156).

34. Similarly to Ortese's *Neapolitan Chronicles* a few years later, Malaparte's book was also received very badly by the city's elite because of his depiction of the Neapolitan poor.

35. "From 1945 until early 1953, Europeans lived, as we have seen, in the shadow of the Second World War and in anxious anticipation of a third. . . . Nevertheless, with the death of Stalin and the end of the Korean War, Western Europe stumbled half unawares into a remarkable era of political stability" (Judt 2005, 242).

36. On collective memory and "social amnesia" in postwar Europe, see Fogu and Kansteiner 2006; Judt 2000.

37. "Una bimba di forse sette anni, completamente rapata, vestita di un solo cencio grigio, che le veniva fin sui piedi, lasciando scoperto il petto, a modo di una dama" (Ortese 1994, 131). Unless otherwise specified, all the following citations in Italian in this section refer to this text, while citations from its English translation refer to Ortese 2018.

38. " 'Guarda . . . guarda' . . . 'Veramente divertente.' . . . 'Come colore, perfetto' " (132).

39. "La ragazzina, come un mostro da baraccone assalito da un capriccio improvviso, lasciò rapidamente il gruppo e, con una mano tesa, sudicia, falsamente implorante, la bocca senza denti aperta in una risata muta, avendo intravisto il giovane, salì di corsa i pochi scalini, si accostò ai vetri, con la gonna in mano, facendo un inchino. Quindi sputò" (132).

40. "La saliva scendeva ora lungo il vetro, e Luigi la guardava" (132).

41. According to Greimas and Courtés (1993, 55–56), in the elementary structure of signification the complex term corresponds to the "coexistence of contraries" (*coincidentia oppositorum*), situated on the upper side of the square.

42. " 'Guardami sulla testa,' disse Luigi . . . con una pazienza e un terrore infiniti, sforzandosi a una calma del tutto innaturale 'Non ho nulla . . . nulla di bagnato?' " (133).

43. "The lazzari were, therefore, the lowest class of the proletarians of Naples, that class that modern sociologists contrast with the industrial proletarian, of which in fact they often form the antithesis and sometimes the adversary, with the name of 'ragged proletarian' (*Lumpenproletariat*)" (Croce 2006, 89).

44. For a definition of the concept of "informal sector," see Moser 1978.

45. "Their social strategies of persistence—rather than survival—typically combine resources spanning what I call *the four economic corners of marginality*: unstable wage work (the market), stopgap or perennial informal activities (the street), restrictive welfare support (the state), and the reciprocal economy of kin, friends, and neighbors (social ties)" (Wacquant 2022, 163).

46. No scholarly reflection exists, to my knowledge, about the derogatory use of this term, alluding to a racial difference between the city's classes.

47. I am aware that Loïc Wacquant has recently argued that "underclass" implies derogatory and reactionary traits in contemporary sociology (Wacquant 2022). However, precisely this derogatory undertone makes it a good translation of terms like "popolino" and "plebe," which historically have been used for the Neapolitan lower classes at large.

48. "The generic expression 'popular classes' is intentionally used in the plural to indicate the classes, both in the historic center and in the peripheral neighborhoods of the city, not immediately belonging to the industrial working class. In modern historiography on the city, various terms are used—'lazzari,' 'plebs,' 'popolino,' 'sub-proletariat'—with usually negative connotations. The choice for the expression 'popular classes' intends both to avoid references to similar connotations and to refer to a varied social structure which can also include, for example, artisans or people belonging to the lower middle class" (Dines 2014, 72).

49. The Autonomy, or Workers Autonomy (Autonomia operaia), consisted of a network of grassroots political organizations of the radical left that were active in Italian political life in the 1970s, challenging the hegemony of the PCI and taking on a vanguard role for both workers' struggles and movements advocating for political rights and cultural renewal, with a key participation in the feminist movement and the first (ante litteram) LGBTQ organizations. Cf. Tarì 2012.

50. "This peculiar urban configuration has been the target of numerous 'reclamation' attempts that have sought to expel these sectors [the lower classes] of the population rather than to improve their social conditions, aiming to 'enhance' the conditions of the historic center, which is a delicate way of defining the operation of increasing the real estate value of the neighborhoods" (Bove and Festa 2022a, 179).

51. A 2020 interview with activist Enzo De Vincenzo (qtd. in Bove and Festa 2022a, 10:206).

52. A 2020 interview with activist Vittorio Forte (qtd. in Bove and Festa 2022a, 10:223).

53. "The structures constitutive of a particular type of environment (e.g., the material conditions of existence characteristic of a class condition) produce *habitus*, systems of durable, transposable *dispositions*, structured structures predisposed to function as structuring structures, that is, as principles of the generation and structuring of practices and representations" (Bourdieu 1977, 72).

54. With reference to the Althusserian conception of ideology here described, Jameson has noted the probable influence Bourdieu's studies had on Althusser's own reflections (Jameson 2009b, 337).

55. "This affective background that first throws consciousness outside of itself" (Merleau-Ponty 2012, 96); "Ce fond affectif qui jette originairement la conscience hors d'elle-même" (Merleau-Ponty 2005, 123).

56. "Ce second espace à travers l'espace visible" (Merleau-Ponty 2005, 339).

57. "Traumatic experience does not subsist as a representation in the mode of objective consciousness and as a moment that has a date. Rather, its nature is to survive only as a style of being" (Merleau-Ponty 2012, 85).

58. "Literature thus realizes the phenomenological project of expressing the pure meaning of the still mute experience" (Robert 2020, 262).

59. "Un vecteur, une sollicitation, une possibilité d'état, un principe de sélection historique, un schéma d'existence" (Merleau-Ponty 2000, 72).

60. Years later he will write: "To comprehend is not to constitute in intellectual immanence . . . to comprehend is to apprehend by coexistence, laterally, *by the style* [*en style*]" (Merleau-Ponty 1968b, 188).

61. The passage quoted from *Le Temps Retrouvé* ("Le style . . . est une question non de technique mais de vision") is in Proust 1989, 4:474.

62. For this point, with reference to cinema, Vivian Sobchack's reflections are particularly important (Sobchack 2009, 262–84).

63. "Le travail de l'écrivain reste travail de langage, plutôt que de 'pensée' : il s'agit de produire un système de signes qui restitue par son agencement interne le paysage d'une expérience, il faut que les reliefs, les lignes de force de ce paysage induisent une syntaxe profonde, un mode de composition et de récit, qui défont et refont le monde et le langage usuels" (Merleau-Ponty 1968a, 40).

64. For example, open vs. closed = possibility vs. impossibility; linear time vs. frequentative mode = meaningful activity vs. useless expression of anxiety.

Chapter 1

1. Letter to Paolo Lacaldano, November 12, 1962. Qtd. in Clerici 2002, 352.

2. Letter to Vito Laterza, October 18, 1957 (Clerici 2002, 333–34).

3. Letter to Vito Laterza, November 11, 1957 (Clerici 2002, 334).

4. That was the place for those who could not afford the ticket, as one could quickly hide in the restroom to evade the inspector.

5. Kafka's Italian collection *Il messaggio dell'imperatore* was a crucial reading for the collaborators of *Sud*. Luigi Compagnone, who was a leader among these intellectuals and one of the central figures in Ortese's "The Silence" (and a lifelong friend of hers, despite the bitterness due to the publication of that story), wrote an extensive essay devoted to Kafka in the fourth issue of *Sud* (Compagnone 1946) and was obsessed with the book, according to La Capria: "I don't remember when I met Luigi Compagnone, but I remember well that he was the one who put in my hand a book by Kafka with a glossy black cover with the profile of the Great Wall of China engraved on it in red. It was *The Emperor's Message* and contained the most beautiful stories of Kafka" (2003, 1110). Immediately after, he mentions the affinity between Compagnone and Ortese. Even beyond the reference to the circulation of Kafka's Italian collection among the intellectuals of *Sud*, Kafka has often been mentioned by critics with reference to Ortese's poetics. See, for example, Flora Ghezzo's introduction to the most recent collection of essays devoted to Ortese (Ghezzo 2015a, 10). In the same collection, Monica Farnetti highlights Kafka's importance for Ortese's critical understanding of literature, and adds: "Kafka's works were obviously not missing from Ortese's library, and perhaps he is more responsible than has hitherto been acknowledged for her resolute conversion to stories of metamorphosis" 2015, 439). For the importance of the reception of this early translation of Kafka's short stories by Italian writers since the 1930s, see Ziolkowski 2020, 20–26. Ziolkowski focuses here in particular on Morante and Buzzati, not by chance two authors Ortese admired. See Farnetti 2015, 448–51; Farnetti 1998, 96–97; Clerici 2002, 284.

6. The verse division is hypothetical and based on Bergman's recitation. Although the acting was in English, two different versions of *Journey to Italy*, one in English and one in Italian, were post-synchronized simultaneously, so both should count as the original. In the Italian version the verses were "Tempio dello spirito / non più corpi / ma pure, ascetiche immagini / al cui confronto persino il pensiero diventa grave / pesante, opaco" (I will come back to the discrepancy between the Italian version and the English translation). Given Rossellini's work procedure, the Italian version was certainly composed first, by himself and/or his collaborator, the writer Vitaliano Brancati, who was present on the set during the months of the shooting. In an interview with Robin Wood from the 1970s, talking about Rossellini's work method (not specifically for *Journey to Italy*), Ingrid Bergman explained: "He would then write down dialogue sometimes, exactly what he wanted, in Italian;

and his assistant, who could speak English, used to translate it into English. He sometimes had an English writer on, but he wrote everything himself. It was very difficult for him to take anybody else's word that maybe this was not right. He had a feeling for it. He knew that he wanted to arrive at a certain pitch of emotion and he did it his way" (Wood 1974, 12).

7. Luciana Bohne suggested that the reference to Joyce might be entirely due to Brancati's contribution: "Perhaps Rossellini was unaware of the inspiration his literary coworker Brancati had drawn from Joyce's greatest story, 'The Dead'" (Bohne 1979, 43). Elena Dagrada also suggests that the reference to Joyce might be due to Brancati's initiative. She quotes a passage in the writer's *Diario Romano* from the same weeks of the shooting (April 1953) in which he mentions Joyce, although just in passing (Dagrada 2008, 320n67). I agree with the hypothesis that Brancati was the first to suggest using Joyce's text, and to support this claim I will later quote a previously unnoticed journal article he wrote where he mentioned it directly. However, it does not seem likely that Rossellini could be unaware of this reference. Although, as Bohne points out, Rossellini never mentions "The Dead" in interviews discussing the film, the connections to Joyce's text are too evident and central, from the protagonists' surname to the ghostly presence of the deceased poet to the words Katherine uses to describe their encounter. All this had certainly been discussed between the two authors.

8. The reconstruction of this process has not been easy until Elena Dagrada's extraordinary work carried out in her *Le Varianti Trasparenti* (2005; then 2008), in which she has clarified many passages in the development of *Journey to Italy* and of the other Rossellini's films with Ingrid Bergman through archival research.

9. In his introduction to the Oxford Edition of the *Dubliners*, Jeri Johnson talks of a "revelation of Gabriel's failure, despite years of marriage, ever to have recognized Gretta's actual difference from the picture he has created of her, a picture painted more in his own image than in hers" (2000).

10. See also Brunette, 162–63: "After being exposed to those things that Charles had written about—especially the powerful rawness of the statuary in the Naples museum—she begins to realize that his aestheticism was a projection of his own personality rather than a description of Italy."

11. "New positive modes of appreciating the south, however, also developed. While the rise of bourgeois civilization in western Europe fueled a new emphasis on the barbarism of other parts of the continent and the world beyond, it also generated new forms of interest in those very backward areas and peoples. Travelers and artists looked south in search of a more natural, untamed world to find, in a word, the picturesque" (Moe 2002, 2).

12. "Alessandro ironically comments on these verses that describe the Campania as a silent and dead land, the ancient statues as 'pure, ascetic forms'" (Dagrada 2008, 515).

13. It is not possible to verify whether the second poem had already been entirely written when the revised synopsis was submitted, or if only the syntagma "pure, ascetic forms" had been conceived.

14. I emended Gallagher's translation due to an evident mistake. The original is as follows: "Vita è la nostra unica parola. Ma l'eco / di questi luoghi risponde sommessamente: morte. / Gli uomini nascono qui contagiati di vecchiezza / e la vita è priva di fanciullezza. / Il silenzio si adagia su tutte / le cose come la polvere." The verse division is in this case in the original document (Dagrada 2008, 516). Gallagher translates "gli uomini nascono qui" as "people hide," thus evidently confusing "nascono" with "si nascondono." He also forgets the adverb "qui," ("here"), which is key for my interpretation.

15. As we will see in a moment, the model used for the Italian verses is the original English and not an Italian translation.

16. Published in *Omnibus: Settimanale di attualità politica e letteraria*, June 11, 1938.

17. "Landed on 'Red Beach,' Paestum, at seven o'clock. Boatloads had been going ashore all day after a dawn shelling from the ships and a short battle for the beachhead. Now an extraordinary false serenity lay on the landward view. . . . Here and there, motionless columns of smoke denoted the presence of war, but the general impression was one of a splendid and tranquil evening in the late summer on one of the fabled shores of antiquity. . . . The corpses of those killed earlier in the day had been laid out in a row, side by side, shoulder to shoulder, with extreme precision as if about to present arms at an inspection by death" (Lewis 1978, 11–12). " 'That's Naples,' said the voice that accompanies all travelers. 'I'd know it from the postcards and the pitchers in the barbershops. Look, that's Vesuvius. . . . Yessir, the old anthill's smokin. Ain't got over the shock of Anzio yet. . . . And see that big thing that looks like a country club at the top of the city? That's Castel Sant'Elmo. . . . I been readin' my guidebooks.' . . . The acres of devastation along the water front were something Hal had never imagined, except in the rubbled castles of his own brain. For a mile along the port area the houses lay in their gray dust. Here and there a room stuck out of a second story where a bomb had split a house in half. Some were like dollhouses, in which a side can be hinged away for a cross section of all the rooms. Here was half a staircase leading nowhere, a flapping shred of blue wallpaper" (Burns 1947, 83–84).

18. "Always, what impressed me—almost as if I did not see well, or had a delirium—was the total abandonment of the children, some little eyes that I saw smiling and lowering themselves among the rags, inside a box of Coca Cola—lowering themselves forever" (Ortese 1997, 34).

19. See recently the feature film by Claudio Giovannesi *Piranhas* (*La paranza dei bambini*, 2019), or the TV show *The Sea Beyond* (*Mare fuori*), 2020–2025.

20. There are countless examples of these kind of "picturesque" scenes during the military occupation. See, for example, Burns: "This parachutist was arriving at a price agreement with a small girl in a tight blue dress. Her body was skinny, on her bolero she wore officers' insignia, wings, and divisional patches. She also chewed gum. Beside her stood a scabrous urchin presiding as auctioneer, screaming out a sales talk, the specifications of her charms" (1947, 13).

21. This circular structure is not explicit in the Italian as in the English version ("seems flesh"). Instead of the comparison with "flesh," the Italian simply has one more adjective, "grave," whose meaning is redundant with the following "pesante"; and yet, the three Italian adjectives can be read as reevoking the bodily dimension that absorbs "thought" again, in opposition to the "ascetic images," thus producing that same circular movement made more evident in the English version.

22. See Lorenzo Fabbri's reflections on this film, focusing in particular on the ideological manipulation of the suffering bodies (2023, 149–60). Fabbri also emphasizes the continuity between this film and Rossellini's postwar production (155).

23. Shortly after *Journey to Italy*, Rossellini went back once more to the cave of Mergellina to shoot *Naples 1943*, an episode for the collective film *Mid-Century Loves* (*Amori di mezzo secolo*, 1954).

Chapter 2

1. For a detailed account of the origin and elaboration of the book, see Clerici (2002, 222–78), Farnetti (1998, 89–92), De Gasperin (2014, 106–7), and Re (2015, 35–38). An important source of information for this period are Ortese's letters to Pasquale Prunas (Ortese 2006).

2. On the "hybrid" structure of the book, see Silvia Contarini's remarks: "The composite structure of *Il mare non bagna Napoli* is, on the contrary, an indispensable piece of Ortesian visionary realism. The book's ambition, it has been said, is fictional and not essayistic; indeed the problem does not consist in attributing a genre to it, but in understanding the underlying logic. Although it presents itself as a hybrid collection, with more traditional stories flanked by stories based on the journalistic inquiry, *Il mare non bagna Napoli*, far from being a simple chronicle or testimony, is a literary project in which the Neapolitan reality acts as the lowest common denominator" (Contarini 2004, 9). On the same topic, see Baldi 2000, 94–95. For a discussion of the relation of the book to the category of Neorealism, see Re 2003, 112; and De Gasperin 2014, 108–114.

3. Split into two installments, on January 12 and 19, 1952. The second part was titled "The Horror of Living" ("L'orrore di vivere").

4. The story described the author's exploration of the Granili, an eighteenth-century military building used in the postwar years as a shelter for hundreds of homeless families. Living conditions in the building were horrible.

5. The exact timeline of these events as reported by Clerici (and others who used him as a primary source) is not completely clear, since Vittorini's first letter to Ortese is from January 2 (Ortese 2006, 111), thus before the publication of "The Involuntary City." Ortese (or possibly Prunas on her behalf) had probably

contacted him first to propose a book project on Naples (which she was already preparing), also including the manuscript of "The Involuntary City" in the mailing.

6. For a reflection on the role of Olivetti in the cultural context of Italian economic development, see Karen Pinkus's "Opening Credits" to her *Clocking Out* (2020, 1–28).

7. For a summary of the development of the different streams of trauma theory in the past decades, see Luckhurst (2008) and Balaev (2014).

8. Here she was probably echoing Leopardi's materialist conception of Nature: "The natural order . . . is a circle of destruction, and reproduction, and of regular and constant changes as regards the whole" (Leopardi 1983, 541).

9. "Rejection of that *reality* was the secret of my first book, published in 1937 by Bompiani, and mocked by the champions of the 'real' at the time" (Ortese 2018, 10). On this topic, see Ghezzo 2015a, 8–10.

10. "That such new possibilities can also be thought of in aesthetic and formal ways, alongside these scientific and epistemological ones, must now be recalled and emphatically stressed, since it was in terms of this very interrelationship between the formal possibilities of 'realism' and of standpoint knowledge that we argued for the deeper continuity between the Lukács of *History and Class Consciousness* and the later theoretician of the realist novel" (Jameson 2009a, 221).

11. "The book's release in fact triggered bitter, resentful accusations of 'betrayal' by some and claims that it was defamatory, even fascist. Some of the men and women featured in the last chapter took it, to Ortese's dismay, as an attack *ad hominem*. Each new printing caused new protestations. Even its rerelease in 1994, despite the new 'Introduction' and 'Afterword' by the author that reaffirmed Ortese's affection for and indebtedness to the *Sud* group (and its original idealism) while spelling out more clearly than ever her real motives for writing the book, seemed to reopen an emotional wound that had never really healed. The publication prompted, once again, polemical comments by La Capria and Compagnone—an indication perhaps that the book had in fact hit the mark and continued to trouble them in a profound way" (Re 2015, 52). On Ortese's experience with *Sud* and its intellectuals, see also Farnetti 1998, 147–49.

12. "The story of the *Sud* group . . . appeared to portray, as in one of those beloved nineteenth century variety shows, the innocent conflict between the dreams of youth and the overwhelming logic of things" (Ortese 2018, 124).

13. The quote is from "The Silence of Reason" (104).

14. "This endless lair where humans and animals compete for food and even air, where the streets seem to force and channel a frenetic humanity towards who knows what unthinkable outcomes" (Mozzillo 1983, 10).

15. For this argument in the context of postwar years, see Percy Allum's *Politics and Society in Post-War Naples*. For a more narrative oriented, less technical overview on the responsibilities of the Neapolitan ruling class for the enduring

underdevelopment of the city, see Antonio Ghirelli's chapter "The Urban Massacre" ("Il massacro urbano," in his *History of Naples* (*Storia di Napoli*, 2015).

16. "The technocratic reasoning of the medical model marginalizes the political agency of those it aims to help. The ghetto poor are regarded as passive victims in need of assistance rather than as potential allies in what should be a collective effort to secure justice for all" (Shelby 2016, 2).

17. Such as the theory of the "culture of poverty" (Shelby 2016, 80–116).

18. While discussing the implausibility of her descriptions of the crowd of the poor, he speaks of the "unreliability that can be reached by a sensibility that is too offended" (La Capria 2003, 692). He also states, commenting on a description in which mice were mentioned, "this population of mice, seen with the terror with which women usually see mice" (693). On this same passages, see Baldi's comments (Baldi 2000, 104n33).

19. Discussing Root's concept of "insidious trauma," Laura Brown has emphasized its utility in the analysis of the psychological conditions of social groups: "It can be spread laterally throughout an oppressed social group as well, when membership in that group means a constant lifetime risk of exposure to certain trauma" (1995, 108). In more recent years, discussing Brown's essay, Laurie Vickroy has again stressed the importance of the class perspective for the analysis of traumatic experiences in connection with literary analysis, speaking of "the constant stress and humiliation associated with being a person of low socioeconomic status" (2015, 7).

20. See Michel Mercier's "Notice," in Colette 1991, 1670–1776.

21. We will see later how Serafin's statements about this film are not reliable. However, for this case, a similar version was provided by Ingrid Bergman in her autobiography, and she probably had a better overall insight into the situation.

22. The actual title on the manuscript is *New Vine*, but Dagrada is certainly right in considering this a typo for *Wine*, as many journal articles published at the time of the film's preparation (thus relying on information released to the press) call it *New Wine* and make reference in different ways to the wine metaphor (Dagrada 2008, 290). For this reason, I will use the title *New Wine* in the following pages, and will later clarify the connection of the wine metaphor with the plot of the story.

23. In a conversation with the author in June 2022, the director of Pietrangeli's Archive, Antonio Maraldi, affirmed that the screenwriter Ugo Pirro, to whom he had shown the screenplay, claimed to have also worked on it. To my knowledge, this claim is not supported by any documentary evidence.

24. "Alice recalled that, when they came to the little bridge connecting the Cransac driveway with the public road, Michel had offered her his arm so that they might give the inquisitive villagers the impression of a closely united couple. But still, they were well aware that the natives were gifted with a phenomenal flair and hawk-like eyes for anything that concerned the château. 'They noticed that I was wearing my muddy old shoes,' Michel thought to himself, 'and the druggist's wife advised Alice to try rose waster for inflamed eyelids. What an awful lot of gossips!'

Alice recalled also, with a start of indignant protest, that at Espagnat Michel had put his arm around her waist and squeezed her hand" (Colette 1951, 394).

25. In April 1950, writing about the Rossellini-Bergman scandal in a humorous comment, Brancati wrote, "The most beautiful and famous woman in the world prefers an Italian man of genius with a fat belly, shining with his bold head and oiled hair" (2003b, 1476). Here, as it was common, the very image of "Italianness" is indicated by the synecdoche of oily dark hair.

26. In the same article previously quoted, talking about the scandalous preference Bergman gave to Rossellini, Brancati further describes him as follows: "With a sly smile on his face ready to get wet with tears, a man willing to sing, cry, get on his knees, break glasses, just to 'fill' the life of his partner" (2003b, 1476).

27. The myth of the scene having been a lucky chance Rossellini was able to exploit thanks to his talent for improvisation originates in Enzo Serafin's interview from 1989, published in Bergala (1990, 129–35). Here, no less than Rossellini's director of photography tells the story of the miraculous discovery: "We knew more or less that there would probably be someone's body, but the fact that it was a couple facing the couple who separated, it was still something! But I assure you that there was no preparation!" (131). After more than thirty years, it should not be surprising that personal memories tend to conform to a story that has already become a cultural myth. Yet a final proof that by no means Serafin could be right here is the fact that immediately after, he claims that the final scene, too, with the religious parade in Maiori where a "miracle" happens, was not orchestrated. In Maiori's community, the memory still lives of that procession being, in fact, a mise-en-scène explicitly created for the film (I conducted interviews to confirm this). This circumstance is further demonstrated by the fact that the statue of the Virgin Mary paraded in the film is not the one that was and still is actually used for that occasion in real life (the Addolorata instead of the Assunta), which only happens on August 15 (and, for another procession, in autumn). There is no possibility Rossellini could have shot there beyond the official ending of the shooting in April or early May. In his influential work, Tag Gallagher takes up and gives credit to this myth (for both episodes) without questioning the plausibility of Serafin's account.

28. "If you call me your 'dear child' once more, I'll throw this teapot in your face!" (Colette 1951, 410).

29. For the last two quotes I provided my own translation for a closer adherence to the original (Colette 1991, 926, 928).

30. Margot Norris suggests a similar reading of this dynamic when she affirms that Gretta, with her account, "displaces her husband forever from the passional center of her life and marginalizes him in his own self-image" (2003, 217). Her essay proposes a much wider theoretical interpretation of Joyce's text from a feminist perspective, which is not possible to summarize here. Yet it is important to mention that she highlights the importance, as an intertext for Joyce's story, of Enrik Ibsen's

A Doll's House, which can be seen as a foundational model for the kind of discovery made by the husbands in the stories we are analyzing.

31. Until this moment the scene numbering corresponds in the two versions: It starts to diverge with the following scene 13, which is completely absent in S1b (thus, in this latter, scene 13 will correspond to scene 14 in S1a, etc.).

32. "Scendi, guagliò! . . . Scendi figlio di puttana" (S1a, scene 2, 15).

33. "Quel fantastico aspetto di miseria fresca, umida e colorata ma dopo tutto, almeno agli occhi di un inglese, assolutamente indecente" (S1a, scene 7, 35–36).

34. "Quel fantastico aspetto di miseria fresca, umida, colorata e straordinariamente viva" (S1b, scene 7, 37).

35. "Come visione fantastica e insieme forse un po' ripugnante" (S1a, scene 7, 36).

36. "Isabella volge intorno lo sguardo e non nasconde un senso di meraviglia e di depressione. Le smorfie di John esprimono chiaramente ripugnanza e schifo" (S1a, scene 7, 36).

37. See Ennio Bispuri's recent book *Il cinema dei telefoni bianchi* (2021).

38. The article is collected in an anthology of Pietrangeli's critical writings included in the volume *Il cinema di Antonio Pietrangeli* (Detassis et al. 1987, 111).

39. This expression, coupled with a previous one, "food, wine, and the sun make the brain ferment" (515), which explains the premises of the terrace scene in which the memory of the dead poet first emerges, finally clarifies the meaning of the wine metaphor in the screenplay's title. To become a new substance—which brings new life according to Christian symbology—new wine needs to go through a period of fermentation, which, for the couple, corresponds to their journey to Italy. In other words, the first title of the project wants to communicate the idea that, for the protagonists, with this journey a new life starts.

Chapter 3

1. "Che cosa fanno i giovani scrittori di Napoli" (Ortese 1994, 99–100). Unless otherwise noted, all subsequent citations in English refer to Ortese 2018, while those in Italian to Ortese 1994.

2. "Qualche notizia più particolare, maliziosa, di quelle che sollevano tanto il tono di un articolo" (99).

3. "The Gold of Forcella" and "The Involuntary City," which ends on an emotional peak: "The involuntary city was preparing to consume its few goods, in a fever that would last until the following morning, the hour when complaints, surprise, mourning, the moribund horror of living start again" (98).

4. "The public adores hearing about these people. We may think it's *fatuous*, but we have to consider what the public wants" (134). "Il pubblico adora volentieri

questi nomi. Per quanto ne possiamo vedere la *fatuità*, questi desideri del pubblico rimangono importanti" (126; my emphasis).

5. The translation here does not capture the ambiguity of the original "nelle estreme e più lucenti terre del Sud" (117): The adjective "estreme," coupled with "terre del Sud," besides referring spatially to the "*far* south" could also mean "extreme" in a non-spatial sense, denoting a peculiar, more abstract quality of the southern region as "excessive" in the many senses this expression can have.

6. Both conjunction and disjunction are subsumed in the semiotic category of "junction" (Greimas and Courtés 1993, 201).

7. A thematic role at the surface level of the text in Greimasian terms.

8. It is a case of "actantial syncretism," which happens when one single "actor" embodies two or more "actants" (Greimas and Courtés 1993, 374–75; Greimas 1983, 26). Actants are structural functions at the deep level of the text, which I intend here according to the simplified, more abstract formulation summarized by Bertrand (2000, 181–190), where they are reduced to the three basic "relational positions" sender, subject, and object—plus the "symmetric and inverted figures of the anti-subject and the anti-sender" (260), on which the polemical dimension of narrative is based.

9. Despite apparently being the sender of the original narrative program on which the film is built, the action he mandates is the opposite of that the protagonists initially arrive to perform—they want to alienate the object (the villa), not to be united with it. This demonstrates that his role is rather connected to an anti-program, although this function will later be taken up by the other looming absent figure: the poet Lewington.

10. On this concept, see Casetti 1998, 18–25, where it is referred to as "cinematographic enunciation."

11. "Stendere . . . le prime linee di quella scuola della Ragione, che, altrove, aveva già purificato i paesi, e alla cui mancanza, qui, era dovuto il profondo sonno e la dispersione della coscienza" (112).

12. "Si voleva sapere tutto, capire tutto di questa mostruosità che, alla luce degli ultimi fatti, appariva Napoli; rimuovere la lapide finissima che posava sulla sua fossa, e cercare se, in quella decomposizione, rimanesse ancora qualcosa di organico" (112).

13. Domietta Torlasco's phenomenological reading of Pasolini's *Oedipus Rex* (1967) has been a model for this analysis. In that case, too, the linear diegetic time hides a different temporality, the archaic one of the unconscious crime, buried in the depths of the visible. Similarly, in *Journey to Italy*, as well as in the visual dimension of Ortese's story, we will see a blocked, circular temporality emerge, which was created by the "crime" on which the history of the city is based. Thus, the protagonists's individual experiences will be obliterated by the emergence of the traces of a collective history: "The depth of the visible constitutes a memory in

excess of our subjectivity" (Torlasco 2008, 68). As in Pasolini's film, in *Joureny to Italy* this phenomenon will be highlighted with the juxtaposition of landscape (an urban landscape in this case), and the close-ups of the protagonist.

14. "The object in literature is given by the mode of appearance . . . this is linked to the organization of the elements of the world in the writer's own experience" (Merleau-Ponty 2020a, 181–82).

15. "La sera del 19 giugno (sera per modo di dire, essendo il Cielo chiarissimo e il sole ancora fisso a mezzo il mare, con uno sguardo intento), presi un tram della linea 3, che percorre tutta la Riviera di Chiaia e termina a Mergellina" (99).

16. It is used, for instance, by Gaspara Stampa among others, and is reminiscent of Dante (Inf. xiv, 94).

17. "Sedetti in un angolo, vicino a una donna senza naso, che portava in grembo una grossa pianta, e mi misi a pensare con quali parole avrei giustificato la mia visita a Luigi Compagnone, impiegato all'Ufficio Prosa di Radio Napoli, che non vedevo da molto tempo, e dal quale appunto stavo andando" (99).

18. "Non si poteva dire che quel tram corresse" (100).

19. The translation accentuates the contrast between the weirdness of the idea and her initial consideration of it: "one might *reasonably* suspect." In the original the adverb "reasonably"—a heavy choice given the importance of the semantic field of "reason" in this story—is absent, yet the suspect is nevertheless initially treated as unproblematic: "da favorire il sospetto che il conducente si fosse addormentato, oppure . . . giacesse ferito sul suo seggiolino" (100).

20. "Ma qui si avvertiva qualcosa di diverso, che in breve costringeva a rifiutare, per una definizione, i due aggettivi nominati. No, non si poteva parlare né di *agitato* né di *squallido*; questa strada, piuttosto, rimaneva ridente e terribile, come appunto l'espressione d'intelligenza e bontà che appare talora sul viso ai defunti. Era una strada *defunta*, così almeno la definii nel mio cuore, sperando poterle trovare in seguito un attributo meno intenso ed irrazionale, cosa che invece non fu possibile" (100).

21. "I basoli della strada erano tutti smossi, conferendole l'aspetto di un torrente in piena, le torbide acque, precipitose e oblique, improvvisamente drizzate e pietrificate" (100).

22. In both cases the translation of the first term of each couple does not render the original in a way close enough to manifest the inherence of the isotopies we are discussing: "agitato" is more neutrally connected with ongoing movement than "distressed." Similarly, "ridente," with its metaphoric significance of vitality, is more general and immediate than "smiling": That a place might look "ridente" is perfectly common and refers to a general welcoming quality.

23. It is important to clarify that this crowd is precisely *not* "working class," as the term "plebe" refers, as we have seen, to the *lumpenproletariat*.

24. "Quel qualcosa di nero e colorato, quell'interminabile nastro di plebe che si agitava perennemente alla radice delle case" (101).

25. "L'eterna folla di Napoli, semovente come un serpe folgorato dal sole, ma non ancora ucciso" (101).

26. "Dopo i selvaggi anni '40–'45" (100).

27. "Quel qualcosa . . . aveva emesso, per la prima volta, in quegli anni successivi alla tempesta, un rumore nuovo, imprevedibile, incantato, pari al fruscio della risacca sulla rena, dopo l'uragano" (101).

28. A closer translation here would be "unpredictable."

29. "Vi era dell'inquietudine, e soprattutto della Speranza, in quel sordo continuo rumore" (101).

30. "Ecco perché i vetri delle case avevano brillato, e le facciate rosa e gialle erano parse battute da un altro sole, vivide, rinnovate" (101).

31. As mentioned, the definitions of sender and anti-sender are purely relational, depending on the perspective we take in defining program and anti-program.

32. On this passage, see also Morra's essay "Anna Maria Ortese's Palette: Colors and Achromaticity in *Neapolitan Chronicles*," (2019, 710).

33. "Una patina, misterioso intruglio di piogge, polvere e soprattutto di noia, si era distesa sulle facciate, velandone le ferite, e riconducendo il paesaggio a quella immobilità rarefatta, a quell'espressivo e equivoco sorriso che appare in volto ai defunti" (101).

34. "Quegli uomini e donne e bambini seminudi, e cani e gatti ed uccelli, tutte forme nere, sfiancate, svuotate" (101).

35. "Tutte gole che emettono appena un suono arido, tutti occhi pieni di una luce ossessiva, di una supplica inespressa—tutti quei viventi che si trascinavano in un moto continuo, pari all'attività di un febbricitante, a quella smania tutta nervosa che s'impadronisce di certi esseri prima di morire, per un gesto che gli sembra necessario, e non è mai il definitivo" (101).

36. "Quella grande folla di larve che cucinava all'aperto, o si pettinava, o trafficava, o amava, o dormiva, ma mai veramente dormiva, era sempre agitata, turbava la calma arcaica del paesaggio" (101).

37. The term translates here "inquietudine," whose semantic field in Italian is more positive than "anxiety," and is often associated with intellectual restlessness, coupling the implied absence of peace of mind with a positive thrust toward knowledge and discovery.

38. Not by chance, the example chosen by Greimas in his analysis of Maupassant's "Two Friends" ("Deux amis," 1882) concerns the starving population of Paris ready to eat any form of life to survive, having been reduced, in this desperate effort, to *a dying form of life* itself, thus arriving at the limit of abolishing the difference between subject and object as eater and eaten (Greimas 1976, 37).

39. "This unconscious master narrative—which we will call, following French usage, a *fantasm*, in order to distinguish it from the connotations of daydream or wish-fulfillment unavoidable in the English term 'fantasy'—is an unstable or contradictory structure, whose persistent actantial functions and events (which

are in life restaged again and again with different actors and on different levels) demand repetition, permutation, and the ceaseless generation of various structural 'resolutions' which are never satisfactory, and whose initial unreworked form is that of the Imaginary, or, in other words, of those waking fantasies, daydreams, and wish-fulfillments" (Jameson 2002, 166–67).

40. Benjamin developed the concept in "Little History of Photography" and in "The Work of Art in the Age of its Technological Reproducibility" (Benjamin 2002), where it refers to the photographic image. I will use it with reference to the visualization of details that could not be perceived with such precision by the point of view apparently adopted by a verbal description focalized on a character-observer.

41. "In realtà, quell'uomo dalla giubba sbiadita e priva di bottoni sedeva regolarmente alla guida" (100).

42. "Il sole brillò un momento sulla lastra di un finestrino, e per un attimo macchiò di rosso le ginocchia della mia vicina" (102).

43. As already mentioned, the journey to Naples that inspires the story (or rather, that was made to write the story) had happened in June 1952, and the book was published a year later.

44. "Un sorriso leggerissimo, compiaciuto, vagava nei suoi occhi neri al di sopra della cicatrice" (102).

45. "Un uomo magro e dall'aspetto seriamente malato . . . disse sotto-voce . . . 'Lassa fa' a Dio'" (102).

46. As mentioned, "working class" is not an appropriate translation for "plebe."

47. "I giovani della plebe, invece, esseri dai cinque ai quindici anni, ne invadono volentieri i punti più ombrosi: vi si recano a fare i loro bisogni, oppure a torturare degli animali; o seggono pensando cose d'amore, ruffianerie, canti; i tisici vi sono condotti dai parenti per consiglio del medico, e si vedono consumarsi su quelle pietre come bianche ali di farfalle" (102–3).

48. "Indorando pallidamente le statue e i busti decapitati" (103).

49. "Di età indefinibile" (103).

50. "Si misero a correre sul muro, tentando di seguire il tram, con richiami striduli, dolenti, appassionati, che volevano attrarre la nostra attenzione su tutto quanto essi possedevano" (103).

51. "Non avevano occupazioni ragionevoli. Una pazzia tenera li sollevava" (103–4).

52. "Altri erano intenti a trafiggere una farfalla" (103).

53. "La donna senza naso mi guardava ora quietamente, e guardava la strada, e guardando me e la strada insieme, doveva aver pensato qualche cosa intorno a quello che io potevo pensare, perché il sorriso con cui aveva accennato ai festeggiamenti era scomparso, per lasciar posto a un breve scintillio sospettoso, raccolto. . . . In questo guardare, essa non metteva alcun pensiero, eppure la sua intensità e curiosità mi causavano un vero malessere. Anche l'uomo, ora, guardava nel mezzo del mio volto" (104).

54. Fontanille's reflections are here based on Greimas' essay "Toward a Theory of Modalities" (Greimas 1983, 67–91).

55. "The fourth term . . . must be (when the operation is successful) the place of novelty and of paradoxical emergence" (Jameson 1987, xvi).

56. "Ogge stó tanto allero / ca quase quase me mettesse a chiagnere / pe' 'sta felicitá."

57. It is true that only the first stanza of the song is present in the film, thus excluding the following ones that expand on the emigration topic, as noted by Carlo Coen (2018, 572); and yet, even a hint of a song so universally famous at the time—at least in Italy—carries with it the entirety of its meanings. In any case, the situation of the lyrical subject returning to Naples is already central in the first verses.

58. "This is one of the many self-referential hymns in which Naples is celebrated as the land of excellence, endowed with nature's most precious gifts" (Prato 2016, 184).

59. "Chist' è 'o paese addó tutt' 'e parole / só doce o só amare, / só sempe parole d'ammore."

60. Yet he had already briefly returned to Naples the previous year to shoot *Napoli 1943*, an episode for the collective *Amori di mezzo secolo*, 1954.

61. "One just 'skips' the moments judged to be of no interest for the plot; it is then the ordinary sequence, a very common syntagmatic type in films" (Metz 1968, 131). For an English-language discussion of this kind of syntagm, see Stam et al. (2005, 45–46).

62. For a detailed description (according to Pasolini's grammar) of this scene, see Albano et al. 1967, 189.

63. "Présence extraordinairement intense de ce qui n'est pas explicité: regard vers . . . spectacle {horrible}, qu'on ne vois pas—quand il est présenté, son influence sur l'expression du visage—Donc <u>soudure par dessus des lacunes, présentation indirecte, *i. e.* désignation de l'absent par le présent. = engrenage de l'un dans l'autre, prégnance de l'un dans l'autre</u>" (Merleau-Ponty 2011, 169).

64. According to the definition elaborated by Michel Chion 2005, 75–76.

65. This is the so-called comic scene, which has been cut from the Italian version of the film, as the interactions between Alex and the servants, who do not understand each other, did not make sense with the dubbing (Dagrada 2008, 293, 302–3). In chapter 5 I will analyze the scene in detail.

66. For the following two decades, in interviews Rossellini often spoke incoherently of the final scene of the film.

67. This is Aprà and Martelli's interpretation (1967, 200).

68. This term ("acousmatique"), which Chion inherits from Pierre Schaeffer, refers to any sound, diegetic or non-diegetic, whose source is not visible on screen. "Acousmatic" is thus used as a broader term than *offscreen*, and also includes non-diegetic sounds (Chion 2005, 63–65).

69. In a previous formulation, Jameson had more explicitly framed History in the terms of the Lacanian Real, which "our narratives can only approximate in asymptotic fashion and which 'resists symbolization absolutely'" (1977, 388–89). The quote ("ce qui résiste absolument à la symbolisation") comes from Lacan's first seminar (1953–54), *Les écrits techniques de Freud* (1978, 80). We cannot fail to notice how Lacan's initial reflection on the Real is also part of that same "window of opportunity" for historical knowledge to which all the texts we are studying here belong.

70. "Nella immensa luce, delicata come quella di una conchiglia, dalle verdi colline del Vomero e di Capodimonte fino alla punta scura di Posillipo, era un solo sonno, una meraviglia senza coscienza" (Ortese 1994, 172).

71. In conceiving this allegory Ortese had probably in mind a passage from Curzio Malaparte's *The Skin* (*La pelle*, 1949): "He had believed he was setting foot in a world dominated by reason and ruled by human conscience; and he had found himself without warning in a mysterious country, where men and the circumstances that make up their lives seemed to be governed not by reason and conscience, but by obscure subterranean forces" (Malaparte 2013, 33).

72. "Esiste, nelle estreme e più lucenti terre del Sud, un ministero nascosto per la difesa della natura dalla ragione; un genio materno, d'illimitata potenza, alla cui cura gelosa e perpetua è affidato il sonno in cui dormono quelle popolazioni. Se solo un attimo quella difesa si allentasse, se le voci dolci e fredde della ragione umana potessero penetrare quella natura, essa ne rimarrebbe fulminata" (117).

73. "E tutti i giovani scrittori che io avevo conosciuto, non tessevano forse l'elogio della loro antica madre? Ve n'era uno che gettasse sulla natura il lume della ragione umana? Tutti, tutti dormivano ora vicino al mare, dormivano da Torre del Greco a Cuma" (169).

74. "Sapevo che la sua indifferenza era una forma di controllo. Tutti erano indifferrenti, qui, quelli che desideravano salvarsi. Commuoversi, era come addormentarsi sulla neve" (156).

75. "Il motivo per cui ero arrivata fin là—ottenere alcune informazioni e indiscrezioni sui giovani scrittori napoletani—era sparito per lasciar posto a un interesse più profondo, dal quale non era escluso un certo imprecisato *spavento*" (110; my emphasis).

76. "Dovevo convenire che Luigi non era stato soltanto un funzionario, e nemmeno del tutto un napoletano, così come quelli che aveva avuto intorno, e la stessa cupa strada che io avevo percorso poco prima in tram, non erano soltanto Napoli, cioè incoscienza e colore, non erano solo un'ondata di antichità, ma anche le cose giovani che scorrono, con molta angoscia, al disotto dell'antichità" (110–11).

77. He will continue his reflection on "institution" (Husserl's concept of "Stiftung") in the courses of the academic year 1954–55 (Merleau-Ponty 2015).

78. "Produce [a] new analysis of perceptual consciousness as figure-background consciousness and consequently as ambiguous consciousness" (Merleau-Ponty 2020b, 133).

79. Luca Vanzago has stressed the elements of both continuity and novelty for Merleau-Ponty's thought, represented by the coupling of *Gestalt* theory with psychoanalysis and Marxism in these notes: "The very fact that something be perceptually given is due to the simultaneous givenness of its background. The individuation of the 'thing' is at the same time the position of a virtuality which is not present in the same way the thing is, but is not nothing either. This statement is in itself not really surprising in the light of what can be read in *Phenomenology of Perception*. But in these lectures Merleau-Ponty emphasizes the dynamical nature of the figure-background relationship. The usual notion of consciousness neglects and conceals precisely this interplay when is only defined in terms of consciousness-of something. And Merleau-Ponty relates this concealedness to Marx's and Freud's analyses of mystifying consciousness" (2012, 114).

80. For the historical and biographical background of its publication, and for its place in the philosopher's political itinerary, see Cooper 2017, 103–10.

81. The passage quoted from *Le Temps Retrouvé* is in Proust 1989, 4:474.

82. "In Husserl's language, beneath 'act intentionality'—which is the thetic consciousness of an object that, in intellectual memory, for example, converts the 'this-thing' into an idea—we must acknowledge an 'operative' intentionality (*fungierende Intentionalität*), which makes the former one possible and is what Heidegger calls 'transcendence'" (Merleau-Ponty 2012, 441). On operative intentionality as understood by Merleau-Ponty, see Jacobs 2018.

83. "The thickness of the pre-objective present, where we find our corporeality, our sociality, and the preexistence of the world" (Merleau-Ponty 2012, 457).

84. "This intentionality can further also be characterized as pre-personal, anonymous, and non-transparent because it is not a self-conscious I who accomplishes this organization of the field of perception" (Jacobs 2018, 665).

85. Merleau-Ponty quotes in particular Swann's reflections about Vinteuil's sonata: "Swann tenait les motifs musicaux pour de véritables idées, d'un autre monde, d'un autre ordre, idées voilées de ténèbres, inconnues, impénétrables à l'intelligence, mais qui n'en sont pas moins parfaitement distinctes les unes des autres, inégales entre elles de valeur et de signification" (Proust 1987, 1:349). Qtd. in Merleau-Ponty 2020a, 155.

86. "These ideas are inseparable from their sensible presentation (that is, from their visual, linguistic, or musical images, for instance) . . . they are instituted by these very images as their own depth" (Carbone 2019, 34).

87. As Dermot Moran noted, Merleau-Ponty's conception of embodied habitus, which belongs to the "alogical essences" communicated by the aesthetic gesture, is deeply linked to the pre-personal contact with the world Husserl called "operative intentionality" (or "functioning intentionality" in Moran's own translation): "The mature Husserl recognizes the complexity of 'functioning intentionality' working anonymously, and has himself described the kind of embodied habitus (*leiblicher Habitus*) which is later described in more detail by Merleau-Ponty" (Moran 2011, 71).

88. "The experience of reality becomes its own transcendental, just as the hawthorns on the Méséglise Way turn into the 'true hawthorns.' According to Merleau-Ponty, the intertwining of memory and forgetfulness that Proust calls *involuntary memory* makes certain experiences that had arisen within our operative relationship with the world decant into the body, where they become . . . *sensible ideas*" (Carbone 2020b, 29). For the centrality of this concept in Merleau-Ponty's later ontology, see in particular Merleau-Ponty 1964, 195–98. On this topic, see also Carbone 2020a.

89. On Merleau-Ponty interpretation of Lukács's praxis, see also López 2019, 341–43.

90. "In the commodity the worker recognises himself and his own relations with capital. Inasmuch as he is incapable in practice of raising himself above the role of object his consciousness is the *self-consciousness of the commodity*; or in other words it is the self-knowledge, the self-revelation of the capitalist society founded upon the production and exchange of commodities . . . when the worker knows himself as a commodity his knowledge is practical. *That is to say, this knowledge brings about an objective structural change in the object of knowledge*" (Lukács 1971, 168–69).

91. "Un vecteur, une sollicitation, une possibilité d'état, un principe de sélection historique, un schéma d'existence" (Merleau-Ponty 2000, 72).

92. "Choses qui sont des catégories, des dimensions, des structures du temps, de l'espace, de la vie. La qualité d'un monde = de tels principes organisateurs, inclus dans un tissu concret" (Merleau-Ponty 2020a, 164).

93. "The social totality itself, something no individual can ever grasp or 'represent,' and which is as it were invisible at the same time that it is omnipresent and inescapable" (Jameson 2009b, 340–41).

94. The definition of Proletarian Standpoint constitutes the central part of the main essay of *History and Class Consciousness* (Lukács 1968, 331–97). On the literary origin of this concept in Lukács's philosophy, see Jameson 2015.

95. "Les chagrins sont . . . des serviteurs atroces, impossibles à remplacer, et qui, par des voies souterraines, nous mènent à la vérité et à la mort" (Proust 1989, 4:488).

96. "The basic structure of reification can be found in all the social forms of modern capitalism (e.g., bureaucracy). But this structure can only be made fully conscious in the work-situation of the proletarian. For his work as he experiences it directly possesses the naked and abstract form of the commodity" (Lukács 1971, 171–72).

Chapter 4

1. "Appoggiai il dito sul bottone di porcellana . . . accostai il viso ai vetri" (Ortese 1994, 107). Unless otherwise noted, all subsequent citations in English refer to Ortese 2018, while those in Italian to Ortese 1994.

2. "In the two moments between ringing the porcelain bell and finally taking her finger off it, the interstitial space opens up, and for sixteen pages the narration gapes into an analepsis that provides the memorial account of Compagnone, Prunas, and the intellectual endeavour of *Sud* immediately after the war" (De Gasperin 2014, 121).

3. "Mi pareva scorgere delle figure, e avrei creduto udire il suono di voci familiari. . . . Queste figure si trattenevano per qualche istante . . . ; poi, come i numeri del quadretto bianco di un tassametro, venivano sostituite" (108–9).

4. "L'aria raccapricciata delle cantine e dei cimiteri" (125).

5. "Il viso sottile e inchinato, che guardava perplesso verso la porta. . . . egli mi aveva riconosciuta e osservata" (124).

6. "Benché . . . nulla, assolutamente nulla, esprimesse la minima attenzione e piacere" (124–25).

7. "Una freddezza così mortale, propria di coloro che, piuttosto che fuggire dal mondo, lo vedono rimpicciolire e ritrarsi e, impietriti, non osano levare più neppure un lamento" (125).

8. I modified the translation, as Compagnone's smile is rendered by Goldstein and PcPhee as "more . . . dead than that of any in Chiaia," thus missing the exact focus of the comparison, which is between the man and the whole street, both taken as symbols of a wider reality: "Nacque in quel volto un sorriso, più astratto e morto di quello di Chiaia" (125).

9. " 'Entra pure' disse continuando a sorridere in *quel modo*, lo sguardo ovunque, meno che dove io ero, e porgendomi la mano sudata" (125).

10. "Mi ero seduta vicino al grosso tavolo, e pensavo che non bisognava guardarlo, perciò gli voltavo le spalle" (125).

11. "Non lo vedevo, eppure lo sentivo. . . . Era come se dietro le mie spalle ci fosse una voragine, un vuoto pieno di mani, che battendo l'una sull'altra ne nascesse un rumore desolato, un sospiro senza fine" (125).

12. "Pensai che la cosa migliore fosse ridurre al minimo le mie vibrazioni, i pensieri; bandire dalla mia stessa mente, o confinarle in un angolo ristrettissimo, quelle voci che, presentando un qualche rapporto con la vita, non potevano che turbarlo. L'avrei calmato provandogli che anche la mia intelligenza era stata, dalle necessità della vita, mortificata e vinta" (125–26).

13. "Cautamente mi girai per guardarlo" 127.

14. "Benché non fosse possibile, qualcosa, in pochi minuti, era mutato terribilmente nella sua persona. La statua che mi aveva aperto la porta, ora era viva e tremava. Sembrava che ai suoi piedi egli vedesse qualcosa di molto grande. . . . Un bambino che scorge una tigre nella sua stanza, o un ragno enorme sul cavallo a dondolo, ma, per qualche motivo profondo (forse un terrore più grande), *non può* mostrare di aver visto l'oggetto del suo spavento, non si sarebbe comportato in maniera diversa" (127).

15. "Nello specchio, vidi che il suo volto sudato e sottile trasaliva, e gli occhi si aprivano avidamente, come chi scopre qualcosa di lucente davanti a sé" (126).

16. "Come se . . . ascoltasse voci di campane salire dal pavimento" (127–28).

17. "Non sa farsi valere, . . . del denaro non gli importa, come se non avesse una famiglia. E sì che non scrive peggio di altri" (129).

18. In the previous section the narrator had made specific reference to the nineteenth-century bildungsroman (although she talks about "variety shows," she has clearly in mind the paradigm that had gained popularity starting with novels like Goethe's *Wilhelm Meisters Lehrjahre*) to explain how Nature had corrupted Compagnone: "She [Nature] held up a mirror of excellent workmanship to the Marxist Neapolitan in which the story of the *Sud* group, rather than reflecting the imperceptible and terrifying battle between the demands of reason and antiquity, appeared to portray, as in one of the many nineteenth century variety shows, the innocent conflict between the dreams of youth and the overwhelming logic of things" (124; translation modified). "Fu essa [la Natura] a presentare al marxista partenopeo uno specchietto di eccellente fattura, in cui la storia del gruppo Sud, anziché rivelare, impercettibile e spaventoso, il combattimento tra le esigenze della ragione e l'antichità, appariva, come in uno dei tanti spettacoli di varietà cari all'Ottocento, l'ingenuo conflitto tra i sogni della gioventù e la soverchiante logica delle cose" (119).

19. As shown in chapter 3, the allegory of Nature is tightly connected to motherhood (although a suffocating, deadly one) throughout the book.

20. The translation here has "scalp" for "cranio." Yet the connection with the imagery of the skull is important for the visual symbolism of the story: "Sguardo calmo, privo di sorriso come di pensiero. Fragili capelli, che lasciavano vedere il cranio" (128).

21. "Qualcosa si era frantumato in lui, l'ansia di poco prima si era spezzata, e il silenzio era ritornato a governare la sua memoria. Anche la mia presenza aveva smesso di turbarlo, gli era divenuta perfettamente indifferente" (129–30).

22. "Completamente rapata, vestita di un solo cencio grigio, che le veniva fin sui piedi, lasciando scoperto il petto, a modo di una dama" (131).

23. "E così passeggiando, ed elemosinando, emettevano un grido pieno di risa, una supplica buffonesca e desolata insieme, parafrasando uno dei tanti inni Cristiani alla Vergine: *Virgo preticando / abbi di noi piatà*. E insistevano su quel *piatà* torcendosi dalle risa" (131).

24. " 'Guardami sulla testa,' disse Luigi . . . con una pazienza e un terrore infiniti, sforzandosi a una calma del tutto innaturale 'Non ho nulla . . . nulla di bagnato?' " (133).

25. Clerici quotes an epigram Compagnone wrote in response to the publication of "The Silence," which insists on her ungratefulness for having been fed so many times: "She badmouthed those friends / that every night had fed her / in that Neapolitan pizzeria" ("Sparlò di quegli amici / che ogni sera l'avevano sfamata / in quella pizzeria napoletana") (Clerici 2002, 241).

26. "Era l'ora che Napoli si accende e gonfia come una medusa; e le sue ferrite risplendono, I suoi cenci si coprono di Fiori, e la popolazione barcolla" (133).

27. "C'era per le strade un effetto di movimento ed eccitazione, che poi, guardando meglio, era nulla" (133).

28. "[La folla] borghese e aristocratica, che neppure mostrava fastidio o ribrezzo, perché non se ne avvedeva" (134).

29. "Chi si soffiava con un cartone, chi dormiva allungato sul marciapiede, con la bocca aperta, chi mangiava, chi cantava una nenia triste; nelle stanze, vicino ai letti, c'era chi cucinava, e sui letti chi, a volte anche un uomo giovane, disteso pensava" (134).

30. "Tutto era disordine, e un cupo incanto" (133).

31. "Non avresti detto che fossero svegli, ma che in un sogno oscuro si agitassero" (134).

32. "Ma non era lieto, non era limpido, non era buono quel rumore" (134).

33. "latente e orribile vi si avvertiva il silenzio, l'irrigidirsi della memoria, l'andirivieni impazzito della speranza" (134).

34. "Con la sua andatura un po' stanca di claudicante, senza fretta" (106).

35. "Ebbi la sensazione che la famiglia fosse già a tavola, e che la mia visita avrebbe portato un certo imbarazzo. Mi chiesi se non avrei fatto bene a ritornare più tardi" (140).

36. She excuses herself by saying that Rea had no telephone, so she would not know how to contact him in advance. But this is proved untrue by two passages in the story: First Anita had said that Rea's wife had asked to phone her (132, 140); then, later, Rea names the telephone among the comforts he now has and would like everyone else to have too (144, 153).

37. "'Stai qua' disse con la stessa freddezza di Compagnone, *un allarme segreto.* E non sorrideva, mi osservava" (141; my emphasis).

38. "Risorto mito della napoletanità" (123).

39. "Io amo il popolo. Io, anzi, sono il popolo" (143).

40. Unless otherwise noted, when two consecutive page numbers are indicated, the first one refers to the original Italian and the second to the English translation of Ortese's text.

41. "Una donna, da un terrazzino, ne chiamò un'altra, giovane, vestita di giallo e rosso, intenta nel giardino a stendere dei panni. 'Mo' vengo' rispose cantando questa. Dal terrazzino, la voce gridò dopo un attimo, impensatamente: '*Pozzi jettà 'u sangue.*' Guardai la donna che aveva gettato l'augurio: era già calma, assorta" (139).

42. "Vidi una fila di terrazzini bianchi, con delle cordelle tese da un muro all'altro, come già nella casa di Luigi, e da quelle pendevano un po' di biancheria, dei calzini. Una goccia, che non era di pioggia, mi cadde su una mano" (140).

43. "Su un uomo simile, io sputo" (144).

44. "A un tratto quel giovane divenne sfrenatamente allegro. La sua piccola faccia butterata s'illuminò come le pietre di Napoli, quando s'alzano nel cielo notturno, dapprima in silenzio, poi con fischi e fragori altissimi, i fuochi d'artificio" (147).

45. I modified the translation here, as the English edition cuts the first half of the title ("Literal translation"): "Traduzione letterale: 'Che cosa significa questa notte?'"

46. "Li conoscevo bene" 150.

47. "Non mi appariva importante per una identificazione di Napoli" (151).

48. "Mi dissi che avevo avuto un'allucinazione" (151).

49. "Qualcosa che fosse Napoli, il Vesuvio e il contro Vesuvio, il mistero e l'odio per il mistero" (151).

50. Prunas in a letter from 1947: "Anna Maria Ortese is starving, just the real starving. And Scognamiglio just like Ortese" (qtd. in Clerici 2002, 164). Of him La Capria writes, "He was always haunted by (mental) illness, poverty, and misfortune" (La Capria 2003, 1041–42).

51. "Io me ne vado per sempre da questa città / ove il mare è scomparso" (Scognamiglio 1946).

52. "Anche qui c'era un gran movimento, un che di eccitato e straordinario . . . ma poi, accostandosi, era nulla" (152).

53. "Della presenza di questa plebe non era nessun segno sulle face dei borghesi" (152).

54. "Non è che vi fossero solo due o tre vecchie madri . . . ma ve n'erano cento, duecento. Non è a dire che gli uomini dal petto concavo e gli occhi loschi . . . fossero cinque o sei, ma erano per lo meno mille" (152).

55. "Si grattano il capo, trascinando uno zoccolo" (152).

56. The English translation does not preserve the metaphorical intensity of the vivid original, where the eyes are *broken* by "memorie" (instead of "ricordi"), a more lyrical term in this context: "occhi rotti dale memorie" (152).

57. "E se aveste cercato . . . sareste stato abbondantemente appagato. . . . Se poi aveste voluto incontrare . . . sareste rimasto atterrito" (152–53).

58. "La plebe dall'informe faccia riempiva questa strada meravigliosa e scendeva dai vicoli circostanti *e s'affacciava a tutte le finestre*" (152; my emphasis).

59. "O la plebe, aprendosi come la montagna, aveva vomitato questa gente più fina, che, allo stesso modo di una cosa *naturale*, non aveva occhi per l'altra cosa *naturale*" (153).

60. "O questa categoria di uomini, per altro molto ristretta, aveva rinunciato, per salvarsi, a considerare come vivente, e facente parte di sé, la plebe" (153).

61. "Qui era veramente accaduto qualche cosa. . . . scorsi a terra una macchia rossa, lucente, circondata da altre più piccole" (153–54).

62. As noted by Baldi, this event might be inspired by Serao's short story "Giovannino o la morte," as the housemaid is named Giovannina (Baldi 2010, 39n43).

63. "Uno dei tanti attimi allucinanti di Napoli" (158).

64. "Di cercare il regista di un così squisito lavoro" (158).

65. *"Pecché nun fa journo? Che vo' di' sta nuttata?"* (155).

66. "Asciutte e un po' fredde, non sudate come quelle di Luigi, né roventi come quelle di Rea" (160).

67. " 'Devi avere pietà,' dicevano quegli occhi spenti 'devi evitare di guardare. È vero che siamo morti?' chiedeva 'è vero che siamo stati assorbiti dalla città, e ora siamo in pace?' " (161).

68. A different road than the Riviera di Chiaia.

69. "L'amico della ragione mi odiava, per le memorie che gli riportavo, per lo specchio che gli offrivo" (163).

70. "Viso inchinato, di un bruno giallo, magro e silenzioso. Solo le labbra erano animate da un sorriso impercettibile, pieno di ostilità . . . sembra[va] morto, morto in piedi. Invece ascoltava" (159).

71. "A Napoli, il ragazzo sardo si era coperto di miseria, ma non era morto; era antico, ma non morto ancora, perché incapace di pensare nella sua testa la parola morte" (164).

72. As shown in chapter 3, "To become emotional" is the translation of *commuoversi*, literally, "to be moved."

73. "Incapace di commuoversi e farsi triste, se non a momenti, subito dimenticandolo. La sua sete di vita, la sua capacità di costruire vita, soffocate, enormi" (164).

74. "Un capo, un comandante" (175).

75. "Aveva scarpe nere, piccole, da bambina, come del resto le sue mani scure e tutta la minuta persona erano più simili a quelle di un adolescente che di un uomo" (159).

76. "Piccolo di statura quanto una bambina" (108).

77. "Un'aquila morente e un fiore. Aveva la stessa dissanguata ferocia, e la grazia" (159).

78. "il sorriso di chi non potrà mai più sorprendersi di alcuna cosa, e neppure patire o gioire se non meccanicamente" (160).

79. " 'Qui si uccidono sempre allo stesso modo' disse il Gaedkens con ironia. 'Il balcone. I balconi e le finestre della nostra città, sembra non abbiano nessun'altra funzione' " (161).

80. "Ma una volta per le vie di Napoli, non potete fare a meno di muovervi in questa o quella direzione, senza alcun proposito. . . . Si cammina senza scopo, si parla senza ragione, si tace senza motivo" (162–63).

81. "Parlava e la sua voce rassomigliava al silenzio. Era la voce di uno che amava la forma, . . . non voce d'uomo, ma eco" (164–65).

82. "Una tenda scura che nascondeva la porta di un'altra stanza. . . . A un certo punto, dietro la tenda rimasta aperta per un attimo, brillò qualcosa di chiaro, e in quella cosa—niente più di una bara di vetro—si vedeva una forma allungata" (166).

83. "Era un uomo vestito di nero, e sorridente, che guardava intorno pazientemente, fumando una sigaretta" (166).

84. "Mi domandavo anche se avessi bevuto qualcosa di forte, in quel mio girovagare ansioso per Napoli" (166).

85. "Mi venne di domandarmi se fosse estremamente vivo o solo estremamente morto" (167).

86. "Allora fui certa ch'egli era veramente morto, finito. . . . Nessuno di quelli che avevo finora incontrato mi aveva nascosto così la sua morte. Avevo visto la dichiarazione di fine, di fallimento, scritta in caratteri abbastanza chiari su ogni volto, come un avviso di tribunale affisso su una povera porta. . . . La città lo aveva distrutto. E perché non avrebbe dovuto distruggerlo? Tutti erano caduti, qui, quelli che avevano desiderato pensare o agire, tutte le lingue si erano confuse ed erano andate a incrementare la dolorosa vegetazione umana. Questa natura non poteva tollerare la ragione umana. . . . Anche questo ragazzo era caduto" (167–68).

87. "Parlando di Napoli come terreno fenomenico, si compiaceva della labilità di questa terra, che continuamente mutava forma, e dove nulla era stabile, e tutto generava inganno e spavento" (168).

88. "'E con questo?' chiese a un tratto, tranquillamente, il Prunas. . . . Il ragazzo ebbe di nuovo un sorriso, così vivo e incredulo, così inadeguato all'ora e alle parole del Gaedkens, che ancora io mi meravigliai. Ma non aggiunse parola" (169).

89. "Mi ricordavo di averlo visto sempre così, negli anni in cui faceva 'Sud,' dirigersi alla tipografia: con questi passi piccoli e rapidi, senza guardare nulla, freddissimo, intento nei suoi pensieri di cose da fare" (170).

90. "Mi parve di capire, con immensa meraviglia, ch'egli non avesse immaginazione né sentimento, almeno secondo il modello comune, o avendoli li considerasse come un'energia che va controllata continuamente, e questo gli permetteva di non aver paura di Napoli" (170).

91. "Era un solo sonno . . . il ragazzo sardo . . . forse a quest'ora ancora pensava" (172).

92. "Come tutte le mostruosità, Napoli non aveva alcun effetto su persone scarsamente umane, e i suoi smisurati incanti non potevano lasciare traccia su un cuore freddo" (170).

93. "Produire un système de signes qui restitue par son agencement interne le paysage d'une expérience" (Merleau-Ponty 1968a, 40).

94. "Les reliefs, les lignes de force de ce paysage induisent une syntaxe profonde, un mode de composition et de récit, qui défont et refont le monde et le langage usuels" (Merleau-Ponty 1968a, 40).

95. "Guardai anche verso le mura rosse di Monte di Dio, dove il ragazzo sardo, così semplice e freddo, forse a quest'ora ancora pensava" (172).

96. "Non si sentiva che lo sciacquio tranquillo dell'acqua sugli scogli, non si vedevano che le colline sempre più vive e vittoriose nella luce" (172).

97. "E, più giù, le case e i vicoli grigi, i miseri vicoli infetti" (172).

98. "Dove brillava ancora, sulle immondizie, qualche lume" (172).

99. "Ma il giorno diveniva sempre più alto e splendido, e a poco a poco anche quelle ultime luci si spensero" (172).

Chapter 5

1. This kind of receptive mechanism in film viewing has been explored by Vivian Sobchack in her studies on the "cinesthetic subject": "We see and comprehend and feel films with our entire bodily being, informed by the full history and carnal knowledge of our accultured sensorium" (Sobchack 2004, 63).

2. "When one reads resumes of them, the scenarios of many Italian films are open to ridicule. Reduced to their plots, they are often just moralizing melodramas, but on the screen everybody in the film is overwhelmingly real" (Bazin 2005, 21). Bazin has often highlighted the fundamental role of nonprofessional actors for the revelatory power of Italian cinema of the postwar years. See, for example, Bazin 1962, 54–55.

3. "One cannot help but notice the overwhelming difference between the two in manners, height, voice, attitude, clothing . . . the supreme irritation of the staid Alex stands out when the woman, increasingly excited and noisy, not only allows herself to address him informally (gesturing so eloquently that Alex notices it and adds indignantly: 'how dare you speak to me like that?') but even *touches him*, taking him by the arm, to drag him to the 'Signorino Tony' " (Dagrada 2008, 322).

4. "Katherine, throughout the film, conscientiously ensures that there is an intermediary—a guide, Natalia—that is to say an organized and reassuring discourse between her and what she visits" (Bergala 1990, 51).

5. In an interview, the cinematographer Enzo Serafin recalls that he went to capture this footage in the streets of Naples during the first days of shooting, implying that they were not orchestrated but randomly shot while driving around the city (Dagrada 2008, 330 n86). Rossellini himself, in a later interview, referred to these images as "documentary stuff" (Rossellini 1992, 154). Of course, as already mentioned, Katherine's close-ups in the driving sequences have been shot at a different time, and their matching with specific subjective views belongs entirely to the editing.

6. A traditional but incorrect interpretation of the two bronze statues of young athletes, which current scholarship has shown are runners before the start of the race (they are currently classified as such by the museum).

7. "The director was clearly fascinated by these objects, and the autonomous self-sufficient world of the fiction seems to collapse under their weight. That is to say, the combination of camera with music and editing that gives the sequence its aesthetic unity overwhelms Katherine and her fictional subjectivity" (Mulvey 2000, 104).

8. As noted by Dagrada (131). Dagrada also noticed how Renzo Rossellini's music for this scene is similar to the music in the museum scene (Dagrada 2008, 324).

9. "I would venture that the true break in the history of cinema is embedded in the history of the century and that it illustrates the interpenetration of form and chronology. It was the war, its violence, the resulting stupor, and the traumatic realization of the reality of extermination camps as the nodal point of the Nazi worldview that suddenly erupted onto the screen" (De Baecque 2012, 2).

10. About this close-up Bergala has written: "This surprise encounter with something visible which has imposed itself on her, leaves her dazed, haggard, in a strange close-up, one of the most disturbing, where Rossellini films her for too long, in a state of stupor, with a gesture of the head which is like a refusal to let herself be invaded by this reality that she has just glimpsed" (1990, 53).

11. "The content of the vision is never revealed, but only indirectly characterized by, possibly, the marks of attention, surprise, and fear on the observer's face" (Fontanille 1989, 144).

12. "The body of the screen character has the power to show what the character is seeing, without it being shown. Here the complicity of bodies that structures viewing also implicates the invisible" (Raviv 2016, 174).

13. This is reminiscent of a scene in the original screenplay where Isabella was so horrified by the vision of a little donkey pulling a big cart that she wanted to denounce it to the British press.

14. As highlighted by Mulvey, the sequence also includes shots in which the camera seems to pursue an "interest" in the surrounding natural phenomena independent of the visual perspective of the characters, as often camera movements leave the human bodies to follow the fluctuations of the smoke on the waste ground: "The camera finds its own independent relation with the movement of the smoke. As the volume of smoke increases, the camera follows as it drifts away until it fills the screen . . . even if on a less formally evolved level, the image moves away from its fictional frame of reference. Film turns into something beyond its usual subservience to iconic representation" (Mulvey 2000, 105–6). And yet, although the hypothesis that this might be a meta-reflection on the powers of cinema is fascinating, in my opinion the formal structure of these shots is still serving the illustration of the verbal explanation of the guide, which is part of the actualization of the ideological discourse that domesticates the elements of reality to fit them inside the reductive paradigm of the picturesque.

15. "The origin of the quarry may be traced back to the XVI century, and its expansion to the XVII century. At that time, the city was scourged in rapid succession by popular rebellions, famines, earthquakes, eruptions of the Vesuvius and epidemics. Being our cavity located in an isolated place, outside the walls of the city but close to them, it was used to collect the corpses of the victims" (Scotto di Santolo et al. 2013, 642–43).

16. For this interpretation, and for the reading of the layered space in the next sequence, a source of inspiration has been Fontanille's interpretation of filmic space in Godard's *Passion* (1982) in *Sémiotique du Visible* (1995, 135–50), although the four typologies of space he delineates there do not coincide with those we find in *Journey to Italy*.

17. Of course, there is also the moment in which the maid at the villa forcefully took Alex's hand, but that happened inside the "normalized" master-servant relationship.

18. "The shadow of the camera on the crowd, while it describes its rainbow, openly and clearly designates it as a tutelary authority, the enunciation has become an annunciation, the miracle can take place" (Bergala 1990, 67).

19. "The spectacle of cinema, like the spectacle of the world, lets thoughts and feelings emerge as modes of behavior, ways of inhabiting space and performing certain movements" (Torlasco 2008, 80).

20. "It is a fairly normal thing in modern society that many marriages are limited companies under another name. People get married because one of them has a job to do, the other has a number of connections, so the wife acts as a public relations officer while the husband is an economics official, to describe it in terms of actual job. . . . And the couple in *Journey to Italy* is that kind of couple" (Rossellini 1992, 154).

Epilogue

1. "The aim is to leave on the paper a trace of our contact with this object and this spectacle, insofar as they made our gaze and virtually our touch, our ears, our feeling of risk or of destiny or of freedom vibrate. It is a question of leaving a testimony and not any more of providing information" (Merleau-Ponty 1973b, 150).

2. For a detailed analysis of this work, see De Gasperin 2014, 58–105; and Ghezzo 2015b.

3. "The madness of Toledo" ("La follia di Toledo"); thus Ortese defines her autobiographical novel in one note posthumously included in the Adelphi edition of her novels (2002, 1068).

4. Thirty-four early poems and the first nine short stories from *Angelic Sorrows* (*Angelici Dolori*, 1937) were included with some variations (De Gasperin 2014, 68).

5. Among many possible examples, see Clerici's account of the way she dealt with the short stories collected in her second book, *The Buried Princess* (*L'infanta sepolta*, 1950): "According to a practice of intensive use of texts confirmed by all the other collections, out of 17 short stories only two are unpublished. . . . But there is more: the case of the *Infanta* testifies to a further passage. When the 'Corriere di Napoli' offers her to collaborate, Anna Maria does not hesitate to review some

chapters of the book . . . retransformed into articles, those short stories born for other newspapers are published in the 'Corriere' between February and November 1952" (Clerici 2002, 225).

6. The theme of forgery is naturally also linked, as noted by Ghezzo and De Gasperin in the studies just cited, to the deformations imposed on the autobiographical narrative.

References

Albano, Gianfranco, Paquito Del Bosco, and Luigi Faccini. 1967. "Materiali per un'analisi in svolgimento su Rossellini." *Cinema e Film* 1 (2): 188–97.

Alexander, Jeffrey C. 2004. "Toward a Theory of Cultural Trauma." In *Cultural Trauma and Collective Identity*, edited by Jeffrey Alexander and Neil Smelser. University of California Press.

Allum, Percy A. 1973. *Politics and Society in Post-War Naples.* Cambridge University Press.

Althusser, Louis. 1976. *Positions, 1964–1975.* Éditions Sociales.

Althusser, Louis. 2001. *Lenin and Philosophy, and Other Essays.* Monthly Review Press.

Amar, Tarik Y. C. 2015. *The Paradox of Ukrainian Lviv: A Borderland City Between Stalinists, Nazis, and Nationalists.* Cornell University Press.

Andén, Lovisa. 2019. "Literature and the Expressions of Being in Merleau-Ponty's Unpublished Course Notes." *Journal of the British Society for Phenomenology* 50 (3), 208–19.

Aprà, Adriano, and Luigi Martelli. 1967. "Premesse sintagmatiche ad un'analisi di 'Viaggio in Italia.'" *Cinema e Film* 1 (2): 198–207.

Arneil, Barbara. 2017. *Domestic Colonies: The Turn Inward to Colony.* Oxford University Press.

Balaev, Michelle. 2014. "Literary Trauma Theory Reconsidered." In *Contemporary Approaches in Literary Trauma Theory*, edited by Michelle Balaev. Palgrave Macmillan.

Balázs, Béla. 1953. *Theory of the Film: Character and Growth of a New Art.* Roy Publishers.

Baldi, Andrea. 2000. "Infelicità senza desideri: 'Il mare non bagna Napoli' di Anna Maria Ortese." *Italica* 77 (1): 81–104.

Baldi, Andrea. 2010. *La meraviglia e il disincanto: studi sulla narrativa breve di Anna Maria Ortese.* Loffredo.

Barattoni, Luca. 2012. *Italian Post-Neorealist Cinema.* Edinburgh University Press.

Barbagallo, Francesco. 2010. *Storia della camorra.* Laterza.

Barrow, Clyde. 2020. *The Dangerous Class: The Concept of the Lumpenproletariat.* University of Michigan Press.

Basch, Victor. 1936. "Deuxième Congrès International d'Esthétique et de Science de l'Art: Paris 1937." *Annali della R. Scuola normale superiore di Pisa. Lettere, Storia e Filosofia* 5 (4).

Bazin, André. 1962. *Qu'est-ce que le cinéma? IV. Une esthétique de la réalité: Le Néo-Réalisme.* Editions du Cerf.

Bazin, André. 2005. *What Is Cinema?* Vol. 2. University of California Press.

Bellour, Raymond. 1990. "The Film Stilled." *Camera Obscura: Feminism, Culture, and Media Studies* 8 (3 [24]): 98–124.

Belmonte, Thomas. 2012. *The Broken Fountain: Twenty-Fifth Anniversary Edition.* 2nd ed., expanded ed. Columbia University Press.

Benigno, Francesco. 2005. "Trasformazioni discorsive e identità sociali: il caso dei *lazzari.*" *Storica XI* (31): 1–38.

Benjamin, Walter. 2002. "The Work of Art in the Age of Its Technological Reproducibility." In *Selected Writings.* Vol. 3. Edited by Howard Eiland and Michael W. Jennings. Belknap Press of Harvard University Press.

Benjamin, Walter, and Asja Lacis. 1996. "Naples." In *Selected Writings.* Vol. 1. Edited by Marcus Bullock and Michael W. Jennings. Schocken Books.

Bergala, Alain. 1990. *Voyage en Italie de Roberto Rossellini.* Yellow Now.

Bernari, Carlo. 1947. *Prologo alle tenebre.* Mondadori.

Bernari, Carlo. 1952. *Speranzella.* Mondadori.

Bertrand, Denis. 2000. *Précis de sémiotique littéraire.* Nathan.

Bispuri, Ennio. 2021. *Il cinema dei telefoni bianchi.* Bulzoni.

Bohne, Luciana. 1979. "Rossellini's 'Viaggio in Italia': A Variation on a Theme by Joyce." *Film Criticism* 3 (2): 43–52.

Bourdieu, Pierre. 1977. *Outline of a Theory of Practice.* Cambridge University Press.

Bourdieu, Pierre. 2000a. *Esquisse d'une théorie de la pratique: Précédé de Trois études d'ethnologie kabyle.* Collection Point. Seuil.

Bourdieu, Pierre. 2000b. *Pascalian Meditations.* Stanford University Press.

Bourke-White, Margaret. 1944. "Naples: Its Citizens Live Underground in Caves While Allied Engineers Clear Its Harbor, Destroyed by the Germans." *Life Magazine* 16 (4): 17–23.

Bove, Antonio, and Francesco Festa, eds. 2022a. *Gli autonomi: L'Autonomia operaia meridionale.* Vol. 10. DeriveApprodi.

Bove, Antonio, and Francesco Festa, eds. 2022b. *Gli autonomi: L'Autonomia operaia meridionale; Napoli e la Campania.* Vol. 11. DeriveApprodi.

Brancati, Vitaliano. 1964. *Il bell'Antonio.* Bompiani.

Brancati, Vitaliano. 2003a. *Romanzi e Saggi.* Edited by Marco Dondero. I Meridiani. Arnoldo Mondadori.

Brancati, Vitaliano. 2003b. *Racconti, teatro, scritti giornalistici.* Edited by Marco Dondero. I Meridiani. Arnoldo Mondadori.

Breaugh, Martin. 2007. *L'expérience plébéienne: Une histoire discontinue de la liberté politique*. Payot.

Brosses, Charles de. 1858. *Le Président de Brosses en Italie: Lettres familières écrites d'Italie en 1739 et 1740. Tome 1*. Didier et C. Libraires Éditeurs.

Brown, Laura S. 1995. "Not Outside the Range: One Feminist Perspective on Psychic Trauma." In *Trauma: Explorations in Memory*, edited by Cathy Caruth. Johns Hopkins University Press.

Brunetta, Gian Piero. 2009. *Il cinema neorealista italiano: Storia economica, politica e culturale*. Laterza.

Brunette, Peter. 1987. *Roberto Rossellini*. Oxford University Press.

Bruno, Giuliana. 2002. *Atlas of Emotions: Journeys in Art, Architecture and Film*. Verso.

Burns, John Horne. 1947. *The Gallery*. Harper & Brothers.

Calaresu, Melissa. 2007. "From the Street to Stereotype: Urban Space, Travel and the Picturesque in Late Eighteenth-Century Naples." *Italian Studies* 62 (2): 189–203.

Cannamela, Danila, and Achille Castaldo. 2021. "Neither Utopia nor Juvenile Transgression: Retracing the Link Between the Movimento Del '77, Autonomy, and Literature." *Italian Studies* 76 (1): 96–111.

Carbone, Mauro. 2019. *Philosophy-Screens: From Cinema to the Digital Revolution*. State University of New York Press.

Carbone, Mauro. 2020a. "The Clouded Surface: Literature and Philosophy as Visual Apparatuses According to Merleau-Ponty." In *Merleau-Ponty's Poetic of the World*, by G. A. Johnson, E. De Saint Aubert, and M. Carbone, translated by M. Nijhuis. Fordham University Press.

Carbone, Mauro. 2020b. " 'The Proustian Corporeity' and 'The True Hawthorns': Merleau-Ponty as a Reader of Proust Between Husserl and Benjamin." In Johnson et al., *Merleau-Ponty's Poetic of the World*.

Caruth, Cathy. 1996. *Unclaimed Experience: Trauma, Narrative, and History*. Johns Hopkins University Press.

Casetti, Francesco. 1998. *Inside the Gaze: The Fiction Film and Its Spectator*. Indiana University Press.

Chion, Michel. 2005. *L'audio-vision: Son et image au cinéma*. Armand Colin.

Chion, Michel. 2019. *Audio-Vision: Sound on Screen*. Columbia University Press.

Clerici, Luca. 2002. *Apparizione e visione: Vita e opere di Anna Maria Ortese*. Mondadori.

Coen, Carlo. 2018. " 'Chist' è 'o Paese d' 'o Sole': La rappresentazione di Napoli in Rossellini e Martone." *Forum Italicum* 52 (2): 566–81.

Colas-Blaise, Marion. 2014. "Quand nier, c'est agir: Vers une définition de la 'textualité négative.' " *Actes Sémiotiques* 117.

Colette, Sidonie-Gabrielle. 1951. *Short Novels*. Dial Press.

Colette, Sidonie-Gabrielle. 1991. *Oeuvres*. Vol. 3. Edited by Claude Pichois et al. Gallimard.

Colletta, Lisa, ed. 2015. *The Legacy of the Grand Tour: New Essays on Travel, Literature, and Culture.* Fairleigh Dickinson University Press.

Compagnone, Luigi. 1946. "Immagine di Franz Kafka." *Sud: Giornale di Cultura* 1 (3–4): 8–9.

Constant, Benjamin. 1895. *Journal intime de Benjamin Constant et Lettres à sa famille et ses amis.* Edited by Dora Melegari. Paul Ollendorff.

Contarini, Silvia. 2004. "Tra cecità e visione: Come leggere *Il Mare Non Bagna Napoli* di Anna Maria Ortese." *Chroniques Italiennes*, 5, 1–13.

Cooper, Barry. 2017. *Merleau-Ponty and Marxism.* University of Toronto Press.

Copley, Stephen, and Peter Garside. 1994. Introduction to *The Politics of the Picturesque: Literature, Landscape, and Aesthetics Since 1770*, edited by S. Copley and P. Garside. Cambridge University Press.

Croce, Benedetto. 2006. *Un paradiso abitato da diavoli.* Adelphi.

Dagrada, Elena. 2008. *Le varianti trasparenti: I film con Ingrid Bergman di Roberto Rossellini.* 2nd ed. LED.

Dainotto, Roberto M. 2007. *Europe (in Theory).* Duke University Press.

De Baecque, Antoine. 2008. *L'histoire-caméra.* Gallimard.

De Baecque, Antoine. 2012. *Camera Historica: The Century in Cinema.* Columbia University Press.

De Gasperin, Vilma. 2014. *Loss and the Other in the Visionary Work of Anna Maria Ortese.* Oxford University Press.

De Stefano, Daniele. 2022. "Puorteme a Casa Mia! Le lotte per la casa a napoli (1962–1980)." In *Gli autonomi: L'Autonomia operaia meridionale; Napoli e la Campania*, edited by Antonio Bove and Francesco Festa. Vol. 11. DeriveApprodi.

Deleuze, Gilles. 1989. *The Time Image.* University of Minnesota Press.

Detassis, Piera, Tullio Masoni, and Paolo Vecchi, eds. 1987. *Il Cinema di Antonio Pietrangeli.* Marsilio.

Dickie, John. 1999. *Darkest Italy: The Nation and Stereotypes of the Mezzogiorno, 1860–1900.* St. Martin's Press.

Dines, Nick. 2014. "L'eterno abietto: Le classi popolari napoletane nelle rappresentazioni del Partito Comunista Italiano." *Itinerari di ricerca storica*, new series, XXVIII (2): 77–96.

Dupaty, Charles-Marguerite-Jean-Baptiste Mercier. 1788. *Lettres sur l'Italie en 1785.* Vol. 2. De Senne.

Fabbri, Lorenzo. 2023. *Cinema Is the Strongest Weapon: Race-Making and Resistance in Fascist Italy.* University of Minnesota Press.

Farnetti, Monica. 1998. *Anna Maria Ortese.* Bruno Mondadori.

Farnetti, Monica. 2015. "An 'Uncommon Reader': The Critical Writings of Anna Maria Ortese." In *Anna Maria Ortese: Celestial Geographies*, edited by Gian Maria Annovi and Flora Ghezzo. University of Toronto Press.

Fogu, Claudio, and Wulf Kansteiner. 2006. "The Politics of Memory and the Poetics of History." In *The Politics of Memory in Postwar Europe*, edited by R. N. Lebow, W. Kansteiner, and C. Fogu. Duke University Press.

Fontanille, Jacques. 1989. *Les Espaces subjectifs: introduction à la sémiotique de l'observateur : discours, peinture, cinéma*. Hachette.

Fontanille, Jacques. 1995. *Sémiotique du Visible: Des mondes de lumière*. Presses Universitaires de France.

Forter, Greg. 2011. *Gender, Race, and Mourning in American Modernism*. Cambridge University Press.

Foucault, Michel. 1977. "Nietzsche, Genealogy, History." In *Language, Counter-Memory, Practice: Selected Essays and Interviews*. Cornell University Press.

Fucini, Renato. 1976. *Napoli a occhio nudo*. Einaudi.

Gallagher, Tag. 1998. *The Adventures of Roberto Rossellini*. Da Capo Press.

Genette, Gérard. 1972. *Figures III*. Éditions du Seuil.

Ghezzo, Flora. 2015a. "Introduction: Anna Maria Ortese and the Red-Footed Angel." In Annovi and Ghezzo, eds., *Anna Maria Ortese: Celestial Geographies*.

Ghezzo, Flora. 2015b. "On the Ruins of Time: Toledo and the (Auto)Fiction of the Ephemeral." In Annovi and Ghezzo, eds., *Anna Maria Ortese: Celestial Geographies*.

Ghirelli, Antonio. 1976. "Introduzione." In Fucini, *Napoli a occhio nudo*.

Ghirelli, Antonio. 2015. *Storia di Napoli*. Einaudi.

Ginsborg, Paul. 1990. *A History of Contemporary Italy: Society and Politics, 1943–1988*. Penguin Books.

Glynn, Ruth. 2020. "Porosity and Its Discontents: Approaching Naples in Critical Theory." *Cultural Critique* 107 (1): 63–98.

Goddard, Victoria A. 1996. *Gender, Family, and Work in Naples*. Berg.

Gramsci, Antonio. 1957. *La questione meridionale*. Editori riuniti.

Greimas, Algirdas Julien. 1976. *Maupassant: La sémiotique du texte: Exercices pratiques*. Seuil.

Greimas, Algirdas Julien. 1983. *Du sens II: Essais sémiotiques*. Seuil.

Greimas, Algirdas Julien. 1987. *On Meaning: Selected Writings in Semiotic Theory*. University of Minnesota Press.

Greimas, Algirdas Julien, and Joseph Courtés. 1993. *Sémiotique: Dictionnaire raisonné de la théorie du langage*. Hachette.

Greimas, Algirdas Julien, and Jacques Fontanille. 1991. *Sémiotique des passions: Des états de choses aux états d'âme*. Seuil.

Heidegger, Martin. 2014. *Introduction to Metaphysics*. Translated by Gregory Fried. Yale University Press.

Herbert, James D. 1995. "The View of the Trocadéro: The Real Subject of the Exposition Internationale, Paris, 1937." *Assemblage*, 26, 95–112.

Herbert, James D. 1998. *Paris 1937: Worlds on Exhibition*. Cornell University Press.

Hinde Stewart, Joan. 1980. "Colette's Gynaeceum: Regression and Renewal." *French Review* 53 (5): 662–69.

Ingarden, Roman. 1968. *Vom Erkennen Des Literarischen Kunstwerks*. Niemeyer.

Ingarden, Roman. 1969. *Erlebnis, Kunstwerk und Wert: Vorträge zur Ästhetik 1937–1967*. Niemeyer.

Ingarden, Roman. 1973. *The Cognition of the Literary Work of Art*. Northwestern University Press.

Iser, Wolfgang. 1980. *The Act of Reading: A Theory of Aesthetic Response*. Johns Hopkins University Press.

Jacobs, Hanne. 2018. "Husserl, Heidegger, and Merleau-Ponty on the World of Experience." In *The Oxford Handbook of the History of Phenomenology*, edited by Dan Zahavi. Oxford University Press.

Jameson, Fredric. 1977. "Imaginary and Symbolic in Lacan: Marxism, Psychoanalytic Criticism, and the Problem of the Subject." *Yale French Studies*, 55/56, 338–95.

Jameson, Fredric. 1979. *Fables of Aggression: Wyndham Lewis, the Modernist as Fascist*. University of California Press.

Jameson, Fredric. 1987. Foreword to *On Meaning: Selected Writings in Semiotic Theory*.

Jameson, Fredric. 2002. *The Political Unconscious: Narrative as a Socially Symbolic Act*. Routledge.

Jameson, Fredric. 2009a. "History and Class Consciousness as an Unfinished Project." In *Valences of the Dialectic*. Verso.

Jameson, Fredric. 2009b. "Ideological Analysis: A Handbook." In *Valences of the Dialectic*. Verso.

Jameson, Fredric. 2013. *The Antinomies of Realism*. Verso.

Jameson, Fredric. 2015. "Early Lukács, Aesthetics of Politics?" *Historical Materialism* 23 (1): 3–27.

Jameson, Fredric. 2019. *Allegory and Ideology*. Verso.

Johnson, Jeri. 2000. Introduction to *Dubliners*, by James Joyce. Oxford University Press.

Joyce, James. 2014. *Dubliners*. Edited by Terence Brown. Penguin Classics.

Judt, Tony. 2000. "The Past Is Another Country: Myth and Memory in Postwar Europe." In *The Politics of Retribution in Europe: World War II and Its Aftermath*, edited by István Deák. Princeton University Press.

Judt, Tony. 2005. *Postwar: A History of Europe Since 1945*. Penguin Press.

Kafka, Franz. 1971. *Complete Stories*. Edited by Nahum N. Glatzer. Schocken Books.

La Capria, Raffaele. 2003. *Opere*. Mondadori.

Lacan, Jacques. 1978. *Les écrits techniques de Freud*. Seuil.

Laffin, Stefan. 2019. "Occupied Naples and the Politics of Food in World War II." In *War and the City: The Urban Context of Conflict and Mass Destruction*, edited by Tim Keogh. Brill.

Lanzetta, Peppe. 1998. *Figli di un Bronx minore*. Feltrinelli.

Lanzetta, Peppe. 2000. *Tropico di Napoli*. Feltrinelli.

Leopardi, Giacomo. 1983. *Zibaldone di pensieri*. Mondadori.

Lewis, Norman. 1978. *Naples '44*. Collins.

López, Daniel Andrés. 2019. "Lukács: Praxis and the Absolute." Brill.

Luckhurst, Roger. 2008. *The Trauma Question*. Routledge.

Lukács, György. 1968. *Geschichte und Klassenbewusstsein*. Luchterhand.

Lukács, György. 1971. *History and Class Consciousness: Studies in Marxist Dialectics*. MIT Press.

Luzzi, Joseph. 2014. *A Cinema of Poetry: Aesthetics of the Italian Art Film*. Johns Hopkins University Press.

Macciocchi, Maria Antonietta, and Louis Althusser. 1973. *Letters from Inside the Italian Communist Party to Louis Althusser*. NLB.

Macry, Paolo. 1997. "The Southern Metropolis: Redistributive Circuits in Nineteenth-Century Naples." In *The New History of the Italian South: The Mezzogiorno Revisited*, edited by Robert Lumley and Jonathan Morris. University of Exeter Press.

Malaparte, Curzio. 2013. *The Skin*. Translated by David Moore. New York Review of Books.

Maraini, Dacia. 2015. "*Who Were You?* Interview with Anna Maria Ortese." In Annovi and Ghezzo, eds., *Anna Maria Ortese: Celestial Geographies*.

Maraldi, Antonio. 1992. *Antonio Pietrangeli*. La nuova Italia.

Marlow-Mann, Alex. 2011. *The New Neapolitan Cinema*. Edinburgh University Press.

Marotta, Giuseppe. 1964. *L'oro Di Napoli*. Bompiani.

Marrazzo, Giuseppe. 1984. *Il Camorrista*. Tullio Pironti Editore.

Marrone, Gianfranco. 2021. *Introduction to the Semiotics of the Text*. De Gruyter Mouton.

Marx, Karl. 1975a. "The Victory of the Counter-Revolution in Vienna." In *Karl Marx, Frederick Engels: Collected Works*. Vol. 7. Lawrence & Wishart.

Marx, Karl. 1975b. "Counter-Revolution in Berlin." In *Karl Marx, Frederick Engels*. Vol. 8.

Marx, Karl. 1975c. "The Class Struggles in France, 1848 to 1850." In *Karl Marx, Frederick Engels*. Vol. 10.

Marx, Karl. 1975d. *Eighteenth Brumaire of Louis Bonaparte*. In *Karl Marx, Frederick Engels*. Vol. 11.

Mercier, Michel. 1991. "Notice." In Colette, *Oeuvres*. Vol. 3. Gallimard.

Meriggi, Marco. 2002. "Una recezione tedesca della rivoluzione napoletana. La 'Storia della repubblica partenopea' di Johann Gottfried Pahl." In *Napoli 1799 fra storia e storiografia: Atti del Convegno internazionale, Napoli, 21–24 gennaio 1999*, edited by Anna Maria Rao. Vivarium.

Merleau-Ponty, Maurice. 1964. *Le visible et l'invisible: Suivi de notes de travail*. Gallimard.

Merleau-Ponty, Maurice. 1968a. *Résumés de cours: Collège de France, 1952–1960*. Gallimard.

Merleau-Ponty, Maurice. 1968b. *The Visible and the Invisible: Followed by Working Notes*. Northwestern University Press.

Merleau-Ponty, Maurice. 1970. *Themes from the Lectures at the Collège de France, 1952–1960*. Northwestern University Press.

Merleau-Ponty, Maurice. 1973a. *Adventures of the Dialectic*. Northwestern University Press.

Merleau-Ponty, Maurice. 1973b. *The Prose of the World*. Northwestern University Press.

Merleau-Ponty, Maurice. 1993. "Eye and Mind." In *The Merleau-Ponty Aesthetics Reader: Philosophy and Painting*, edited by Galen A. Johnson and Michael Bradley Smith. Northwestern University Press.

Merleau-Ponty, Maurice. 2000. *Les aventures de la dialectique*. Folio, Essais. Gallimard.

Merleau-Ponty, Maurice. 2005. *Phénoménologie de la perception*. Gallimard.

Merleau-Ponty, Maurice. 2011. *Le monde sensible et le monde de l'expression: Cours au Collège de France, Notes 1953*. Edited by Stefan Kristensen and Emmanuel de Saint Aubert. Metis Press.

Merleau-Ponty, Maurice. 2012. *Phenomenology of Perception*. Routledge.

Merleau-Ponty, Maurice. 2015. *L'institution, la passivité*. Belin.

Merleau-Ponty, Maurice. 2020a. *Le problème de la parole: Cours au Collège de France, Notes, 1953–1954*. Metis Press.

Merleau-Ponty, Maurice. 2020b. *The Sensible World and the World of Expression: Course Notes from the Collège de France, 1953*. Northwestern University Press.

Metz, Christian. 1968. "Problèmes de dénotation dans le film de fiction." In *Essais sur la signification au cinéma*. Klincksieck.

Milani, Raffaele. 2009. *The Art of the Landscape*. McGill-Queen's University Press.

Moe, Nelson. 2002. *The View from Vesuvius: Italian Culture and the Southern Question*. University of California Press.

Moran, Dermot. 2011. "Edmund Husserl's Phenomenology of Habituality and Habitus." *Journal of the British Society for Phenomenology* 42 (1): 53–77.

Morlicchio, Enrica, and Enrico Pugliese. 2006. "Naples: Unemployment and Spatial Exclusion." In *Neighborhoods of Poverty: Urban Social Exclusion and Integration in Europe*. Edited by S. Musterd, A. Murie, and C. Kesteloot. Palgrave Macmillan.

Morra, Eloisa. 2019. "Anna Maria Ortese's Palette: Colors and Achromaticity in Neapolitan Chronicles." *Forum Italicum* 53 (3): 699–715.

Morrison, Jeffrey. 1996. "Johann Joachim Winckelmann and Roman Ingarden on the Reception of Works of Art." In *Winckelmann and the Notion of Aesthetic Education*, edited by Jeffrey Morrison. Oxford University Press.

Moser, Caroline O. N. 1978. "Informal Sector or Petty Commodity Production: Dualism or Dependence in Urban Development?" *World Development* 6 (9): 1041–64.

Mozzillo, Atanasio. 1983. *La sirena inquietante: Immagine e mito di Napoli nell'Europa del Settecento*. Ci.esse.ti cooperativa.

Mozzillo, Atanasio. 1993. *Passaggio a Mezzogiorno: Napoli e il Sud nell'immaginario barocco e illuminista europeo*. Leonardo.

Mozzillo, Atanasio. 1995. *I ragazzi di Monte di Dio: Una cronaca napoletana degli anni Cinquanta*. Avagliano.

Mulvey, Laura. 2000. "Vesuvian Topographies: The Eruption of the Past in *Journey to Italy*." In *Roberto Rossellini: Magician of the Real*, edited by D. Forgacs, S. Lutton, and G. Nowell-Smith. British Film Institute.

Norris, Margot. 2003. *Suspicious Readings of Joyce's "Dubliners."* University of Pennsylvania Press.

Ortese, Anna Maria. 1958. *I giorni del cielo*. Mondadori.

Ortese, Anna Maria. 1987. *In sonno e in veglia*. Adelphi.

Ortese, Anna Maria. 1991. *La lente scura: Scritti di viaggio*. Marcos y Marcos.

Ortese, Anna Maria. 1994. *Il mare non bagna Napoli*. Adelphi.

Ortese, Anna Maria. 1997. *Corpo celeste*. Adelphi.

Ortese, Anna Maria. 1998. *Il porto di Toledo*. Adelphi.

Ortese, Anna Maria. 2000. *L'Infanta sepolta*. Adelphi.

Ortese, Anna Maria. 2002. *Romanzi*. Vol. 1. Edited by Monica Farnetti. Adelphi.

Ortese, Anna Maria. 2006. *Alla luce del Sud: Lettere a Pasquale Prunas*. Edited by Renata Prunas and Gianni Di Costanzo. Archinto.

Ortese, Anna Maria. 2018. *Neapolitan Chronicles*. Translated by Ann Goldstein and Jenny Mcphee. New Vessel Press.

Pandey, Gyanendra. 2006. *Routine Violence: Nations, Fragments, Histories*. Stanford University Press.

Pardo, Italo. 1993. "Socialist Visions, Naples and the Neapolitans: Value, Control and Representation in the Agency/Structure Relationship." *Journal of Mediterranean Studies* 3 (1): 77–98.

Paura, Raffaele. 2022. "L'autonomia dei dannati. Lotte, carcere, territorio nella rivolta degli anni Settanta." In *Gli autonomi: L'Autonomia operaia meridionale; Napoli e la Campania*, edited by Antonio Bove and Francesco Festa. Vol. 11. DeriveApprodi.

Pinkus, Karen. 2020. *Clocking Out: The Machinery of Life in 1960s Italian Cinema*. University of Minnesota Press.

Prato, Paolo. 2016. "The Good, the Bad, and the Ugly: Transatlantic Stereotypes, 1880s–1950s." In *Neapolitan Postcards: The Canzone Napoletana as Transnational Subject*, edited by Goffredo Plastino and Joseph Sciorra. Rowman & Littlefield.

Proust, Marcel. 1987. *A la recherche du temps perdu*. Vol. 1. Gallimard.

Proust, Marcel. 1989. *A la recherche du temps perdu*. Vol. 4. Gallimard.

Rancière, Jacques. 2001. *La Fable cinématographique*. Seuil.

Rancière, Jacques. 2003. *Short Voyages to the Land of the People*. Stanford University Press.

Raviv, Orna. 2016. "The Cinematic Point of View: Thinking Film with Merleau-Ponty." *Studia Phaenomenologica* 16, 163–83.

Re, Lucia. 2003. "Neorealist Narrative: Experience and Experiment." In *The Cambridge Companion to the Italian Novel*, edited by Peter Bondanella and Andrea Ciccarelli. Cambridge University Press.

Re, Lucia. 2015. " 'Clouds in Front of My Eyes': Ortese's Poetics of the Gaze in 'Un Paio Di Occhiali' and *Il Mare Non Bagna Napoli*." In Annovi and Ghezzo, eds., *Anna Maria Ortese: Celestial Geographies*.

Robert, Franck. 2020. "Vers l'ontologie: Postface." In *Le Problème de la parole: Cours au Collège de France, Notes, 1953–1954*, by Maurice Merleau-Ponty. Metis Press.

Root, Maria P. P. 1992. "Reconstructing the Impact of Trauma on Personality." In *Personality and Psychopathology: Feminist Reappraisals*, edited by Laura S. Brown and Mary B. Ballou. Guilford Press.

Rossellini, Roberto. 1987. *Il mio metodo: Scritti e interviste*. Edited by Adriano Aprà. Cinema. Marsilio.

Rossellini, Roberto. 1992. *My Method: Writings and Interviews*. Marsilio.

Sabatini, Gaetano. 2013. "Economy and Finance in Early Modern Naples." In *A Companion to Early Modern Naples*, edited by Tommaso Astarita. Brill.

Saviano, Roberto. 2006. *Gomorra*. Mondadori.

Saviano, Roberto. 2016. *La paranza dei bambini*. Feltrinelli.

Schenk, Dieter. 2007. *Der Lemberger Professorenmord und Der Holocaust in Ostgalizien*. Dietz.

Schneider, Jane, ed. 1998. *Italy's "Southern Question": Orientalism in One Country*. Berg.

Scognamiglio, Gianni. 1946. "Due poesie per una città." *Sud: Giornale di cultura* 1 (7): 5.

Scotto di Santolo, A., A. Evangelista, and E. Evangelista. 2013. "The Fontanelle Cemetery: Between Legend and Reality." In *Geotechnical Engineering for the Preservation of Monuments and Historic Sites*, edited by E. Bilotta, A. Flora, S. Lirer, and C. Viggiani. CRC Press.

Selwyn, Jennifer D. 2004. *A Paradise Inhabited by Devils: The Jesuits' Civilizing Mission in Early Modern Naples*. Routledge.

Serao, Matilde. 2021. *Il ventre di Napoli*. Rizzoli.

Seymour, Miranda. 2000. *Mary Shelley*. Grove Press.

Shelby, Tommie. 2016. *Dark Ghettos: Injustice, Dissent, and Reform*. Belknap Press of Harvard University Press.

Smelser, Neil. 2004. "Psychological Trauma and Cultural Trauma." In Alexander and Smelser, eds., *Cultural Trauma and Collective Identity*.

Sobchack, Vivian. 2004. "What My Fingers Knew: The Cinesthetic Subject, or Vision in the Flesh." In *Carnal Thoughts: Embodiment and Moving Image Culture*. University of California Press.

Sobchack, Vivian. 2009. *The Address of the Eye: A Phenomenology of Film Experience*. Princeton University Press.

Spivak, Gayatri Chakravorty. 1988. "Can the Subaltern Speak?" In *Marxism and the Interpretation of Culture*, edited by Cary Nelson and Lawrence Grossberg. Macmillan Education.

Stach, Reiner. 2013. *Kafka, the Years of Insight*. Princeton University Press.

Stam, Robert, Robert Burgoyne, and Sandy Flitterman-Lewis. 2005. *New Vocabularies in Film Semiotics Structuralism, Post-Structuralism, and Beyond.* Routledge, Taylor & Francis.

Tarì, Marcello. 2012. *Il ghiaccio era sottile: Per una storia dell'Autonomia.* DeriveApprodi.

Tarrow, Sidney. 1996. "Making Social Science Work Across Space and Time: A Critical Reflection on Robert Putnam's Making Democracy Work." *American Political Science Review* 90 (2): 389–97.

Torlasco, Domietta. 2008. *The Time of the Crime: Phenomenology, Psychoanalysis, Italian Film.* Stanford University Press.

Van Ness, Emma Katherine. 2020. *Antonio Pietrangeli, the Director of Women: Feminism and Film Theory in Postwar Italian Cinema.* Anthem Press.

Vanzago, Luca. 2012. "The Many Faces of Movement." *Chiasmi International* 12.

Varriale, Roberta. 2023. "Oral History as a Source for the Interpretation of UBH: The World War II Shelters in Naples Case Study." *Societies* 13 (5): 130.

Vickroy, Laurie. 2015. *Reading Trauma Narratives: The Contemporary Novel and the Psychology of Oppression.* University of Virginia Press.

Wacquant, Loïc. 2022. *The Invention of the "Underclass": A Study in the Politics of Knowledge.* Polity Press.

Wood, Robin. 1974. "Ingrid Bergman on Rossellini." *Film Comment* 10 (4): 12–15.

Woolf, Virginia. 2015. *A Room of One's Own.* John Wiley/Blackwell.

Zincone, Giuliano. 1972. "Il Terzo Mondo in Casa Nostra." *Corriere Della Sera,* Dec. 15, 1972.

Ziolkowski, Saskia Elizabeth. 2020. *Kafka's Italian Progeny.* University of Toronto Press.

Index